AF845202

Dictionary of Construction Terms

Dictionary of Construction Terms

Fenwick Elliott LLP

Edited by:
Simon Tolson, Jeremy Glover and Stacy Sinclair

informa law
from Routledge

First published in paperback 2024

First published 2012 by Informa Law

Published 2013
by Informa Law from Routledge
4 Park Square, Milton Park, Abingdon, Oxon OX14 4RN

and by Informa Law from Routledge
605 Third Avenue, New York, NY 10158

Informa Law is an imprint of the Taylor & Francis Group, an informa business

Illustrations by Stacy Sinclair

British Library Cataloguing-in-Publication Data
A catalogue record for this book is available from the British Library

ISBN: 978-1-84311-794-0 (hbk)
ISBN: 978-1-03-292133-4 (pbk)
ISBN: 978-1-315-85032-0 (ebk)

DOI: 10.4324/9781315850320

FOREWORD

Even for the experienced construction professional or specialist legal practitioner, the availability of an intelligent and usable dictionary of construction terms is vitally important. It is only once one understands the terms being used that one can begin to understand the problem or issue which needs to be addressed.

Some 35 years ago, a deputy judge dealing with a case only about the alleged inadequacy of purlins in a roof left it until the fourth and final day of the trial to ask what a purlin was. Whilst one would not blame any normal person for not knowing what a purlin was, it did not create any confidence amongst the lawyers and clients involved in the case that the judge left it until the last day to ask. If he had had access to this *Dictionary*, the judge would have been told that it is "A horizontal beam in a roof carried on the principal rafters". He would have been a better informed judge at the beginning of the case.

This particular *Dictionary* has an extensive list of definitions not only of the technical construction and engineering terms but also of the related legal, litigation, adjudication or arbitration terms about which parties need to know in the modern world. It is important that parties involved in construction, engineering and technology understand what the words used by other parties actually mean. It will often be as important to understand what a "quoin" is as to appreciate what an actual or would-be lawyer means by referring to a "quantum meruit".

This *Dictionary* draws together thousands of words and terms both from the technical and legal sides of the business and that is vitally important, in my view, for people at all levels involved in the construction, engineering and technology business. For trainees and fully experienced personnel within the construction and engineering business and for people within and indeed outside the legal and construction professions, a good widely drawn dictionary is essential.

I would commend this *Dictionary* as an extremely useful aid to everyday practice both for trained and untrained and experienced and even inexperienced people involved in the construction, engineering and technology areas.

Mr Justice Robert Akenhead
Judge in charge of the Technology and Construction Court
London

PREFACE

This *Dictionary of Construction Terms* is intended to cover a wide range of the more common as well more esoteric yet important terms a building professional, lawyer, student, judge, arbitrator, adjudicator, engineering economist or the like may require definition upon in the construction law field. The intention is to clear the fog, and to do so concisely in clear English in an alphabetical format. So whether you are looking for the answer to a spandrel panel, chequerplate, revetment, or NAECI or what is meant by *nemo dat quod non habet* or the rule in Pinnel's case, we have it here, and a whole lot more.

How did it start? In about 1994 I started assembling a construction database on my *Psion Organiser* (for those that can remember such pocket computers) regularly adding building and engineering terms, legal references etc relevant to the firm's work as construction lawyers. I was always excited to learn new terms and add to the record. Then about 10 years ago with the advent of powerful networked computing and software systems, Fenwick Elliott created its own intranet platform, and that database was uploaded to it. It was coined by the office, "*Simon Says*". This data rapidly grew with our busy international practice and with projects that are more complex the legal issues thrown up blossomed in tandem with the new technologies.

It was pretty clear that often things on *Simon Says* could not be turned up easily elsewhere, not even on Wikipedia. Whilst we live in a world where the computer is king be it iPad, Blackberry or Galaxy etc, we all in truth welcome the comfort of a book we can sniff, thumb through, sticker up when we want pages flagged and keep by our elbow.

Jeremy Glover (Solicitor and Partner), Stacy Sinclair (an Architect, Engineer and Assistant Solicitor) and I were unanimous in the view that none of the existing 'building dictionaries' covered the cross over into the specialist law we habitually practice in and so the idea was born – drawing on our respective fields and bringing together construction terms with building law. Jeremy with his huge knowledge of the FIDIC forms, and adjudication law and the Stacy on design, architecture, buildability, AutoCAD and BIM to name but a few. My contribution was more cross over, the ephemera and a miscellany of facts, laws, technical terms and regulations with a small toe in many camps. Naturally, other big cheeses at Fenwick Elliott have chipped in too!

Anyhow, this book would not have happened without the triumvirate efforts of Stacy and Jeremy, and a smidgen from me, the excellent illustrations are Stacy's own. Our publisher is to be thanked for bearing with us! At times, fee earning has got in the way, and it has been a long road.

For you the dear reader I hope we have got the balance about right and covered what you guys need on the hoof, in battle, on site or working late at your desk when everyone else has gone home.

We know it is not perfect, we have sought to make it up to date as at 15 August 2012.

Simon Tolson

Aldwych 26 September 2012

ABOUT THE AUTHORS

Simon Tolson, senior partner and practitioner at Fenwick Elliott LLP, Chairman of the Technology & Construction Solicitors Association, Chartered Arbitrator and panel Adjudicator. Sometime visiting lecturer to the Centre of Construction Law MSc programme at King's College, London. Ranked by Chambers and Partners UK Guide of Construction Solicitors and Legal 500 UK 2012 in the top first band. Recommended as leader in his field of construction. Since 1986 he has specialised in construction law and the disputes generated by the industry including for the last decade many arising in the process engineering field. For many years he has and continues to run cases at senior level including in the TCC, Arbitration and other fora. In his younger days he worked as a building labourer and still like to get his hands dirty.

Jeremy Glover, a partner at Fenwick Elliott LLP, advises on all aspects of projects both at home and abroad, from initial procurement to where necessary dispute avoidance and resolution. Jeremy is the co-author of Understanding the FIDIC Red Book, the second edition of which was published in January 2012 and is the lead editor of *Building Contract Disputes: Practice and Precedents*. Jeremy is a member of the Board of Examiners on the Centre of Construction Law MSc programme at King's College, London where he also teaches on adjudication and FIDIC issues.

Stacy Sinclair, an Assistant Solicitor, advises on a broad range of construction and engineering issues. Before qualifying as a solicitor, Stacy practiced as an Architect, principally designing large-scale projects such as stadiums, hospitals and education buildings both in the UK and the US. Stacy has a particular interest in BIM and its impact on the construction industry and regularly writes for Building Magazine and the RIBA Journal. Stacy is also a lecturer and oral examiner on the RIBA Part III postgraduate course at a number of universities.

TABLE OF CONTENTS

Foreword	v
Preface	vii
About the Authors	viii
Table of Cases	xi
Table of Abbreviations and Acronyms	xix
DICTIONARY OF CONSTRUCTION TERMS	1
Appendices: Procurement Diagrams	317

TABLE OF CASES

A Bell and Son (Paddington) Ltd v CBF Residential Care and Housing Assn (1989) 46 BLR 102 52
A Monk & Co Ltd v Devon County Council (1978) 10 BLR 9 (CA) 181
AC Yule & Son Ltd v Speedwell Roofing & Cladding Ltd [2007] EWHC 1360 (TCC); [2007] BLR 499 231
Adkin v Brown [2002] NZCA 59 278
Aerospace Publishing Ltd v Thames Water Utilities Ltd [2007] EWCA Civ 3; [2007] BLR 726 (CA); 110 ConLR 1 . . . . . 133, 170
AG v Barker [2000] 1 FLR 759 (DC) 1
Alderslade v Hendon Laundry Ltd [1945] KB 189, 192 11
Alfred McAlpine Capital Projects Ltd v Tilebox [2005] EWHC 281 (TCC); [2005] BLR 271; 104 ConLR 39 164
Alghussein Establishment v Eton College [1988] 1 WLR 587 11
Aluminium Industrie Vaassen BV v Romalpa Aluminium Ltd [1976] 1 WLR 676 (CA); [1976] 2 All ER 552 . . . . . 12, 232
Amec Civil Engineering Ltd v Secretary of State for Transport [2004] EWHC Civ 2339 (TCC) 86
Amec Civil Engineering Ltd v Secretary of State for Transport [2005] EWCA Civ 291; [2005] BLR 227, 235; [2005] 1 WLR 2339 (May LJ) 86
American Cyanamid Co v Ethicon Ltd (no 1) [1975] AC 396 (HL) 13
Anglia Television Ltd v Reed [1972] 1 QB 60 (CA); [1971] 3 All ER 690 304
Anns v Merton London Borough Council [1978] AC 728; [1977] 2 All ER 118 . . . . . 15, 90, 179
Antaios *Compania*. Naviera SA v Salen Rederierna A.B. [1974] 1 WLR 728 . . 214
Appleby v Myers [1867] LR 2 CP 651 116
Arenson v Arenson [1977] AC 405 . . . . . 104, 216
Ashwell & Nesbitt v Allen (1912) Hudson, Building Contracts, 4th edn, 1914, Vol. 2, p. 462 9
Associated Provincial Picture House Ltd v Wednesbury Corporation [1948] 1 KB 223 (CA); [1947] 2 All ER 680 305
Atlantic Mutual Insurance Co v King [1919] 1 KB 307 136
Atlantic Paper Stock Ltd v St Anne-Nackawic Pulp and Paper Co Ltd [1976] 1 SCR 580 117
Attorney General of Belize v Belize Telecom Ltd [2009] UKPC 10; [2009] 1 WLR 1988; [2009] 2 All ER 1127 . . . . . 27, 142
Attwood v Lamont [1920] 3 KB 571, 578 38
Austin Hall Building Ltd v Buckland Securities Ltd [2001] EWHC 434 (TCC); [2001] BLR 272; 80 ConLR 115 139
Aveat Heating Ltd v Jerram Falkus Construction Ltd [2007] EWHC 131 (TCC), [2007] TCLR 3; 113 ConLR 13 224
Baber v Kenwood [1978] 1 Lloyd's Rep 175, 179 104
Baldwin & Francis Ltd v Patents Appeal Tribunal [1959] AC 663 (HL); [1959] 2 WLR 826; [1959] 2 All ER 433 244
Barratt v Shaw and Ashton [2001] EWCA Civ 137; [2001] CP Rep 57 81
BCCI v Ali [2001] AC 251 110
Ben Hashem v Ali Shayif [2008] EWHC 2380 (Fam), [2009] 1 FLR 115 68
Berkeley Community Villages Ltd v Pullen [2007] EWHC 1330 (Ch); [2007] 3 EGLR 101 124
Bickerton v Northwest Metropolitan Hospital Board [1970] 1 WLR 607 228

Biggin v Permanite Ltd [1951] 2 KB 314 (CA). 35
Bloor Construction (UK) Ltd v Bowmer & Kirkland (London) Ltd [2000] BLR 314. . . . . .6, 37, 56, 255
Blyth & Blyth Ltd v Carillion Construction Ltd [2001] Scot (CS) 90; 79 ConLR 142 . . . . 82, 187
Blyth v Birmingham Waterworks [1856] 11 Ex 781 221
Bolam v Friern Hospital Management Committee [1957] 2 All ER 118 38
Bole v Huntsbuild Ltd [2009] EWCA Civ 1146; 127 ConLR 154. 115
Bouygues (UK) Ltd v Dahl-Jensen (UK) Ltd [2000] BLR 522 (CA) 5, 171
Bovis Lend Lease Ltd v Trustees of the London Clinic [2009] EWHC 64 (TCC) 13
Bremer Handelgesellschaft mbH v Vanden Avenne Izegem NV [1978] 2 Lloyd's Rep 113. 62
Bridgeway Construction Ltd v Tolent Construction Ltd [2000] CILL 1662. 285
British Eagle International Airlines Ltd v Compagnie Nationale Air France [1975] 1 WLR 758 (HL); [1975] 2 All ER 390 113
British Russian Gazette & Trade Outlook Ltd v Associated Newspapers Ltd [1933] 2 KB 616 3
British Steel Corp v Cleveland Bridge & Engineering Co Ltd (1981) 24 BLR 94; [1984] 1 All ER 504. 141
British Telecommunications plc v Bell Cable Media (Leeds) Ltd [2001] BLR 343 194
Bullock v London General Omnibus Co [1907] 1 KB 264 45
Butler Machine Tool Co-v-Ex-Cell-O-Corp [1979] 1 WLR 401; [1979] 1 All ER 965. 33
Byrne v Van Tienhoven [1880] 5 CPD 344 234
C–81/98 Alcatel v Austria [1999] ECR I–7671 11
Calderbank v Calderbank [1976] Fam 93; [1975] 3 WLR 586; [1975] 3 All ER 333. 47
Callaghan & Welton v Hewgate Construction Ltd (1996) 75 BLR 11 (CA) 256
Cambridge Water Co Ltd v Eastern Counties Leather plc [1994] 2 AC 264; [1994] 2 WLR 53. 239
Cantillon Ltd v Urvasco Ltd [2008] EWHC 282 (TCC), [2008] BLR 250; 117 ConLR 1 182
Cantrell v Wright & Fuller Ltd [2003] EWHC 1545 (TCC); [2003] BLR 412 114
Caparo Industries v Dickman [1990] UKHL 2. 48
Channel Tunnel Group v Balfour Beatty [1993] 2 WLR 262 53
Chartbrook Ltd v Persimmon Homes Ltd [2009] UKHL 38; [2009] AC 1101; [2009] BLR 551; [2009] 3 WLR 267. . . . . 183, 223
City Inn Ltd v Shepherd Construction Ltd [2010] CSIH 68; [2010] BLR 473 . . . . 17, 152
Clemence v Clarke (1879) Hudson's Law of Building, Engineering & Ship Building Contracts 4th edn, Vol. 2, p. 54 . . . . 151, 234
Collins (Contractors) Ltd v Baltic Quay Management (1994) Ltd [2004] EWCA Civ 1757; [2005] BLR 63, 74; [2004] 2 All ER 982 (Clarke LJ) 86
Conquer v Boot [1928] KB 336 63
Co-operative Insurance Society Ltd v Argyll Stores (Holdings) Ltd [1996] 3 WLR 27; [1996] 3 All ER 934 92
Co-operative Insurance Society Ltd, The v Henry Boot Scotland Ltd [2002] EWHC 1270 (TCC) 68
Co-operative Retail Services v Taylor Young Partnership [2002] UKHL 17; [2002] Lloyd's Rep IR 555; [2002] 1 WLR 1419. 114
Copée-Lavalin SA/NV v Ken-Ren Chemicals and Fertilizers Ltd [1994] 2 All ER 449. 148
Cornhill Insurance plc v Improvement Services Ltd [1986] WLR 144. 68

Coslett (Contractors) Ltd, Re (1998) 85 BLR 1 (CA); [1998] 2 WLR 131; [1997] 4 All ER 115; [2002] BLR 166 (HL) 248
Crest Nicholson (Eastern) Ltd v Western [2008] EWHC 1325 (TCC); [2008] BLR 426; [2008] TCLR 9 182
Crowshaw v Pritchard (1899) Hudson's Law of Building, Engineering and Ship Building Contracts 4th edn, Vol. 2, 274 . . . . 101, 278
Dalton v Angus [1881] 6 App Cas 740 (HL) 235
Dashwood v Dashwood [1927] WN 276 285
David Allen & Sons Billposting Ltd v Drysdale [1939] 4 All ER 113 . . . . 250, 269
Davies v Elsby Brothers Ltd [1961] 1 WLR 170 (CA) 177
Davis Contractors Ltd v Fareham UDC [1956] AC 696 119
Department of Environment v Thomas Bates [1991] 1 AC 499 (CA) 179
Derry v Peek [1889] 14 App Cas 337 . . . . 118, 177
Dickinson v Dodds [1876] 2 Ch D 463 84
DPP v Lynch [1975] AC 653 90
DSND Subsea Ltd v Petroleum Geo-Services ASA [2000] BLR 530, 545 92
Dumford Trading AG v Oao Atlantrybfl ot [2005] EWCA Civ 24 177
Dunlop Pneumatic Tyre Co Ltd v New Garage & Motor Co Ltd [1915] AC 79 164
East Ham Corporation v Bernard Sunley & Sons Ltd [1966] AC 406 (HL) 91
Eichleay Corp v US ASBCA No 5183 (1960) 93
Equitable Debenture Assets Corp Ltd v William Moss Group Ltd [1984] 2 ConLR 1 (TCC) 42
ERDC Group Ltd v Brunel University [2006] EWHC 687 (TCC); [2006] BLR 255 118
Eurotunnel v TML [1993] 2 WLR 262 102
The Evia Luck [1992] 2 AC 152, 165G 92
Fastrack Contractors Ltd v Morrison Construction Ltd [2000] BLR 168; 75 ConLR 33 155
Federal Commerce & Navigation Co Ltd v Tradax Export SA [1978] AC 1 (HL) 260
Ferguson v Welsh [1987] 1 WLR 1553 (HL); [1987] 3 All ER 777 189
FG Minter Ltd v Welsh Health Technical Services Organisation (1980) 13 BLR 1 (CA) 84
Field v Metropolitan Police Receiver [1907] 2 KB 853 (DC) 236
Finelvet AG v Vinava Shipping Co Ltd [1983] 1 Lloyd's Rep 503; [1983] 1 WLR 1469 304
Franks & Collingwood v Gates [1983] 1 ConLR 21 299
Galaxy Energy International Ltd v Eurobunker Spa [2001] EWHC 502 (Comm); [2001] 2 Lloyd's Rep 725; [2001] 2 All ER (Comm) 912 171
Geldof Metaalconstructie NV v Simon Carves Ltd [2010] EWCA Civ 667; [2010] BLR 401 100
GLC v Cleveland Bridge & Engineering Co Ltd (1984) 34 BLR 50 (CA) 104
Golden Ocean Group Ltd v Salgaocar Mining Industries PVT Ltd [2011] EWHC 56 (Comm); [2011] 2 All ER (Comm) 95 263
Goodman v J Eban Ltd [1954] 1 QB 550 (CA); [1954] 1 All ER 763 252
Greater London Council v Connolly [1970] 2 QB 100 242
Great Peace Shipping Ltd v Tsaviliris Salvage International Ltd [2002] EWCA 1407; [2003] QB 679 177
Greaves v Baynham Meikle [1975] 2 Lloyd's Rep 325; [1975] 1 WLR 1095 (CA); [1975] 3 All ER 99 116
Gwelhayl Ltd v Midas Construction Ltd [2008] EWHC 2316 (TCC); 123 ConLR 91 115
H Fairweather Ltd v Asden Securities Ltd (1979) 12 BLR 40 119
Hadley v Baxendale [1854] 9 Ex 341; [1854] 23 LJ Ex 179 . . . . 144, 228
Hadley v Baxendale [1854] 156 ER 145 131

Hadley v Baxendale [1854] EWHC J70; [1854] 9 ExCh 341 84
Halsey v Milton Keynes General NHS Trust [2004] EWCA Civ 576; [2004] 1 WLR 3002; [2004] 4 All ER 920. . . . . 131, 174
Hanak v Green (1958) 2 QB 9; 1 BLR 1. 100
Hancock v BW Brazier (Anerley) Ltd [1966] 1 WLR 1317 (CA); [1966] 2 All ER 901. . . . . 115, 131
Harmon CFEM Facades (UK) Ltd v House of Commons [1999] 67 ConLR 1 177
Harris Springs Ltd v Howes [2007] EWHC 3271 (TCC); [2008] BLR 229 158
Hawthorn v Newcastle-on-Tyne & Hallway Co [1840] 3 QB 734 162
Hedley Byrne & Co Ltd v Heller & Partners Ltd [1964] AC 465 (HL); [1963] 3 WLR 101; [1963] 2 All ER 575 . . . . .134, 177, 183
Henry Boot Construction Ltd v Alstom Combined Cycles Ltd [2000] BLR 247 (CA) 110, 134
Henry Boot Construction Ltd v Alstom Combined Cycles Ltd [2005] EWCA Civ 814; [2005] BLR 437 (CA); [2005] 1 WLR 3850 163
Henry Boot Construction Ltd v Central Lancashire New Town Development Corp (1980) 15 BLR 8 24
Henry Boot Construction (UK) Ltd v Malmaison Hotel [2000] EWCA Civ 175; 70 ConLR 32 142
Henthorn v Fraser [1892] 2 Ch 27 208
The Heron II (C Czarnikow Ltd v Koufos [1976] 2 Lloyd's Rep 555; [1967] 3 WLR 1491; [1967] 3 All ER 686 [1969] 1 AC 350 (HL)) 158
Herschel Engineering Ltd v Breen Pty Ltd [2000] BLR 272 118
HG Construction Ltd v Ashwell Homes (East Anglia) Ltd [2007] EWHC 144 (TCC), [2007] BLR 175; 112 ConLR 128 231
Hickman & Co v Roberts [1913] AC 229; 82 LJKB 678. 134
Hoenig v Isaacs [1952] 2 All ER 176 269
Holbeck Hall Hotel Ltd v Scarborough BC [2000] BLR 109 (CA); [2000] 2 WLR 1396; [2000] 2All ER 705. 235
Homburg Houtimport BV v Agrosin Private Ltd [2003] 1 Lloyd's Rep. 571; [2004] 1 AC 715 (HL) 257
Home Office v Lownds [2002] EWCA Civ 365; [2002] 1 WLR 2450; [2002] 4 All ER 775 . . . . 144, 259
Hong Guan and Co Ltd v R Jumabhoy and Sons Ltd [1960] AC 684; [1960] 2 All ER 100 117
Hounslow London Borough Council v Twickenham Garden Developments Ltd [1971] Ch 233 182
How Engineering Services Ltd v Lindner Ceilings Floors Partitions plc [1999] 64 ConLR 67 25
Hutchinson v Harris (1978) 10 BLR 19 (CA). 1
HW Nevill (Sunblest) Ltd v Wm Press & Son Ltd (1991) 20 BLR 78 208
Inglis v Buttery & Co [1878] 3 App Cas 552 (HL) 81
Inntrepreneur Pub Co (GL) v East Crown Ltd [2000] 2 Lloyd's Rep 11. 99
Investors Compensation Scheme Ltd v West Bromwich Building Society [1997] UKHL 28; [1998] 1 WLR 896; [1998] 1 All ER 98 . . . . 110, 149
IRC v Hobhouse [1956] 1 WLR 1393. 313
J Crosby & Sons Ltd v Portland UDC (1967) 5 BLR 121. 123
J & J Makin Ltd v London & NE Rly Co [1945] 1 KB 467 4
Jarvis & Sons Ltd v Westminster Corp [1970] 1 WLR 637; [1970] 1 All ER 943. 208
John Doyle Construction Ltd v Laing Management 2002 Scot (CS) 110; [2002] BLR 393; 85 ConLR 98 151
John Jarvis Ltd v Rockdale Housing Association Ltd (1986) 36 BLR 48 (CA). 295, 297, 301
Joinery Plus Ltd v Laing Ltd [2003] EWHC 3513 (TCC); [2003] BLR 184; 87 ConLR 87 . . . . 156, 282

Junior Books Ltd v Veitchi Co Ltd [1983] 1 AC 520; [1982] 3 WLR 477; [1982] 3 All ER 201 90
Kawasaki Kisen Kobushiki Kiasha of Kobe v Bantham Steamship Co Ltd (No 2) [1939] 2 KB 544 (CA) 303
L Schuler AG v Wickman Machine Tool Sales Ltd [1973] UKHL 2; [1974] AC 235 13
Lagden v O' Connor [2003] UKHL 64; [2004] AC 1067 93
Lanes Group plc v Galliford Try Infrastructure Ltd [2011] EWCA Civ 1617 118
Langstane Housing Association Ltd v Riverside Construction (Aberdeen) Ltd [2009] CSOH 52; 124 ConLR 211 183
LCC v Henry Boot & Sons Ltd [1959] 1 WLR 1069; [1959] 3 All ER 636. . . . 178
Leander Construction Ltd v Mulalley & Co Ltd [2011] EWHC 3499 (TCC) 139
Lebeaupin v Crispin [1920] 2 KB 714 301
Linden Gardens Trust Ltd v Lenesta Sludge Disposals Ltd [1994] 1 AC 85; [1993] 3 WLR 408; [1993] 3 All ER 417 212
Lindsay Petroleum Co v Hurd [1874] LR 5 PC 221 159
Lintest Builders Ltd v Roberts (1978) 10 BLR 120 (CA) 278
Lodder v Slowey [1904] AC 442 (PC) 216, 304
London and Manchester Plate Glass Co Ltd v Heath [1913] 3 KB 411 (CA). 55
London Borough of Dagenham & Barking v Terrapin Construction Ltd [2000] BLR 479 (CA) 106
Lownds v Home Office [2002] EWCA Civ 365; [2002] CP Rep 43; [2002] 1 WLR 2450; [2002] 4 All ER 775 259
Lurcott v Wakely [1911] 1 KB 905 228
Macob Civil Engineering Ltd v Morrison Construction Ltd [1999] BLR 93; 75 ConLR 101 169
Magill v Porter [2002] 2 AC 357 (HL) 34
Mannai Investment Co Ltd v Eagle Star Life Assurance Co Ltd [1997] AC 749; [1997] 2 WLR 945; [1997] 3 All ER 352. . . . . 13, 201, 265
Mareva Compania Naveira SA v International Bulkcarriers SA [1975] 2 Lloyd's Rep 509 171
McAlpine Humberoak Ltd v McDermott International Inc (No 1) (1992) 58 BLR 1 (CA). 86
McCutcheon v David MacBrayne Ltd [1964] 1 WLR 125, 133; [1964] 1 All ER 430. 252
McGlinn v Waltham Contractors Ltd [2007] EWHC 149 (TCC); [2008] BLR 233; 111 ConLR 1 145
Mead General Building Ltd v Dartmoor Properties Ltd [2009] EWHC 200 (TCC); [2009] BLR 225; [2009] BPIR 516 264
Mehta v J Pereira Fernandes SA [2006] EWHC 813 (Ch); [2006] 1 WLR 1543. 262
Midland Expressway Ltd v Carillion Construction Ltd [2006] EWHC 1505 (TCC), [2006] BLR 325 85
Midland Expressway Ltd v Carillion Contractors Ltd [2006] 107 ConLR 235 (CA). 213
Mirant Asia-Pacific Construction (Hong Kong) Ltd v Ove Arup and Partners International Ltd [2007] EWHC 918 (TCC); [2008] BLR D1 306
Modern Engineering (Bristol) Ltd v Gilbert Ash (Northern) Ltd [1974] AC 689 (HL) 1
Moffatt v Laurie [1855] 15 CB 563 212
Monk Construction Ltd v Norwich Union Life Assurance Society (1992) 62 BLR 107 (CA). 162
Mooney v Henry Boot Construction Ltd (1996) 80 BLR 66 (CA) 250
Mowlem plc v Newton Street Ltd [2003] EWHC 737 (TCC); 89 ConLR 153 129

Multiplex Constructions (UK) Ltd v Honeywell Control Systems Ltd [2007] EWHC 447 (TCC); [2007] BLR 195; 111 ConLR 78. 283
Murphy v Brentwood DC [1991] 1 AC 398; [1990] 2 All ER 908. . . . . . . 15, 179
National Justice Compania Naviera SA v Prudential Assurance Company Ltd (The "Ikarian Reffer") [1993] 2 Lloyd's Rep 68 141
National Semiconductors (UK) Ltd v UPS Ltd [1996] 2 Lloyd's Rep 212 306
NATL Amusements (UK) Ltd v White City (Shepherd's Bush) Ltd Partnership [2009] EWHC 2524 (TCC); [2010] BLR 24; [2010] 1 WLR 1181 287
Neodox v Swinton and Pendlebury BC (1958) 5 BLR 38 272
Nigel Witham Ltd v Smith No.2 [2008] EWHC 12 (TCC); [2008] TCLR 3; 117 ConLR 117 174
Nikko Hotels (UK) Ltd v MEPC plc [1991] 2 EGLR 103, 108 105
Nikon Inc v US No 99/98/982C (Fed. Cl. Dec 21, 2001) 93
Nittan (UK) Ltd v Solent Steel [1981] 1 Lloyd's Rep 633 (CA) 177
North Eastern Properties Ltd v Coleman [2010] EWCA Civ 277; [2010] BLR 579 99
Nugent v Smith (1876) 1 CPD 423 301
Nye Saunders & Partners v Bristow (1987) 37 BLR 92 (CA) 101
Orakpo v Manson Investments Ltd [1978] AC 95; [1977] 3 WLR 229; [1977] 3 All ER 1 (HL) 268
Ove Arup & Partners International Ltd (No 2) v Mirant Asis- Pacific Construction (Hong Kong) Ltd [2006] BLR 187; [2005] EWCA Civ 1585 254
P & M Kaye Ltd v Hosier & Dickinson Ltd [1972] 1 WLR 146, 165; [1972] 1 All ER 121 278
Pagnan v Feed Products [1987] 2 Lloyd's Rep 601 197
Paul Smith Ltd v H and S International Holding Inc [1991] 2 Lloyd's Rep 127 73
Pepper v Hart [1992] UKHL 3; [1993] AC 593; [1992] 3 WLR 1032 . . . . 131, 202
Perar BV v General Surety (1994) 66 BLR 72 (CA) 78
Philips Hong Kong Ltd v Attorney-General of Hong Kong (1993) 61 BLR 41 164
Photo Productions Ltd v Securicor Transport Ltd [1980] AC 827; [1980] 2 WLR 283; [1980] 1 All ER 556. . . . . 119, 171
PJ Dick Inc v Principi 324 F.3d 1364 (Fed. Cir. 2003) 93
Porter v Magill [2001] UKHL 67; [2002] 2 AC 357 207
Porter v Tottenham UDC [1915] KB 776 (CA) .2, 217
Post Office v Aquarius Properties Ltd [1987] 1 All ER 1055. 228
Pratt Contractors Ltd v Transit New Zealand [2003] UKPC 83; [2004] BLR 143. 149
Premium Nafta Products Ltd v Fili Shipping Co Ltd [2007] UKHL 40; [2008] 1 Lloyd's Rep 254; [2007] 4 All ER 951 19
Prenn v Simmonds [1971] 1 WLR 1381, 1384; [1971] 3 All ER 237. . . . . 110, 198
Prestcold (Central) Ltd v Minister of Labour [1969] 1 WLR 89 279
Projects Ltd v Elmwood (Glasgow) Ltd [2011] CSOH 64 285
R v Architects' Registration Tribunal ex parte Jaggar [1945] 2 All ER 131 DC 21
R. Durtnell & Sons Ltd v Kaduna Ltd [2003] EWHC 517; [2003] BLR 225 95
Reardon-Smith Line Ltd v Yngvar Hansen-Tangen and Sanko SS & Co Ltd [1976] 2 Lloyd's Rep 621; [1976] 1 WLR 989 189
Rees & Kirby Ltd v Swansea Corp (1985) 30 BLR 1 . . . . 84, 114
Rhodia International Holdings Ltd v Huntsman International LLC [2007] EWHC 292 (Comm); [2007] 2 Lloyd's Rep 325. 34
Rickards v Lothian [1913] AC 263 239
Robertson v French [1803] 7 East 130 173

Robinson v PE Jones (Contractors) Ltd [2010] EWCA Civ 102; [2010] TCLR 3 90
Royal Brompton Hospital NHS Trust v Hammond [2002] EWHC 2037 (TCC) 117
RTS Flexible Systems Ltd v Molkerei Alois Muller Gmbh [2010] UKSC 14; [2010] BLR 337 (SC); [2010] 1 WLR 753; [2010] 3 All ER 1. 268
Rupert Morgan Building Services (LLC) Ltd v Jervis [2004] BLR 18 (CA) 1
Rylands v Fletcher [1866] LR 1 Ex 265 239
Sanderson v Blyth Theatre Co [1903] 2 KB 533 (CA) 241
Schuler (L) A.G. v Wickman Machine Tool Sales Ltd [1973] 2 Lloyds Rep 53; [1974] AC 235. 201
Sempra Metals Ltd v Commissioners of Inland Revenue [2008] AC 561 (HL) 60
Sempra Metals Ltd v IRC [2007] UKHL 34; [2008] 1 AC 561; [2007] 3 WLR 354; [2007] 4 All ER 657 (HL). 257
Sempra Metals Ltd v Revenue [2007] UKHL 34; [2008] AC 561 (HL); [2007] 3 WLR 354 147
Shaw v Massey Foundation & Pilings Ltd [2009] EWHC 493 (TCC). 230
Siemens Building Technologies FE Ltd v Supershield Ltd [2009] EWHC 927 (TCC); [2009] 2 All ER (Comm) 900. 35
Simon Carves Ltd v Ensus UK Ltd [2011] EWHC 657 (TCC); [2011] BLR 340; 135 ConLR 96 252
Sinclair Roche and Temperley v Somatra [2003] EWCA Civ 1474; [2003] 2 Lloyd's Rep 855 . . . . . 144, 259
Sir Alfred McAlpine Homes North Ltd v Property & Land Contractors Ltd (1995) 76 BLR 59 25
Sir Lindsay Parkinson & Co Ltd v Commissioners of Works and Public Buildings [1949] 2 KB 632; [1950] 1 All ER 208. 197
Smith v South Wales Switchgear [1978] 1 All ER 18. 255
Stansbie v Troman [1948] 2 KB 48 (CA) 280
Steamship Mutual Underwriting Association Ltd v Trollope & Colls (City) Ltd (1986) 33 BLR 77 (CA) 13, 50
Stein v Blake [1996] AC 243 (HL); [1995] BCC 543; [1995] 2 WLR 710. . . . 180
Sudbrook Trading Estate Ltd v Eggleton [1983] 1 AC 444 (HL). 242
Sutcliffe v Thackrah [1974] AC 727; [1974] 1 All ER 859. . . . .21, 216, 273
Team Services plc v Kier Management and Design Ltd (1993) 63 BLR 76. . . . 49
Tersons Ltd v Stevenage Development Corp (1963) 5 BLR 54 (CA) 66
Thorn v Mayor and Commonality of London (1876) 1 App Cas 120 (HL). . . 143
Three Rivers D.C. v Bank of England (no. 3) [2003] 2 AC 1, 282, (HL) 270
Three Rivers District Council v Bank of England [2004] UKHL 48; [2004] 3 WLR 1274 . . . . . 212, 281
Tilling v Whiteman [1980] AC 1. 210
Toepfer v Continental Grain Co [1974] 1 Lloyd's Rep 11 (CA) 171
Token Construction Co Ltd v Charlton Estates Ltd (1973) 1 BLR 48 (CA). 52
Tramp Shipping Corp v Greenwich Marine Inc [1975] 2 All ER 988 266
Transco plc v Stockport Metropolitan Borough Council [2003] UKHL 61; [2003] 3 WLR 1467; [2004] 1 All ER 589. 240
Trim Joint District School Board of Management v Kelly [1914] AC 667 (HL) 3
Trollope & Colls Ltd Haydon [1977] 1 Lloyd's Rep. 244 103
Turriff Construction Ltd v Regalia Knitting Mills Ltd (1971) 9 BLR 20 . . . . . 162, 290
Uniplex (UK) Ltd v NHS Business Services Authority (Case C-406/08, 28 January 2010) 296
United States v Spearin, 248 U.S. 132 (1918). 257
Universal Tanking of Monrovia v ITWF [1983] AC 336, 400B-E 92
Victoria Laundry (Windsor) Ltd v Newman Industries Ltd [1949] 2 KB 528 (CA). 158

Voaden v Champion [2002] 1 Lloyd's Rep 623 (CA) 34
VosslohAtkiengesellschaft v Alpha Trains (UK) Ltd [2010]
EWHC 2443 (Ch) 204
Walter Lawrence & Son Ltd v Commercial Pties (UK) Ltd [1984]
4 ConLR 36 103
Walter Lilly & Co Ltd v Mackay & others [2012] EWHC 1773. 123
Watson Lumber v Guennwig, 79 Ill. App. 2d 377; 226 N.E.2d 270 (1967). . . . 300
Weldon Plant Ltd v Commission for New Towns [2000] BLR 496;
[2001] 1 All ER (Comm) 264. 110
West Faulkner Associates v London Borough of Newham (1994)
71 BLR 1 (CA). 84, 95, 225
Wickham Contracting Co v Fischer (1994) 12 F.3d 1574
(Fed. Cir. 1994) 306
Williams v Wallis & Cox [1914] 2 KB 478. 176
Wimbledon Construction Co 2000 Ltd v Vago [2005] EWHC 1086 (TCC);
[2005] BLR 374; 101 ConLR 99 263
Witney Town Council v Beam Construction (Cheltenham) Ltd [2011]
EWHC 2332 (TCC); [2011] BLR 707; [2011] TCLR 8. 308
WN Hillas & Co Ltd v Arcos Ltd [1932] 147 LT 503 (HL) 242
Wong Lai Ying v Chinachem Investment Ltd (1979) 13 BLR 86 (PC) 119
Worlock v SAWS (1981) 20 BLR 94. 118
Yates Building Co Ltd v RJ Pulleyn & Sons (York) Ltd [1975] 237 EG 183. . . . 186
YCMS Ltd v Grabiner [2009] EWHC 127 (TCC); [2009] BLR 211;
123 ConLR 202 . . . . 37, 313
Yeadon Waterworks Co, Re v Wright [1895] 72 LT 832 (CA) 270
Yuanda (UK) Co Ltd v WW Gear Construction Ltd [2010]
EWHC 720 (TCC); [2010] BLR 435; 130 ConLR 133 . . . . .244, 285, 313
Zealander & Zealander v Laing Homes Ltd [2000] 2 TCLR 724. 181

TABLE OF ABBREVIATIONS AND ACRONYMS

A&E, A/E	Architect and Engineer; Architecture and Engineering
AAC	Autoclaved Aerated Concrete
ABE	Association of Building Engineers
AC	Appeal Cases
ACA	Association of Consultant Architects
ACE	Association of Consulting Engineers
ACoP	Approved Code of Practice
ADR	Alternative Dispute Resolution
AFC	Approved for Construction
AGA	Authorised Guarantee Agreement
AGC	Associate General Contractors of America
AHU	Air Handling Unit
AI	Approved Inspector; Architect's Instruction
AIA	American Institute of Architects
ALARP	As Low as Reasonably Practicable
All ER	All England Reports
ALWC	Accelerated Low Water Corrosion
ANB	Adjudicator Nominating Body
AOD	Above Ordnance Datum
API	American Petroleum Institute
APR	Annual Percentage Rate
ARB	Architect's Registration Board
ASME	American Society of Mechanical Engineers
ASR	Alkali Silica Reaction
AssocRICS	Associate member of RICS
ASTM	American Society for Testing and Materials
BAE	British Academy of Experts
BAFO	Best and Final Offer
BAS	Building Automation System
BATNA	Best Alternative to Negotiated Agreement
BBA	British Board of Agrément
BCB	Building Control Body
BCMS	Building Control and Management System
BERR	Department for Business, Enterprise and Regulatory Reform
BIM	Building Information Modelling
BIMMI	BIM Maturity Index
BIS	Department for Business Innovation and Skills

BLR	Building Law Reports
BMS	Building Management System
BOOT	Build, Own, Operate and Transfer
BOQ, BQ	Bill of quantities
BOT	Build, Operate and Transfer
BRE	Building Research Establishment
BREEAM	BRE Environmental Assessment Method
BS	British Standards
BSF	Building Schools for the Future
BSI	British Standards Institution, Building Systems Integration
BSRIA	Building Services Research and Information Association
BThU, Btu	British Thermal Unit
BWG	Birmingham Wire Gauge
BWIC	Builder's Work In Connection
C&G	City and Guilds of London Institute; Clearing and Grubbing
CA	Contract Administrator; Court of Appeal
CAD	Computer-Aided Design
CAR	Contractor's All Risks policy
CAWS	The Common Arrangement of Work Sections
CBR	California Bearing Ratio
CDE	Common Data Environment
CDM	Construction (Design and Management)
CDP	Contractor Designed Portion
CEDR	Centre for Effective Dispute Resolution
CEN	European Committee for Standardisation
CESSM	Civil Engineering Standard Method of Measurement
CFA	Conditional Fee Agreement
CGCT	Combined Cycle Gas Turbine
Ch	Chancery Division
CIArb	Chartered Institute of Arbitrators
CIBSE	Chartered Institute of Building Services Engineers
CILL	Construction Industry Law Letter
CIMAR	Construction Industry Model Arbitration Rules
CIOB	Chartered Institute of Building
CIS	Construction Industry Scheme
CMC	Case Management Conference
CMU	Concrete Masonry Unit
COB	Close of Business
COBie	Construction Operations Building Information Exchange

COCO	Contractor Owned Contractor Operated
ConLR	Construction Law Reports
ConstLJ	Construction Law Journal
CORE	Cumbrians Opposed to a Radioactive Environment
CORGI	The Confederation for the Registration of Gas Installers
COW	Clerk of Works
CPIC	Construction Project Information Committee
CPM	Critical Path Analysis/Method
CPR	Civil Procedure Rules
CPs	Contractor's Proposals
CVA	Company Voluntary Arrangement
CVI	Confirmation of Verbal Instruction
DAB	Dispute Adjudication Board
DB	Decibel; Design and Build Contract; Dispute Board
DBFM	Design Build Finance Manage
DBFO	Design Build Finance Operate
DBO	Design Build Operate
DCLG	Department for Communities and Local Government
DECC	Department for Energy and Climate Change
DfT	Department for Transport
DHW	Domestic Hot Water
DLP	Defects Liability Period
DNO	Distribution Network Operator
DoE	Department of the Environment
DPA	Defective Premises Act
DPC	Damp Proof Course
DPM	Damp Proof Membrane
DRB	Dispute Resolution Board
DRBF	Dispute Resolution Board Foundation
DTI	Department of Trade and Industry
E&OE	Errors and Omissions excepted or excluded
EA	Environment Agency
EAR	Erector's All Risks policy
ECJ	European Court of Justice
EIA	Environmental impact assessment
EJ	Expansion Joint
ELPS	Emergency Lighting Power Supply
EN	European Standard, Euronorm
ENE	Early Neutral Evaluation
EOT	Extension of time
EPC	Engineering, Procurement, Construction
EPS	Emergency Power Systems; Expanded Polystyrene

ERs	Employer's Requirements
ES	Edison Screw
ESD	Electrostatic Discharge
ETFE	Ethylene Tetra Fluoroethylene
EU	European Union
EVOH	Ethylene Vinyl Alcohol Copolymer
EWCA	England and Wales Court of Appeal
EWHC	England and Wales High Court
EWN	Early Warning Notice
Fam	Family
FAT	Factory Acceptance Test
FEED	Front End Engineering Design
FFE	Furniture Fixtures Equipment
FFL	Finished Floor Level
FIDIC	Federation Internationale des Ingenieurs-Conseils
Fi fa	*Fieri facias*
FIT	Feed In Tariff
FLA	Football Licensing Authority
FM	Facilities Management
FMB	Federation of Master Builders
FOIA	The Freedom of Information Act 2000
FPA	Fire Protection Association
FRC	Fibre-Reinforced Concrete
FRICS	Fellow of the RICS
FS	Factor of Safety
GA	General Arrangement (drawing)
GBG	Good Building Guides
GC/Work	GC/Work (Formerly Government Conditions Contract)
GEA	Gross external area
GMP	Guaranteed maximum price
GOCO	Government owned, contractor operated
GPDO	General Permitted Development Order
GRC	Glass(fibre)-reinforced concrete
GRG	Glass(fibre)-reinforced gypsum
GRP	Glass Reinforced Plastic; Glass-Reinforced Polyester
Ha	Hectare
HA	Highways Agency
HAC	High Alumina Cement
HAZID	Hazard Identification Studies
HAZOP	Hazard and Operability Studies
HGCRA	Housing Grants, Construction and Regeneration Act
HMRC	Her Majesty's Revenue and Customs

HPHW	High-Pressure Hot Water
HRA	Human Rights Act
HRSG	Heat Recovery Steam Generator
HSE	Health and Safety Executive
HVAC	Heating Ventilation and Air Conditioning
HVOTL	High Voltage Overhead Transmission Line
IBC, IC	Intermediate Building Contract
iBIM	Integrated BIM
ICC	International Chamber of Commerce
ICD	Intermediate Building Contract with Contractor's Design
ICE	Institution of Civil Engineers
ICE 6	The 6th edition of the Measurement Contract published by the ICE
ICE 7	The 7th edition of the Measurement Contract published by the ICE
IChemE	Institution of Chemical Engineers
ICI	Imperial Chemical Industries
ICP	Independent Connections Provider
IEE	Institution of Electrical Engineers
IET	Institution of Engineering and Technology
IFC	Intermediate Form of Contract; Issued for Construction
IFC 84	Intermediate Form of Contract 1984 version
IFCE	International Federation of Consulting Engineers
IIE	Institution of Incorporated Engineers
IMechE	Institutions of Mechanical Engineers
Incoterms	International Commercial Terms
IPT	Integrated project team
ISO	International Organization for Standardization
IT	Information Technology
ITB	Invitation to Bid
ITN	Invitation to Negotiate
ITT	Invitation to Tender
IVA	Individual Voluntary Arrangement
JCT	Joint Contracts Tribunal
JV	Joint Venture
KPI	Key Performance Indicator
LADs	Liquidated and Ascertained Damages
LCIA	London Court of International Arbitration
LCJ	Lord Chief Justice
LDEDC or LDEDCA	Local Democracy, Economic Development and Construction Act 2009

LDF	Local Development Framework
LIBID	The London Interbank Bid Rate
LIBOR	The London Interbank Offered Rate
LIFT	Local Improvement Finance Trust
LJ	Lord Justice; Lady Justice
LJJ	Lords Justices; Ladies Justices
LLP	Limited Liability Partnership
LOI	Letter of Intent
LS	Locus Sigilli
M&E	Mechanical and Electrical
M&O	Management and Operations
MC	Management Building Contract
MCD	Main Contractor's Discount
MDB	Multilateral Development Banks
MDF	Medium-Density Fibreboard
MDP	Multi-Disciplinary Practice
MEAT	Most Economically Advantageous Tender
MEP	Mechanical, Electrical and Plumbing
MEWPs	Mobile Elevating Work Platforms
MF/1	Model Form of General Conditions of Contract/1
MF/2	Model Form of General Conditions of Contract/2
MH	Manhole
MOAT	Methods of Assessment and Testing
MRICS	Member of RICS
MRT	Mean Radiant Temperature
MW	Minor Works Building Contract
MWD	JCT Minor Works Building Contract with Contractor's Design
MWSUB/D	JCT Minor Works Building Subcontract with Subcontractor's Design
NAECI	National Agreement for the Engineering Construction Industry
NBS	National Building Specification
NDA	Non-Disclosure Agreement; Nuclear Decommissioning Authority
NEC	New Engineering Contract
NHBC	National House Building Council
NIA	Nuclear Industry Association
NJCC	National Joint Consultative Committee for Building
NOx	Nitrogen Oxides
NR	Noise Rating
NSB	National Standards Body
NSC	Nominated Subcontractor

NSCC	National Specialist Contractor's Council
O&M	Operation and Maintenance Manual
OCR	Optical Character Recognition
ODN	Ordnance Datum Newlyn
OFFER	Office of Electricity Regulation
OFGEM	Office of Gas and Electricity Markets
OHP (OH&P)	Overheads and Profit
OJEU	The Official Journal of the European Union
OJEU Notice	The Official Journal of the European Union Notice
OSB	Oriented Strand Board
P3	Primavera Project Planner™
PABX	Private Automatic Branch eXchange
PAP	Pre-Action Protocol
PBA	Project Bank Account
PC	Polycarbonate sheet; Practical Completion
PC item/sum	Prime Cost item/sum
PD	Practice Direction
PE	Polyethylene
PERT	Program Evaluation and Review Technique
PFI	Private Finance Initiative
PFP	Passive Fire Protection
pH	Potential Hydrogen
POMI	Principles of Measurement International
PP	Polypropylene
PPC2000	A Standard Form of Contract for Project Partnering, published by the ACA
PPP	Public–Private Partnership
PQQ	Pre-Qualification Questionnaire
PS	Polystyrene
PSW	Performance Specified Work
PTFE	Polytetrafluorethylene
PTR	Pre-Trial Review
PU	Polyurethane
PVB	Polyvinyl Butyral
PVC	Polyvinyl Chloride
PVCu	Unplasticised PVC
PVF	Polyvinyl Fluoride
PVF2	Polyvinylidene Fluoride
PWR	Pressured Water Reactor
QA	Quality Assurance
QB	Queen's Bench Division
QC	Queen's Counsel; Quality Control
QM	Quality Management

QS	Quantity Surveyor
RAG	Residential Agency Guidelines
RCD	Residual Current Device
RDSAP	Reduced Data Standard Assessment Procedure
RE	Resident Engineer
RFI	Request for Information
RH	Relative Humidity
RIAS	Royal Incorporation of Architects in Scotland
RIBA	Royal Institute of British Architects
RICS	Royal Institution of Chartered Surveyors
ROT clause	Retention of title clause
RPB	Regional Planning Body
RPG	Regional Planning Guidance
RPI	Retail Prices Index
R/R	Relative Readings
RS	Regional Strategy
RSC	Rules of the Supreme Court
RSJ	Rolled Steel Joist
RSS	Regional Spatial Strategy
RTECS	Registry of Toxic Effects of Chemical Substances
RWP	Rainwater Pipe
SBC	Small Bayonet Cap ; Standard Building Contract
SC	Supreme Court
SCADA	Supervisory Control and Data Acquisition
SCL	Society of Construction Law
SES	Small Edison Screw
SI	Statutory Instruments
SIP	Structurally Insulated Panels
SME	Small and Medium Sized Enterprise
SMM, SMM7	Standard Method of Measurement
SPV	Special Purpose Vehicle
SRB	Sulphate-Reducing Bacteria
ss	Stainless Steel
SSL	Structural Slab Level
SSSI	Site of Special Scientific Interest
SUDS	Sustainable Urban Drainage Systems
SWIFT	Structured What-If Technique
TBM	Temporary Benchmark
TCC	Technology and Construction Court
TCLR	Technology and Construction Law Reports
TECBAR	Technology and Construction Bar Association
TeCSA	Technology and Construction Solicitors' Association
TOC	Taking Over Certificate

TPO	Tree Preservation Order
TQ	Technical Query
TRADA	Timber Research and Development Association
TRU	Thermostatic Radiator Valve
UDP	Unitary Development Plan
UNCITRAL	The United Nations Commission on International Trade Law
UNIDROIT	International Institute for the Unification of Private Law
UPS	Uninterruptible Power Supply
uPVC	Unplasticised polyvinyl chloride
VAT	Value Added Tax
VAV	Variable Air Volume systems
VE	Value Engineering
WCs	Water Closet, toilet
WHRB	Waste Heat Recovery Boiler
WLR	Weekly Law Reports
Y2K	Year 2000

A

AAC See **Autoclaved aerated concrete**.

Abandonment A failure or refusal to continue performance of a contract on a permanent basis, particularly by a contractor under a construction contract. An abandonment will usually give rise to a right on the part of the employer to regard himself as discharged from further performance of his part of the contract and claim damages for breach, or to determine the contractor's employment under the express terms of the contract. A contractor now has a right to suspend performance on the grounds of non-payment under s112 of the **Construction Act**.

Abatement A remedy which the common law provides for breaches of warranty in contracts for sale of goods and for work and labour, available as of right to a party and independent of the doctrine of equitable set off, allowing a defendant to a claim for the price not to set off by a proceeding in the nature of a cross action, the amount of damages which he has sustained, but simply to defend himself by showing how much less the subject matter of the action is worth by reason of the breach: see *Modern Engineering (Bristol) Ltd v Gilbert Ash (Northern) Ltd* [1974] AC 689 (HL). It is not available to a defendant to a claim for professional fees (*Hutchinson v Harris* (1978) 10 BLR 19 (CA)) or where a **withholding** or **payless notice** has not been served by the paying party under the **Construction Act** and the sum due has been determined by a third party certifier: *Rupert Morgan Building Services (LLC) Ltd v Jervis* [2004] BLR 18 (CA). ■ See **Set off**.

ABE See **Association of Building Engineers**.

Ab initio Latin: "from the beginning", as in the case of a void contract.

Above ordnance datum (AOD) Refers to a spot height or level above the mean sea level. In Great Britain, the ordinance datum is defined as the mean sea level at Newlyn in Cornwall (known as Ordnance Datum Newlyn, **ODN**) and is the level from which a measurement is taken.

Absolute obligation An unconditional or unqualified obligation.

Absorption The process whereby one substance permeates another by chemical or molecular action. Contrast with **adsorption**.

Abuse of process The use of the court's process for a purpose or in a way significantly different from its ordinary use: see *AG v Barker* [2000] 1 FLR 759 (DC). The main categories are: vexatious proceedings, collateral attacks upon earlier decisions and delay. The court has the power to strike out proceedings which are an abuse.

Abutment The part of a structure which bears the weight, thrust or pressure of an arch, vault or bridge by resisting horizontal and vertical forces. The place from where projecting parts abut. In bridge design, the abutments are the end supports for the bridge span and are typically constructed of *in situ* concrete. Also used to transmit loads from the superstructure to the foundation.

ACA See **Association of Consultant Architects**.

Accelerated Low Water Corrosion (ALWC) A form of corrosion of metal sheet piling in marine environments such as ports and harbours, caused by the presence of sulphates, which are converted by sulphate-reducing bacteria (SRB) into hydrogen sulfide (H_2S). This in turn converts into sulphuric acid (H_2SO_4) and promotes a continuous electrolytic process at the steel surface thereby accelerating the corrosion. It is a form of microbiologically induced corrosion and is identified by orange soft organic bacteria (Ferric 3+ oxides), with a black layer (ferric sulphide) hiding bright, pitted steel.

Acceleration When the velocity of an object changes at an increasing rate it is said to accelerate. An increase in the rate at which works are carried out, usually by the application of additional resources. Acceleration may be used to achieve an earlier completion date, and contract terms may allow the employer to instruct this to be done. Acceleration is more commonly used to make up for delay. Some contracts include clauses allowing acceleration to be instructed and, if this is the case, this will usually involve an increase in the contract sum. ■ See **Constructive acceleration** and **Contract sum**.

Accelerator An ingredient or admixture which hastens chemical reactions. For example, an admixture used to gain early strength in the concrete and/or reduce the initial setting time by speeding up the chemical reaction between cement and water. Accelerators are often used where concrete is poured at low temperatures in order to counteract the effects of cold weather slowing down the curing process. If reinforcement is not required in concrete, calcium chloride can be used as an accelerator. However, where reinforcement is required, a non-chloride accelerator such as calcium nitrate should be used in order to prevent corrosion of steel. ■ See **Admixture**.

Acceptance The unqualified agreement by the person to whom an offer is made, thereby creating a binding contract. Acceptance may be oral, in writing or implied by conduct but should be unconditional or might be construed as a counter-offer which will extinguish any previous offer. If the offer stipulates a particular mode of acceptance, it is necessary to comply with that stipulation to avoid arguments regarding the formation of the contract. If the offer stipulates that acceptance is to be by letter, the "postal rule" provides that the date of acceptance is from the date of posting, not the date of receipt of the letter by the offeree. ■ See **Counter-offer** and **Postal rule**.

Accepted programme A defined term found in contracts including the **NEC3** contract for the programme identified in the **Contract Data**.

Accepted risk An occurrence or event, the risk of which is assumed by one of the parties to a contract should it take place. The term is used to identify events such as fires and floods which can be insured against and for which the contractor is usually granted an extension of time. ■ See **Specified peril**.

Access floor A floor usually located above the structural floor level which creates a space for mechanical and electrical services, including data and power cables. Often comprising adjustable floor pedestals which support a variety of decking materials, typically demountable to allow access to the services below.

Access to site The means of entry to a site, which will usually be the subject of express contractual terms. There is no implied warranty against third parties making unfounded claims challenging the employer's title to land upon which a temporary access road is to be built: *Porter v Tottenham UDC* [1915] KB 776.

Accident A generally negative outcome or unexpected occurrence, but the common meaning of this word is ruled neither by logic nor by etymology, but by custom, and no formula will precisely express its usage for all cases: *Trim Joint District School Board of Management v Kelly* [1914] AC 667 (HL).

Accommodation works Works carried out by statutory undertakers in relation to land adjoining the site of construction works. They can include fencing, gates and hedges. For example, the planting of hedges adjacent to a new road to minimise the impact of the scheme.

Accord and satisfaction The purchase of a release from an obligation whether arising under contract or tort by means of any valuable consideration, not being the actual performance of the obligation itself. The accord is the agreement by which the obligation is discharged and the satisfaction is the consideration which makes the agreement operative: *British Russian Gazette & Trade Outlook Ltd v Associated Newspapers Ltd* [1933] 2 KB 616. A defence to a claim on the basis that it has been compromised.

ACE See **Association of Consulting Engineers**.

Acknowledgement of service The formal written acknowledgement of the service of legal proceedings indicating whether the defendant proposes to defend the proceedings, oppose the jurisdiction of the court or admit part or all of the claim, which should be served on a defendant with the Claim Form. See CPR Part 10. The defendant has 14 days from the date of service of the Claim Form to complete the acknowledgement of service form and file it in the court. Once the acknowledgement of service has been filed at court and served on the claimant the time for service of the defence is extended to 28 days from the date of service of the Claim Form. ■ See **Claimant, Claim Form defendant and Jurisdiction and Service**.

ACoP See **Approved Code of Practice (CDM Regulations)**.

Acoustic boards/panels/tiles Boards, panels or tiles used on walls or ceilings to control or reduce sound. Their core material is typically made of a porous insulation, mineral-fibre, cork or foam in order to absorb sound.

Acquiescence Acceptance by a party by their silence or inaction of an event or a claim which may thereafter prevent that party from challenging or defending the event or claim. ■ See **Estoppel** and **Waiver**.

Action Court proceedings, now usually described as a claim.

Activation The changing of a passive surface of a metal to a chemically active state. ■ See **Passivation**.

Active solar heating A heating system that utilises solar panels or other mechanical devices to heat water by collecting the sun's radiation. As a result of increasing energy costs, many domestic hot water systems utilise active solar heating. ■ See also **Passive solar heating**.

Activity A defined action within a construction sequence, usually to be found in the context of project planning or **retrospective delay analysis**.

Activity Schedule A defined term used in some **Standard form contracts** (eg certain versions of NEC3 and JCT) to describe the list of various actions the contractor is required to carry out in sufficient detail to allow the contractor to price each activity.

Act of God An occurrence so unprecedented and unexpected that human agency would not reasonably anticipate it or be bound to take any steps to meet it: see *J & J Makin Ltd v London & NE Rly Co* [1945] 1 KB 467. Sometimes the subject of exclusion in contractual terms.

Act of Parliament Primary legislation which embodies the law. Supplemented by but takes precedence over secondary legislation and statutory instruments. The Act begins as a Bill which must pass through three readings in both Houses of Parliament and receive Royal Assent before it takes legal effect. Secondary legislation and/or instruments serve to implement or provide the detail which is expressed in broad principles within the Act.

Actual cost See **Prime cost**.

Actual cost contract Synonymous with the term "Cost reimbursable contract". ■ See **Cost contract**.

Actual notice Real knowledge, as opposed to knowledge which ought to have been had. ■ See **Constructive notice**.

Addendum bills Bills of quantities prepared to modify previous bills.

Additional claim Any claim other than the claim by the claimant against the defendant in litigation: see CPR Part 20.2.

Additional party A party against whom an additional claim is made and who has been joined into the proceedings under CPR Part 20.

Additional work Work in excess of that obliged to be carried out under a construction contract. Under the inclusive price principle, the contractor must carry out all necessary work to complete and cannot claim further payment for any part of such work. Where, however, the employer instructs the carrying out of further work or the parties have agreed that further work is needed in certain circumstances, such as compliance with the Building Regulations, further payment may be recoverable. ■ See **Inclusive price principle** and **Variations**.

Address for service The address specified by a party for the service of legal documents or other proceedings or for service of important documents and notices in contracts. In court proceedings, if the address has not been specified, CPR Part 6 requires legal documents to be served at the principal office or any place of business of the company within the jurisdiction which has a real connection with the claim. For an individual, if an address for service has not been specified, the CPR Part 6 requires service to be effected at the usual or last known residence. In formal contracts, specific provisions often provide an address for service and details of valid methods of service of important documents and notices such as withholding notices and termination notices.

Addressable fire alarm system A fire detection system in which each detector or sensor is wired back to a central control panel by one or more loops. Should an incident occur, be it an actual fire or rather the presence of smoke or dust, the control panel instantly reports the nature of the incident and the precise location of the device(s) activated.

Adequacy of consideration The extent of the value of the consideration given in return for a promise in the formation of a contract. The general rule is that courts will not judge adequacy, but this is subject to exceptions.

Adequacy of damages A factor to be considered by the court in deciding whether or not to grant an injunction. The fact that a monetary award may not adequately compensate the party seeking the injunction militates in favour of its being granted.

Ad hoc Latin: "for this thing", for a particular purpose. Thus, an ad hoc submission to arbitration is an agreement made between parties that a dispute will be referred to arbitration, rather than pursuant to an arbitration clause in a contract between them.

Ad idem Latin: "to the same thing", of the same mind, a consensus or agreement between parties, meeting of minds on the same point.

Adjoining owner Under the Party Wall etc. Act 1996, the owner of premises adjoining those of the building owner who is proposing to carry out works. ■ See **Party Wall Act**.

Adjudication An interim dispute resolution procedure by which the parties submit their dispute to a third party who will decide it within a comparatively short period of time; it was first introduced into standard forms of building subcontracts in the 1970s and subsequently implied into construction contracts governed by Part II of the **Construction Act**. Statutes in many other Commonwealth jurisdictions provide for adjudication, as do standard form and one-off contracts. Under the UK legislation, the process takes 28 days unless extended with the referring party's or both parties' agreement. A decision has "temporary finality" in the sense that it is binding on the parties unless superseded in subsequent arbitration or litigation. Decisions will be enforced by the court even though they are wrong in law and fact, provided that the adjudicator has addressed and answered the right question: see *Bouygues (UK) Ltd v Dahl-Jensen (UK) Ltd* [2000] BLR 522 (CA). There are limited grounds for resisting enforcement such as lack of jurisdiction and breach of natural justice. ■ See **Adjudication Rules, Adjudicator**, **Arbitral Tribunal**, **Referring Party** and **Responding Party**. ➤ **Figure A1**

Adjudication Rules Rules governing the conduct of statutory or contractual adjudication. Such rules are published by **TeCSA**, **IChemE**, **CIArb**, **CEDR** and other construction industry bodies. These rules may be incorporated into the adjudication provisions in a contract, and in order for the rules to be valid, they must comply with ss108 and 108A of the **Construction Act** 1996, otherwise the provisions of the **Scheme for Construction Contracts** will apply. ■ See **Adjudication**.

Adjudicator A person who is appointed in a quasi-judicial role to decide on a dispute between the parties. There is no statutory requirement that this should be a legally or technically qualified person. Adjudicators are appointed by an Adjudicator Nominating Body or by the agreement of the parties. The parties may have named the adjudicator in their contract or the contract may specify one or more of the Adjudicator Nominating Bodies who will then select an adjudicator on their behalf. ■ See **Adjudicator Nominating Body, Referring Party** and **Responding Party**.

Adjudicator Nominating Body (ANB) Any organisation that puts itself forward as willing to nominate adjudicators: there are no statutory restrictions in the United Kingdom, unlike in other jurisdictions where

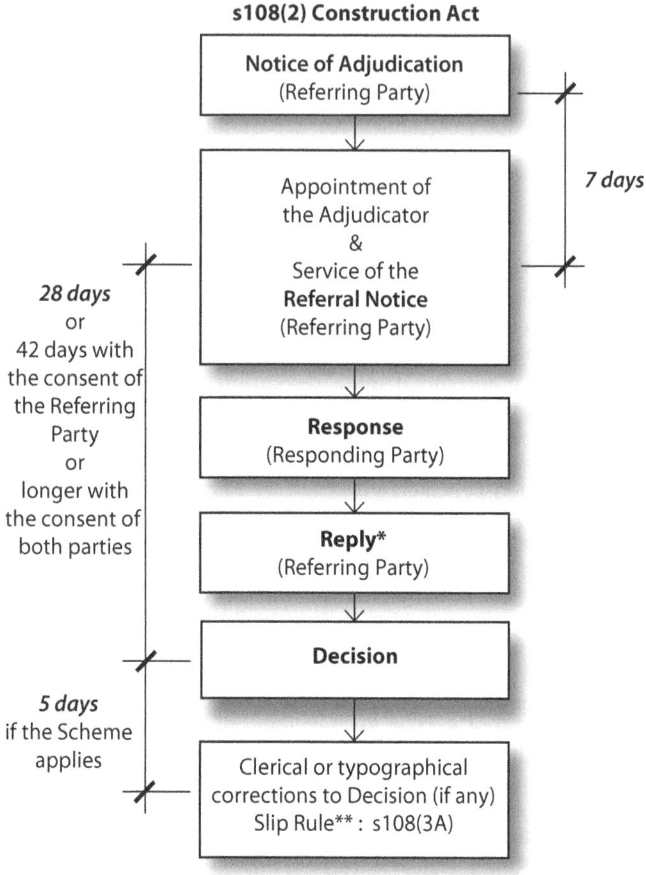

* The Referring Party does not have an automatic right to serve a Reply. A direction is required from the Adjudicator. Similarly, if the Responding Party wishes to serve a Rejoinder (following the Reply), a direction is required.

** See *Bloor Construction (UK) Ltd v Bowmer & Kirkland (London) Ltd* [2000] BLR 314

➤ **Figure A1.** Adjudication under the Construction Act

the position is often monitored and administered by a government agency. In practice, nomination is usually undertaken by a trade or professional body by agreement of the parties. Contracts often allow for the adjudicator to be nominated by the President or Vice President of the trade or professional body or the Chairman of **TeCSA** or **TECBAR**, but in practice they are selected according to their relevant experience or on a rota basis. Nominating bodies include **RIBA**, **RICS**, **ICE**, **TECBAR**, **TeCSA** and **CIArb**. ■ See **Adjudicator** and **Referring Party**.

Adjudicator's jurisdiction The scope of the adjudicator's legal power to determine the dispute. This may depend upon the terms of the contract and applicable adjudication rules; previous adjudicator's decisions in the same dispute; the Notice of Adjudication; the nature of the dispute which has crystallised; the ambit of the dispute and the rules of natural justice. An adjudicator may lack jurisdiction if the formal requirements for his nomination and appointment are not observed or if he is only empowered to decide specific issues referred to him. An adjudicator's decision can include the enforcement of contractual remedies such as the payment of monies and may determine the rights of the parties, but adjudicators cannot grant injunctions or exercise powers of enforcement which are the domain of the court. ■ See **Natural justice** and **Notice of adjudication**.

Adjusted as-planned programme A programme which demonstrates the differences in time and sequencing between the as-planned programme and the as-built programme. ■ See **As-built programme, As-planned-programme** and **Programme**.

Administration A procedure under the Insolvency Act 1986 as amended by the Enterprise Act 2002 in which the affairs and assets of an insolvent company are placed in the hands of an administrator (often an accountant) with a view to rescuing the company as a going concern, achieving a better result for its creditors than winding up, or realising property to make a distribution to secured or preferential creditors. If the administrator enters into contracts on behalf of the company, he or she may be personally liable in respect of the obligations under that contract unless he or she has the benefit of an indemnity from the company. ■ See **Insolvency** and **Liquidation**.

Administration Order A court order placing a company in the hands of an administrator or joint administrators.

Administrative charges See **Overheads**.

Administrative Receiver Individual appointed by the holder of a floating charge. Once appointed, the administrative receiver has control of a company's property and wide powers over that company's business. Under the Enterprise Act 2002, administrative receivership was effectively abolished as a remedy for all floating charges created after the Act, subject to some exceptions (these exceptions include private finance initiative (PFI) and certain utilities projects, but not all construction projects would fall within these categories). The Enterprise Act 2002 does not apply to floating charges created prior to the Act coming into force. For floating charges created on or after 15 September 2003, administrative receivership is no longer available as a remedy to enforce that security. Instead, a qualifying floating charge holder can put the company into administration by appointing an administrator using the out-of-court route. The Enterprise Act 2002 does not affect the right of a holder of a fixed charge to appoint a receiver.

Admissibility of evidence The extent, if any, to which evidence may be taken into account by a tribunal in reaching a decision. The rule against hearsay evidence is no longer absolute. The main grounds for excluding evidence are that it is irrelevant, is subject to privilege, or has not been the subject of a witness statement, summary or report previously supplied to the other party.

Admixture A specially formulated additive which modifies the chemical and physical properties of concrete, mortar or grout when added in small amounts during the mixing process. Examples include plasticisers, retarders, accelerators and air-entraining agents.

ADR See **Alternative Dispute Resolution**.

ADR agreement An agreement between parties to refer their disputes to a specified form of ADR such as mediation. This may be stipulated in the contract or agreed by the parties when a dispute arises.

ADR clause A clause in a contract providing that disputes can or will be referred to a form of ADR such as mediation. ■ See **Alternative Dispute Resolution** and **Mediation**.

Adsorption The surface retention of solid, liquid or gas molecules by a solid or liquid. Contrast with **absorption**.

Advance payment guarantee An instrument guaranteeing repayment by a third party of advance payments made to the contractor under a construction contract. The third party may be either a parent company of the contractor, a bank, insurance company or other financial concern or a government or one of its agencies. The question which will usually arise is whether the guarantee is an on-demand bond or a conventional contract of surety. They are common on major projects particularly in the **EPC** sector. ■ See **Performance bond**.

Advance payments Payments made to a contractor in advance of the commencement of the work, or in advance of the contractual date for payment of executed works, often to enable the contractor to mobilise or to order items with a long lead-in.

Adverse physical conditions Physical conditions (other than weather conditions or conditions due to weather) or artificial obstructions which could not have been reasonably foreseen by an experienced contractor, which can entitle the contractor under the **FIDIC Red**, **Yellow** and **Gold** books and the former **ICE** standard forms of civil engineering contract to further payment and an extension of time.

Adverse weather conditions See **Exceptionally adverse weather conditions**.

A&E, A/E Acronym, commonly used for "Architect and Engineer" or "Architecture and Engineering".

Aerated concrete A lightweight concrete used in situations where less dead load is required; for example, the handling of concrete blocks in residential construction. Produced by introducing gas or air into the mortar mix, it can either be foamed concrete or autoclaved aerated concrete. Such lightweight concrete blocks are often used in residential construction to minimise the weight for handling reasons. ■ See **Autoclaved aerated concrete** and **Foamed concrete**.

Aeration Supplying or infusing with air: for example, sand or soil.

AFC See **Approved for construction**.

Affidavit A written, sworn statement of evidence. Written evidence is now usually given in the form of a signed witness statement verified by a statement of truth. ■ See **Witness statement**.

Affirmation (1) A formal declaration by a witness before he or she gives evidence to tell the truth and often used instead of a religious oath. (2) An election by an innocent party faced with a repudiatory breach of contract to endorse the contract and treat it as continuing. ■ See **Repudiation**.

A fortiori Latin: "more strongly", to a greater extent, with greater reason.

A-frame building A building whose section is in the shape of an "A". The name originates from its distinctive roofline. The roof beams extend from the ridge line down or towards foundation level. The walls of the interior rooms may be formed by the steep slope of the lower roof. This building type is often used in cold climates to facilitate the transfer of snow to the ground thereby minimising heavy snow build-up on the roof.

AGA See **Authorised guarantee agreement**.

AGC See **Associate General Contractors of America**.

Agency The relationship between a principal and an agent and the law relating to this relationship and dealings with third parties. ■ See **Agent** and **Principal**.

Agent A person appointed by a principal to act on his behalf. An agent may have actual or apparent (ostensible) authority to act. An agent owes duties to his principal to act with care and due diligence. In exercising the rights conferred, the agent can bind the principal. Any limitations on the appointment of the agent cannot bind third parties unless they have notice of those limitations. If the agent has exceeded his authority, this may give the innocent party a right to claim a breach of implied warranty against that agent. Under some forms of building contract, the person acting on behalf of the employer is termed the employer's Agent. He will generally be required to act fairly despite being remunerated by the employer. An architect, engineer or project manager in private practice has no implied authority to make a contract with the contractor binding on the employer, or to vary or depart from a concluded contract: *Ashwell & Nesbitt v Allen* (1912) Hudson, *Building Contracts*, 4th edn, 1914, Vol. 2, p. 462.

Aggregate A granular material (typically of crushed stone or sand) which forms one of the essential components of plaster, mortar and concrete in order to give it compressive strength bulk and cohesion. Concrete aggregates must comply with BS EN 12620. ■ See also **Coarse aggregate** and **Fine aggregate**.

Aggregate/cement ratio The ratio, by weight or volume, of cement to aggregate which will normally be specified by a designer according to the required characteristics of the finished product.

Aggregates levy A tax on the use of extracted rock, sand and gravel introduced by the Finance Act 2001, which can be a significant cost in projects such as those involving road building. Express contractual provisions will usually be made in construction contracts. Those responsible for exploiting aggregates for commercial reasons must register with the **HMRC**.

Agreement (1) A term often used when referring to a **contract**. (2) One of the essential elements of a contract, comprising an offer by one party to do something and the acceptance of that offer by the other party. ■ See **Offer** and **Acceptance**.

Agrément Certificate A certificate issued by the British Board of Agrément (BBA). The certificate is awarded to a product or material after it has undergone a comprehensive series of tests, evaluations and inspections to confirm its fitness for purpose and compliance with the building regulations and other product quality requirements. The Agrément process is often utilised in circumstances where a new product or material is manufactured and there is no British Standard covering its performance. ■ See **British Board of Agrément** and **British Standard**.

AHU See **Air Handling Unit**.

AI See **Architect's Instruction**.

AIA See **American Institute of Architects**.

Air-admittance valve A pressure-activated device which replaces conventional venting usually to sanitary pipework to allow air to enter the system and equalise pressure. In a soil and waste system, this value is required to break the vacuum in the pipe which is created when emptying sinks, toilets and shower traps. This prevents foul odours escaping from the soil stack back into internal spaces. ■ See **Soil stack**.

Air balancing The measuring, testing and adjustment of air conditioning and ventilation systems to provide optimal performance and air distribution.

Air brick A brick perforated with holes to aid ventilation. Used in external walls and below floor level in older properties to ventilate the under floor space.

Air conditioning The process of mechanically treating the temperature, humidity, cleanliness and distribution of air within a building or space.

Air curtain or **air door** A device, typically located over the entrance doors of retail or commercial buildings, which blows warm air in order to minimise the loss of heated or conditioned air. Also used to separate zones within one room.

Air diffuser An air terminal, typically located in a ceiling or bulkhead which blows conditioned air into a room. Diffusers vary greatly in shape, size and function. For example, swirl diffusers are used for quick exchange of high air volumes. Where supply air from the diffuser is required to travel long distances in a large room or space, such as airports, jet nozzles may be used instead.

Air-dried timber Timber which has been dried using the traditional method of seasoning whereby the timber is stacked in the open air using battens or stickers, allowing natural air movement to remove the moisture. ■ See **Kiln-dried timber and Stickers**.

Airey house A pre-fabricated house built following World War II using surplus army lorry tubing and concrete panels tied together by wire. In the 1980s many were sold to tenants and extensive repairs had to be carried out.

Air-entraining admixture Incorporates microscopic air bubbles uniformly throughout the mix, enabling the concrete to resist the damaging effects of freezing and thawing by relieving internal pressure on the concrete. The agent, which slightly decreases the concrete strength, is added to the cement at the cement plant or to the concrete at the ready-mixed concrete plant. Air entrainment cannot be achieved when mixing concrete by hand. It is used whenever concrete may experience freezing, for example, driveways, patios, footpaths and roads in cold or temperate climates.

Air handling unit (AHU) Plant (usually fixed installation but may be portable) comprising fan/blower, heating and/or cooling coils, and air filtration. Used to meet requirements for heating, cooling, (de) humidification, ventilation, filtration, recovery and sound attenuation in commercial and industrial premises.

Air space See **Cavity wall** and **Figure E3**.

Air termination network A system which captures the lightning current when it strikes a building and dissipates it safely to the earth. It often consists of a 10 × 20 m grid of conductors covering the roof. Some high risk structures may require a denser grid of conductors. Where metal roof cladding is used, conductors may not be required as the cladding itself provides the air termination network. The network is then connected to down conductors which are located around the perimeter of the building, either fixed to the face of the façade or behind the external wall cladding. The down conductors are then connected to an earth electrode by way of an earth terminator. BS EN 62305 provides guidance and standards relevant to lightning protection. ■ See **Earth electrode** and **Earth terminator**.

ALARP See **As Low as Reasonably Practicable**.

Alcatel Letter Letter sent at the conclusion of a **public procurement** process to unsuccessful bidders.

Alcatel period The compulsory waiting period, of at least 10 days, between the decision to award a contract to which the Public Procurement Regulations apply and the date on which the contract is entered into. See C–81/98 *Alcatel v Austria* [1999] ECR I–7671. ■ See **Standstill period**.

Alderslade principle A long-standing principle of contract interpretation, that for an exclusion of liability clause to apply in the event of a party's negligence, the wording of the clause must be sufficiently clear to cover negligence. See *Alderslade v Hendon Laundry Ltd* [1945] KB 189, 192.

Alghussein Establishment v Eton College [1988] 1 WLR 587: the House of Lords held that clear and express provisions are required to contradict the presumption that a party to a contract should not be able to benefit from its own breach.

Alkali metal A metal in group 1A of the periodic system – namely, lithium, sodium, potassium, rubidium, caesium and francium. They form strong alkaline hydroxides.

Alkaline Having properties of an alkali or having a pH >7.

Alkali-resistant glassfibre Used in the production of glass fibre-reinforced concrete (GRC), cement renders and lime-based renders. The fibres are added to the mortar or concrete mix to increase its strength, impact resistance and durability.

Alkali-resistant paint Paints designed to resist corrosion from atmospheric pollution and provide coating to protect the treated surface from damage due to alkaline substances. Where asbestos cement products are found in good condition in residential properties, though specialist advice should also be sought, it is recommended that the safest course of action is to leave it in place and paint them with an alkali-resistant paint to prevent any dust escaping.

Alkali silica reaction (ASR) More commonly known as "concrete cancer". A chemical reaction within concrete generally caused by the alkalis (sodium and potassium) in the cement reacting with the silica in the aggregate when moisture is present. This creates a gel which absorbs water and expands, thereby exerting an expansion pressure which results in cracking. Today's concrete specifications limit the alkali content in order to minimise the rise of ASR.

Alliancing Method of procuring or managing where two or more parties work collaboratively together as an integrated team to deliver a project.

All-in aggregate A mixture of coarse and fine aggregates, such as stones and sharp sand.

All-inclusive price principle See **Inclusive price principle.**

Allocation Questionnaire Following the issue of court proceedings, parties are required to complete an allocation questionnaire (Form N149, N150 or N151) which provides information about the case so that it may be allocated to the appropriate track (small claims, fast-track or multi-track) and judge.

Alternate bay construction A form of construction used to reduce the period for constructing a large slab of concrete. Concrete is cast in alternate bays (every other bay) to allow a greater quantity of concrete to be poured in one day. The adjacent sections (or bays) are typically connected by steel dowel bars which are partially embedded in one bay and incorporated into the neighbouring bay when it is subsequently poured. ■ See **Continuous run concreting.**

Alternative Dispute Resolution (ADR) An alternative to a formal court hearing or litigation. The word "alternative" in this context is used to distinguish between litigation and any other method of resolving a dispute, ranging from simple negotiation to arbitration. There are many dispute resolution techniques which also embrace mediation and conciliation, with many refinements and combinations being developed through use. Different disputes demand different techniques, depending on the degree of control and flexibility required by the parties. For example, the parties have maximum control in a straightforward negotiation, yet minimum control in the courts, as the tribunal, the procedure and the eventual outcome are imposed. ADR is a collective term for the ways that parties can settle disputes with (or without) the help of a third party. ■ See also **Court Settlement Process, Early Neutral Evaluation** and **Mediation.**

Aluminium A light metallic element extracted from bauxite and resistant to corrosion and used extensively in roofing and cladding applications. Aluminium is a versatile material and can take many forms: castings, extrusions, tubes, sheet, plate, foil, powder, forgings etc. with variety of surface finishes available (coatings, anodising, polishing etc.). It is also a light weight material (approximately a third of steel) and a good conductor of electricity and heat.

Aluminium Industrie Vaassen BV v Romalpa Aluminium Ltd [1976] 2 All ER 552: the Court of Appeal upheld as valid a retention of title clause allowing a supplier to reserve title to goods until it has received payment for them. ■ See **Retention of title.**

Aluminium roofing Properties of aluminium make it suitable for use as a roofing material: self-supporting, lightweight, durable and fire-resistant. It is often profiled to increase its stiffness. ■ See **Standing seam.**

Aluminium–zinc coating A coating on steel which offers corrosion and abrasion resistance, as well as thermal and light reflectivity.

ALWC See **Accelerated Low Water Corrosion.**

Ambiguity The possibility of more than one meaning. The literary critic W. S. Empson identified seven types of ambiguity, but English law conventionally distinguished between a latent ambiguity, where a written instrument appeared clear on its face but was ambiguous in the context of other evidence, and a patent one, where the wording used could obviously bear two or more meanings. Bacon suggested that a latent ambiguity, because it arose from extrinsic matters, could be resolved by extrinsic evidence, whereas a patent ambiguity could not be resolved. The distinction is now regarded as "based on outmoded and highly technical and artificial rules" and "not merely capricious but also … incoherent": see *L. Schuler AG v Wickman Machine Tool Sales Ltd* [1974] AC 235 and *Mannai Investment Co Ltd v Eagle Star Life Assurance Co Ltd* [1997] AC 749; [1997] 2 WLR 945; [1997] 3 All ER 352.

Ambush The commencement of adjudication to the responding party's disadvantage. The threshold to a reference to adjudication is the existence of a crystallised dispute. Thus, if a dispute has arisen by 23 December in a given year, the referring party may refer that dispute to adjudication on 24 December. That might give rise to an assertion that there has been an "ambush" because the defending party may well have insufficient time, given the Christmas break common in the construction industry, to prepare its defence. It is not uncommon, similarly, for claiming parties to refer matters to adjudication during the summer holidays when it is known that the key personnel of the defending party are away. Again, this might be said to be an "ambush". For better or for worse, Parliament does not expressly give an adjudicator the power to extend the 28 days by reason of that fact. However, there is a sensible school of thought which suggests that in those circumstances an adjudicator can in effect decline to accept the appointment on the grounds that justice cannot be done or the adjudicator can simply say to the referring party words to the effect: "Unless you agree to an extension of time I will not be able to produce my decision within 28 days". Indeed, that is commonly what adjudicators will do and it is a very rare case when the referring party does not accede to some extension of time accordingly: see *Bovis Lend Lease Ltd v Trustees of the London Clinic* [2009] EWHC 64 (TCC).

Amendment The alteration of a statement of case to rectify mistakes or add further information or claims. Any words to be deleted by the amendment are struck out in red and additional words are written in red and underlined. Successive re-amendments are traditionally coloured green, violet and yellow, although the courts today sometimes allow a more pragmatic, if less colourful numeric approach. In legal proceedings, amendment is either carried out without permission before service or with the consent of the opposing party or with permission following an application to the court. Generally, a party will not be allowed to add a new cause of action in litigation after the limitation period has expired unless it arises from the same facts as those of the original claim, or a new cause of action in arbitration where it had not arisen before the date of the notice of arbitration (because no dispute could have existed). For the purposes of amendment, it is a mixed question of law and fact whether there is a new cause of action, and the court will look not only to the duty on a party but also to the nature and extent of the breach relied upon, as well as to the nature and extent of the damage complained of, in deciding whether, as a matter of degree, a new cause of action is being relied upon: see *Steamship Mutual Underwriting Association Ltd v Trollope & Colls (City) Ltd* (1986) 33 BLR 77 (CA). ■ See **Statement of case**.

***American Cyanamid* principles** *American Cyanamid Co v Ethicon Ltd (no 1)* [1975] AC 396 (HL): authority for the rule that before an interim injunction will be granted, the court must look first at whether there is a serious issue to be tried; second, ask whether damages would provide an adequate remedy (should the party being refused the injunction succeed on final judgment) and third, consider where the balance of convenience lies.

The American Institute of Architects (AIA) A professional association for licensed architects in the United States. Architects are licensed in each State and the use of the term is restricted to those licensed.

American Petroleum Institute (API) A national trade association which promotes standards and certification in the oil and natural gas industry, including design, measurement and operation of systems.

American Society of Mechanical Engineers (ASME) A professional association in the United States which represents mechanical engineers, produces technical standards and promotes collaboration and knowledge sharing across all engineering disciplines.

American Society for Testing and Materials (ASTM) See **ASTM International**.

Analogue addressable fire detector The device which communicates back to a central control panel by way of electronic signals, reporting the conditions at its location. ■ See **Addressable fire alarm system**.

Anchorage A method for securing an element or component. In bridge terminology, an anchorage block is the concrete block at the end of a suspension bridge which anchors the cables to the ground.

Ancient lights Now more commonly known as a "right to light". A building owner's right, in certain circumstances, to receive natural daylight through windows which have existed for 20 years or more and to maintain the same level of illumination. This is usually an easement acquired under the Prescription Act 1832 and can be important in the context of high rise development as courts may grant an injunction to prevent substantial interference with this right. The principle only applies Anchorage to the light coming into the windows of a building. ■ See **Right to light**.

Ancient monument A structure of special historic interest or national importance, ranging from earthworks to ruins to buried remains. Many are scheduled as nationally important archaeological sites under the Ancient Monuments and Archaeological Areas Act 1979 and consent is required for any work that may affect them. ■ See **Scheduled monuments**.

Anechoic Chamber Acoustic testing environments, comprising echo-free enclosures with a sound energy absorption level of 99 per cent to 100 per cent, or a reflected sound pressure level of 10 per cent or less. Sound absorption is obtained by lining the walls, ceilings and floor with sound-absorbing elements. They can be acoustic chambers or radio frequency chambers and are used: (1) to provide a free-field environment for the measurement of sound or radio waves emanating from a sound source; (2) to test a wide variety of equipment for its noise transmission; (3) for acceptance tests of electrical equipment to achieve accredited standards; and (4) for recording studios.

Angle bead Metal trim for protecting the corner of a wall. Commonly used over plasterboard to provide a straight, sharp corner joint and to strengthen the edge. Once the angle bead is fixed in place, the plasterboard can then be skimmed up to the metal edge.

Angle brace A bar or angle used to stiffen a frame or truss.

Angle section A structural steel member having an L-shaped cross section. The "legs" of the angle may be of equal or unequal lengths. ■ See **Steel sections**.

Anisotropic When properties of a material are dependent on a direction. For example, the strength of wood depends on the direction of the grain. "With the grain" is weaker than "against the grain". ■ See **Isotropic**.

Annealed glass Annealed glass is glass without internal stresses resulting from heat treatment. It is the standard form of modern glass and the basic material for safety glass. Glass is annealed by being heated above a transition point then allowed to cool slowly, without being quenched. Float glass is annealed during the process of manufacture. However, most toughened glass is made from float glass that has been specially heat-treated. Annealed glass breaks into large, jagged shards that can cause serious injury and is thus considered a hazard in architectural applications. Building codes restrict the use of annealed glass in areas where there is a high risk of breakage or injury, for example, in bathrooms, door panels, fire exits and at low heights in schools or houses.

Annealing The heat treatment of metal to alter its microstructure and to improve its strength, hardness and ductility. The purpose of annealing is to soften the metal and remove all stresses caused by rolling or hammering in the manufacturing process. Annealed metal can be bent or machined more easily in its softer form. Aluminium is annealed so that it can be bent without fracturing. Both ferrous and non-ferrous materials can be annealed.

Annexe (1) A document attached or appended to another document; (2) an extension to a building.

Anns v Merton London Borough Council [1978] AC 728; [1977] 2 All ER 118: authority for the proposition that not only a local authority exercising building control functions but also a builder carrying out works owed a duty of care to the owner or subsequent purchaser. Overruled in *Murphy v Brentwood DC* [1991] 1 AC 398; [1990] 2 All ER 908. ■ See **Duty of care**.

Anode The electrode at which oxidation or corrosion of some component occurs (opposite of cathode). Electrons flow away from the anode in the external circuit.

Anode corrosion The dissolution of a metal acting as an anode.

Anodising Anodising, or anodizing, is an electrolytic process used to increase the thickness of the natural oxide layer on the surface of metal. Anodising increases corrosion resistance and wear resistance and provides better adhesion for paint primers and glues than bare metal. Most commonly applied to aluminium.

Anticipatory breach The expression by a party of an intention to break a contract or behaviour reasonably leading to a conclusion of such an intention before the time for its performance. ■ See **Repudiation**.

Antiquities Ancient relics or items of historical interest, the discovery of which on a construction site can lead to delay while the appropriate authorities are informed and a decision made as to how to proceed. Most **standard form** contracts make express provisions in respect of such matters, such as clause 3.22 of the 2011 JCT SBC form, which refers to "*All fossils, antiquities and other objects of interest or value* ...".

Anti-static flooring A conductive flooring material, such as carpet and specialist vinyls, which controls electrostatic discharge (ESD) created by friction between the feet of users and the flooring material. It is used in areas such as computer rooms, laboratories, X-ray rooms and operating theatres where static discharge can cause problems. Specialist adhesives and installation techniques are typically required. ■ See **Electrostatic discharge**.

Anton Piller order A civil search warrant, now known as a **search order**. ■ See CPR 25.1(h).

AOD See **Above ordnance datum**.

AP1000 A pressurised water reactor designed by Westinghouse Electric Company. Utilises modular construction such that components are manufactured off-site in order to reduce cost and minimise the construction programme on-site.

Appeal A process by which the decision of a court is subject to reconsideration by a higher court. The term is used to describe both the process and the hearing itself in the higher court. In the United Kingdom, leave, or permission, from the court is generally required to appeal, either from the judge who made the decision or directly from the appeal court. Grounds of appeal are usually limited to points of law but appeals on findings of fact (and the conclusions drawn from them) are sometimes permitted. The powers of the appeal court are wide: it may set aside the lower court's decision and substitute its own decision or remit the case for reconsideration to the lower court. There are limited grounds on which to appeal an Arbitrator's award, pursuant to the Arbitration Act 1996.

Appendix to Tender Term often used, see for example the **FIDIC** form of contract, to describe a document setting out certain project details; for example, timing for payments or the completion date which form part of the contract. ■ See **Contract Data**.

Applicable law The law which applies to the interpretation and enforcement of a contract. Many English contracts state that the applicable law is the Law of England and Wales. If the applicable law is not identified, the inference is that it will be the law of the country where the contract was entered into. In contracts involving a foreign element, it is desirable to identify the applicable law of the contract and also any applicable law that applies to the procedure and conduct of any arbitration (if different).

Application The procedure in court and other proceedings whereby a party makes a formal request (in writing or orally at a hearing, or both) for the court or other tribunal to make an order or direction. An application is generally made on notice to the other party, but in the case of urgency may be made to the court without notice, when only the applicant attends (ex parte). Part 23 of the Civil Procedure Rules (CPR) deals with general rules for applications. ■ See **Ex parte, Interim remedy, Judgment in default, Notice** and **Security for costs**.

Application notice The document by which an applicant states his intention to seek a court order. ■ See CPR 23.1.

Application for Payment A document produced by a contractor and submitted to the employer or a specified person under the contract (such as the Architect or Contract Administrator) requesting payment for the works carried out and providing a breakdown of the sum claimed. Applications for Payment are usually made on an interim basis each month, and their content is often prescribed by specific provisions in the contract. The final Application for Payment will usually be in the form of a final account. Applications for Payment can also stand as Payment Notices, provided they meet the requirements of a Payment Notice under the **Construction Act**. ■ See also **Final account** and **Payment Notice**.

Apportionment Where a situation exists in which two causes are operative, one being a relevant event and the other some event for which the contractor is taken to be responsible, and neither of which could be described as the dominant cause, the claim for extension of time will not necessarily fail. In such a situation, which could, as a matter of language, be described as one of concurrent causes, in a broad sense, it may be open to the decision-maker, depending on whether the project is in England or Scotland approaching the issue in a fair and reasonable way, to apportion the delay in the completion of the works occasioned thereby as between the relevant event and the other event. In that connection, it must be recognised that the background to the decision making, in particular, the possibility of a claim for liquidated damages, as opposed to one for extension of time, must be borne in mind and approached in a fair and reasonable manner. See the contrasting decisions in *City Inn Ltd v Shepherd Construction Ltd* [2010] CSIH 68; [2010] BLR 473 and *Walter Lilly & Co Ltd v Mackay & others* [2012] ELHC 1773.

Approved Code of Practice (ACoP) Published by the Health and Safety Executive (HSE). It provides practical guidance on how to comply with the Construction (Design and Management) (CDM) Regulations 2007, SI 2007/320. Failure to comply with the ACoP is not in itself an offence; however, it is likely to evidence a failure to comply with primary health and safety legislation.

Approved for construction (AFC) The final status of an engineering or construction drawing. This terminology is typically used in the fabrication of a product or component. The effect of the approval will depend on the terms of the construction contract. In building contracts, design consultants do not normally "approve" the contractor's drawings for construction, but rather "comment" on the drawings. In the JCT 2011 Design and Build contract where the contractor submits its design to the employer under Schedule 1, the employer (or the Architect/Contract Administrator on his behalf) returns the drawing, marking it either with a status "A", "B" or "C" to indicate whether or not the contractor shall carry out the works in accordance with that drawing. ■ See also **Issued for Construction**.

Approved Documents Documents published by *NBS for Communities and Local Government* and approved by the Secretary of State which provide practical guidance on how to comply with the UK Building Regulations. There are 14 "Parts" (Parts A–P, excluding I and O) and "Regulation 7" which provides guidance on fire safety, ventilation, structure, glazing, conservation of fuel and power, access to and the use of buildings, etc. The guidance and solutions provided are not mandatory and there may well

Part A: Structure
(2004 edition, incorporating 2010 amendments)

Part B1: Fire Safety
Volume 1: Dwellinghouses
Volume 2: Buildings other than dwellinghouses *(2006 edition, incorporating 2010 amendments)*

Part C: Site preparation and resistance to contaminates and moisture *(2004 edition, incorporating 2010 amendments)*

Part D: Toxic substances
(1992 edition, incorporating 2002 and 2010 amendments)

Part E: Resistance to the passage of sound
(2003 edition, incorporating 2004 and 2010 amendments)

Part F: Ventilation
(2010 edition, incorporating further 2010 amendments)

Part G: Sanitation, hot water safety and water efficiency
(2010 edition, incorporating further 2010 amendments)

Part H: Drainage and waste disposal
(2002 edition, incorporating 2010 amendments)

Part J: Combustion appliances and fuel storage systems
(2010 edition, incorporating further 2010 amendments)

Part K: Protection from falling, collision and impact
(1998 edition, incorporating 2010 amendments)

Part L1A: Conservation of fuel and power (New dwellings)
(2010 edition, incorporating further 2010 amendments)

Part L1B: Conservation of fuel and power (Existing dwellings)
(2010 edition, incorporating further 2010 and 2011 amendments)

Part L2A: Conservation of fuel and power (New buildings other than dwellings) *(2010 edition, incorporating further 2010 amendments)*

Part L2B: Conservation of fuel and power (Existing buildings other than dwellings) *(2010 edition, incorporating further 2010 and 2011 amendments)*

Part M: Access to and use of buildings *(2004 edition, incorporating 2010 amendments)*

Part N: Glazing – safety in relation to impact, opening and cleaning
(1998 edition, incorporating 2010 amendments)

Part P: Electrical safety – dwellings
(2006 edition, incorporating 2010 amendments)

Approved Document to support Regulation 7: Materials and workmanship *(1999 edition)*

➤ **Figure A2.** Approved Documents

be alternative methods of achieving compliance. However, compliance with the Approved Documents is generally considered to be evidence that the Building Regulations have been complied with. Their legal status is defined by the Building Act 1984. ■ See the **Building Act 1984** and **Building Regulations.** ➤ **Figure A2**

Approved inspector The role of the approved inspector is to provide independent third party certification of building or refurbishment work under the **Building Regulations**.

Approximate quantities Quantities within a bill of quantities that cannot be measured with accuracy. This may be due to lack of information at the time the bill of quantities is prepared or where the precise extent of work could never be accurately measured (eg ground works which may depend on the ground conditions encountered when construction starts). Approximate quantities are provided for the guidance of tenderers but the actual quantities of work carried out are re-measured during the course of the contract to produce the final valuation based on actual measures. ■ See **Bill of Quantities** and **Remeasurement contract**.

Aqueous Pertaining to water; an aqueous solution is made by using water as a solvent.

ARB See **Architect's Registration Board**.

Arbitral Tribunal A single arbitrator or a panel of arbitrators appointed to decide a dispute in an arbitration. Where more than one arbitrator is appointed, it is common in commercial and international arbitrations for three arbitrators to be appointed. Each party nominates one arbitrator and the chairman is then appointed independently. The members of the tribunal are either agreed by the parties, named in the contract or are appointed by any nominating body named in the contract, in the absence of which the **Arbitration Act 1996** contains provisions for the appointment of the Arbitral Tribunal. ■ See **Arbitration** and **Arbitrator**.

Arbitration A formal dispute resolution procedure whereby an Arbitral Tribunal makes an Award which the parties recognise will be binding. The Arbitration Act 1996 provides the statutory framework within which arbitrations are conducted. An arbitration requires the agreement of the parties to submit the dispute for a final decision by the Arbitrator. Arbitration clauses are therefore commonly found in standard form construction contracts but parties can agree to submit their dispute to arbitration at any time. An arbitrator is often appointed because of his specialist knowledge of the area in which the dispute arises. An advantage of arbitration is that it is private to the parties, unlike court proceedings. In contrast to Adjudication, the English courts can refuse to enforce an arbitration award if there is a substantial error in law which should be corrected in the public interest. However, in practice the courts are reluctant to interfere with the arbitration process and/or award. ■ See **Arbitral Tribunal**. ➤ **Figure A3**

Arbitration Act 1996 Came into force on 31 January 1997. The Act applies to all arbitration proceedings commenced on or after that date and is expressly stated to be construed in accordance with three principles: (1) the object of arbitration is to obtain the fair resolution of disputes by an impartial tribunal without unnecessary delay or expense; (2) the parties should be free to agree how their disputes are resolved, subject only to such safeguards as are necessary in the public interest; (3) the court should not intervene in arbitrations save as expressly provided in the Act.

Arbitration Agreement An agreement in writing by the parties to submit their dispute for resolution by an arbitrator and the terms of that agreement. Section 6(1) of the **Arbitration Act 1996** defines an arbitration agreement as "an agreement to submit to arbitration present or future disputes (whether they are contractual or not)". The arbitration agreement is a separate contract between the parties although it is often incorporated within the substantive contract which has given rise to the dispute by means of an arbitration clause. See *Premium Nafta Products Ltd v Fili Shipping Co Ltd* [2007] UKHL 40; [2008] 1 Lloyd's Rep 254; [2007] 4 All ER 951. ■ See **Arbitration**, **Arbitrator** and **Arbitration clause**.

Arbitration clause A clause which specifies that disputes between the parties are to be referred to arbitration. It must provide the mechanism for the appointment of the arbitrator (usually nomination by an appointing body) and it may specify the seat of the arbitration (ie geographical location) the applicable arbitration rules and the substantive law to apply to the arbitration. Standard form building contracts enable the parties

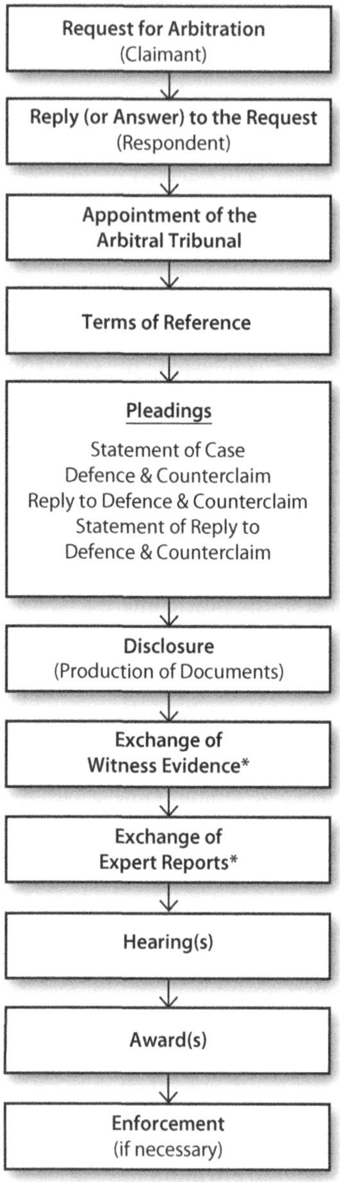

* In countries with a civil code, witness evidence and expert reports are more usually served with the Statement of Case and Defence.

➤ **Figure A3.** Arbitration

to specify that all disputes are to be resolved by arbitration. In a bespoke contract, the parties may also draft their own arbitration clause which specifies that all disputes are to be referred to arbitration.

Arbitrator A technically and/or legally qualified person who is nominated by an appointing body or agreed by the parties to decide a dispute by way of arbitration. The jurisdiction of the arbitrator is governed by the contract and the agreement of the parties. In default of the parties agreeing an arbitrator, some contracts will specify that the Arbitrator is to be appointed by a professional body such as **CIArb**, **ICE**, **RIBA**, **RICS**, **TeCSA** and **TECBAR**. The arbitrator's function is to consider the case presented to him by each party and to reach a decision (in his award) on all the issues referred to him. Subject to agreement by the parties, the Arbitrator is free to determine the procedure to be followed.

Architect A professional design consultant, who plans, designs and supervises the construction of a building or structure. His or her characteristics have been described as:

> "...one who possesses, with due regard to aesthetic as well as practical considerations, adequate skill and knowledge to enable him (i) to originate, (ii) to design and plan, (iii) to arrange for and supervise the erection of such buildings or other works calling for skill in design and planning as he might, in the course of his business, reasonably be asked to carry out or in respect of which he offers his services as a specialist." See *R v Architects' Registration Tribunal ex parte Jaggar* [1945] 2 All ER 131 DC.

In the United Kingdom, the use of the title "architect" is restricted to professionally qualified persons who are registered with the Architect's Registration Board (ARB). It is a criminal offence to use the title without registration with the ARB, and those found guilty may be subject to a fine. Many architects in the United Kingdom are also members of the Royal Institute of British Architects (RIBA). Use of the initials RIBA signifies that the person is an architect. ■ See **Architect's Registration Board** and **Royal Institute of British Architects**.

Architect's/Engineer's Independence Although an architect under a building contract is appointed and paid by the employer, in carrying out his or her duties as certifier and decision-maker under the contract, the architect must act in an impartial and independent manner. It is assumed that, as a professional, the architect is able to exercise independent judgement (notwithstanding his or her status as a quasi-employee of the employer) at times when the interests of the employer and the contractor might conflict. The same principle applies to an Engineer, Contract Administrator and Quantity Surveyor when acting in this capacity under a construction contract. ■ See ***Sutcliffe v Thackrah*** [1974] AC727.

Architect's Instruction (AI) A written or oral instruction from an architect to a contractor. AIs often introduces changes or variations to the works and will entitle a contractor to claim additional time and/or payment under the contract. If an instruction is given orally, it should be followed by a written confirmation of verbal instruction. ■ See **Confirmation of verbal instruction (CVI)**.

Architect's Registration Board (ARB) The statutory authority for the registration of architects which exercises regulatory and disciplinary powers over architects. The ARB maintains the UK Register of Architects and prescribes the qualifications necessary to become an architect. It was established by the Architects' Act 1997 and its purpose as regulators is to "*ensure that good standards within the profession are consistently maintained for the benefit of the public and architects alike*".

Architectural concrete A term used to refer to *in situ* concrete which is specified to a higher quality than typical engineering specifications. It may contain specific admixtures or fines (eg mica) to give a "whiter" appearance and/or requires other special requirements (such as a particular type of pattern in the formwork or the specific placing and filling of bolts in vertical formwork) in order to achieve a high-quality finish. Because its quality, finish and colour are often of utmost importance to the design and/or client, it requires special care during preparation, placement and curing. The term is also used to refer to the concrete specification used in precast concrete panels where the colour and finish need an even greater degree of control, although this is assisted by casting the panels in a factory environment.

Architectural drawings Plans, sections, elevations and details drawn by the architect which show the general layout, arrangement and specific detail of the design. ■ See **Elevation, Detail drawings plan** and **Section**.

Architectural metalwork Secondary structural elements, such as steel balconies, balustrades, staircases and gates, which are sited in a prominent or highly visible location and therefore quality, aesthetics and workmanship are of utmost importance to the designer and/or client. A wide range of metals (eg steel, iron, lead and zinc) may be used depending on building element or application. The term may also be used when referring to decorative metal elements such as trims.

Architectural sections (1) Drawn, extruded or folded shapes, often made of aluminium or stainless steel, used as a decorative trim around the outside of windows and other building elements. See **Figure A4**. (2) A type of drawing, produced by the architect, which shows the view through a building (or a part of the building) when a vertical plane or slice is taken through the building revealing what lies beneath. See **Figure G3**

Architrave (1) A trim or moulding that frames a door or window, covering the gap between the frame and the wall. See **Figure A5**. (2) A lintel which spans between two columns. (3) In classical architecture, the lowest element of the entablature (comprised of the cornice, frieze and architrave). See **Figure A5**.

Articles of agreement Parts of a written contract which usually appear at the beginning and contain details of the parties, a summary of the works and the contract sum. In standard forms of contract, the Articles identify the contract documents. The detailed terms are then contained in a schedule of conditions.

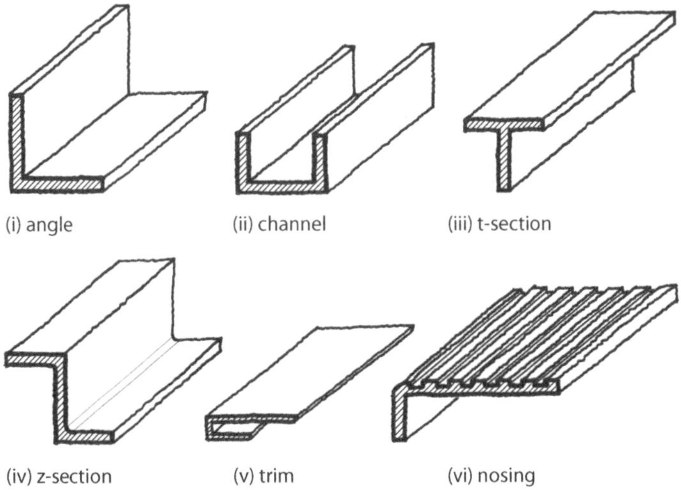

➤ **Figure A4.** Architectural sections *(not to scale)*

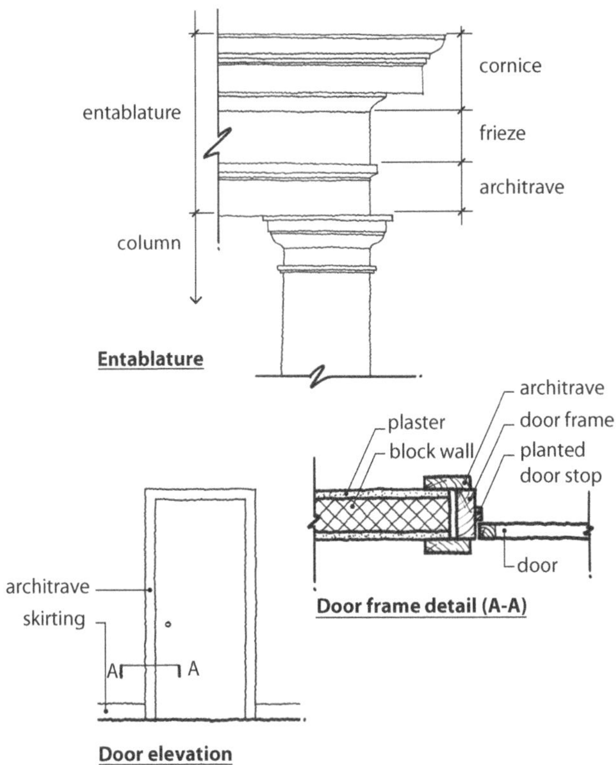

➤ **Figure A5.** Architrave

Articles of Association The formal statement of the terms which govern the operation of a limited company and the relationship between its directors and shareholders. It will also include the objects of the company which define the scope of its business, usually in very general terms. All limited companies in England and Wales are required to have Articles under the Companies Act 2006.

Artificial obstruction See **Adverse physical conditions**.

Artists, tradesmen or others engaged by the employer An expression used in the old JCT 63 contract to mean persons who execute work not forming part of the main contract. The expression was replaced in the 1980 edition by "persons employed or otherwise engaged by the Employer". The "artists, tradesmen or others" clause applied to statutory undertakers such as electricity or gas boards where they were employed by the employer and not carrying out their statutory functions: *Henry Boot Construction (UK) Ltd v Central Lancashire New Town Development Corp* (1980) 15 BLR 8.

Asbestos A widely used mineral until the mid-1980s because of its insulation and fire retardant properties. Any building built before 2000 (houses, factories, offices, schools, hospitals) may contain asbestos. A growing understanding of its carcinogenic character led to a ban on its production or use in new applications. It is dangerous if distributed because its minute fibres are easily inhaled, but in sealed and undisturbed locations, it presents little risk. Asbestos work, the removal of asbestos and its disposal is strictly controlled by the Control of Asbestos Regulations 2012, SI 2012/632 and the **HSE**'s Approved Code of Practice – Work with Materials containing Asbestos. Contractors who carry out this work must be licensed.

As-built but-for analysis In analysing the work activities on a project, a record of the date on which each activity started and finished is made and the impact of the delay events caused by the employer is analysed to establish the date on which completion would have been achieved but for the delay.

As-built critical path The analysis of the critical path of a project as it actually progressed, produced after the works have been completed. ■ See **Critical path** and **Programme**.

As-built drawings The drawings prepared once the works are complete, to record the as-built construction. The as-built drawings are different from the drawings used for design and fabrication in that they document all revisions to previous drawings, instructions given to the contractor and the effects of unanticipated site conditions. The drawings are used by the owner for future maintenance, operations or alteration of the building or structure. In some contracts (such as the JCT Design and Build Contract), the as-built drawings are required to be completed and supplied by the contractor prior to **practical completion (PC)**.

As-built programme The reconstruction after practical or substantial completion of the programme representing the actual sequence and duration of the works. This is then compared with the planned programme to identify the reasons for overall delay on a project and the impact of identified delay events. ■ See **Programme**.

Ascertain To find out for certain. Under the JCT standard forms of contract, direct loss and/or expense is to be ascertained. It has been held that the word "ascertain" in this context does not connote as much use of judgement or the formation of an opinion had "assess" or "evaluate" been used, and appears to preclude making general assessments as have at times to be done in quantifying damages recoverable for breach of contract: see *Alfred McAlpine Homes North Ltd v Property & Land Contractors Ltd* (1995) 76 BLR 59. A different view has also been expressed: see *How Engineering Services Ltd v Lindner Ceilings Floors Partitions plc* [1999] 64 ConLR 67.

Ashlar Stonework which has been prepared (dressed and cut) and is often smooth or polished. Typically used as the outer leaf of a **cavity wall** or with a precast concrete backing to speed up construction on larger buildings (stainless steel dowels fix the ashlar back to the concrete). Ashlar is also sometimes used as a feature around windows.

As Low as Reasonably Practicable (ALARP) A health and safety term used by the HSE in the analysis of determining the level to which they expect risks to be controlled. The concept of "reasonably practicable" derives from the Health and Safety at Work etc. Act 1974 and is used in numerous health and safety regulations. For example, as regards to nuclear energy and reducing radiation exposure, in order to demonstrate that risks have been reduced to ALARP, one must show that the costs of improving safety further would be grossly disproportionate to the benefit gained with further measures in place.

Asphalt A natural or manufactured substance comprising bitumen and other inert mineral matter. When heated, asphalt becomes a highly viscous material. It is often used in road construction as a binder for other aggregate particles. Mastic asphalt is a type of asphalt comprised of asphaltic cement (a blend of bitumen, lake asphalt and asphaltite) and appropriately graded mineral matter. With its higher bitumen content, mastic asphalt is ideal for damp-proof membranes and paving.

Asphalt roofing A roofing material which provides a continuous waterproof membrane, typically made of several coats of mastic asphalt. ■ See **Asphalt**.

Aspirated detection system A system in which air is drawn from an area, through a network of pipes or tubes, towards the detection system using a high pressure aspirator fan. Used to detect smoke.

As-planned impacted A method of delay analysis by reference to a programme which records the impact of delay events on an as-planned programme in order to establish the likely completion date or to subsequently analyse the effect of identified delay events on the overall progress of the works. Also known as the baseline adding impacts method.

As-planned programme The programme of work showing the sequence relationships and planned duration of construction activities on a project leading to the construction completion date. Some standard form contracts require the contractor to produce and make available his or her planned programme before work begins, but generally the programme is not a contract document, as this may provide the contractor with a claim if he or she cannot follow his planned sequence and timing of work due to acts or omissions by the employer. The programme may be used by the architect to monitor the contractor's progress and assess the impact of delay events.

As-planned v as-built A retrospective method of delay analysis often used as a first step in identifying activities which did not proceed in accordance with the programme. It involves a simple comparison of a contractor's planned programme (as-planned) against what actually happened (as-built). Note that this method does not identify who might be responsible for the delays in question.

ASR See **Alkali silica reaction**.

Assessment of costs The procedure whereby the court quantifies the amount of a party's legal costs, formerly known as taxation, and carried out by a specialist costs judge. In arbitration, the Arbitral Tribunal can determine by award the recoverable costs of the arbitration under the s63 Arbitration Act 1996.

Assignment The transfer of rights or benefits (but not the burden) of a contract from one of the original contracting parties to a third party, usually effected in writing. Some standard contracts prohibit assignment without the approval of the other party. Where an assignment of the employer's rights has taken place, difficult questions may arise as to the recoverability of damages for defects. ■ See **Contract** and **Parties**.

Associate General Contractors of America (AGC) National trade association established in 1918 representing more than 33,000 firms.

Association of Building Engineers (ABE) The professional body for those specialising in the technology of building. It was founded in 1925 under the name of "The Incorporated Association of Architects and Surveyors" and provides the prime qualification "Building Engineer".

Association of Consultant Architects (ACA) A United Kingdom national professional body representing consultant Architects in private practice. In 2000, the ACA published the first construction industry Project Partnering Contract, PPC2000.

Association of Consulting Engineers (ACE) Represents the consultancy and engineering industry in the United Kingdom and produces a standard for appointment of consultancy and engineering professionals, the most recent one being known as the ACE Agreement 2009.

Assumption of responsibility One of the factors to be considered in deciding whether a duty of care is owed in tort. ■ See **Duty of care**.

ASTM International Formerly known as the American Society for Testing and Materials. An organisation which develops technical standards for materials, products, systems, and services in a wide variety of construction and other technical activities. The voluntary consensus standards are used around the world and are developed in accordance with the guiding principles of the World Trade Organisation.

Atrium The internal courtyard of a building, often several storeys in height and either with or without a translucent/transparent roof, which brings daylight into the centre of a building.

Attendance The provision, whether notional or not, of facilities by a main contractor to a subcontractor which is usually priced as an item in bills of quantities.

Attenuator A mechanical device for reducing the output from a machine or system. Often a silencing unit in air conditioning ductwork to reduce noise levels.

Attestation The signing or sealing of legal documents in front of a witness who adds his or her name, address and profession and a short statement confirming that the document was signed or sealed in their presence and in accordance with the method prescribed by statute or other regulation. ■ See **Contracts signed under hand, Deeds, Statute** and **Witness**.

Attorney General of Belize v Belize Telecom Ltd [2009] UKPC 10; [2009] 1 WLR 1988; [2009] 2 All ER 1127: the Privy Council considered the correct test for implying terms into contracts to reflect the parties' intentions. Lord Hoffman commented that the proper question for the court is whether the implied provision would spell out in express words what the contract, read against the relevant background, would reasonably be understood to mean. ■ See **Implied term**.

Audi alteram partem Latin: "hear the other party". One of the rules of natural justice embodying the principle that no one should be condemned without a fair hearing. ■ See **Natural justice**.

Austenitic A common grade of stainless steel, often used in swimming pools and aggressive environments, which typically has a chromium content of around 18 per cent and a nickel of around 8 per cent. It has a higher corrosion resistance as compared to other grades and is generally non-magnetic.

Authorised guarantee agreement (AGA) Where an outgoing tenant assigns his lease to a new tenant, a landlord may insist that the outgoing tenant to enter into an AGA which guarantees that the assignee will perform the covenant in the lease. AGAs are regulated by s16 of the Landlord and Tenant (Covenants) Act 1995.

Authorised nominating body A body authorised to nominate adjudicators in several Commonwealth jurisdictions. There is no such regulation in the UK jurisdictions.

Authorities The decided cases or judgments a party relies on to identify a legal principle or to support a legal argument. Most are reported in recognised law reports. Computer searches may generate lists of many cases which appear to have some relevance to the issues but the courts discourage the excessive citation of authorities.

Authority The extent of an agent's power to bind his principal. ■ See **Agency**.

AutoCAD Computer software developed for computer-aided design. AutoCAD is one of several standard computer programs in the construction industry used by architects, consultants and manufacturers to draw and develop both schematic and technical designs in either 2D or 3D. Electronic files which have been created using AutoCAD generally tend to have the file format ".dwg".

Autoclave A device that uses steam to sterilise equipment and other objects, maintaining high pressure for at least 15 minutes.

Autoclaved Aerated Concrete (AAC) Pre-cast, aerated concrete in which the gas formed within the mortar is done so by a chemical reaction. It is manufactured in steel moulds and cured in an autoclave. AAC has a high thermal efficiency and is used in the production of masonry units, reinforced floor/roof and wall panels and lintels. AAC can also be sawn by hand, sculpted and penetrated by nails, screws and fixings.

Avoided loss The principle that a claimant cannot recover damages for any part of his loss consequent upon the defendant's breach of contract which the claimant could have avoided by taking reasonable steps. If the claimant in fact avoids or mitigates his loss consequent upon the defendant's breach, he cannot recover for such avoided loss. Where the claimant incurs loss and expense in the course of taking reasonable steps to mitigate the loss resulting from the defendant's breach, the claimant may recover this further loss or expense from the defendant. ■ See the **Three Rules of Mitigation**.

Award The formal decision of an **arbitrator** which may be interim or final. It normally follows a traditional format in which the history of the **arbitration** as well as the substantive dispute is rehearsed in detail.

Award of tender Formal acceptance of a contractor's tender. Once the invitation to tender is issued, and the tenders are returned, the professional team and the client assess the tenders and select a contractor to carry out the work. A contract may be formed by simple acceptance of the tender but further negotiation over its price and scope of work is commonplace. ■ See **Invitation to Tender**, **Tender** and **Tendering**.

B

Back charge See **Contra charge**.

Backfill, backfilling Backfill, or backfilling, is aggregate or other suitable material that has been removed from a building site as part of the construction process. Rather than being carted away and discarded, the excavated material, if suitable, is used to protect foundations, in landscaping, or filling in voids that would otherwise weaken underground structures. One of the most common uses of backfilling is to provide protection along the base of a foundation wall: after excavation of the building site and completion of the foundation, the excavated material is returned and firmly placed around the perimeter of the foundation.

Backflow Backflow is a reversal of the normal flow of water in a pipe system. Two common causes are: (1) **Back siphonage**, which occurs when the pressure on the supply end of a water pipe drops suddenly. This causes a vacuum which can suck dirty fluids back through connections upstream thus contaminating the water system. A sewage backflow may occur if a main drain is overwhelmed with the volume and pressure of dirty water. (2) Back pressure, the result of reversed water pressure on an outlet from a water main connection exceeding the mains supply pressure.

Background drawing A drawing used to help coordinate the design of another discipline. For example, an architectural plan may be used as an "underlay" to design and coordinate the building services.

Backing ring A flat concentric ring or backing ring essential in the formation of a sealed joint. It helps keep pipes properly aligned and prevents leaks. Often made of rubber or copper. The ring has holes drilled through it, through which bolts will pass. These holes are sometimes referenced as per a clock face to indicate a recommended tightening sequence.

Backings An element which supports or strengthens something else. For example, see **Firring Piece**.

Back siphonage A backflow of liquid caused by the siphonage from a cistern or appliance into the pipe feeding it, possibly leading to a contamination of the water supply. The sucking back of dirty water from within a building can lead to backflow into a water main if the pressure drops. All water authorities have regulations to prevent pollution of the main, for example, by having an air gap under the draw-off taps of sinks or drinking fountains, or ball valves of cisterns.

Back-to-back contracts Contracts, usually subcontracts or sub-subcontracts, the provisions of which are closely related to those of another contract, usually the main contract or the next contract "up the line". Such contracts often used to contain "pay-when-paid" or "pay-when-certified" terms, now prohibited by ss110(1A–D) and 113 of the **Construction Act**.

Backward pass A form of delay analysis, analysing the delay retrospectively from the end of the project to the start to ascertain the cause of delay.

Bad faith A dishonest or malicious intent which motivates a decision or the pursuit of a legal claim or defence.

BAE British Academy of Experts.

BAFO Best and final offer. A public procurement term. Used to signify the last stage in the bidding process which leads to the award of a contract.

Baffle A device for breaking up the flow of air, gas, water or light, often used as a diffuser. Baffles (opaque/translucent elements) are used to reduce glare from luminaires. They are also used to reduce sound passing through an **Attenuator**, to break the force of rain driving into an open-drained joint, or, as a sound absorbing unit to reduce reverberation and noise levels.

Bagging, bag rendering Rubbing cement mortar over the face of brickwork to leave a rough textured surface.

Bailey bridge Portable, usually pre-fabricated truss bridge based on the design of Sir Desmond Bailey developed during the Second World War.

Balance of convenience The point at which the factors in favour or against the granting of an interlocutory injunction outweigh or are outweighed by those on the other side. The court will weigh the claimant's need for protection against injury by violation of his right against the corresponding need of the defendant to be protected against injury resulting from his having been protected from exercising his own legal rights: see **American Cyanamid**.

Ballast Aggregate used as a filling or drainage medium. ➤ **Figure P1**.

Ballcock (also referred to as **Ball valve** or **Float valve**) A fill valve that controls the flow of water from the water supply line into a tank or cistern.

Balustrade A protective barrier (balusters, metal or timber rails or any other infill material) on a stair or parapet, or along the side of a bridge, often doubles as a decorative feature.

Bank holiday Public holidays in the United Kingdom. Strictly a bank holiday is a day defined in Schedule 1 Banking and Financial Dealings Act 1971, namely, Easter Monday, the last Monday in May, the last Monday in August, 26 December, if it is not a Sunday and 27 December in a year in which 25 or 26 December is a Sunday. This definition does not include Christmas Day and Good Friday, which are also considered to be public holidays. Under some legislation, for example, s116 of the **Construction Act,** bank and/or public holidays are excluded from the computation of certain deadlines.

Bankruptcy The legal process governed by the Insolvency Act 1986 in which an insolvent individual has their financial affairs managed by the Official Receiver. A declaration of bankruptcy ensures that such assets of the individual as might exist are distributed in a pre-determined order. A bankrupt is restricted in terms of the professional roles they may undertake and the finance they can secure until the expiry of three years from the making of the bankruptcy order, at which point the bankrupt will be automatically discharged from bankruptcy. ■ See **Insolvency**.

Bar chair See **Chair** and **Reinforcement spacer**.

Bargeboard A decorative or plain board fixed to the end of projecting gable. Conceals and protects the exposed end of the roof members.

Barograph A recording aneroid barometer produces a paper or foil chart called a barogram that records the barometric pressure over time. The recording chart is mounted on a drum which is powered usually by clockwork windings. The ink trace, or barogram, on the recording paper is a visual record of changes in pressure (as an aneroid barometer) where the trend shown can be an invaluable help in forecasting weather changes. Often used to monitor buildings in conjunction with **Data loggers** after damage caused by water penetration to monitor building environment. Nowadays, meteorological mechanical recording barographs have commonly been superseded by electronic weather instruments that use computer methods to record the barometric pressure.

Barrel vault A vault of stone or brick, semi-circular in cross section, supported by parallel walls, steel beams or arcades. Also known as a barrel roof; cradle vault; tunnel vault; wagon-head vault and wagon vault. The barrel vault is the simplest form of a vault.

Barrister A person who has been called to the Bar of England and Wales. A practising barrister has rights of audience in all Senior Courts.

Bar schedule A written table of the reinforcement required on a project for reinforced concrete showing the number, shape, size and dimensions of each element. ■ See **Reinforcement Schedule ➤ Figure B1**

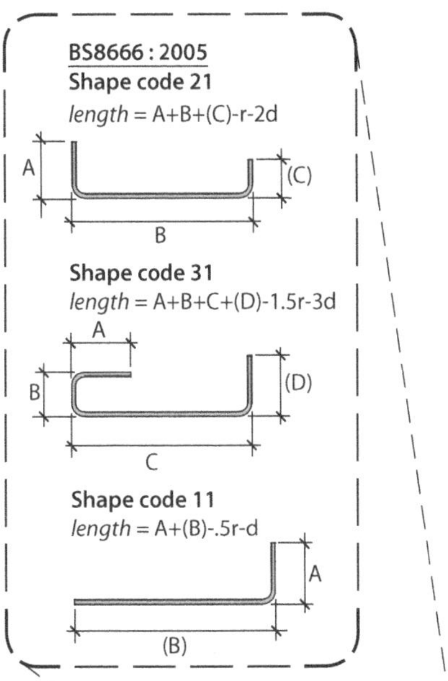

Member	Bar Mark	Type & Size	No. of mbrs	No. of bars in each	Total No.	Length of each bar(mm)	Shape code	A	B	C	D	E/r
Edge detail	1	H16	2	45	90	1850	21	1000	500	(400)		
	2	H12	2	120	240	1650	31	600	300	600	(200)	
	3	H20	2	40	80	550	11	400	(200)			

➤ Figure B1. Bar Schedule and Shape Codes

BAS See **Building Automation System**.

Bascule A counterbalanced device or structure used in moveable bridges, such as drawbridge: when one end is lowered the other is raised, just like a see-saw.

Baseball arbitration An arbitration in which the parties having made sealed offers, the tribunal determines the figure in dispute and the offer closest to the determined figure is awarded. Also known as a best offer, final offer, flip flop or pendulum arbitration. The name derives from the procedure used to determine transfer fees for baseball players in the United States.

Base course (1) In highway and pavement construction, the layer of material below the wearing course and above the roadbase. The base course or binder course is a load spreading layer which spreads the load imposed on the wearing course (surface course) over the wider area of the roadbase. Most commonly a bituminous material, it can be either hot rolled asphalt or dense bitumen macadam (asphalt concrete).It can also be a specialised layer, for example, both stiff and impervious under a porous asphalt wearing course to prevent the ingress of water into the road fabric. Often laid to tight tolerances with a good surface so that the wearing course can be laid accurately to "line and level" and so produce a better surface. (2) The lowest or bottom course of a brick/block wall.

Base date The base date is the date from which certain contractual events are related, for example, JCT DB 2011 clause 4.4 which deals with the supply of goods and services which become exempt from **VAT** at the base date. Alternatively, it may be the date from which, fluctuations in the prices of materials are to be taken into account in calculating the contract sum where it is subject to a contractual provision (see **Fluctuations Clause**) to that effect. The base date tends to be the date on which tenders are received, although the parties can choose any date for the base date.

Baseline adding impacts See **As-planned impacted**.

Base rate Term used to describe the interest rate set by the Bank of England which is used as the basis for other banks' rates.

BATNA Best Alternative to Negotiated Agreement

Bathroom pod A pre-fabricated bathroom unit, manufactured and assembled off-site in a factory typically with all fittings and internal finishes complete. It is craned into place onto a concrete slab ready for use once the services (drainage, electricity, water) have been connected. The use of pre-fabricated bathroom pods has increased with the need for faster construction programmes and modular construction. ■ See **Modular construction**.

Batten A thin strip of solid material (usually wood) fixed onto a smooth surface. Battens are used for many purposes in building construction, such as rendering, fixing tiles and sub-frames for other cladding.

Battle of the forms The course of a negotiation between two parties seeking to make a contract on their respective standard terms and one party rejects the other party's offered terms by sending back their own terms. Generally, the last terms sent are deemed to have been accepted and will prevail. See *Butler Machine Tool Co-v-Ex-Cell-O-Corp* [1979] 1 WLR 401; [1979] 1 All ER 965.

Bayonet Cap Type of light bulb fitting, most common in the United Kingdom since circa 1910. See also Edison screw (ES or E27), Small Bayonet cap (SBC) and Small Edison Screw (SES or E14) common in most of Europe and the United States of America.

BBA See **British Board of Agrément**.

Beam A horizontal or sloping structural member used to support buildings (or structures above them) and transfer the load to structural members below (eg, columns). Beams are traditionally made of timber, reinforced concrete or steel. Building and engineering components such as joists and girders are specific types of beam. ➤ **Figure S2**

Bearing capacity The ability of the ground to support the loads applied to it. The bearing capacity of soil is the maximum contact pressure between the foundation and the soil without causing a shear failure or settlement. The ultimate load which a foundation can support can be calculated using bearing capacity theory. For preliminary design, presumed bearing values from the nature of the ground can be used to indicate the pressures which would normally result in an adequate factor of safety. Alternatively, there are a range of empirical methods which are based on in situ test results. The ultimate bearing capacity (q_f) is the value of bearing stress which causes a sudden catastrophic settlement of the foundation (due to shear failure).

Beckett's anchor A type of ground anchor to hold structures such as pontoons in place. Designed by engineer Allan Beckett who developed Mulberry Harbour in the Second World War.

Becquerel (Bq) The unit of radioactive decay equal to one disintegration per second.

Bedding A layer of material laid over a horizontal surface to fill the irregularities between it and the components on top and to retain and strengthen the materials used when set. Mortar bedding is used for brickwork and either mortar or adhesive bedding is used for tiling. Alternatively, placing the material on bedding and tapping and pressing it to the desired level.

Bed joint The mortar the brick lies on. The layer of mortar, concrete or putty on which the bed surfaces of a building rests. Term occasionally used as meaning one of the radial joints in an arch. ➤ **Figure B3**

Benchmarking Comparison of results and standards of performance between providers of similar services.

Bending load A lateral force applied to a straight component which is then caused to bend.

Bending moment The amount of force required to be applied to metal or other flexible material to induce it to bend.

Bending schedule The schedule of steel bar reinforcement required for reinforcing concrete in readiness for cutting and bending. It sets out size, cross section, shape and dimension of rebars to be cut. Bar bending schedules help to determine appropriate material quantities for cost estimating and ordering.

Beneficiary A person with equitable ownership of assets which are held on trust for him or her by a trustee. A third party who receives a payment or other benefits under a contract or insurance policy.

BERR See **Department for Business Innovation and Skills**.

Bespoke contract A contract produced specifically for a project and adapted to its particular needs. It may incorporate elements taken from **Standard form contracts** such as those produced by JCT, NEC, ICE, IFCE and also terms the Employer has used for similar projects. Bespoke contracts are often negotiated by the Employer and Contractor.

Bespoke system A system or building element which is designed and custom-made for a specific project in contrast to standard products which can be purchased readymade.

Best endeavours An obligation to use best endeavours probably requires a party to take all the reasonable courses he can, whereas an obligation to use reasonable endeavours to achieve the aim probably only requires a party to take one reasonable course, not all of them: see *Rhodia International Holdings Ltd v Huntsman International LLC* [2007] EWHC 292 (Comm); [2007] 2 Lloyd's Rep 325.

Best evidence A common law principle that requires that the best available evidence is produced at court. If an original document is no longer available, a copy will be admissible as the "best evidence".

Betterment Conventionally, an increase in property value arising from government action or an improvement. In relation to damages for defective work, the term is also used to describe any benefit which a claimant might gain from the carrying out of a particular remedial scheme. The general rule is that credit should be given for the substitution of new for old, but this is subject to exceptions in the cases of the repair of chattels and the destruction of buildings provided that a replacement building is necessary to prevent the collapse of a business or loss of profits. The principle is that only some aspect of betterment which is of real pecuniary advantage to the claimant will be taken into account: see *Voaden v Champion* [2002] 1 Lloyd's Rep 623 (CA).

Bias A real likelihood of an operative prejudice, whether conscious or unconscious, on the part of a tribunal deciding a claim. An interest giving rise to bias can be one which would give rise to automatic disqualification of a tribunal, or apparent bias. The first category is exemplified by the rule at common law, *nemo debet esse judex in propria sua causa*, no one can be judge in his own cause. The question would be not whether the tribunal has some link with a party involved in a dispute before it but whether the outcome could, realistically, affect the tribunal's interest. In the case of an interest giving rise to apparent bias, the test would be whether a fair-minded and informed observer, having considered all the circumstances which have a bearing on the suggestion that the tribunal was biased, would be led to conclude that there was a real possibility that he was biased: see *Magill v Porter* [2002] 2 AC 357 (HL). ■ See **Natural justice**.

Bid See **Tender**.

Bid bond A bond given by a tendering contractor to an employer inviting tenders with the intention that the successful contractor will be bound to enter into a contract with the employer.

Bid criteria The basis upon which bids or tenders for projects will be judged by the party awarding the contract.

Biggin v Permanite Ltd [1951] 2 KB 314 (CA): establishes the principle that a claimant can rely against the defendant on the amount he has paid a third party as a result of the defendant's breach of contract pursuant to a reasonable the settlement. Subsequent decisions have extended its ambit controversially to the recovery of amounts paid to settle claims without proving liability to the third party: see *Siemens Building Technologies FE Ltd v Supershield Ltd* [2009] EWHC 927 (TCC); [2009] 2 All ER (Comm) 900.

Billet A bar of metal. "Billet parts" are machined directly from the bar, without intermediate casting or forging.

Bill of quantities (BQ) (BOQ) A written document which provides a detailed description of the quantity and quality of the works to be carried out on a project broken down into sections. They are typically prepared in accordance with an agreed standard method of measurement (such as the RICS **Standard Method of Measurement 7** - SMM7), and their principal purpose is to enable the contractor to prepare his tender sum. The contractor provides either a specific price for each item listed, or alternatively a rate for a quantity of work or materials. In JCT contracts bills of quantities are also used to value variations. Where Bills of quantities are used on a project, they are often specified as a contract document. ■ See **Standard Method of Measurement 7**. ➤ **Figure B2**

Bill of variations A written statement prepared on completion itemising the variations on the project and to demonstrate the effect the variations had on the contract sum. ■ See **Variation**.

		Qty	Unit	Rate (£)	Price (£)
	MASONRY				
	F10: BRICK/BLOCK WALLING				
	Engineering bricks, BS 3921, Category F, 215 x 102.5, class B; in cement mortar (1:3)				
A	102.5 thick; stretcher bond	20	m^2	50	1,000
	Facing bricks, Bradgate Red, Specification F10/110				
B	215 thick; English bond; facework both sides	45	m^2	80	3,600
C	102.5 thick; Flemish bond; facework one side	60	m^2	60	3,600
D	extra; special bricks; vertical angles; single cant; BS 4729, type AN5.2	200	m	25	5,000

➤ **Figure B2.** Bill of Quantities

BIM See **Building Information Modelling**.

Bimetallic corrosion A type of corrosion arising when two different metals are placed in contact in a corrosive environment (such as steel and aluminium). A small electric current flows from one piece of metal to the other (electrolytic action) accelerating the corrosion rate of the more reactive of the two metals. Bimetallic corrosion is sometimes found when new piping is added to old pipelines. The old pipeline covered by rust is cathodic to the new pipe, thus accelerating the corrosion rate in the new pipe.

BIM Maturity Levels The extent to which **BIM** is implemented as defined by Mark Bew and Mervyn Richards in their 2008 BIM Maturity Diagram. Maturity levels include: Level 0, **Level 1**, **Level 2** and Level 3.

Bio-fouling and Corrosion Control Bio-fouling and Corrosion Control are terms used in the engineering and oil and gas industry to limit risk of damage to equipment such as condensers and compressors.

Biomass Biodegradable organic material from plants, animals and micro-organisms, including gases and liquids that can be used as an energy source. For example, pellitized wood strips used as boiler fuel.

Biomass gasification A process which involves thermally converting **biomass** to simple chemical building blocks that can be transformed to fuels, products, power and hydrogen. Components include feed preparation, the biomass gasifier, and a gas treatment and cleaning train. The initial syngas contains particulates and other contaminants and must be cleaned and conditioned prior to use in fuels, chemical or power conversion systems (eg catalyst beds or fuel cells). Increasingly used in secondary power generation. Biomass Gasification Power Generation Technology converts agricultural waste (such as rice husk, wood chips, straw, domestic rubbish and silage) to combustible biomass gas by gasification technology.

Birmingham Wire Gauge (BWG) A standard for the measurement of the sizes of wire and pipes. It is also known as Stub's Wire Gauge. BWG is implied where gauge numbers are provided for a pipe without reference to a particular system.

BIS See **Department for Business Innovation and Skills**.

Bitumen A black, oily, viscous petroleum based material that is a naturally-occurring organic by-product of decomposed materials. Traditionally used in roof repairs and damp proofing masonry. Although the unqualified term "bitumen" is usually understood to refer specifically to asphaltic bitumen, the word "bituminous" is habitually used to describe both surface coatings deriving from coal tar and those based on bitumen.

Bitumen felt A flexible material for roofing incorporating bitumen.

Bituminous paint Used for waterproofing and to protect metals. Bituminous paints divide into two main classes; those of petroleum origin and those of coal tar origin. Black bitumen solution is used for the general protection of iron and steelwork such as water tanks, gutters, down pipes and can also be used as protection against moisture and corrosive atmospheres on both steelwork and timber.

Black book The name given to a collection of guidance notes covering quantity surveying and construction activities, which are produced by the RICS Quantity Surveying and Construction Professional Group.

Black start Black start gas is used for energising plant in gas treatment plants and power stations.

Blank panel Opaque infill to a frame used instead of glazing.

Blast cleaning (or Blasting) A process of treating a surface by propelling a high velocity stream of abrasive or water towards it by forcing the stream out of a pipe with compressed air.

Bleed Valve Values used in any pressurised system or circuit to permit controlled "bleeding" of fluids or gas. Common uses are in central heating, air conditioning and compressed air lines.

Blinding A layer of (usually) coarse sand, gravel or weak concrete applied to an area intended for construction activity or plant movement. It increases the bearing capacity and drainage characteristics of the ground and is used to even the surface of hardcore if a damp-proof membrane or reinforced concrete will be placed on top. ➤ **Figures E3 & R2**.

Blind nailing Concealed or secret nailing, so that nail heads do not show, particularly in finished work, on window and door frames.

Blistering (1) Bubbles in a paint surface caused by moisture or resin vapourising under the surface. (2) Swelling in finished plasterwork, a defect which may cause the finishing coat to fall away from the background.

Block diagram A type of flow-chart or diagram using blocks connected by straight lines to represent the relationship of the component parts. When used to represent electrical circuits, it is sometimes known as a **Single-line diagram**.

Blockmaker A machine for making concrete building blocks. Vary in applications from factory based to mobile units.

Blockwork Factory produced masonry (larger than traditional bricks) of precast concrete or derivatives in various densities. Used in the construction of walls, and in beam and block floors. Usually laid in cement mortar. Not typically used in "face" work.

Bloor Construction (UK) Ltd v Bowmer and Kirkland (London) Ltd [2000] BLR 314: In the absence of a specific agreement by the parties to the contrary, there is to be implied into the agreement for adjudication the power of the adjudicator to correct an error arising from an accidental slip or omission or to clarify or remove any ambiguity in the decision which he has reached, provided this is done within a reasonable time and without prejudicing the other party (the "**slip rule**"). The slip rule has subsequently been codified by s140 of **LDEDCA**. See also ***YCMS Ltd v Grabiner*** [2009] EWHC 127 (TCC); [2009] BLR 211.

Blow down In connection with boilers or **cooling towers**, the process of discharging or draining water to remove accumulated salts and other impurities or the name given to the water which is blown down or discharged.

Blowhole, superficial void A bubble of air trapped on the surface of concrete, not driven out during vibration.

The Blue Book (1) See **Tree Preservation Orders: A Guide to the Law and Good Practice (2000)**. (2) The National Agreement for the Engineering Construction Industry (or "the NAECI" or "Blue Book") sets terms and conditions of employment for hourly-paid engineering construction workers on major engineering construction projects and repair and maintenance sites throughout the United Kingdom.

BLR See **Building Law Reports**.

Blue pencil test The severability of a contract if the several parts are independent of one another and can be severed without the severance affecting the meaning of the remaining part. This is sometimes expressed by saying that the severance can be effected when the part severed can be removed by running a blue pencil through it. "This is a figurative way of expressing the principle, and like most figurative expressions may possibly lead to misunderstanding": see *Attwood v Lamont* [1920] 3 KB 571, 578. The test is particularly applicable to contractual provisions which are illegal or unenforceable.

BMS See **Building Management System**.

Bodkin A hand tool used for the binding of legal documents with thread or ribbon. Also known as a "bodger".

The *Bolam* test Mcnair J laid down the applicable test for the standard of care for professionals. Here, it was held that a doctor was not necessarily negligent if he conformed to a practice accepted as proper by some responsible members of his profession, even if other members would have taken a different view. Evidence of an accepted practice must be responsible and reasonable. *Bolam v Friern Hospital Management Committee* [1957] 2 All ER 118. ■ See **Negligence.**

Bona fide Latin: "in good faith".

Bond (1) See **Performance bond**. (2) The adhesion of one material to another. (3) The pattern formed in brickwork by the configuration of the bricks. A variety of face bonds are used although, historically, Flemish bond (alternate headers and stretchers in each course) predominated domestically, whilst English bond (alternate courses of headers and stretchers) was favoured industrially. ➤ **Figure B3**

Bonded screed There are two basic methods of screed construction: bonded to a concrete base or unbonded, both being covered by BS 8204-1.

Bonding (1) The adhesion of two materials; (2) The connecting together of all non-current-carrying metal parts to form an electrically conductive path that enables current to be conducted safely. ■ See **Earthing**.

Bonding agent A treatment applied to a base substrate to increase the adhesion of subsequent applications of materials.

Bonding plaster A backing plaster used on smooth surfaces which are difficult to bond to.

Bondsman The issuer of a bond (also known as a surety or guarantor). The Bondsman is usually a bank, insurance company or specialist bonding company.

Bonus An additional payment, such as on to a contractor for early completion. The NEC contract provides for addition to the price payable for the work in certain circumstances.

Boom (1) The **Jib** of a crane; (2) A truck used to hoist heavy material up and into place.

BOOT See **Build, own, operate, transfer**.

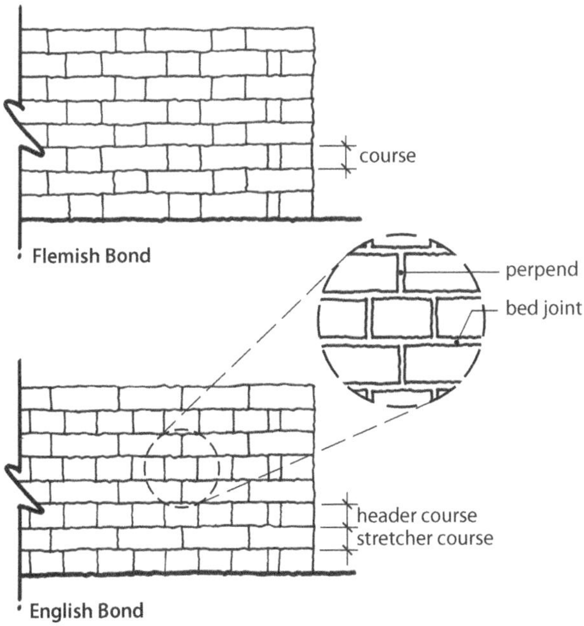

➤ **Figure B3.** Brick Bonds

Boot lintel An L-shaped (boot-shaped) lintel, with the main body of the lintel inside the cavity wall, thereby reducing the depth of the lintel exposed on the external wall. Boot lintels can result in condensation and **Cold bridging**.

Bored piling Piling formed by pouring concrete into previously formed bores.

BOT See **Build, operate and transfer**.

Bottom chord See **Chord**. ➤ **Figure T4**.

Bottom plate The lowest horizontal member of a framed partition which rests on the rough floor, to which the studding is nailed.

Box girder A hollow beam.

Brace A structural member (strut or tie) used to stabilise and stiffen a framework.

Braced frame A structural frame (columns and beam) with additional stability provided by diagonal cross-bracing. A structural system designed to work both in tension and compression.

BRE See **Building Research Establishment**.

Breach of contract A failure by a party to comply with a term of a contract. The term may be: a condition, breach of which would entitle the other party to regard itself as discharged from further performance (repudiation); a warranty, breach of which would only entitle the other party to damages or an innominate term, breach of which could have either effect, depending on the circumstances. ■ See **Damages, Repudiation** and **Specific performance**.

Breakwater A structure designed to protect a beach or harbour from the force of waves.

Breather membrane A membrane which repels water (for example, that which has penetrated the external lead of a Cavity Wall) but still allows water vapour to escape from the other side.

BRE Environmental Assessment Method (BREEAM) BREEAM was first launched in 1990 to provide an environmental assessment and labelling scheme for buildings. It is updated periodically to ensure that the scheme continues to represent best practice. BREEAM has been used to assess the environmental performance of both new and existing buildings. It is regarded by the UK's construction and property sectors as the measure of best practice in environmental design and management. BREEAM addresses wide-ranging environmental and sustainability issues and enables developers and designers to prove the environmental credentials of their buildings to planners and clients.

Brickbat (1) A piece of a brick, often used as a weapon; (2) A critical remark or comment.

Brick slip (Brick Tiles, Brick Cladding) Thin facing bricks used for cladding. May be used where the use of a full brick is impossible or impractical. They provide an actual brick finish but without the full depth of a traditional brick.

Brick veneer Thin facing bricks applied to a surface. Typically non-structural.

Bricklayer's scaffold (Putlog Scaffold) A scaffolding for use by bricklayers supported by putlogs, which have a flattened end to fit into raked-out holes in the bed joints, the other end being carried on ledgers held up by the standards.

Brief A set of instructions or documents, or both, for an advocate.

Brise soleil A French word which literally means breaking, crushing or smashing the sun. In construction, it is a building component designed to prevent solar gain inside buildings. It consists of a shade positioned over a window in such a way as to prevent the sun from directly hitting the glazing. Unlike a blind or awning which can be extended or retracted, the brise soleil is a permanent structure. In summer, when the sun is high in the sky, the brise soleil blocks the sunlight from warming the inside of the building. In winter, however, when the sun is low in the sky, the positioning of the brise soleil is such that the sun passes beneath it and thus enables the building to benefit from the sun's energy.

British Board of Agrément (BBA) An independent assessment and approval body which can certify that a material or product is fit for purpose. ■ See **Agrément Certificate**. An Agrément Certificate is awarded to a product only after it has successfully passed a comprehensive assessment involving laboratory testing, on-site evaluations and inspections of production, the latter to check that the manufacturer has a factory production control system in operation that will ensure that the specification of the product will be maintained consistently. The main focus of the Agrément process is the evaluation of the extent to which the product allows compliance with relevant building regulations and other statutory or non-statutory requirements to be achieved.

British Standards (BS) Standards established and approved by the **British Standards Institution** relating to the performance of products or services.

British Standards Institution (BSI) Independent national standards-making body. BSI is a non-profit distributing organisation globally recognised as an independent and impartial body serving both the private and public sectors, working with manufacturing and service industries, businesses and governments to facilitate the production of British, European and International Standards. As well as facilitating the creation of BS, BSI is the United Kingdom's National Standards Body (NSB) and represents the United Kingdom's interests across all of the European and International Standards committees.

British thermal unit (Btu) The amount of heat energy required to raise the temperature of one pound of water by 1°F. This is the standard measurement used to state the amount of energy that a fuel has, as well as the amount of output of any heat-generating device.

Broom-finish concrete Smooth, levelled concrete which finished by drawing a broom across it to make it a slip-resistant surface. As known as "brushed finish."

Brown-field site A potential building site which has previously been used for another purpose or has previously been developed on. Brown-field sites are often located in industrial areas or city centres and therefore are often subject to difficult environmental issues such as contamination.

Brushability The ease with which a coating can be brushed.

Brussels Convention Shortened name for Brussels Convention on Jurisdiction and the Enforcement of Judgments in Civil and Commercial Matters 1968. This is superseded by Council Regulation (EC) No 44/2001 of 22 December 2000 on jurisdiction and the recognition and enforcement of judgments in civil and commercial matters.

BS See **British Standards**.

BS 5606 Guide to accuracy in building – the level of accuracy required for survey work is based on BS 5606: 1990 – Guide to Accuracy in Building. The accepted deviations in accuracy for site surveys when measuring with a steel tape the accepted range of deviation are as follows:

± 5 mm up to dimensions of 5m;
± 10 mm over 10 m;
± 15 mm for over 25 m,

irrespective of the measuring device.

BSF See **Building Schools for the Future**.

BSI See **British Standards Institution**.

BSRIA A consultancy, test and research organisation providing construction and building services companies.

Btu, BThU See **British thermal unit**.

Buggeration Builders' jargon for disruption and consequent uneconomic working. Sometimes used loosely to include prolongation.

Buildability The practicability of the work involved in realising a design by those likely to be employed to do it, in the conditions which can be foreseen, by the exercise of the care and skill ordinarily to be expected of them; first recognised as an aspect of the designer's duty in *Equitable Debenture Assets Corp Ltd v William Moss Group Ltd* [1984] 2 ConLR 1 (TCC).

Builder One who carries out building work: there is no statutory restriction on the term's use.

Builder's line A length of cord or rope stretched between two points which acts as a marker for building works.

Builder's level A spirit level or a dumpy level.

Builder's Work in Connection (BWIC) Work to be carried out by a main contractor to facilitate the execution of subcontract works (often in relation to services items: for example cutting small holes in concrete to allow services to pass). May be charged for as a separate item.

Building In addition to its well-known definition as a structure or edifice which provides protection from the elements, s336(1) of the Town and Country Planning Act 1990 defines a building as including "any structure or erection, and any part of a building, as so defined, but does not include plant or machinery comprised in a building". This is particularly significant in relation to planning issues and listed buildings. Furthermore, s2(1) of the Building Regulations 2010, SI 2010/2214 defines a building, for the purpose of these regulations, as "any permanent or temporary building but not any other kind of structure or erection, and a reference to a building includes a reference to part of a building". ■ See **Listed building**.

Building Act 1984 Legislation which was enacted with the aim of ensuring that the health, safety, welfare and convenience of persons in or about buildings are secured. In addition, it aims to further the conservation of fuel and power and prevent waste, undue consumption, misuse or contamination of water. (See s1 of the Act) The Building Act 1984 only applies in England and Wales and does not extend to Scotland and Northern Ireland. ■ See **Approved Documents** and **Building Regulations**.

Building Automation System (BAS) A system for monitoring and coordinating building services by the use of computer programs.

Building contract A contract whereby one person, the builder, agrees to build or construct some work on behalf of some other person, the employer or building owner, usually to be carried out on that other person's land. A building contract can also be described as a construction contract, and sometimes an engineering contract.

Building control Laws and procedures to ensure that buildings are built correctly. The main function of building control is to ensure compliance with the building regulations. This function is carried out by a Building Control Body (BCB), either the local authority building control service or a private sector approved inspector (AI). Certain types of building work can be self-certificated as compliant with building regulations by a member of a Competent Person Scheme without the need to notify a BCB.

Building Control and Management System (BCMS) See **Building management system (BMS)**.

Building control officer Main functions of a building control officer include the following: checking of plans and details of buildings to be erected or altered, regular inspection of work in progress to ensure that the building work is in accordance with building regulations, management of buildings and structures identified as being in a dangerous condition, management of the demolition of buildings, management of improved access to buildings for people with disabilities, guidance and advice on all types of buildings and constructional problems including those not subject to building regulation control.

Building employer See **Employer**.

Building Information Modelling (BIM) The process of creating and managing information concerning a building, typically in a three-dimensional computer model which embeds data relating to its construction and uses parametric design. If employed to its full extent, it is a tool used as part of the design process, throughout construction and for maintenance and alteration of the completed project. ■ See **BIM Maturity Levels** and **Parametric Design**.

Building inspector Employee of a local authority, a lender, or an insurance company, whose responsibilities include reviewing building plans and/or inspecting building sites to determine whether or not they meet existing legal and regulatory requirements.

Building Law Reports (BLR) A set of law reports published mainly for the construction industry, reporting on key judgments from the Technology and Construction Court, appellate courts in England and Wales and other relevant jurisdictions worldwide. Topics covered include adjudication, arbitration, civil procedure rules, construction contracts, delay and disruption, construction insurance, costs, damages etc.

Building management system (BMS) A system which monitors and often automatically controls such mechanical and electrical building services as the hot water services, heating, lighting, lifts, security, air conditioning, fire alarm and sprinkler systems. This centrally controlled system enables easier operation of the building systems and minimises energy waste as the services are only used when required. For example, the system might be programmed such that lights are automatically shut off if no occupants are in a particular room.

Building Notice Required where a local authority is to supervise the works, alternatively a person intending to carry out work may submit full plans. In certain circumstances the option of submitting a Building Notice is not available; reg 11, SI 1985/1065. It is best suited for small uncomplicated work. It cannot be used for designated buildings or buildings within 3 m of a public sewer or when a fire certificate is required.

Building owner A party intending to carry out or carrying out works covered by the **Party Wall Act 1996**. Also used to mean the employer under a building contract.

Building permit (Building Consent) Authorisation by the local authority to permit construction; it is essential before site work can start.

Building Regulations A set of legal requirements and minimum design and construction standards which aim to ensure the health, safety and welfare of people in and around buildings. In addition, the regulations provide for safe access to buildings and energy and fuel conservation. The regulations have been created by the Secretary of State for the Environment under powers delegated by the Building Act 1984. They are intended to provide practical guidance on how to comply with reg 7 of the Building Act 1984 which states that building work shall be carried out with adequate and proper materials and in a workman-like manner. The current legislation is "The Building Regulations 2010, SI 2010/2214". The regulations are supported by 14 **Approved Documents** from A (structural safety) to P (electrical safety) which set out further detailed technical guidance on how to comply with Schedule 1 and Regulation 7. Similar to the Building Act 1984, the building regulations only apply in England and Wales and do not extend to Scotland and Northern Ireland. In order ensure that any proposed works comply with the regulations, approval must be obtained either from the building control services provided by the local authority, or from an **approved inspector** in the private sector. ■ See **Approved documents, Approved inspector, Building Act 1984** and **Building Control**.

Building Research Establishment (BRE) A former UK government establishment located with its headquarters in Garston near Watford (but now a private organisation, funded by the building industry) that carries out research, consultancy and testing for the construction and built environment sectors in the United Kingdom. Among the BRE's areas of interest are participation in the preparation of national and international standards and building codes, including the UK Building Regulations. The organisation is now funded by income from its commercial programmes, the BRE bookshop, contracted work, and by bidding for research funding from government and the industries it serves. It is also a UKAS Accredited Testing Laboratory.

Building Schools for the Future (BSF) School buildings investment programme, pursuant to which the government was seeking to support a transformation of secondary education and ensure that all secondary age children and young people have access to facilities of 21st century standard. The intention was to renew and/or replace all secondary schools over a 10- to 15-year period beginning from 2005/2006. Partnerships for Schools (PfS) was responsible for the management and delivery of **BSF**. In July 2010, the Coalition Government announced it was discontinuing the BSF programme.

Building survey An inspection of a building. Building surveys vary according to circumstances, but would normally be expected to describe the building's layout, and state of repair.

Building surveyor A construction professional trained in the techniques, costs and law of property and construction. They work on site with new buildings and are concerned with the aftercare and performance of existing buildings. This is a very wide field and may include advising on various aspects of buildings at different stages, including design, maintenance, repair, dilapidations, refurbishment, restoration and sustainability.

Building Systems Integration (BSI) The interface and co-ordination of systems (eg structural, mechanical, electrical, fire detection and suppression systems) within a building or the introduction and co-ordination of new systems into an existing set-up.

Building tolerances The limits within which specified dimensions are permitted to deviate from the absolute measurements given, expressed as a "plus or minus" figure.

Buildmark A scheme operated by the National House Building Council from 1988 giving the purchaser or subsequent owner of a new dwelling a right to claim against the builder and make an insurance claim against the NHBC in respect of defects.

Build, operate and transfer (BOT) A form of procurement whereby the contractor agrees to build, operate and then transfer the works to the employer. Often used in process engineering, infrastructure and oil and gas contracts. The transfer of the works may take place sometime after the works have been completed and after they have been operated for an agreed period. ■ See also **Design Build Operate (DBO)**.

Build, own, operate and transfer (BOOT) A form of procurement whereby, in addition to building, operating and then transferring the works (see **BOT**), the contractor takes a share in the ownership of the project.

Built-in Furniture, fittings or other building elements which are constructed into the structure or fabric of the building. For example, built-in cabinets are generally those which are permanently constructed into a recess in the wall, unable to be moved without demolition works.

Built-up roofing A continuous, semi-flexible roof membrane assembly, consisting of plies of saturated felts, coated felts, fabrics or mats between which alternate layers of bitumen are applied, generally surfaced with mineral aggregate, bituminous materials, or a granule-surfaced roofing sheet. It is usually used to weatherproof a flat roof.

Bulkhead (1) An area of reduced ceiling height to provide additional space, typically for the structure or large mechanical ductwork; (2) A wall within a structure or ship which can provide stiffness, acoustic separation and/or fire separation.

Bullock Order A form of costs order first recognised in *Bullock v London General Omnibus Co* [1907] 1 KB 264 whereby a successful defendant's costs are ordered to be included in the costs recoverable by the claimant from an unsuccessful defendant.

Bund An earth mound or embankment, such as one built around a storage tank containing hazardous liquid to prevent its escape and spreading.

Bundle The file or files of documents used at hearings in litigation, arbitration and adjudication. In the Technology and Construction Court, in the event of problems not capable of resolution by agreement, the assigned judge will give directions as to the preparation of the agreed trial bundle. In addition to statements of case and orders, there are usually separate chronological bundles of correspondence and meeting minutes, with other bundles consisting of contracts, witness statements, experts' reports, drawings, technical documents and the like. Core bundles may also be directed to be prepared.

Burden of proof The obligation of a party making an assertion to prove his case. It can shift from the claimant to the defendant, depending on the allegations being made. Not to be confused with the **Standard of proof**, which is the level of proof required to discharge the burden.

Burgundy Book See **IChemE**.

Burlap bags Like hessian, a strong, coarsely woven cloth made of fibres of jute, flax or hemp. Used to make bags, to reinforce linoleum, and in interior decoration. Also used for filling with sand for engineered revetments.

Busbar An electrically conductive bar connecting two or more electrical circuits. Busbars are used within installations for distributing electrical power from a supply point to a number of output circuits. They may be used in a variety of configurations ranging from vertical risers, carrying current to each floor of a multi-storey building, to bars used entirely within a distribution panel.

Business day Not a weekend or public or bank holiday.

But-for test The test for causation in tort, namely whether the act or omission was a contributory cause without which the damage would not have occurred. ■ See **Causation**.

BWIC See **Builders Work In Connection**.

Byelaw The law as developed by local authorities or localised government departments. This delegated legislation can be subject to review by the courts and the government. ■ See **Delegated legislation**.

C

CA See **Contract administrator** and **Court of Appeal.**

Cable tray A cable management system rigidly supported from the building structure, sized to accommodate the electrical and data cabling, typically routed from plant rooms via vertical cable trays in service risers to horizontal cable trays fixed above the suspended ceiling.

CAD Computer-Aided Design. Used for drawing two-dimensional or three-dimensional technical or engineering drawings, often used as an abbreviation for the computer programme **AutoCAD**.

Caisson A pressurised water and airtight chamber in which work is carried out underwater.

Calcium silicate bricks Bricks composed of lime mixed with quartz, crushed flint or crushed siliceous, which were the subject of many failures in the 1970s when used in the wrong ground conditions. Also susceptible to natural shrinkage.

Calderbank Offer An offer to compromise litigation made "without prejudice save as to costs", first recognised in *Calderbank v Calderbank* [1976] Fam 93; [1975] 3 WLR 586; [1975] 3 All ER 333. The need for such offers has largely been removed by the revised provisions of CPR Part 36. The term is sometimes also used to describe a sealed offer in arbitration: ■ See **Sealed Offer** and **Part 36 Offer**.

California Bearing Ratio (CBR) A simple penetration test developed by the California State Highways Department to evaluate the strength of road sub-grades by comparing the bearing capacity of a material with that of a well-graded crushed stone. See BS 1377: Soils for civil engineering purposes: Pt 4, Compaction related tests.

Call-off contract A contract, usually for a fixed period of time, made with one or more contractors, suppliers or service providers for a defined range of works, goods or services covering terms and conditions (including price). Typically an individual contract is awarded or called off under a **Framework Agreement** for the provision of the particular services, goods or works in question.

Call on a bond To require the provider of a performance bond to make payment.

Calorifier A waste storage heater, typically a cylinder or vessel in which water is heated indirectly, normally by passing steam or hot water through a coiled pipe contained within the calorifier. An indirect water cylinder.

Candela A standard unit of luminous intensity in the International System of Units (SI).

Canons of construction Established rules which are applied in construing a document to arrive at its legal effect.

Cantilever A beam or other horizontal member which is fixed only at one end. ➤ **Figure C1**

Capacity The ability of a person or other legal entity to enter into a binding contract. Generally, certain classes of people or entities cannot enter into a binding contract, such as minors, agents unless their terms of appointment entitle them to do so, unincorporated associations and persons suffering from mental illness or learning difficulties. ■ See **Agent** and **Unincorporated association**.

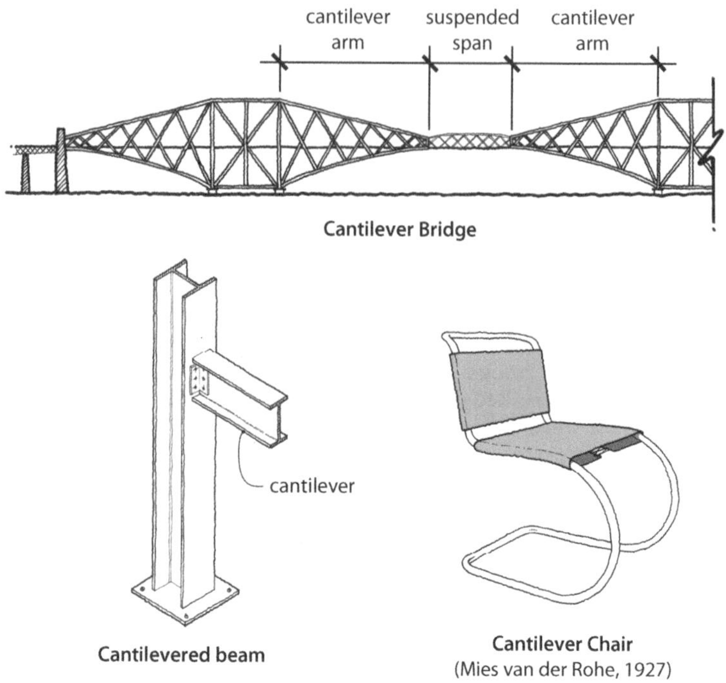

➤ **Figure C1.** Cantilever

Caparo Industries v Dickman [1990] UKHL 2: the House of Lords put forward a threefold test to establish whether a duty of care is owed by one party to another in tort. The test seeks to establish whether the damage which occurred was foreseeable; whether there is sufficient proximity in the relationship between the parties; and finally, whether it is just, fair and reasonable in all the circumstances to impose a duty of care.

Capillary action (Capillarity) The tendency of a liquid to rise in narrow tubes or to be drawn into small openings such as those between grains of a rock. Capillary action, also known as capillarity, is a result of the intermolecular attraction within the liquid and solid materials. Rising damp and water bridging a cavity wall result from capillarity.

Capillary break A space between two surfaces made wide enough to prevent the movement of moisture through that space by **Capillarity**.

Capping (1) A cover to protect or finish the end or top of a wall; (2) Something which terminates the end of a pipe.

Capping strip A strip to cover joints to prevent water ingress or damage to fixings.

Carcass, Carcassing (1) Load bearing structure in timber framing; and (2) Framework to joinery items such as cabinet and IPS systems.

CAR policy See **Contractor's All Risks policy**.

Casement window An opening window which is attached to its frame by a series of hinges. Compare with **Sash window.**

Case management conference (CMC) A hearing, the first of one of which is usually held at an early stage of proceedings, at which the court reviews case preparation, gives directions and seeks agreements; see CPR Practice Direction 29 and s5 of the **Technology and Construction Court (TCC) Guide**. ➤ **Figure T1**

Cash discount A deduction from a payment by a main contractor to a subcontractor under the terms of the subcontract. The discount has been conventionally viewed as one dependent upon prompt payment, although the Court of Appeal's majority decision in *Team Services plc v Kier Management and Design Ltd* (1993) 63 BLR 76 suggests otherwise.

Castellated universal section A standard universal beam or column section formed by cutting along a castellated line, producing two halves which are then welded together.

Casting A method of making a component, in which molten material (such as metal) is poured into a mould and then allowed to harden.

Casting-in Electrical conducts or other inserts are fixed to the concrete shutter. Once the concrete is pared and the Shutterstruck, the items are "cast" into the concrete slab or wall.

Cast stone Reconstructed stone. Concrete mix with carefully selected aggregate and cement (with the occasional inclusion of mica) cast in a mould and finished to provide the appearance of stone.

Category A fit-out One of the typical levels of completion for an office building which includes some fitting out of the office space: raised floors, suspended ceilings and luminaires.

Category B fit-out The stage of fit-out following Cat A fit-out which commonly comprises installation of cellular offices, conference/meeting room facilities, IT and audio visual services and furniture.

Cat ladder A ladder frame fitted with cleats and used on steep roofs.

Catwalk A gangway for accessing the upper parts of high buildings.

Caucus An American term probably of Algonquian origin used either as a noun or a verb in mediation to describe the process whereby a party and its advisors meet in private usually with the mediator, but in the absence of the other party. ■ See **Mediation**.

Caulking A process of sealing a joint with a flexible sealant material.

Causa causans Latin: "the causing cause", the immediate cause.

Causa sine qua non Latin: "a cause without which not", a necessary precondition.

Causation The connection between a wrongful act and any loss suffered. Where more than one factor has contributed to a loss, the test of whether the connection is sufficient in contract is whether the breach was an "effective or predominant cause" or a "real and effective cause". In tort, the test is a "but for" one, namely whether the act or omission was a contributory cause without which the damage would not have occurred.

Cause of action A factual situation the existence of which entitles one person to obtain from the court a remedy against another person. For the purposes of the amendment of statements of case, it is a mixed question of law and fact whether there is a new cause of action: see *Steamship*

Mutual Underwriting Association Ltd v Trollope and Colls (City) Ltd (1986) 33 BLR 77.

Caveat emptor Latin: "let the buyer beware", the common law rule whereby a buyer purchase at his own risk, now qualified by the Sale of Goods Act 1979, the Unfair Contract Terms Act 1977 and the Supply of Goods and Services Act 1982 in the case of consumer and standard terms of trading transactions.

Cavity barrier Barriers positioned in walls, floor voids and cavities to prevent the passage of smoke or fire. They are also suitable for reducing flanking noise transmission: for example, if positioned in the floor or ceiling voids above/below office partitions.

Cavity closer Used to fill the gap between two walls, or two leafs of a wall, which are separated by a void/hollow space. They are primarily used for the purpose of moisture prevention and insulation. However, a cavity closer also provides a natural framework for setting up doors and windows.

Cavity flashing A waterproofing material which crosses the gap of a cavity wall. See **Damp proof course**.

Cavity inspection Inspection carried out either during or after the process of construction of a **Cavity Wall**.

Cavity insulation A substance inserted into a **Cavity wall** to improve the thermal performance of the wall and achieve the U-valves required by the Building Regulations.

Cavity tray A stepped damp proof course, frequently preformed, installed above window or door openings to prevent the ingress of water into the cavity.

Cavity wall External wall constructed of an inner and outer leaf. The outer leaf is typically brickwork with the inner leaf being constructed of blockwork or timber framing. The air space ("cavity") is usually at least 50 mm (2 inches). The purpose of the cavity is to prevent water or dampness from passing between the outer (wet) leaf and the inner (dry) leaf and to prevent condensation from occurring in the inner leaf (dew point calculations are required to confirm this). Insulation is used in the cavity to comply with Building Regulations, although to make further energy savings and comply with "green" best practice, these requirements are now commonly exceeded. If timber construction is used for the inner leaf, insulation is normally placed between the timber studs. See **Figure E3**

CAWS The Common Arrangement of Work Sections, a classification of works for specifications and bills of quantities intended to standardise the arrangement of documents used in building projects, published by the Construction Project Information Committee (CPIC).

CBR See **California Bearing Ratio**.

CDE See **Common Data Environment**.

CDM Coordinator Construction Design Management (CDM) Coordinator. CDM Coordinator is a specialist in construction health and safety risk management matters. The role of CDM Coordinator, formerly known as the planning supervisor, is to assist and advise the client on the appointment of competent designers and contractors and the adequacy of management arrangements. Only required on those projects which are "notifiable" under the CDM Regulations. ■ See **Construction (Design and Management) Regulations 2007**.

CCM See **Common Carbon Metric**.

CDM Regulations See **Construction (Design and Management) Regulations 2007**.

CDP See **Contractor Designed Portion.**

CEDR See **Centre for Effective Dispute Resolution.**

CE mark CE The letters "**CE**" are the abbreviation of French phrase "**C**onformité **E**uropéene" which means "European Conformity". The term initially used was "EC Mark" and it was officially replaced by "CE Marking" in the Directive 93/68/EEC in 1993. "CE Marking" is now used in all EU official documents. **CE mark** is therefore not the official term. CE Marking on a product is a manufacturer's declaration that the product complies with the essential requirements of the relevant European health, safety and environmental protection legislation, in practice by many of the so-called Product Directives. CE Marking on a product indicates to governmental officials that the product may be legally placed on the market in their country.

Ceiling diffuser A terminal part of HVAC system supplying the air. Usually features bars or blades for air deflection. Manufactured from steel, aluminium or plastic.

Ceiling hangers Metal fasteners, fixed to the underside of the structural slab, designed to carry a suspended ceiling.

Ceiling insulation Internal insulation for the pitched roof of a house to reduce heat loss.

Ceiling joist (Roof Joist) A structural framing member used to carry ceiling loads. Can be the roof joist or the **bottom chord** of a roof truss.

Cellular concrete See **Aerated concrete**.

Cellular construction (1) Efficient method of construction for building repetitive accommodation units such as apartments, hotels, prisons etc. (2) A construction having a lightweight inner core containing voids which is faced on both sides by a material such as clay, plywood or hardboard.

Cement A binder, usually Portland cement. A substance which sets and hardens independently, and can bind other materials, such as concrete or mortar, together.

Cement content A quantity of cement contained in a unit volume of concrete or mortar. Cement content determines strength and durability of the mix.

Cement screed A layer of cement mortar which is cast in situ onto a prepared base slab. The screed may be left as finished, or floated to produce a smooth surface on which to lay the specified flooring or finish.

CEN See **European Committee for Standardization.**

Centre for Effective Dispute Resolution (CEDR) A not for profit organisation specialising in alternative dispute resolution and, in particular, mediation, based in London.

Centre-to-centre A method of measuring a line from the centreline of each part or component.

Centrifugal fan A type of fan in which the air flow is in a radial direction relative to the driveshaft. Suited for use in ducted and air conditioning systems due to the airstream pressure generated by centrifugal force.

Certainty One of the elements of a binding contract which relates to the clarity of precision of the terms. If the terms are uncertain the contract will be void. ■ See **Void**.

Certificate A document formally recording a matter as required by contract or statute. In the case of construction contracts, different certificates will usually fulfil a number of functions, such as the certifier's interim or final valuation of the works, the stage of completion or non-completion of the works. A document will not be a certificate unless it is one "in form, in substance or in intent": *Token Construction Co Ltd v Charlton Estates Ltd* (1973) 1 BLR 48 (CA). ■ See **Condition precedent** and **Retention**.

Certificate of lawfulness A certificate confirming that a proposed use or development would be lawful under permitted development law.

Certificate of making good defects A certificate issued under JCT forms (clause 2.39 of JCT 2011) indicating that the contractor has discharged his obligations in relation to the defects liability period and usually marking the point at which the second half of the retention monies are to be released to the contractor.

Certificate of non-completion A certificate issued under JCT standard forms of contract stating that the contractor has failed to complete the works or a section by the relevant completion date. Its issue is a condition precedent to the employer's right to deduct or recover liquidated damages: *A Bell and Son (Paddington) Ltd v CBF Residential Care and Housing Assn* (1989) 46 BLR 102.

Certificate of Practical Completion A certificate issued under certain standard forms of contract (ie clause 2.30 of JCT 2011) stating that practical completion of the works or a section of them has been achieved. ■ See **Practical Completion**.

Certificate of service Under CPR 6.17, where the claimant serves the claim form, the claimant must file a certificate of service within 21 days of service of the particulars of claim, unless all the defendants to the proceedings have filed acknowledgements of service within that time. A claimant cannot obtain judgment in default under CPR 12 following a failure to serve an acknowledgement of service form unless a certificate of service has been filed.

Certifier A person designated in a contract to give a certificate, such as an architect, engineer or contract administrator.

Certiorari A discretionary remedy of the High Court whereby the decision of an inferior court is quashed as it contains an error of law or is ultra vires. ■ See **Ultra vires**.

Certum est quod certum redid potest Latin: that which can be made certain is sufficiently certain. A rule of construction which permits the court to uphold an agreement by ascertaining a matter which is not described precisely, such as an unlimited period for something to be done, which can be regarded as a reasonable time to be established by evidence.

CESSM Civil Engineering Standard Method of Measurement

CFA See **Conditional fee agreement.**

C & G See **City and Guilds of London Institute, Clearing and grubbing.**

CGCT Abbreviation commonly adopted in the power industry for combined Cycle Gas Turbine, being an efficient type of power station which captures exhaust steam. It describes the process whereby the exhaust gas steam from this process is used for a second time to drive a low pressure turbine to improve the efficiency of the generating station. Both the gas and steam turbines drive electrical generators, directly by shaft or gearing achieving a greater thermal efficiency than is possible independently.

Chair A bent reinforcement bar specifically made to support the upper layer of reinforcement. The chair sits on the bottom reinforcement to support the upper reinforcement at the correct level for adequate concrete cover. Also known as "bar chair" and "reinforcement spacer". ■ See **Reinforcement spacer**.

Chair rail A protective wall mounted moulding that runs horizontally usually at about 3 feet from the floor (ie level with the top of the chair).

Chamfer A bevelled edge usually at 45° angle.

Champerty The support of a party to litigation in return for a share of the proceedings, no longer a crime or tort.

Change A variation of the works. A term frequently used in design and build contracts and also in American forms of contract.

Chancery Division That part of the High Court which deals with disputes relating to interests in land, trusts, companies and complex financial claims. ➤ **Figure C3**.

Changed conditions clause A clause, usually in a contract for civil engineering works, entitling the contractor to additional cost incurred as a result of encountering unforeseen adverse physical conditions, such as clause 12 of the ICE forms.

Change of use A change of use of a building or land, which may require a planning permission. Planning laws classify uses of land and buildings into various categories called "Use Classes". A Use Class is a grouping together of similar land uses.

Change order An instruction for a change or variation of the works, often but not exclusively found under American forms of contract, which usually make the issue of such an order a condition precedent to recovery by the contractor. ■ See, however: **Constructive change order**.

Channel Tunnel Group v Balfour Beatty [1993] 2 WLR 262: Lord Mustill held that where a contract provides for a prescribed dispute resolution procedure, irrespective of how elaborate or complicated, the parties shall be bound by that process.

Charging Order An order made in accordance with the Charging Orders Act 1979 which imposes a charge over a property as security for a Judgment debt.

Chartered builder (MCIOB, FCIOB) Member or Fellow of the **Chartered Institute of Building**.

Chartered engineer In the United Kingdom, a Chartered Engineer is a professionally qualified engineer, registered with the Engineering Council United Kingdom.

Chartered Institute of Arbitrators (CIArb) The leading British association of arbitrators, qualification for membership of which requires the passing of examinations.

Chartered Institute of Building (CIOB) The leading professional body worldwide concerning the management of the total building process.

Chartered Institute of Building Services Engineers (CIBSE) A membership organisation based in London representing building services engineers. CIBSE publishes Guidance and Codes, which are internationally recognised as authoritative, and sets the criteria for best practice in the profession.

Chartered surveyor A surveyor who is a member of the **Royal Institution of Chartered Surveyors.**

Chase A channel cut into masonry or timber usually to run service media like cable and pipes.

Chatham House Rules Devised in 1927 with the aim of providing anonymity to a speaker in order to encourage openness and the sharing of information. When a meeting is said to be being held under the Chatham House Rule, participants are free to use the information received, but must not reveal the identity or affiliation of the speaker or indeed of any other participant at the meeting.

Chequerplate A pressed structural steel or aluminium floor plate with a raised pattern to provide slip resistance. Often used as industrial flooring.

Chiller and basics of air conditioning A device used for cooling water for the purpose of space cooling or air conditioning. Consisting of a compressor, a condenser and an evaporator.

Chimney breast Part of the front of a chimney that projects out into the room.

Chinese wall Arrangements within a business, particularly legal and accountancy firms, that require information held by one person or part of a business to be withheld from others within the same business. See Bolkiah v KPMG (A firm) [1999] 2 WLR 215.

Chippy Carpenter.

Choice of law The applicable law of the contract which has been expressly stated by the parties.

Chord A principle member of a truss or girder which establishes the upper (top chord) or lower (bottom chord) edge of the structural element. Typically, the top chord is in compression and the bottom chord is in tension; however, this condition may be revered, for example in a cantilevered truss. ■ See **Truss** and **Figure T4.**

Chose in action A right against another party which can be assigned to a third party: **Assignment.**

Chromating A process used for corrosion protection especially of zinc electroplated steel parts, but also directly on steel and aluminium.

CIArb See **Chartered Institute of Arbitrators.**

CIBSE See **Chartered Institute of Building Service Engineers.**

CILL See **Construction Industry Law Letter.**

CIMAR See **Construction Industry Model Arbitration Rules.**

CIOB See **Chartered Institute of Building.**

CIS See **Construction Industry Scheme.**

Citation The act of identifying an authority in support of a legal submission. Also, the reference of the authority itself, given either in the neutral form adopted by the court in question or by the series of law reports in which it is contained.

City and Guilds of London Institute (C&G) An examining and accreditation body in the United Kingdom providing vocational education and recognised qualifications in many various trades and disciplines.

Civil code Legal principles, based on Roman Law and the Code Napoléon, governing civil disputes used in many European and Arab jurisdictions. A judge in a civil code court has inquisitorial powers which enable him to play a more active and even investigative part in the hearing or trial.

Civil commotion Acts which constitute a commotion should be acts done by the agents together and not merely acts which are done in preconcert and simultaneously and in proximity to one another, and where there has been no tumult and no disturbance until after the acts; those acts themselves cannot constitute civil commotion, though the subsequent uproar might or might not in itself be a civil commotion: *London and Manchester Plate Glass Co Ltd v Heath* [1913] 3 KB 411 (CA). One of the Relevant Events under the JCT forms of contract which can justify an extension of time.

Civil engineering The design and supervision of the carrying out of construction works other than those that are purely architectural or relate to mechanical and electrical services.

Civil law Legal principles governing civil disputes embodied in a statutory code as adopted in many European and Arab jurisdictions.

Civil Liability (Contribution) Act 1978 Legislation that enables a defendant to claim a contribution from another party in respect of its liability to a claimant. The party from whom the contribution is being claimed must also be liable to the claimant for the "same damage" that is being claimed against the defendant.

Civil Procedure Rules (CPR) The formal rules and accompanying practice directions that govern the procedure of civil litigation, including pre-action conduct of the parties.

Cladding, cladding panel A term used to describe any lightweight material or panelling system which forms the external enclosure of a building or structure. A cladding system or cladding panel is non-load bearing and must resist the usual environmental conditions such as wind, rain, snow and heat. Examples of cladding include glazed curtain walls, rainscreen cladding systems and insulated infill panels or non-load bearing brick panels which are fixed back to the superstructure. ■ See **Façade**, **Load-bearing wall**, and **Rainscreen cladding**.

Claim A request or demand by one party against another. A claim must have been made before a dispute can arise which can be the subject of adjudication or arbitration: ■ see **Dispute**.

Claim form A document the issue of which through the court begins litigation, formerly known as a writ. It briefly summarises the claim and the remedy sought and is valid for service for up to four months from issue. ■ See **Particulars of Claim** and **Figure T1**.

Claimant The party who begins litigation or arbitration, formerly known as "the plaintiff" in litigation. ■ See **Defendant** and **Referring party**.

Claims consultant A technically qualified person who assists a party with the preparation and presentation of a claim. ■ See **Quantum** and **Adjudication**.

Claims made policy A professional indemnity insurance policy the premium for which only covers claims made, as opposed to acts or omissions, during the period covered.

Clapper bridge Bridge made by laying large slabs of stone across piers or simply piles of other stones.

Clashing A situation in which the design of the positioning of one element of the works is in conflict with that of another, usually in the case of services and structure.

Class O A fire hazard classification under the **Building Regulations**. Class O materials are tested to BS 476, which are "non-combustible", have Class I flame spread and a low fire propagation index. Finishes, furniture and fixings often require a Class O classification.

Clause 22 perils Certain potential causes of damage to the works, such as fire, identified in clause 22 of previous JCT standard forms of contract and occasionally still referred to in the insurance industry.

Cleanout of wall cavities (when forbidden by method of construction) Method of ensuring that wall cavities are clear of mortar "snots" during construction by the use of cavity battens. Alternative method: each fifth brick in the lowest course is laid in sand and then, once construction of the wall is completed, removed and, following a cleanout, replaced in mortar.

Clear timber Timber free of knots and other defects.

Clearing and grubbing (C&G) The stage of development prior to commencing groundwork when the vegetation (including roots and stumps) and rubbish is cleared from site.

Clearing site (1) Preparation of the site prior to construction, including demolition of existing structures. (2) Removal of temporary works following completion of works.

Clerestory (or clearstory) A band of windows along the top of a high wall letting in daylight.

Clerical mistake or error A category of mistake in an arbitration award that can be corrected by the arbitral tribunal under the **Arbitration Act 1996** s57 without the need for application to the court. Similar errors can be corrected by adjudicators in adjudication decisions as a result of an implied term: see ***Bloor Construction (UK) Ltd v Bowmer and Kirkland (London) Ltd*** [2000] BLR 314. The Local Democracy, Economic Development and Construction Act 2009, s140, inserting s108(3A) in the Housing Grants, Construction and Regeneration Act 1996, confers a statutory power to correct such errors. The court may correct an accidental slip or omission in a judgment or order under CPR 40.12. A provision allowing such correction is known as a **Slip rule**.

Clerk of Works (COW) A person, typically a builder by trade, appointed to inspect the works. He may be employed either by the employer or a construction professional such as the architect, but usually the former. Some contracts set out the role and obligations of the Clerk of Works. For example, in the JCT Standard Building Contract, the duty of the Clerk of Works is to act solely as an inspector and generally does not have the power to instruct the contractor. He is, or should be, the eyes and ears of the employer.

Client A party engaging either an architect or a contractor, also referred to as "the employer" or "the owner".

Client's representative The employer's representative under the contract. The powers and duties of the client's representative will vary from contract to contract. This can range from the client's representative having certifying duties to simply being a point of contact for the contractor when he wishes to communicate with the client.

Climbing crane A tower crane used on top of a high-rise construction that can be raised with the building as work progresses.

Climbing formwork (slipform) Formwork used for high rise vertical structures (such as skyscrapers) made of individual components that are taken off the bottom and moved to the top for the form to take the next lift of concrete as the work progresses. The formwork is anchored to the concrete below.

Clinker An intermediate substance in the production of Portland cement. Made of heated calcium silicate, clinker is usually in the form of small grey-black pellets. Clinker is subsequently cooled and pulverised into a fine powder that almost completely passes through a 0.075-mm sieve and fortified with a small amount of gypsum to form Portland cement.

Clinker block (Breeze block) A light building block made of Clinker concrete.

Closer (1) A cut or moulded brick used to close the course at the return of the wall or at an opening in it. Closers can be of various types: king closer, queen closer etc. (2) A door closer.

Closing of excavations A stage in construction, during which backfilling takes place to the original ground level.

Closure piece See **Closer**.

CMC See **Case Management Conference.**

CMU See **Concrete Masonry unit.**

Coarse aggregate Crushed stone or gravel used in concrete, ranging in size between 3/8 inch to 1.5 inches. It is known as roadstone when used in the construction of roads.

COB Close of business. Used as a deadline for service of legal submissions.

Cob A form of construction using a mixture of clay sub-soil, aggregate, straw and water to create solid structural walls. The walls are today typically finished in breathable materials such as lime or clay plasters and renders coated with limewash.

COBie See **Construction Operations Building Information Exchange**.

COCO See **Contractor Owned Contractor Operated**.

Code of practice A set of documents/guidelines outlining good practice accepted within the relevant industry.

Coffer A recess in the ceiling of a vault, soffit of a dome or concrete slab.

Cofferdam A temporary dam usually consisting of sheet piling to allow work to be carried out in an area subject to submergence or waterlogging.

Coil heating Concealed heating system featuring low pressure hot water pipes or electrical insulated cables used for underfloor heating.

Cold bridging When a building element passes from the outside to the inside of a building, without a thermal break, a cold bridge is formed, potentially causing condensation and some heat loss.

Cold roof A roof construction whereby the insulation is fitted below the ventilated void space.

Collapsed as-built A form of critical path analysis in which an as-built programme of the works having been constructed on the basis of records, the activities are linked and the programme rerun with employer's delay removed. The difference between the result and the original as-built programme is relied upon as the extension of time due.

Collapsible form Standardised formwork capable of being erected quickly and is reuseable.

Collar Horizontal timbers which are bolted and/or notched to the side of rafters at high level to provide stiffening via triangulation. Often attic room ceilings are run parallel with the bottom side of the collar.

Collateral warranty A subsidiary contract the consideration for which is usually the entering into of another contract. Also, a direct contract between the employer under a main contract and a construction professional or subcontractor employed by the main contractor. ■ See **Employer** and **Privity of contract**.

Collusive tendering An illegal process by which contractors share information amongst themselves so as to affect the outcome of a tender. Typically this will result in contractors fixing the price of their tenders or agreeing which contractors are to secure specific projects, or both.

Colonnade A row of columns placed at regular intervals that usually support one side or end of a roof.

Column A vertical structural member that supports the weight of the building or structure above it. Columns are in compression as they transmit vertical loads from the building elements above them to either the foundations or structure below. ➤ **Figures S2 and A5**.

Column form (Column Formwork) Formwork for the construction of concrete **Columns**. Usually made of steel or aluminium, formwork can be adjusted on site to make different column sizes.

Column starter A starter bar for a reinforced concrete column.

Combination boiler (Combi boiler) A water heater and a central heating boiler combined within one unit, which provides heating and hot water directly from the boiler. The system eliminates the need for a separate hot water cylinder, thus saving space within the property.

Combined extract and input A ventilation system combining extract and input functions.

Combined system (of drainage) In a combined system, the rainwaters/stormwater pipes are discharged into (and are carried in) the foul drain.

Combustible Able to burn easily. Building products are tested for combustibility as a fire hazard.

Comfort index An index which gives a numerical value reflecting ambient atmospheric environment as a measure of comfort used in design of air-conditioning systems.

Commencement date The start date of the works as expressly stated in the contract.

Commercial Court A specialist list forming part of the Queen's Bench Division of the High Court dealing with commercial litigation and arbitration appeals. Most building and engineering cases, however, are dealt with by the **Technology and Construction Court**, another specialist list. ➤ **Figure C3**.

Commissioning The balancing of completed systems in a building (sprinklers, BMS, etc) to ensure optimal performance and compliance with the specification.

Common arrangement A publication by **Construction Project Information Committee (CPIC)** containing classification of work sections for building work. It is used for project specifications and bills of quantities on large contracts.

Common bond (Stretcher bond) A simple brickwork bond made only of stretchers.

Common brickwork Brick which is to be plastered once construction is completed as it does not have a suitable facing/appearance.

Common Carbon Metric (CCM) Launched at COP-15 (the United Nations Climate Change Conference held in Copenhagen in 2009), a protocol for measuring energy use and reporting greenhouse gas emissions (GHG) from the operational phase of buildings thereby establishing the carbon footprint.

Common Data Environment (CDE) A commonly used BIM term which signifies an identified location for storing project information (server or extranet) which can be accessed by the project team.

Common law Law developed through judicial reasoning evidenced by case law, requiring adherence to form. To be distinguished from the rules of equity, also developed by case law, which look to substance. Both systems, which were previously administered by different courts, were fused in the nineteenth century. Jurisdictions with their roots in English law, such as those of Commonwealth countries and the United States, are described as "common law systems".

Common mistake A misunderstanding as to the existence of a state of affairs shared by both parties intending to enter into a contract which can render it void. ■ See **Voidable**.

Communications installation Installation of electrical services such as telephone, sound distribution, data, alarms. Typically separated from other electrical services.

Compaction of concrete Process of releasing trapped air from concrete usually achieved by vibration.

Companies Court A specialist list forming part of the Chancery Division of the High Court and some county courts, dealing with litigation specifically related to the operation of companies, including liquidation. ➤ **Figure C3**.

Company Voluntary Arrangement (CVA) An agreement made by a company with its creditors for the latter to accept less than the amount due to them in satisfaction of the former's debts under Part I of the Insolvency Act 1986.

Comparable Another property of similar type taken into account in the valuation of a property.

Compensation event An event or circumstances entitling a contractor to further payment used in the NEC suite of contracts and bespoke contracts and PFI contracts.

Competitive Dialogue Procedure Introduced in 2006 in public procurement for use in particularly complex projects where it is thought that the technical solutions are difficult to define or where development of the best solution is required. The contracting authority conducts a dialogue with the candidates admitted to the procedure, with the aim of developing one or more suitable alternatives capable of meeting its requirements. At the end of the dialogue when potential solutions have been generated, the remaining tenderers are invited to submit a final tender based on their individual solutions.

Competitive tendering See **Tendering**.

Complete agreement clause Another name for an **Entire agreement clause**.

Completion The point at which the works have been completed, often used interchangeably with "practical completion" or "substantial completion". ■ See **Practical Completion** and **Substantial Completion**.

Completion date Either the date specified in a construction contract upon which the works are to be completed or that upon which they are completed. In the **JCT** forms the "completion date" is either that specified in the contract or that fixed under the extension of time provisions, as opposed to the "date for completion" which is only that specified in the contract. ■ See **Practical Completion**.

Composite construction The use of different materials in the same part of a structure.

Composite panel Panel comprising different materials, often used for cladding as in a sandwich form of construction with insulation between two outer leaves.

Compound beam A beam made up of several elements which have been glued, bolted or connected together in some way: for example, a **glued laminated timber** beam.

Compound interest Interest on interest accumulated at intervals as well as interest on the principal. Such interest can be awarded under s 49 of the Arbitration Act 1996 or by way of damages: see *Sempra Metals Ltd v Commissioners of Inland Revenue* [2008] AC 561 (HL).

Compression To squeeze, or apply pressure by imposed loading. ➤ **Figure C2**

Compromise An agreement whereby parties settle a dispute between them on terms. ■ See **Accord and satisfaction, Waiver** and **Breach of contract**.

Compulsory winding up The liquidation of a company by court order made upon the presentation of a petition by the company, its directors or creditors.

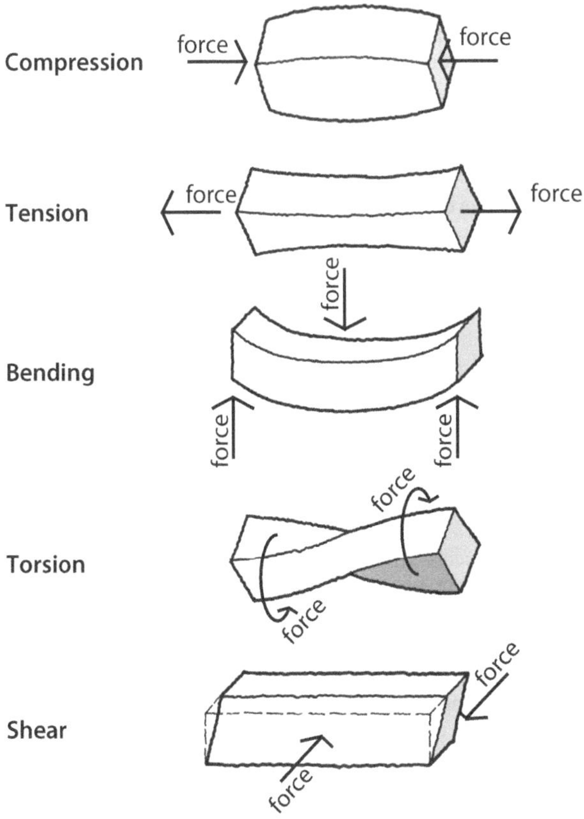

➤ **Figure C2.** 5 Basic Types of Stress

Concession agreement Where a private company enters into an agreement with a contracting authority or government to have the exclusive right to operate, maintain and carry out investment in, for example, a public utility for a set number of years.

Conciliation A method of **alternative dispute resolution** whereby the **Conciliator** attends the parties of a dispute separately in an attempt to achieve concessions from both sides which result in a **settlement**.

Conciliator A person who negotiates concessions with each party to achieve a **settlement**.

Conclusive evidence Not subject to challenge by any other evidence. The JCT forms provide that the final certificate is to be conclusive evidence of a number of matters, subject to the commencement of proceedings within a limited time and cases of fraud.

Concrete Cement concrete, the most common form, is made with water, sand, stone and Portland cement. ■ See **Curing**.

Concrete cancer Failure of reinforced concrete, usually as a result of water penetration causing the reinforcement bars to rust and expand. ■ See **Alkali silica reaction**.

Concrete cover In reinforced concrete the thickness, or cover, of concrete between the reinforcement bar and the outside face of the concrete. ■ See **Spalling**. ➤ **Figure R1**.

Concurrent delay Delay caused by two or more events occurring at the same time. Each event will have delayed completion at and from the same point in time. True concurrency occurs rarely and can be distinguished from the concurrent effect of sequential delaying events. Concurrency more often occurs when the effects of events occurring at different times operate simultaneously, wholly or in part but when the effect of those events is felt concurrently. Both give rise to the problem, if one of the events would entitle the contractor to an extension of the time but the other(s) would not, of whether the contractor would be entitled to an extension of time. *Walter Lilly & Co Ltd v Mackay & others* [2012] EWHC 1773.

Condition Strictly, a term of a contract breach which would entitle the other party to regard himself as excused from further performance, as opposed to a warranty, breach which would merely give rise to a right to damages. Nevertheless, the word "condition" is often used to describe all the terms of contract, as in the JCT forms.

Conditional fee agreement An agreement between a lay client and his lawyer whereby the latter becomes entitled to an enhanced fee in the event of the client's success in contentious proceedings.

Condition precedent Conventionally, some event required to occur before a binding contract could come into existence. Now more widely used to identify the performance of an act by one party to a contract, such as the service of a written notice, required before an entitlement, such as an extension of time or the deduction of liquidated damages, can arise. In the case of *Bremer Handelgesellschaft mbH v Vanden Avenne Izegem NV* [1978] 2 Lloyd's Rep 113, the House of Lords held that a notice provision should be construed as a condition precedent, if: (1) it states the precise time within which the notice is to be served, and (2) it makes plain by express language that unless the notice is served within that time the party making the claim will lose its rights under the clause. ■ See **Time bar**.

Condition subsequent A clause in the contract that terminates the rights of the parties following a specified event such as civil war.

Conductance Thermal conductance, conductivity of a substance divided by its thickness, also known as the C-value.

Conductivity Thermal conductivity, the property of a substance to transmit heat, also known as the K-value.

Confirmation of verbal instruction (CVI) A written notice issued by a contractor to the employer or his construction professional confirming the contents of a verbal instruction of the architect or contract administrator. This no longer a term of art used in building contracts; however, it is widely used in the engineering and construction industry. For example, in JCT SBC 2011, instructions other than those in writing are dealt with in clause 3.12.

Conflict of laws The applicability of the laws of different jurisdictions to the same dispute. ■ See **Applicable law** and **Jurisdiction**.

Con. L.R. See **Construction Law Reports**.

Conquer v Boot [1928] KB 336: A well-settled rule of law that damages resulting from one and the same cause of action must be assessed and recovered once and for all. You cannot seek to dissect what is in substance a single promise into a series of separate obligations and treat them all distinctly.

Consent award An arbitration award made with the consent of the parties. ■ See **Compromise**.

Consent order A court order made with the consent of the parties. ■ See **Compromise**.

Consequential loss Loss which is not a direct or natural result of a breach of contract. ■ See **Breach of contract** and **Damages**.

Conservation area Instigated in 1967, it is a system of designating areas of special architectural and historic interest. The demolition or substantial demolition of a building within a conservation area will usually require permission from the local council and you may also need permission to make alterations such as adding cladding, inserting windows or installing satellite dishes and solar panels.

Consideration The price in whatever form to be incurred by one party to a contract in return for the other party's promise, without which the contract would not be binding unless made under seal. ■ See **Contract**.

Consistency The workability, degree of firmness, conformity or viscosity of concrete, mortar or another material.

Consolidation of actions The joining of two or more claims which are closely related into one set of proceedings in an attempt to save costs and Court time. ■ See **Joinder**.

Consortium An unincorporated joint venture. Comprised of companies or individuals or a combination of both. ■ See **Joint Venture**.

Const. L.J. See **Construction Law Journal**.

Constructing excellence contract A JCT form of partnering contract.

Construction (1) The process of interpretation of a written document to establish its legal effect. (2) The act of building or erecting a design.

Construction Act Name given to the **Housing Grants, Construction and Regeneration Act 1996** as amended by the **Local Democracy, Economic Development and Construction Act 2009**.

Construction contract Generally, a contract for the carrying out of works of construction. Specifically, under the Part II of the Housing Grants, Construction and Regeneration Act 1996, two categories of agreement, namely those for the carrying out or arranging for the carrying out of "construction operations" and those for doing architectural, design or surveying work or the provision of advice on building, engineering, interior or exterior decoration or on the laying out of landscape, in relation to "construction operations". ■ See **Construction operations**.

Construction (Design and Management) Regulations 2007 As a result of the disproportionately high risk of danger in the construction industry, the CDM Regulations were introduced in 1994. The original Regulations, and each subsequent version, have aimed to raise the standards of health and safety in the United Kingdom and encourage the integration of health and safety into the overall management of projects. The 2007 Regulations came into force on 6 April 2007 and replaced the 2004 Regulations. Six types of individuals are identified under the Regulations who hold responsibilities: (1) the Client, (2) the Designer, (3) **the CDM Co-ordinator**, (formerly known as the planning supervisor), (4) **the Principal Contractor**, (5) Contractors and (6) Workers. The Approved Code of Practice gives guidance on how to comply with the Regulations and is available from the Health and Safety Executive's website. Failure to comply with the Regulations is a criminal offence and could result in prosecution. ■ See **Approved Code of Practice**.

Construction Industry Law Letter (CILL) A monthly bulletin of current developments in construction law.

Construction Industry Model Arbitration Rules (CIMAR) The CIMAR were developed to try and achieve a common approach to arbitration across the construction industry. First prepared in 1998 by the Society of Construction Arbitrators, the most recent edition was published in 2011 by the **JCT**.

Construction Industry Scheme (CIS) A tax deduction scheme introduced to counter perceived tax evasion in the industry. Payments made by contractors to subcontractors must have a specified rate of tax deducted from them by the contractor. The definition of "contractor" is wide and may catch those whose primary business is not construction but who spend a specified amount or more on construction over a three-year period (eg Universities, local authorities and hospitals).

Construction Law Journal A periodical containing academic articles and reports of cases concerning construction law.

Construction Law Reports A series of law reports devoted to construction cases, cited as "ConLR".

Construction management A form of procurement where the employer appoints a construction manager to manage the work. The work is divided into specialist "packages" and the employer enters into direct works contracts with each specialist. Conversely, in management contracting it is the management contractor that enters into each works contract. ■ See **Appendix 3**

Construction manager See **Construction Management**.

Construction operations To be a **construction contract** and so fall under the adjudication and payment provisions of the **Construction Act**, a contract must relate to the carrying out of construction operations as defined by the Act. Section 105(2) sets out those operations which are not construction operations within the meaning of the **Construction Act**. These include certain works relating to oil, gas, nuclear processing and power generation.

Construction Operations Building Information Exchange (COBie) A standardised format for collecting and organising a project's assets and other non-graphic data. Often a spreadsheet which links back to the project model(s) and other spreadsheets. It assists with recording and disseminating project information and commissioning and maintaining the building on completion. For example, information contained in the spreadsheet can include manufacturer's information, product data, warranties and maintenance information.

Construction professional A consultant providing professional services in the construction industry such as an architect, engineer or surveyor.

Construction Project Information Committee (CPIC) A committee formed of representatives of the RIBA, RICS and ICE, together with other professional bodies, which gives guidance on construction production information.

Constructive acceleration See **Acceleration**.

Constructive change order A doctrine developed by courts in the United States to overcome the strict condition precedent provisions preventing recovery in the absence of a change order in writing for varied work. Recovery is permitted where the work is clearly additional and has been instructed to be carried out, albeit not in compliance with the contractual procedures.

Consultancy agreement A contract of engagement under which a construction professional is employed. ■ See **Consultant**.

Consultant An independent construction professional engaged by one of the parties to a construction contract.

Contaminated land Land in such a condition as be regarded as such under s78A of the Environmental Protection Act 1990 and therefore subject to the regime of remediations provided for under that statute.

Contestable work On 1 April 1995 the Office of Electricity Regulation (OFFER) now the Office of Gas and Electricity Markets (OFGEM), brought about Competition in Electricity Connections. With this introduction of competition, customers now have the option to seek competitive quotations for some of the works required to make a new connection to the electricity distribution system. This means that when installing a new supply of gas, electricity or water, the work can be split into contestable and non-contestable. Work which is contestable can be offered to third party contractors, rather than the distributor or transporter. Contestable work includes works such as reinforcement or installation on an existing network, design and specification of any new assets, consents and way-leaves may only be undertaken by an accredited Independent Connections Provider (ICP) who must be registered with Lloyds register to carry out such works.

Contingency period Time within the contract period allowed for by the contractor in his programme after completion. ■ See **Float**.

Contingency sum A percentage of the contract sum that is to cover the costs of unexpected events. If the contingency sum is not required then it is deducted from the final account. ■ See **Final account**.

Continuous run concreting A highly mechanised form of concreting normally only used on the largest projects such a major highways and runways: the dowels are auto-inserted into the concrete as it is laid and a joint wet-formed or cut as required. ■ See **Alternate bay construction**.

Contra charge Widely used in the construction industry to mean set-off or more commonly a back-charge. A word often used in the offsetting sense of a particular part of works to another contractor. Typically, a main contractor will contra charge a subcontractor if they had to incur additional costs for making good a defect.

Contra item An amount relating to a cross claim by the paying party under a construction contract, particularly one that is the subject of a deduction by a main contractor from sums due to a subcontractor.

Contra proferentem Latin: short for *verba chartarum fortius accipiuntur contra proferentem*, "the words of an instrument shall be taken most strongly against the party employing them". A rule of construction whereby doubt about the meaning of words will be resolved against the party who has put them forward. It does not apply to a standard form of contract in common use, such as the ICE conditions, which has been prepared and revised jointly by several representative bodies and would normally be incorporated into a contract of the kind under consideration: *Tersons Ltd v Stevenage Development Corp* (1963) 5 BLR 54 (CA).

Contract A legally binding agreement. Where a contract is not intended to take effect as a deed, it will need to be supported by consideration. ■ See **Consideration**.

Contract administrator A prescribed role within certain forms of contract often carried out by an architect, quantity surveyor or project manager. Whilst the contract administrator is often engaged, and paid by, the employer, he is required to operate the terms of the contract fairly and impartially between client and contractor. The most common duties of a contract administrator are those of a certifier.

Contract bills See **Bill of Quantity**.

Contract data Term often used to describe a document setting out certain project details, for example, timing for payments or the completion date which form part of the contract. ■ See also **Appendix to Tender**. Under the NEC form, the contract data is split into two parts, (part 1 being completed by the employer and part 2 by the contractor) and completion of the contract data is essential to finalising the contract. Again under the NEC form, expressions in the contract terms relating to contract data entries appear in *italicised* text throughout the contract.

Contract documents The documents setting out the terms of a contract. The question of whether or not a particular document forms part of or is incorporated into a contract is often difficult to resolve.

Contract drawings The drawings forming part of the contract and identified in the articles of agreement. Copies are usually signed by both parties.

Contracting authority A public body subject to the EU procurement regulations.

Contract Notice See **OJEU Notice**.

Contracts (Rights of Third Parties) Act 1999 An Act enabling third parties to enforce contractual rights, but only where there is an express or implied contractual intention to do so. Its provisions may be excluded from operation in relation to a contract where there is provision to that effect. More often than not, the Act's provisions are expressly excluded from construction contracts.

Contract sum The price payable to the party carrying out the works, which under most contracts will be subject to adjustment in accordance with the terms.

Contract under hand A contract signed by the parties but not intended to take effect as a deed. It must satisfy the usual legal requirements for a contract including consideration (which in a building contract is usually satisfied by the employer agreeing to pay for the works). It is subject to a six-year limitation period. Also known as a simple contract.

Contract under seal A contract bearing the seals of the parties or a contract expressed to take effect as a deed. The limitation period for such contracts is 12 years.

Contractor The party to a construction contract who will be carrying out the works.

Contractor Designed Portion (CDP) A term used in JCT contracts, although often adopted generically in the industry, to describe the part of the works which is to be designed by the contractor as opposed to the employer's professional team. ■ See **Traditional Contract**.

Contractor Owned Contractor Operated A form of public-private partnership under which the contractor keep possession of the works and operates the facility provided.

Contractor's All Risks (CAR) policy An insurance policy which typically covers damage to the contract works, materials on site and in transit by any risk (subject to certain exclusions). These exclusions will usually include damage resulting from wear and tear and defects in design or workmanship. Also known as an Erector's All Risks (EAR) policy. Both are examples of material damage policies which cover loss or damage to property in which the insured has an insurable interest.

Contractor's Proposals (CPs) Under JCT design and build forms, the document produced by the contractor in response to the Employer's Requirements which explains how the contractor intends to satisfy those requirements. ■ See **Design and build contract** and **Employer's Requirements (CPs)**

Contractor's representative Term used to describe the individual nominated by the Contractor to act on behalf of the contractor during a project.

Contractor's share percentages and share ranges The dates and methodology set out in the **Contract Data** under the NEC form of contract for calculating the contractor's **pain/gain share** of the **actual cost** of the project above/below the **target price**.

Contributory negligence The negligence of a party who has contributed to his own loss, which can reduce the damages awarded. ■ See **The Law Reform (Contributory Negligence) Act 1945**.

Convenience clause A clause entitling an employer to terminate the contractor's employment at the employer's discretion. An example is clause 15.5 of the FIDIC conditions **Red Book**.

Conversion A tort whereby a party deals with another's personal property in a manner inconsistent with that other's ownership.

Conveyancing The process by which a legal title to real property is transferred from one party to another.

Cooling tower A heat removal or rejection device used to extract waste heat to the atmosphere usually through the cooling of a water stream to a lower temperature.

The Co-operative Insurance Society Ltd v Henry Boot Scotland Ltd [2002] EWHC 1270 (TCC): A contractor's obligation to complete the design started by the employer or his team requires the contractor to take responsibility for that initial design and ratify it. The contractor's responsibility was not limited to completing the design but extended to overall responsibility for prior design work.

Copy-cat arbitration An arbitration in accordance with established institutional rules but not involving the institution in question.

Copyright An exclusive right to copy or allow others to duplicate or re-use drawings or designs.

Corbel A projection from the face of a wall, such as a block of stone built into a wall, a stone bracket to support other stone work or some element of the super structure.

Core (1) A vertical element in a building containing lifts, stairs, ducts or risers. (2) A nuclear reactor core is that part of the nuclear reactor which contains the nuclear fuel assemblies and where the nuclear reactions take place. (3) CORE is also the name of Cumbrians Opposed to a Radioactive Environment.

CORGI The Confederation for the Registration of Gas Installers. Replaced by the Gas Safe Register in April 2009.

Cornhill Insurance plc v Improvement Services Ltd [1986] WLR 144: a company can be found insolvent in light of evidence showing that a debt owing and undisputed by the company has not been paid.

Corporate veil Limited liability, one of the major consequences of incorporation being that the company has a separate legal personality from that of the directors or shareholders, who are not personally liable on contracts into which the company has entered. This general principle is subject to exceptions where, as the expressions go, the corporate veil is "lifted" or "pierced". The court is entitled to "pierce the corporate veil" and recognise the receipt of the company as that of the individual(s) in control of it if the company was used as a device or façade thereby avoiding or concealing any liability of those individual(s). In *Ben Hashem v Ali Shayif* [2008] EWHC 2380 (Fam), [2009]1 F.L.R. 115 guidance was given as follows: (1) Ownership and control of a company are not of themselves sufficient to justify piercing the veil. (2) The veil cannot be pierced, even where there is no unconnected third party involved, merely because it is thought to be necessary on the interests of justice. (3) The veil can be pierced only if there is some "impropriety". (4) The veil cannot be pierced merely because the company is involved in some impropriety: the impropriety must be linked to the use of the company structure to avoid or conceal liability. (5) It is necessary to show both the control of the company by the wrongdoer(s) and impropriety, that is, (mis)use of the company by them as a device or a façade to conceal their wrongdoing. A company can be a façade even though it was not originally incorporated with any deceptive intent: the question is whether it is being used as a façade at the time of the relevant transaction(s).

Corrosion The chemical or electrochemical reaction between a material, usually a metal, and its environment that produces a deterioration of the material and its properties.

COR-TEN or Corten steel A historical nickname for self-weathering steel which does not require painting owing to its chemical composition whereby a protective layer forms on its surface. Designed to age resulting in a coppery, rust-like appearance.

Cost The expenditure of a contractor. The word cost takes on greater importance if a contractor is to be paid his cost as defined in the contract. For example, under the standard **FIDIC** form, cost means "all expenditure reasonably incurred (or to be incurred) by the Contractor, whether on or off the Site, including overhead and similar charges, but does not include profit".

Cost adjustment clause See **Fluctuations clause**.

Cost breakdown A written document detailing the costs of the project.

Cost capping order An order limiting the amount of future costs which a party may recover pursuant to an order for costs subsequently made. In litigation, this is provided for by CPR 44.18. Similar provision is made in relation to arbitration in s 65 of the Arbitration Act 1996.

Cost contract A contract under which the contractor is paid the actual cost of the work carried out. In addition to this the contractor is usually paid a fee to cover his overhead and profit. This fee may be fixed or calculated as a percentage of the cost of the works. Also known as cost-plus or cost-reimbursable contracts. Generally, expenditure incurred by a contractor, which usually differs from the contractual entitlement to payment. Some contracts "at cost" provide for the contractor to be paid the costs incurred, sometimes with an additional percentage for profit in a "costs plus" contract. In cost and target cost contracts this term defines the sums payable to the contractor. Often only certain costs constitute "actual cost". For example, the cost of direct labour on site may fall within the definition of actual cost but overhead costs (such as head office administration, human resources, marketing, etc.) will often be excluded as they are deemed to be included with any fee that the contractor is paid in addition to the actual cost. ■ See **Actual cost contract**, **Cost reimbursable contract**, **Lump sum contract**, **Prime cost contract** and **Re-measurement contract**.

Cost controller A person whose role is to manage the project cost from budget to final account.

Cost engineer In the United States, a construction professional engaged in preparing tenders and estimates.

Cost estimate An estimate of the likely costs, including expert's fees which is prepared by a solicitor at the outset of proceedings and is indicated to the other party and Court upon the service and filing of the Allocation Questionnaires. A costs estimate may be amended periodically to account for mediation costs, prolonged disclosure or other matters which may increase or reduce likely expenditure. ■ See **Allocation Questionnaire**, **Disclosure** and, **Mediation**.

Cost plan A written statement detailing the projected cost of a project.

Cost-plus A basis of remuneration comprising the cost incurred by the contractor subject to an addition (usually expressed as a percentage) for overheads and profit.

Cost-plus-fixed-fee contract A contract under which the basis of remuneration is cost-plus subject to a fixed addition.

Cost-plus-percentage contract A contract under which the basis of remuneration is cost-plus subject to the addition of a percentage of the cost.

Cost reimbursable contract See **Cost contract**.

Costs Legal costs incurred by a party to arbitration or litigation which can be the subject of an order directing the other party to pay them. Such costs include lawyers' charges and fees paid to experts. The basic rule is that "costs follow the event" and that the successful party is entitled to recover his costs from the other party.

Costs in the case A direction usually given at a hearing before trial, the effect of which is that the parties' costs of the hearing should form part of the costs to be the subject of the order for costs made at the conclusion of the trial.

Costs on the indemnity basis A direction that costs, which are the subject of an order, should be assessed on the indemnity basis. ■ See **Indemnity basis**.

Costs on the standard basis A direction that costs, which are the subject of an order, should be assessed on the standard basis. ■ See **Standard basis**.

Costs reserved A direction that the costs of a hearing should be dealt with at some later date.

Costs thrown away A direction that a party is not entitled to its costs incurred in dealing with a matter which is rendered ineffective, such as a default judgment which has been set aside.

Counterclaim A cross claim by a defending party. ■ See **Set off, cross claim**.

Counter-floor Floorboards on which another layer of flooring is to be laid; a sub-floor.

Counter offer A second offer made in response to an offer. This can happen where the offeree claims to have accepted but actually introduces different terms. The counter offer has the effect of extinguishing the first offer and in fact sets out new terms for acceptance by the original offeror.

Counterpart A duplicate of a legal document such as a lease.

Countersunk fixing (1) A screw fixing where the face of the screw is flush with the adjacent material; (2) A recessed screwed fixing which is then filled with a timber plug to conceal the screw.

County court A local court dealing with civil claims, a small number of which have specialist **Technology and Construction Court** lists to deal with construction disputes. Technology and Construction Court claims for sums less than £50,000 should normally be dealt with in the county court, and must only be issued in specified county court offices. See paras 1.3.5–1.3.6 of the **TCC Guide**. In *West Country Renovations Ltd v McDowell and another* [2012] EWHC 307 (TCC) the TCC issued guidance to the effect that generally, claims valued at less than £250,000 should be issued in county courts or High Courts outside London that have designated TCC judges, rather than in the TCC in the High Court in London. ➤ **Figure C3**.

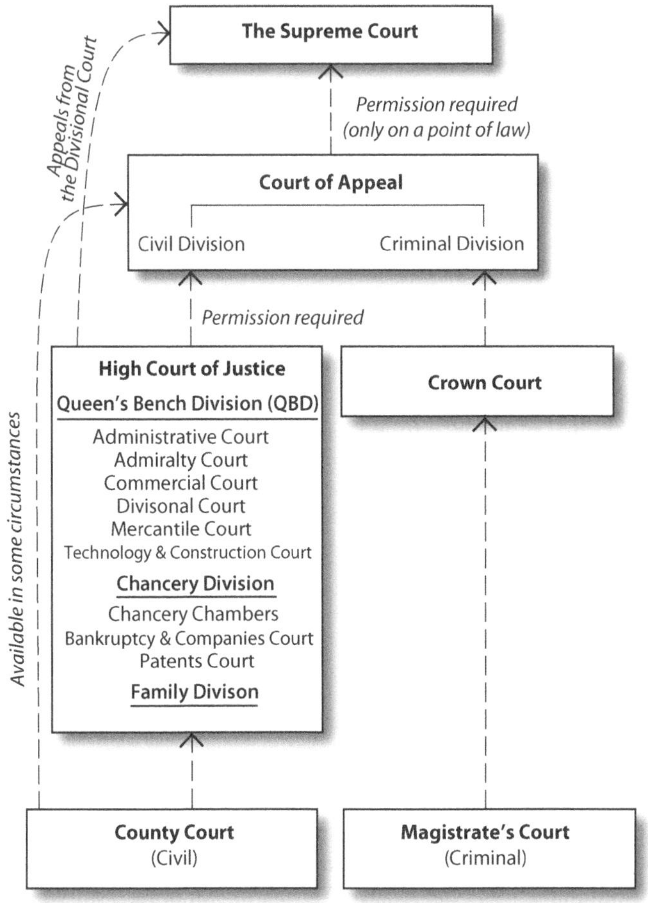

➤ **Figure C3.** English Court System

Couple roof A pitched roof with no tie beam.

Coupling, coupler A fitting which joins two pipes.

Course A row or layer of brickwork or blockwork. ➤ **Figure B3**.

Course of dealing An established pattern of transactions between parties which can give rise to the inference that a subsequent transaction was to be on the same basis, particularly in relation to terms of contracts.

Court of Appeal The first tier of appellate tribunal for cases heard in the High Court and for final appeals from county courts. The judges are Lords or Ladies Justices (LJJ). Appeals from the Court of Appeal, previously heard by the judicial committee of the House of Lords, are now dealt with by the Supreme Court. ➤ **Figure C3**

Court of first instance The court in which a claim is first dealt with.

Court of Session The superior civil court of Scotland which sits in Edinburgh and is divided into the **Outer House** and the **Inner House**.

Court settlement process A form of mediation carried out by TCC judges. See para 7.6 of the **TCC Guide**.

Cove lighting Lighting directed to the ceiling from above a cove or cornice.

Cover See **Concrete cover**.

Cover pricing The submission of a deliberately high price for a project with no intention of winning the work.

CPA Conditions Various standard terms for use in the hire of construction plant published by The Construction Plant-hire Association.

CPs See **Contractor's Proposals**.

CPIC See **Construction Project Information Committee**.

CPM See **Critical Path Method**.

CPR See **Civil Procedure Rules**.

Creep A phenomenon whereby materials forming part of a structure, particularly concrete, experience deformation under stress.

Critical activity Works that directly impact upon the completion date.

Critical delay Delay to works that have an impact upon the completion date.

Critical path The longest series of critical activity in a programme of works. ■ See **Programme**.

Critical path analysis/method (CPM) Programme analysis which calculates the length of time for each element of the works and the longest sequence of the works which is the critical path. The critical path is then analysed to establish the shortest time the project can be completed.

Cross claim A claim raised by a party against another party making a claim against him.

Cross-examination Oral questioning of one party's witness by the other party's advocate. ■ See **Examination-in-chief and Re-examination**.

Cross-hatching Marking of part of a plan or drawing with two sets of diagonal lines crossing each other.

Crown course A capping course at the top of a brick wall.

Crushed aggregate Aggregate consisting of crushed matter used in concrete.

Cube test Crushing a cube of concrete to assess its strength.

Culpable delay Delay in the progress of works for which the contractor would not be entitled to an extension of time and therefore at risk of liability for liquidated damages.

Cumulative impact claim A contractor's claim based on the cumulative effect of changes which, when considered individually, might be thought to have been of little consequence but when combined had a significant impact.

Curial law The law governing an arbitration, also known as the **Lex arbitri**. A body of rules which sets a standard external to the arbitration agreement, and the wishes of the parties, for the conduct of the arbitration. The law governing the arbitration comprises the rules governing interim measures (eg Court orders for the preservation or storage of goods), the rules empowering the exercise by the Court of supportive measures to assist an arbitration which has run into difficulties (eg filling a vacancy in the composition of the arbitral tribunal if there is no other mechanism) and the rules providing for the exercise by the Court of its supervisory jurisdiction over arbitrations (eg removing an arbitrator for misconduct): *Paul Smith Ltd v H and S International Holding Inc* [1991] 2 Lloyd's Rep 127.

Curing The "setting" of concrete once it has been poured, in which its hardness, strength and durability improves over time. Must be kept damp during the process.

Curing agent A substance added to fresh concrete to accelerate curing.

Curing blanket A sheet of hessian, PVC-based insulation or burlap laid over newly laid concrete during curing to prevent the water in the mix from freezing and causing damage. See **Burlap bag**.

Curing membrane A sheet or compound laid over newly laid concrete to prevent drying out.

Curtain wall A form of external cladding to a building which is non-load bearing and is located in front of the structural frame. ■ See also **Cladding**, **Façade** and **Load-bearing wall**.

Custom and usage An established market usage in a trade, which can give rise to an implied term in a contract (subject to its express terms) or a particular meaning being given to certain words.

Cut and fill The excavation of soil from one part of a site and its deposit on another to change the respective levels.

CVA See **Company Voluntary Arrangement**.

C-value Thermal conductance.

CVI See **Confirmation of verbal instruction**.

Cyclical movement Movement of the materials constituting a structure in cycles, usually as a result of temperature changes.

D

Dabs Spots or blobs of adhesive, plaster or mortar applied at intervals to fix sheeting or board.

Dado A border or panel running along the lower half of an internal wall, usually decorative.

Dado rail A wooden rail separating the upper and lower parts of an internal wall.

Dado trunking A dado enclosing cable running along the wall above the skirting.

Daily rates It is the agreed amount of money that one party will pay to the other per chargeable day. The daily rate is usually expressed on a person-by-person or item of plant-by-item of plant basis.

Damage limitation clause A clause that provides for the payment of a fixed sum to be assessed on a periodic basis as damages for delay intended to limit damages for delay, and not a genuine pre-estimate of such damage for this reason. It is thought that such clauses, not being penalties, are enforceable: see *Hudson* 12th edn pp. 935–936, paras 6-048–6-049.

Damages The financial remedy awarded to compensate a party for his loss caused by another's breach of contract or tortious act. Where a party sustains a loss by reason of a breach of contract, he or she is, so far as money can do it, to be placed in the same situation, with respect to damages, as if the contract had been performed. In tort, the measure is that sum of money which will put the party who has been injured in the same position as he would have been in had he not sustained the wrong for which he is now getting his compensation. ■ See **Remoteness of damage**.

Damp-proof course (dpc) A horizontal barrier made of tough plastic or bituminous strip impervious to water bedded into the mortar between two courses of bricks or blocks near the ground level. Can also form a vertical barrier to prevent lateral movement of water for a below ground-level room. In a cavity wall, there is usually a dpc in both the outer and inner wall. In the outer wall, it normally rests 150–200 mm above ground level so that rain may splash up off the ground without saturating the wall above dpc level. The dpc in the inner wall is usually below floor level under a suspended timber floor structure. With a solid concrete floor, it is usually found immediately above the floor slab so that it can be linked to the damp-proof membrane (DPM) under the floor slab. ■ See **Damp-proof membrane**. ➤ **Figure E3**

Damp-proof course brick A brick with low water absorption that is used in building a dpc.

Damp-proof membrane (DPM) A high quality, low density **polyethylene** such as 'visqueen' or mastic asphalt laid under the floor slab to allow the floor slab to dry out and keep out groundwater. Often laid on a bed of sand to prevent sharp edges from puncturing it. To create a continuous horizontal barrier, pieces of dpc or dpm are welded together sealing the inside of a building from the damp ground beneath it. ➤ **Figure E3**

Damp-proofing Inserting a horizontal or vertical dpc.

Data drop See **Information Exchange**.

Data Logger A Data Logger or Datalogger is a device, usually electronic, that records data, such as temperature, humidity, light intensity, seismic activity, over measured time or in relation to location using a built-in sensor or transducer or via external instruments and sensors. They are usually powered by battery, with a microprocessor, internal memory for data storage and ports for downloading to other media. Data loggers are commonly left unattended for long periods to collect data over time.

Data protection The Data Protection Act 1998 controls how personal information is used by companies or the government. The Act requires everyone who collects data to follow strict rules and to keep information safe. The legislation has eight common sense rules known as the "data protection principles".

These principles require any organisation, corporation or governmental body that collects personal information to handle it safely. Anyone collecting personal information, therefore, must: (1) fairly and lawfully process it, (2) process it only for limited, specifically stated purposes, (3) use the information in a way that is adequate, relevant and not excessive, (4) use the information accurately, (5) keep the information on file no longer than absolutely necessary, (6) process the information in accordance with the individual's legal rights, (7) keep the information secure and never transfer the information outside United Kingdom without adequate protection. The law provides stronger protection for more sensitive information such as ethnic background, political opinions, religious beliefs, health, sexual life or any criminal history. It is enforced by an independent information commissioner who can take action against any company or governmental body that fails to protect personal information or abuses its right to collect and hold that information. The Act gives individuals the right to find out what information the government and other organisations store about them. Some agencies or companies charge a fee for providing the information.

Date for completion The contractual date for completion of the works or a section of them under a construction contract. In JCT forms, to be contrasted with the completion date, which is either the date for the completion of the work or such other date as fixed in accordance with the conditions.

Date of possession The contractual date upon which the contractor under a construction contract is to be given possession of the site and from which the contract period usually runs.

Daubert Guidelines Guidelines used in the United States of America to determine the admissibility of expert evidence. Is the evidence based upon sufficient facts or data? Is the evidence the product of reliable principles and methods? Has the expert applied those principles and methods reliably to the facts? Federal Rule of evidence 702; Daubert v Merrell Dow Pharmaceuticals Inc, 509 U.S. 579 (1983)

Day A calendar day. To avoid confusion, some parties prefer to use actual dates (ie 1 January 2012), rather than a period of days (ie within 35 days), to avoid any confusion when setting a deadline.

Day joint The interface in reinforced concrete from one day's concrete pour and that of the next. Day joints may not be designed in advance, though a good design takes cogniscence of the locations and incorporates them into the design of the floor finish above.

Dayworks Works (usually variations) carried out and paid for on a day-work basis, namely a cost-plus basis, where the work cannot be measured and valued by reference to contract rates. Most construction contracts include specific daywork rates.

DB JCT design and build contact

DBA Decibel scale.

DBO See **Design Build Operate.**

Death Where a contract is for personal services, the death of an individual who is a party to the contract brings the contract to an end. Thus, in the case of the engagement of an individual construction professional identified under a construction contract, the employer will be obliged to make a further appointment. Most standard forms expressly provide for such an eventuality.

Death-watch beetle The larvae of the death-watch beetle can cause considerable damage to timber through burrowing. In buildings, they are particularly found in old hardwood, large oak timbers. This can result in the total failure of load-bearing beams.

De bene esse Latin: "for what it is worth", a rubric under which a tribunal will proceed subject to a final determination on a point, such as receiving evidence which is objected to before finally ruling on its admissibility.

Debenture A document in writing setting out the terms of a loan.

Debriefing The process of advising successful and unsuccessful bidders of the reasons why they have or have not been awarded a particular contract. It affords an opportunity for a supplier to improve performance in the future. In public sector procurement, a debrief is a legal obligation from the public body. There is no such obligation in private sector procurement.

Debt A sum of money due by obligation, usually under a contract. A distinction to be drawn between a sum due as a debt under a contract and a sum recoverable as damages for breach of a contract. A sum due as part of the contract sum, including loss and expense ascertained under a contract's express provisions, is a debt, whereas compensation for breach of a contract will be damages. The Late Payment of Commercial Debts (Interest) Act 1998 only applies to debts.

DECC See **Department for Energy and Climate Change.**

Deceit The common law tort of fraudulent misrepresentation, requiring a representation, reliance and damage, entitling the innocent party to damages.

Decibel (dB) A unit of sound measurement, being one-tenth of a Bel (after Alexander Graham Bell) and the logarithm of an electric or acoustic power ratio. Decibel values are calculated from the ratio between two measurements by finding the logarithm of the ratio and multiplying it by 10. When comparing pressure measurements (eg sound pressure or

Volts), the logarithm is multiplied by 20. This reflects the fact that any power value corresponds to the square of a pressure value.

Decision Term used to describe the written judgment or ruling of an **adjudicator**. The decision must be given within 28days (or 42days with the agreement of the **referring party** or longer with the agreement of both parties) and is binding until the dispute is finally decided by litigation, arbitration or agreement.

Decking Material used to make a suspended floor, often seasoned wood.

Declaration A remedy granted at the discretion of a tribunal as to a party's rights, used most frequently in the construction field in relation to the effect of contractual terms.

Decommissioning The planned shut down and dismantling of a building or facility. The aim is to make the facility and surrounding area safe and secure. Whilst the origins of the word lie in the military sphere, today it is often, but not exclusively used, in a nuclear context.

Decontamination The process of the removal of hazardous material, usually of a biological, chemical or radioactive nature, from people, buildings and/or plant.

Decrement delay How insulation behaves in a dynamic situation (dynamic in the sense of fluctuating temperatures). It is quite a simple subject in theory, but there are immense numbers of variables in terms of materials and their positioning and also with regard to climate. It still does not feature in the building regulations, although it can have a very marked effect on how insulation behaves.

Deduction One of the two methods of enforcing a right to liquidated damages. The other is recovery as a debt by proceedings.

Deed A document, signed by each party in the presence of a witness, which does not need to be sealed, provided that it is made clear on its face that it is intended to be a deed and was executed validly as a deed. Unlike simple contracts (contracts signed under hand), there is no requirement for consideration and the limitation period for claims or remedies under a deed extend for 12 years. ■ See **Consideration** and **Limitation**.

Deep-plan building A building in which the horizontal distance from the external wall is many times greater than the floor to floor height. Deep-plan buildings make more efficient use of site area and cost less to build per unit floor area because of their smaller wall to floor area ratio. There are complications for light and ventilation penetration that are more easily solved for single storey buildings. Artificial lighting, air conditioning or ventilation is required for more than one storey.

De facto Latin: "in fact", as opposed to *de jure*, "by law".

Default A breach of duty, the ordinary meaning in a contractual document being a breach of contract: see *Perar BV v General Surety* (1994) 66 BLR 72 (CA).

Default notice or Default payment notice A notice in default of the payer's notice under the Construction Act. See s110(b) of the **Construction Act**. If the paying party is responsible for issuing the payment notice and they fail to do so, then the receiving party will be able to issue a default payment notice requiring payment. If not challenged, the sum in the default notice has to be paid.

Defect A non-conformity of construction works with contractual, statutory or generally accepted standards. Most standard forms, although referring to "defects" do not define them. One exception is the **NEC** (3rd edn), which identifies a defect as part of the works which is not in accordance with the works information or a part of the works designed by the contractor which is not in accordance with the applicable law or the contractor's design which the project manager has accepted. ■ See **Specification**.

Defect action period See **Defects liability period**.

Defective Premises Act (DPA) The Defective Premises Act 1972. The DPA provides that a person who takes on work for, or in connection with, the provision of a dwelling owes a statutory duty to ensure that the work is done in a workman-like or, as the case may be, professional manner, with proper materials and so that, as regards that work, the dwelling, when completed, will be fit for human habitation. Its major disadvantage is that the limitation period of six years runs from the date of the completion of the works and is not subject to the latent damage provisions of the Limitation Act 1980 as amended.

Defects certificate Term used in the **NEC** form to describe a list of defects notified by the **supervisor** which the contractor has not corrected or a statement that there are no such defects. ■ See **Snagging**.

Defects liability period (DLP) The traditional description of a period of several months after practical or substantial completion of the works during which the contractor will be responsible for remedying any defects that appear in the works at his own expense. Usually, a contractual provision for a maintenance period provides an additional right and the contractor will remain liable to rectify defects resulting from defects in materials or workmanship during the limitation period. It is now called the "**rectification period**" in **JCT** forms and the defects correction period in the **NEC**.

Defence The formal response to the claim form and particulars of claim in which a defendant in litigation and a respondent in arbitration sets out a summary of his response to the claim. It is also known as the points of defence in arbitration. Once the defendant has served and filed the acknowledgement of service they have, in the absence of an extension of time, 28 days (from the service of the claim form) to serve and file the defence. If they fail to do so, the claim is presumed to have been admitted and judgment may be entered in default. The defence should seek to address all matters raised by the claim and set out its own version of events if the factual circumstances or legal elements of the claim are disputed. ■ See **acknowledgement of service** and **judgment in default**.

Defence and counterclaim A statement of case consisting of a defence together with a formal counterclaim contained in the same document.

Defence of tender before claim A defence that, before the claimant started proceedings, the defendant unconditionally offered to the claimant the amount due or, if no specified amount is claimed, an amount sufficient to satisfy the claim. See CPR 37.2.

Defence to counterclaim A statement of case in response to a counterclaim, usually contained in the same document as the reply to the defence.

Defendant The named party against whom the claimant seeks redress. ■ See **claimant and defence**.

Defender Scottish term for defendant.

Defined cost A term used in the **NEC** form of contract to describe a contractor's actual costs.

Delay The non-completion of works by a date stated in the contract. In such a situation, the contractor will, in the absence of extension of time provisions, be in breach of contract unless the cause of delay is due to the interference of the employer, in which event the obligation becomes one to complete within a reasonable time. If time is of the essence, the employer could be entitled to rescind the contract. In virtually all construction contracts, however, there are provisions for liquidated damages for delay and extension of time for completion of works for events beyond the contractor's direct control. ■ See **Completion date**, **Extension of time** and **Liquidated damages**.

Delay analysis The detection of causes of delay and the measurement of their effect. This is usually accomplished by the use of **critical path analysis** by reference to programmes. ■ See **As-planned versus as-built, Collapsed as-built**, **Fragnets**, **Impacted as-planned, Time-impact analysis** and **Windows analysis**.

Delay and disruption claim A contractor's claim either under express loss and express provisions in the contract or by way of damages for breach by the employer, based on delay and interference with regular progress caused by matters for which the employer bears the risk.

Delay damages See **Liquidated damages**.

Delegated legislation Also referred to as secondary or subordinate legislation, it is a law made by an executive authority under powers given to it by primary legislation (ie an Act of Parliament) in order to implement and administer the requirements of that primary legislation.

Delegation of authority It is the vesting of authority in another. An agent cannot delegate the authority given to him by his principal to a sub-agent in the absence of express authority to do so. Thus, construction professionals, such as architects or engineers, cannot divest themselves of their liability to their client by appointing a sub-consultant, unless the client has agreed to such a course.

Delegatus non potest delegare Latin: "A delegate cannot delegate": see **Delegation of authority**.

Deleterious materials Materials or building techniques which are dangerous to health or which tend to fail in practice. Often listed in property agreements, appointments and building contracts where the developer consultant or contractor warrants not to use them. A more generalised definition is often given in commercial agreements to avoid repetition of materials.

Deletion The crossing through of words in a written contract or other document usually signed or initialled by those executing it. The general rule of construction is that the deleted words are to be ignored in giving effect to the presumed intention of the parties: *Inglis v Buttery* & Co [1878] 3 App Cas 552 (HL), although there is authority to suggest that they may be relied on to resolve ambiguities and to demonstrate that the parties decided that such words were unnecessary.

Deliverable Used as a noun, it is that which is to be produced, delivered and/or supplied by one party to a contract, usually within a specified time. The term is used in a number of different contexts and somewhat vaguely.

Delivery up A remedy whereby the court will order a party to provide another with chattels, such as plant or documents pursuant to a contractual obligation or under the Torts (Interference with Goods) Act 1977.

De minimis Latin: short for **de minimis non curat lex**.

De minimis non curat lex Latin: "The law does not care for minimal things". The rule that very small matters or inconsistencies will be ignored.

Demolition The planned break up and removal of a structure. Particular care is required to divert building services, to shore up or underpin structures that are adjacent or will remain and to remove and disposal of dangerous and contaminated material.

Demountable partition Temporary or light weight walls that can be removed without causing significant damage or disruption. Those that can easily be relocated offer the least amount of noise protection.

Department for Business Enterprise and Regulatory Reform (BERR) Created in June 2007, this department was created from part of the Department of Trade and Industry (DTI), the Better Regulation Executive (BRE) and the Regional Economic Performance Unit, transferred from the Department for Communities and Local Government (DCLG).

Department for Business Innovation and Skills (BIS) BIS was created in June 2009 from the merger of the Department for Business, Enterprise and Regulatory Reform and the Department for Innovation, Universities and Skills.

Department for Energy and Climate Change (DECC) Created on 3 October 2008, DECC is responsible for all aspects of energy policy in the United Kingdom.

Department of Trade and Industry (DTI) In June 2007, the majority of this department was replaced by the Department for Business Enterprise and Regulatory Reform (BERR).

Deposition A document recording the evidence of a witness examined before the hearing of a trial takes place, which can be given as evidence at the trial. The primary purpose of CPR 34.8, which provides for such evidence, is to introduce evidence at the trial from a witness whom it would be impossible to bring to court for trial, although the procedure might be appropriate where justice requires the evidence to be available before trial: *Barratt v Shaw and Ashton* [2001] EWCA Civ 137; [2001] CP Rep 57.

Derogation Taking away or prejudicing a right you have given or obligation you are under.

Derogatory treatment Any addition to, deletion from or alteration or adoption of a designer's drawing or building which amounts to distortion or mutilation of the work or is otherwise prejudiced to the honour or reputation of the author. A designer has the right not to have his or her work subjected to such treatment under s80 of the Copyright, Designs and Patents Act 1988.

Design A scheme of works to be constructed, traditionally distinguished from workmanship, the act of carrying out the works in accordance with the design under a conventional construction contract. The distinction is more theoretical than practical, because even under such a contract, the contractor exercises a design function in selecting goods and materials where a particular make or type is not specified in the design and can also be under a duty to warn if the design is likely to be unsuitable. ■ See **Duty to warn** and **Suitability**.

Design and access statement A short written report which is required to accompany most planning applications in accordance with art 4C of the Town and Country Planning (General Development Procedure) Order 1995. The statement is to describe the design principles which have been applied to the proposed development in terms of amount, layout, scale, landscaping and appearance. In addition, the statement must explain how the design takes into account the surrounding context of the development and set out the policy adopted with regards to access and how any issues which may affect access have been addressed. ■ See **Planning permission**.

Design and build contract A construction contract under which the contractor undertakes a specific design obligation in addition to the usual one of building the works. Contrary to expectation, many "design and build" contracts entered into in the United Kingdom relate the contractor's design input to one portion of the works, proceed on the basis of a design previously procured by the employer directly from consultants and limit the contractor's liability for the design to exercising skill and care, as opposed to a warranty of its suitability. ■ See **Traditional contract**.

Design and build procurement Under a design and build building contract, the contractor is responsible for the design and construction of a project. However during the procurement process, it is often the case that other design consultants, appointed by the employer, will carry out the initial design. In these circumstances, the contractor and consultants will typically enter into a novation agreement to enable the contractor to complete the design. In this way, the employer will know that there is only one single point of responsibility for design and construction. Following the case of *Blyth & Blyth Ltd v Carillion Construction Ltd* 2001 Scot (CS) 90; 79 ConLR 142, contractors can find themselves required to take liability for the design of the works without having recourse to the designers who have prepared the design. ■ See **Novation**. See **Appendix 2**.

Design build finance manage (DBFM) A method of procurement for private finance initiative and public–private partnership projects, whereby a private provider finances and is responsible for the design, building and management of a facility.

Design build finance operate (DBFO) A method of procurement for private finance initiative and public–private partnership projects, whereby a private provider finances and is responsible for the design, building and operation of a facility.

Design build operate (DBO) A method of procurement for private finance initiative and public private partnership projects, whereby a public agency funds a private provider to design and build a facility which the latter then operates for a management fee. It is typically used for (toll) roads, waste to energy plants and large infrastructure projects.

Design life The period of time for which a project is designed or required to be used for its intended purpose, which will be relevant to the standards to be achieved.

Designer Someone who creates, devises and/or carries out a design. In construction, the word designer is usually used to refer to the **architect** or **engineer**.

Detail A large-scale drawing of a particular building/engineering joint or junction which demonstrates how the construction materials and building elements are to be assembled. ■ See **Detail drawings** and **Figure E3**.

Detail drawings Larger-scaled drawings (eg – 1:20, 1:10, 1:5 and 1:1) which are used to show how building or engineering elements are assembled. These drawings should be fully dimensioned and cross-referenced to other relevant and necessary drawings required for the construction of the particular building or engineering component. Detail drawings can be produced either by construction professionals or contractors and subcontractors depending on the procurement route and contract. See **Figure E3**.

Determination The bringing to an end of the parties' primary obligations to be performed under a contract pursuant to an express provision; it is also called termination. All standard forms provide for the contractor's employment to be brought to an end in a variety of circumstances which include non-payment, failure to make due progress and insolvency, and for the taking of an account to establish sums due to either party.

Determination of costs The process of establishing the level of costs recoverable by a successful party from the other party to an arbitration under s63 of the Arbitration Act 1996; it is the equivalent of assessment of costs in litigation.

Developer A party who arranges the development of a site by obtaining planning permission, organising funding and retaining a contractor.

DHW See **Domestic Hot Water**.

Diaphragm wall A solution for retaining the vertical face of an excavation. Ideally suited to sites that are close to existing roadsor buildings. They are formed in the ground on a panel-by-panel basis in order to restrict the effect of ground movement caused by bulk excavation work. The load deformation for reinforced concrete diaphragm walls is relatively small. A deep slot is dug to suit the chosen wall thickness using a special crane-mounted grab. For harder ground, other specialist is required. The excavation is carefully monitored and its sides are supported during excavation by a bentonite suspension. As soon as the designed depth is reached, the bentonite is replaced by reinforced concrete in order to form a water-resistant load-bearing wall. Joints between the panels are formed using stop ends. With the diaphragm wall in place, the required excavation can take place alongside the working retaining wall.

Dickinson v Dodds [1876] 2 Ch D 463: revocation of a contract need not be communicated directly. It is sufficient that the offeror knew of the revocation before the purported acceptance.

Differential settlement Where one part of the built structure suffers more movement than another, causing distortion, distress and cracking. Usually as a result of dynamics in the soil conditions or inadequate foundations.

Digger A small excavator such as a JCB with a backhoe.

Dilapidation A disrepair or a state of disrepair which usually has to be rectified at the end of the tenancy.

Diligence The application of the physical capacity to progress the works substantially and in accordance with the contractual obligations industriously and efficiently: see *West Faulkner Associates v London Borough of Newham* (1994) 71 BLR 1 (CA).

Dimension A size expressed in a measured standard unit normally in length, width and height.

Diminishing courses Rows of slates where the size of the slate decreases towards the ridge at the top.

Diminution in value A measure of damage, being the amount by which the value of property is less, arising mainly in two situations: first, where a purchaser has bought a property in reliance on a negligent valuation and, secondly, where remedial works to cure defects are not practicable or economic.

Direct loss and/or expense Loss and damage flowing naturally in the usual course of things within the first limb of the rule in *Hadley v Baxendale* [1854] 9 ExCh 341: see *FG Minter Ltd v Welsh Health Technical Services Organisation* (1980) 13 BLR 1 (CA). The expression is used in JCT forms to describe loss recoverable by the contractor caused by the regular progress of the works being materially affected by certain "relevant matters" including variations and prevention by the employer. It includes loss of interest on working capital on a compound basis: *Rees and Kirby Ltd v Swansea Corp* (1985) 30 BLR 1.

Direct payment Payment of a subcontractor by the employer without the involvement of the main contractor, the question of which usually arises where the main contractor has become insolvent or his employment has been terminated under contractual provisions. In the case of insolvency, such a payment will probably be in contravention of the pari passu rule whereby creditors are entitled to recover in the same proportion as their admitted claims and the employer would run the risk of having to pay the main contractor as well.

Direct supply Water supplied directly from the mains and not from a tank.

Directions Instructions to the parties from a judge, arbitrator or adjudicator which relate to case management, such as dates for statements of case and the exchange of evidence.

Disabled facilities Assistance for with disabilities. It is found in most public buildings.

Discharge The bringing to an end of primary contractual obligations by the acceptance of a repudiation or agreement. The parties' secondary obligations such as that to pay damages for breach may remain in force.

Discharge valve, regulating valve A valve to regulate pipe flow.

Disclaimer An exclusion or exemption of liability clause.

Disclosure Making relevant documents available to another party to a dispute. The methods of doing so vary from the formal procedure for litigation outlined in CPR Part 31 whereby the parties exchange lists of documents followed by inspection and copying to adjudication, where the parties serve documents upon which they rely with their statements of case. In arbitration, where the process is more commonly called document production, the parties are sometimes encouraged to disclose documents upon which they rely at an early stage, followed by an application for specific disclosure of other categories of document. ■ See **Privilege**.

Discontinuance The abandonment of proceedings by the party bringing them. In litigation, this is provided for by CPR 38, the usual consequences being that the discontinuing party must pay the other's costs and (if after the service of a defence) may not bring further proceedings arising out of facts which are the same or substantially the same as those relating to the discontinued claim. The position in arbitration is not so clear: there is no provision in the 1996 Act and there is a school of thought that an award should be made against the claimant. Aparty is entitled to withdraw adisputed claim which has been referred to adjudication: see *Midland Expressway Ltd v Carillion Construction Ltd* [2006] EWHC 1505 (TCC), [2006] BLR 325.

Discount See **Contractor's discount**.

Discovery The previous name for **Disclosure**.

Discretion A power to take a course of action or not, particularly that of a tribunal deciding a dispute. A discretion is usually indicated by the use of the word "may" before the course of action in any applicable statute or rules.

Dispute An argument, the existence of which is required before it can be the subject of dispute resolution processes such as arbitration or adjudication. In the absence of a dispute, an appointed arbitrator or adjudicator will not have jurisdiction. The word when it occurs in arbitration clauses as well as s108(1) of the **Construction Act** should be given its normal meaning. It does not have some special or unusual meaning conferred upon it by lawyers. The mere fact that one party ("the claimant") notifies the other party ("the respondent") of a claim does not automatically and immediately give rise to a dispute. It is clear, both as a matter of language and from judicial decisions, that a dispute does not arise unless and until it emerges that the claim is not admitted. The circumstances from which it may emerge that a claim is not admitted are Protean. For example, there may be an express rejection of the claim. There may be discussions between the parties from which objectively it is to be inferred that the claim is not admitted. The respondent may prevaricate, thus giving rise to the inference that he does not admit the claim. The respondent may simply remain silent for a period of time, thus giving rise to the same inference. See *Amec Civil Engineering Ltd v Secretary of State for Transport* [2004] EWHC Civ 2339 (TCC), para 68 (Jackson J), approved in *Collins (Contractors) Ltd v Baltic Quay Management (1994) Ltd* [2004] EWCA Civ 1757; [2005] BLR 63, 74, para 63; [2004] 2 All ER 982 (Clarke LJ) and *Amec Civil Engineering Ltd v Secretary of State for Transport* [2005] EWCA Civ 291; [2005] BLR 227, 235, para 31; [2005] 1 WLR 2339 (May LJ).

Dispute Board (DB) or Dispute Adjudication Board (DAB) A tribunal provided for by the terms of a construction contract consisting of a panel to decide disputes on an interim basis during the course of works. The FIDIC standard forms of construction contract produced by the International Federation of Civil Engineers often used for international projects funded by the World Bank contain provision for initial dispute resolution by "dispute adjudication boards", with finality until overturned or varied in subsequent proceedings.

Dispute escalation clause A clause in a contract providing a machinery for the resolution of disputes prior to the commencement of formal arbitration or litigation proceedings. Typical options proposed include meetings of senior managers of the parties to the contract or one or more of the various forms of **ADR**. ■ See **Scott v Avery clauses**.

Dispute resolution board (DRB) Used largely on large projects in the United States, the DRB is typically a panel of three experienced, respected and impartial reviewers, established before construction begins who meet at regular intervals. The purpose of the DRB is to encourage the resolution of disputes at the job level and help the parties head off problems before they escalate into major disputes.

Disruption Interference with the regular progress of works. Where the cause is a matter for which the employer under a construction contract is responsible, either under loss and expense provisions or by way of breach of contract. It can be grounds for a claim, usually where there has also been delay, called a "delay and disruption claim". Proof of causation and the valuation of the effect of disruption in terms of indirect costs is a fertile area for dispute: see *McAlpine Humberoak Ltd v McDermott International Inc (No 1)* (1992) 58 BLR 1 (CA).

Distress and Inconvenience A frequent head of loss claimed by an owner or occupier dealing with claims arising out of defective work where the occupier's use and comfort are materially distorted. Modest damages might be awarded to individuals but not companies. See *Bella Casa Ltd v Vinestone Ltd* [2005] EWHC 2807 (TCC); [2006] BLR 72.

District surveyor A post established to enforce regulations under the London Building Act 1667. Such matters are now dealt by building control officers.

Documents See **Supply of documents**.

DoE Department of the Environment

Dog-leg stair Two flights of stairs between two floor levels, with half landing. A stair between two floor levels comprised of two flights of stairs with a half landing in-between. The direction of the second flight of stairs is 180 degrees from the first flight.

Domestic hot water (DHW) Hot water usually supplied at 60°C for bathing, washing and cleaning. The supply via a storage cylinder or combi boiler should ideally be energy efficient, environmentally friendly and maintenance free.

Domestic subcontractor A sub contractor selected by the main contractor. Compare with a **named** or **nominated subcontractor** selected by the employer for whom he may assume some responsibility.

Dominant cause The term is used to resolve questions about causation. Described by **Keating** thus: "If there are two causes, one the contractual responsibility of the Defendants and the other the contractual responsibility of the Claimant, the Claimant succeeds if he establishes that the cause for which the Defendant is responsible is the effective, dominant cause...".

Door schedule A document specifying door locations, types, fittings, ironmongery, etc.

Dormer head The gable above a dormer window.

Dormer window A window which is built vertically onto a pitched roof. It therefore has its own roof (either pitched or flat) and walls, with the window set at the front of the structure. Dormer windows are often used in mansard roofs as well as in attic loft conversions for added space. ■ See **Mansard roof**.

Dot and dab fixing The process of fixing plasterboard to a solid (usually uneven) wall by way of plaster board adhesive. Dot and dab or dry lining as it is also called has become the preferred method of lining a wall prior to the application of a finishing skim. ■ See **Dry lining**.

Dots and screeds Dots of solid materials are bedded to a wall or floor at intervals to receive level strips. The strips are then used as a rail for screeding the surface flat.

Double curvature A surface curved two opposite ways usually, for added strength. For example, corrugated sheeting.

Double-decker lift A lift with one car on top of the other in order to save space serving two floors at a time.

Double glazing Two layers of glass or other transparent material forming a sealed unit to provide improved heat and sound insulation. The width of the sealed cavity, the thickness of the glass and the fitted design will determine its effect.

Double-leaf separating wall An untied cavity wall that is intended to improve sound insulation. The leaves and frame of the wall are usually made of timber. The double wall is made laminated plasterboard with the cavity incorporating an insulating fire-stopping material.

Double-lock welt A tight interlocking welt or seam normally used in sheet metal roofing.

Dovetail Used in joinery where the interlocking tenon or pin is fan-shaped to improve rigidity.

Dowel bar Used at a contraction or movement point to transfer the load from one concrete slab to another whilst permitting thermal expansion along the axis of the dowel. A debond sleeve and expansion cap can be fitted as a bond breaker. Stainless steel dowel bars provide a durable connection.

Downlighter A luminaire or light usually in a recessed ceiling or located at height.

Downpipe A pipe to bring rainwater down to a drain or soak-away.

Downstand beam A beam that projects downwards, for example, hanging from a soffit or a worktop.

DPC Damp proof course

DPM Damp proof membrane

Drain pipe A pipe laid in the ground as a drain. Where ground movement is anticipated, the pipe work including joints should be flexible.

Drained and ventilated joint Applied to a panel or glazed cladding system which allows water to penetrate the joints between panels in adverse conditions such as driving rain. Water that reaches the cavity is either drained-off or evaporated. Ventilation gaps are required above and below the cladding as well as around window openings. This system should not be confused with a **pressure equalised** system which functions through the nature of the joints between the panels. The air pressure acting on the face of the panel is balanced by the pressure created at the joint. This equalisation provides a cushion within the air gap that allows the passage of air but not water through the joints. Any water that might penetrate the skin is drained-off within the cladding system. Continuous vertical and horizontal separations must be designed into the system to control the pressure equalisation process thus preventing air from flowing from one compartment to another.

Drained cavity In a damp basement, hollow blocks may be laid to drain water away.

Draw cable Wire used to pull cable through a draw-in duct system. The draw cable is usually left in place.

Drawing register A management tool used to control the access to, the revision of and the issue of the drawings and other files.

Drawing scale See **Scale**.

DRB See **Dispute Resolution Board.**

DRBF Dispute Resolution Board Foundation. An organisation dedicated to promote the avoidance and resolution of disputes worldwide primarily using DRBs.

Dress To work timber (usually) by smoothing down.

Dressed dimension The final dimensions of the wood after dressing and shrinkage from moisture. The dressed dimension may vary considerably from the nominal dimension.

Dressings Smoothed/worked masonry or stucco found around windows and doors or other parts of a structure for decorative effect.

D-ring A pipe joint ring with a flat side shaped like a "D" to prevent rolling.

Drip A trailing groove and sometimes a rise on the underside of an exposed surface to make water drop away from the building.

Drip edge A trailing vertical edge designed to drip water away.

Drop apron See **Drip edge**.

Drop ceiling A second or false ceiling carried on the ceiling joists unlike a **suspended ceiling** carried by the floor joists above.

Dry construction Building without the wet trades. The use of a prefabricated system building, dry linings, suspended ceiling, raised floors all without using a significant amount of water and its effects sometimes offer a quick and cost-effective alternative.

Dry joint A joint fixed without mortar or glue.

Dry lining The application of plasterboard, in place of wet plaster, to line walls and ceilings.

Dry masonry A wall without mortar.

Dry partition A partition that can easily be demounted.

Dry riser Vertical mains fitted into a staircase enclosure or other suitable position and constructed of galvanised steel. Outlet valves are on each floor and inlets are fitted at ground level. They are usually kept empty for the access of fire equipment.

Dry rot *Serpula lacrymans*, a wood-destroying fungus that will only affect timber with a moisture content in excess of 20 per cent. For this reason, removing the source of moisture forms the core of any eradication strategy. Dry rot has the ability to travel through building materials other than timber giving outbreaks the potential to spread quickly throughout a building. For this reason, additional measures (eg masonry sterilisation) often have to be taken when treating dry rot outbreaks over and above those necessary when dealing with outbreaks of other wood-rotting fungi. Typical symptoms of dry rot include: a musty damp odour, wood shrinkage with darkening and cracks; under less humid conditions, a silky grey mushroom skin with coloured patches of lilac and yellow and under humid conditions, white fluffy cotton wool mycelium may develop.

Dry sprinkler A sprinkler system supplied via a dry riser.

Dry trades Building finishing trades that start as soon as the building is weather-tight and dry.

Dry wall Dry lining or a wall without mortar. ■ See also **Wallboard**.

Drying-out The process that begins after wet trades are complete and before the dry trades commence. It may require the use of de-humidifiers and heating especially in winter to achieve satisfactory results.

Dry-pack mortar Mortar with little moisture that is rammed into narrow gaps, for example, between underpinning and an existing foundation to fully fill small voids.

DTI See **Department of Trade and Industry.**

Dubbing-out Filling in hollows and imperfections before plastering.

Dubitante Latin: "doubting", a term used in law reports to indicate that the court, although not overruling a previous decision or established principle, has doubts as to its correctness.

Duct air duct: Light weight pipe for air handling or mechanical ventilation. **Services duct:** The passageway (riser and or shaft) through which the building services run. This duct should be sealed against the transmission of fire (fire stops) and sound at regular intervals.

Ductwork Lightweight pipe (usually rectangular sheet metal) for air ducts.

Due diligence (1) The standard of application sometimes required in carrying out works: see the ICE Conditions 7th edn clause 41(2) and **Diligence**. (2)A process whereby the potential purchaser of a business or his consultants carry out a series of checks on the business.

Duress The use of illegitimate pressure (and this means more than mere commercial pressure) to compel a party to do something against its will. A contract entered into under duress is voidable and not void – see *DPP v Lynch* [1975] AC 653. Once the duress has ceased, a party has the option of affirming or avoiding the contract in question. ■ See **Economic duress**.

Duty of care A duty arising in tort independently of any contract not to cause damage to others. It must now be regarded as settled law that the builder/vendor of a building does not by reason of his contract to construct or to complete the building assume any liability in the tort of negligence in relation to defects in the building giving rise to purely economic loss. The same applies to a builder who is not the vendor and to the seller or manufacturer of a chattel. The decision of the House of Lords in *Anns v Merton London Borough Council* [1978] AC 728, [1977] 2 WLR 1024 like its earlier decision in *Junior Books Ltd v Veitchi Co Ltd* [1983] 1 AC 520; [1982] 3 WLR 477; [1982] 3 All ER 201, must now be regarded as aberrant, indeed as heretical. Where there is a duty, liability can only arise if the defect remains hidden until the defective structure causes personal injury or damage to property other than the structure itself. If the defect is discovered before any damage is done, the loss sustained by the owner of the structure, who has to repair or demolish it to avoid a potential source of danger to third parties, would seem to be purely economic: see *Robinson v PE Jones (Contractors) Ltd* [2010] EWCA Civ 102; A construction professional will, however, usually owe a duty of care to his client.

Dwang A noggin or strut between a joist.

Dwarf wall A low wall often used in the construction of a conservatory.

Dwelling Premises used for the purpose of habitation. In relation to statutory regulation of construction contracts, "dwelling" means a dwelling house or a flat: "dwelling house" does not include a building containing a flat, and "flat" means separate and self-contained premises constructed or adapted for use for residential purposes and forming part of a building from some other part of which the premises are divided horizontally: s106 (2) of the **Construction Act**. A construction contract with a residential occupier is not subject to the Act. Such a contract is one which principally relates to operations on a dwelling which one of the parties to the contract occupies, or intends to occupy, as his or her residence.

Dynamic purchasing system An electronic system used by a contracting authority to purchase commonly used goods, works and/or services within a limited duration of no more than four years.

E

Early Neutral Evaluation (ENE) The system occasionally used by the Technology and Construction Court **(TCC)** and Commercial Court whereby a neutral, typically a judge, evaluates the likely result of the case if it were to proceed to trial but in the form of a recommendation only which is non-binding. See para 7.5.1 of the **TCC Guide**.

Early warning A term used in the New Engineering Contract **(NEC)** Standard Form of Contract which requires each party to ensure that the other has notice of problems early on so that their impact on the progress of the works can be reduced.

Early Warning Notice (EWN) The notice given under the **NEC** Standard Form of Contract given by a party if it becomes aware of any matter which may lead to delay or an increase in cost.

Earned value An assessment of the state of progress of a project by reference to the planned work actually completed in terms of man-hours and amounts of materials used.

Earth electrode The part of an electrical circuit in direct contact with the ground, such as a metal rod.

Earth stake A pin or stake, usually of galvanised steel or copper to enable electrical circuits to be connected to the ground (earth) for several reasons. In mains powered equipment, exposed metal parts are connected to the ground to prevent contact with a dangerous voltage if electrical insulation fails, for example, photovoltaic panels. Connections to ground also limit the build-up of static electricity relevant to handling flammable products or when repairing electronic devices. An electrical ground system should have an appropriate current-carrying capability in order to serve as an adequate zero-voltage reference level.

Earth termination The termination of a lightning conductor in the earth.

Earthing The connection of electrical cables to earth so that in the event of a fault the protection (fuse, trip switch) is operated rapidly. ■ See **Bonding**.

Easement A proprietary right enjoyed by one parcel of land (the dominant tenement) over another (the servient tenement). Easements are created by express or implied grant or prescription and the most common ones are a right of way and an easement of support.

East Ham Corporation v Sunley (Bernard) & Son Ltd [1966] AC 406: where the defect in question is not irreparable; it was held that losses caused by defective work should be assessed by reference to the cost of putting that work right.

Eaves The overhanging edge of a pitched roof or the area behind. ■ See **Eaves gutter, Eaves soffit** and **Eaves vent**.

Eaves gutter A gutter fixed to the eaves board to collect rainwater running down the roof slope and directed by the eaves drip. ■ See **Eaves, Eaves soffit** and **Eaves vent**.

Eaves soffit The underside of the eaves where they project beyond the external wall, normally formed by a flat board fixed to the bottom side of the rafters. ■ See **Eaves, Eaves gutter** and **Eaves vent**.

Eaves vent Ventilation installed at eaves level on opposite sides of a building to allow air flow through the roof space. ■ See **Eaves, Eaves gutter** and **Eaves soffit**.

ECJ European Court of Justice

Economic duress A doctrine, the basis of which is that threats to a party's economic interests which have induced it to enter into a contract can be so serious that they vitiate consent because that party had no other choice. A contract entered into under duress is voidable and not void. The burden on a party alleging such duress is thus a heavy one. The law is well summarised by Dyson J. in *DSND Subsea Ltd v Petroleum Geo-Services* ASA [2000] BLR 530, 545, para 131 as follows:

> "The ingredients of actionable duress are that there must be pressure, (a) whose practical effect is that there is compulsion on, or a lack of practical choice for, the victim, (b) which is illegitimate, and (c) which is a significant cause inducing the claimant to enter into the contract: see *Universal Tanking of Monrovia v ITWF* [1983] AC 336, 400B-E, and *The Evia Luck* [1992] 2 AC 152, 165G. In determining whether there has been illegitimate pressure, the court takes into account a range of factors. These include whether there has been an actual or threatened breach of contract; whether the person allegedly exerting the pressure has acted in good or bad faith; whether the victim had any realistic practical alternative but to submit to the pressure; whether the victim protested at the time; and whether he affirmed and sought to rely on the contract. These are all relevant factors. Illegitimate pressure must be distinguished from the rough and tumble of the pressures of normal commercial bargaining."

Economic Loss See **Pure economic loss**.

Edge beam Beam at edge of construction (often part of main structural frame) enclosing elements such as cast concrete floors.

Efficient breach The theory that a defendant should not be prohibited from breaking a contract if the profit he can make from doing so exceeds the damages he would have to pay to the other party to the broken contract. See the judgment of Millett LJ in the case of *Co-operative Insurance Society Ltd v Argyll Stores (Holdings) Ltd* [1996] 3 WLR 27; [1996] 3 All ER 934.

Efflorescence Salt crystals which appear on the surface of a wall or on grout joints as a whitish powder or crust. These crystals are formed when water reacts with the natural salts in the construction material and in mortar and are transported to and deposited on the surface of the floor or wall as a result of moisture evaporation. Efflorescence is generally harmless except in appearance and can be brushed off when dry.

Egan Report Influential report on the UK construction industry entitled *Rethinking Construction*, which was produced by an industry task force chaired by Sir John Egan. Published in November 1998.

Eggshell Eggshell finish and eggshell paint have an unreflective textured finish which is durable and often used in common parts. The term also refers to wall linings and paper which are uncoated and uncalendered with a fairly rough texture, hence, resembling the surface of an eggshell.

Eggshell skull rule The rule that a tortfeasor must take his victim as he finds him, so that if some injury was reasonably foreseeable, then there is a liability for the full extent of injury even though that may be the result of a peculiar susceptibility, such as a thin skull. Although it was thought for some time that this rule did not apply to the victim's impecuniosity, it is now clear that it does: *Lagden v O'Connor* [2003] UKHL 64; [2004] AC 1067.

EIA See **Environmental impact assessment**.

Eichleay formula A formula for calculating the cost of the head office, overheads and the profits arising during a period of reimbursable contract overrun in loss and expense claims; first considered in by the US Armed Services Board of Contract Appeals in the case of *Eichleay Corp v US* ASBCA No 5183 (1960), concerning a claim under a government contract. The calculation is based on the annual figure for head office costs, overheads and profits achieved for the company, which is multiplied by the number of days of compensable delay. *Eichleay* damages are computed as follows: (a) Total billings under the contract; (b) Total billings for all contracts during the contract period; (c) Total head office overhead during contract period; (d) [(a ÷ b) × c] = Overhead allocated to the contract; (e) Actual number of days for performance of the contract; (f) (d ÷ e) = Daily overhead allocated to the contract; (g) Number of delay days for the contract; (h) (f × g) = Unabsorbed and potentially recoverable overhead. The use of the formula has been limited in the United States to situations where the contractor's performance has been suspended during a period of delay (*PJ Dick Inc v Principi* 324 F.3d 1364 (Fed. Cir. 2003) and the contractor is unable to take on any replacement work during the suspension (*Nikon Inc v US* No 99/98/982C (Fed. Cl. Dec 21, 2001). The method is subject to the objections that it fails to demonstrate that the increase in overheads was caused by delay, and it does not identify the actual losses incurred on a specific project. ➤ **Figure E1**

Ei incumbit probatio qui dicit, non qui negat Latin: "the burden of proof falls on him who alleges, not on him who denies".

EJ Expansion joint

Ejusdem generis Latin: "of the same kind". A rule of construction which provides that if there are specific words that belong to a class followed by more general words, the general words are taken to be part of the same class as the specific words. Doubts have been expressed from time to time as to the utility of the rule and its application to commercial contracts, as opposed to wills and deeds.

Elastic design A method of structural (steel) design by which the yield stress does not exceed the permitted values and so "remains elastic".

Elbow, knee This usually refers to a pipe bend fitting that allows a pipe to perform a turn at any angle, but commonly 90 degrees. An elbow can also refer to a right angle section of concrete or steel, which is used to tie a front and side elevation of a masonry wall together in remedial works.

Election A doctrine whereby a party seeking to take the benefit of an instrument cannot accept that benefit without at the same time conforming to all the provisions of the instrument and renouncing every right inconsistent with them. Also known as "approbation and

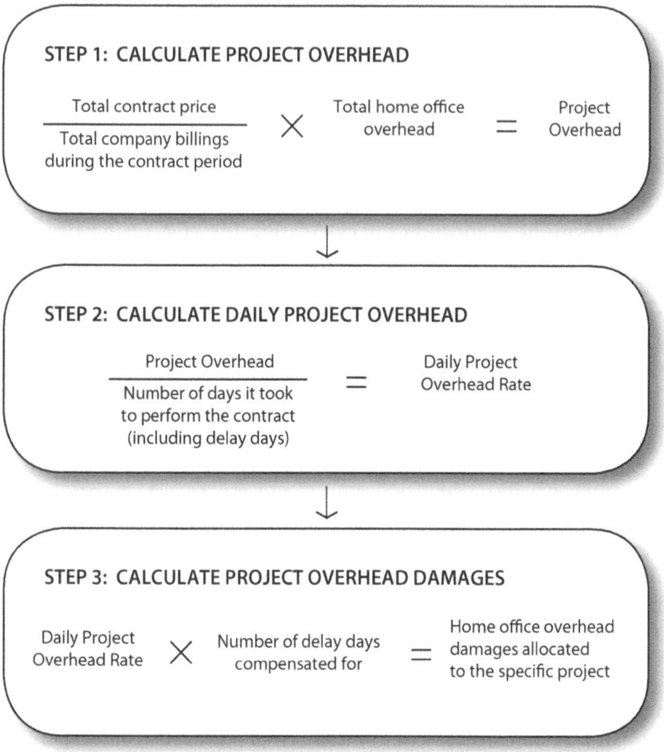

➤➤ **Figure E1.** Eichleay Formula: Calculation of overhead damages for a specified project

reprobation", the doctrine is applicable to the decisions of adjudicators. In simple terms, a party to an adjudication cannot pick and choose which parts of a decision upon a dispute he will accept and which he will not. The decision upon a particular dispute must either be accepted in whole or not at all, assuming that the latter option is otherwise available. For the doctrine to apply, it is necessary for a party, with knowledge that it is open to him to object to the decision and to take the benefit of part of it. However, what constitutes a "*benefit*" for this purpose does not depend simply upon whether the party whose receipt of a "*benefit*" in question has obtained a net cash sum or an entitlement to a payment. It is a "*benefit*" to a party, for the purposes of the doctrine, that his liability to another party in respect of any particular matter is crystallised on an interim basis at a particular amount, even though that is an amount which he is called upon to pay. Thus, a party who contends that his obligation towards another party is limited to the payment of a particular sum by reason of the decision of an adjudicator has both claimed and derived a "*benefit*" from that decision. It is probably also correct to say that a party who is, in consequence of the decision of an adjudicator, entitled to take possession of a building, and does so, has claimed and derived a "*benefit*" from the decision: see *R. Durtnell & Sons Ltd v Kaduna Ltd* [2003] EWHC 517; [2003] BLR 225.

Electrical riser At its simplest a service run, rack, shaft, or conduit to get electrical wiring and other service media between floors.

Electrical services Building services involving electrical work, usually forming part of a services package known as "mechanical and electrical services" or "M & E".

Electrostatic discharge (ESD) A discharge created when two materials with different charges come sufficiently close to each another. Specialist static control flooring is used to protect sensitive equipment. ■ See **Anti-static flooring**.

Elemental bills of quantities A bill of quantities arranged according to materials to be provided for construction or the main ingredients of construction.

Elephant Used by the judiciary as an example of the difficulty in defining certain words and phrases. See Lord Justice Brown in the case of *West Faulkner v London Borough of Newham* (1994) 71 BLR 1 (CA) where he defined **regularly and diligently** thus:

> "Taken together the obligation upon the contractor is essentially to proceed continuously, industriously and efficiently with appropriate physical resources so as to progress the works steadily towards completion substantially in accordance with the contract requirements as to time, sequence and quality of work."

But also conceded that

> "Beyond that I think it impossible to give useful guidance. These are after all plain English words and in reality the failure of which clause 25(1)(b) speaks is, like the elephant, far easier to recognise than to describe."

Elephant's feet Substantial objects into which the base of the ladder fits to stop it slipping.

Elevation (1) A scaled drawing representing the external view of a building or engineering product. In general, an elevation is any view of an object projected onto a plane. Therefore, a "roof plan" is in fact an elevation of the top of a building. ■ See **Orthographic projection** and **Figure G3**. (2) In the context of levels, the elevation of a point is its height above an agreed datum (eg mean sea level).

ELPS Emergency Lighting Power Supply

Emden formula The barrister and County Court Judge Alfred Charles Richard Emden, best remembered as the author of the building law text *The Law relating to Building Leases and Building Contracts*, which was first published by Stevens and Haynes in London on 1882. Subsequent editions appeared in the 1980s. This text gave rise to the Emden Formula to measure head office costs in construction delay claims, an alternative to the better-known Hudson Formula. Received apparent judicial approval in the case of *St Modwen Developments Ltd v Bowmer & Kirkland Ltd* [1996] C.I.L.L. 1203 where the arbitrator, against whose decision the employer unsuccessfully appealed, had based his award on the Emden Formula. A

$$\frac{\text{head office overhead costs and profit*}}{100} \times \frac{\text{the contract sum}}{\text{the contract period}} \times \text{the period of delay} = \text{head office overhead damages attributable to the specific project}$$

* Actual head office overheads and profit

➤➤ **Figure E2.** Emden Formula: Calculation of overhead damages for a specified project

formula for calculating the cost of head office, overheads and the profits arising during a period of reimbursable contract overrun in loss and expense claims. This calculation is based on the annual figure for head office costs (as opposed to the **Hudson formula** which uses the amount of head office overheads and profit included in the tender), overheads and profits achieved for the company, which is then applied to the specific contract as follows:

$$\frac{h}{100} \times \frac{c}{cp} \times pd$$

h = head office costs, overheads and profit;

c = contract sum;

cp = contract period;

pd = period of delay.

Although relatively easy to calculate, this formula assumes a uniform rate of ancillary costs which may not reflect the true position under the contract. ➤ **Figure E2**

Emergency power systems (EPS) Configurations of a system, which may encompass lighting, generators, fuel cells, UPS and other apparatus, to provide backup power feeds in a crisis or when regular systems fail such as those in a hospital, control room, TV studio etc.

Employer The party to a construction contract who engages and pays for the contractor to carry out the works. Also referred to as the "building owner" or "client".

Employer's Agent A person appointed by the Employer to act on his or her behalf. Often an Employer's Agent will be a professional such as an architect or quantity surveyor and may have experience of building and project management. In some forms of contract, the term Employer's Agent has replaced "the Architect" or "Contract Administrator". In spite of the name, the Employer's Agent is required to exercise independent judgement in matters of contract administration, such as certifying extensions of time, issuing notices or paying the contractor. ■ See **Agency**.

Employer's Representative Person appointed by the employer to act on behalf of an employer under a contract.

Employer's requirements (ERs) Under **Joint Contracts Tribunal (JCT)** design and build forms, the document produced by the employer being a written statement of the employer's specific requirements for a project which may include substantial factual and technical documentation. The contractor responds with his proposals. Often the ERs will contain parameters which the completed building must achieve, such as area, clear height, operation of systems, and may range from a simple requirement by the employer (eg a factory of 1 million square feet with ancillary offices for 100 people) to very detailed requirements. The basic scheme is that changes to works constituting a change in the ERs can entitle the contractor to additional payment. ■ See **Contractor's Proposals** and **Design and Build Contracts**.

Emulsion paint Water-based paint used principally on walls and ceilings.

Enabling works Works required to be carried out before commencement of construction, such as demolition, ground preparation for heavy plant and diversion of services.

Enamel paint Oil- or water-based paint with varnish which air dries to give a hard glossy surface.

Encasement The containment of a structure or equipment by external wrapping or boxing. Often required as a fire precaution, it is also used for protecting asbestos insulation from damage or escape.

Enclosed stage The point at which the interior of a building under construction is enclosed by the completion of the walls roof and floor. Sometimes used as stage for payment.

End bearing length The length at each end of a beam which needs to be supported in order to carry a given load.

End grain The grain or pattern of wood when cut at right angles to its length.

End joint Joint where the full section of the joining pieces abut each other.

End lap joint A carpentry joint (either straight or at right angles) where the thickness of the joining pieces is reduced by half the length of the joint.

ENE See **Early Neutral Evaluation**.

Enforcement The process of enforcing a judgment or award. The term is most frequently applied to the steps taken to obtain compliance with an adjudicator's decision. Enforcement by way of a claim in court proceedings normally seeks a monetary judgment, so that a CPR Part 7 claim is usually appropriate. However, if the enforcement proceedings are known to raise a question which is unlikely to involve a substantial dispute of fact and no monetary judgment is sought, CPR Part 8 proceedings may be used instead. In most cases, the claimant will be seeking summary judgment on the basis of the adjudicator's decision. The court may give summary judgment against a defendant if it considers that the defendant has no real prospect of successfully defending the claim and there is no other compelling reason why the case should be disposed of at trial. An adjudication decision creates a debt which may also form the basis of a statutory demand under s268 Insolvency Act 1986. ■ The procedures by which a judgment can be executed against the unsuccessful party to litigation. The court does not automatically enforce its judgments, nor even decide how they should be enforced. It is up to the judgment creditor. Part 70 of the Civil Procedure Rules, and those provisions of the Rules of the Supreme Court which were retained by that Part, give a wide variety of different methods to a successful party to litigation for enforcing judgments, which includes the appointment of a receiver, third party debt orders, charging orders, stop orders, stop notices, and other writs of execution such as a writ of *fieri facias*. There are provisions to seek for the attachment of earnings as well. In addition, there is a statutory option available to a judgment creditor to initiate proceedings for bankruptcy or, in the case of a company, liquidation of the debtor.

Enforcement notice Served by a local authority to (1) stop the use of land and/or remove any buildings or structures that do not have the requisite planning permission and (2) put right what has been done wrong.

Engineer A construction professional who designs and oversees the construction of work of a technical nature and who is qualified to do so by virtue of professional qualifications and practical experience. The use of the term is limited in many countries (but not the United Kingdom) to those who possess certain qualifications and memberships of professional bodies. The term is usually qualified by a specific area of expertise: for example, electrical, structural, civil and mechanical.

Engineering brick A hard brick such as Staffordshire Blues, made of semi vitreous material, designed for locations where compressive strength and resistance to moisture are required; for example, external walls below **damp proof course** or ground level.

Engineering Council The regulatory authority for the engineering profession in the United Kingdom including Chartered and Incorporated Engineers and Engineering Technicians. The designated authority under European regulations for the recognition and validation of professional qualifications in engineering.

Engineering, Procurement, Construction (EPC) A form of contract and procurement route used for large scale engineering and power projects under which the contractor accepts responsibility for design and construction of the works. The contractor will also be required to guarantee performance and reliability levels and the contract will therefore often contain detailed testing and commissioning provisions prior to the works being accepted by the employer. It is, amongst other things, these testing and commissioning provisions which distinguish an EPC contract from a Design and build contract. EPC contracts also place more risk on the contractor in terms of price and programme than design and build contracts. ■ See **Design and Build and FIDIC Silver book**.

English bond A pattern of bricklaying comprising alternate courses of stretcher and header bricks. To be contrasted with **Flemish bond**. ➤ **Figure B3**.

Entire agreement clause A type of **exclusion clause** limiting the parties' liabilities to those arising from the remedies expressly identified in the contract. It is to preclude a party to a written agreement from threshing through the undergrowth and finding in the course of negotiations some (chance) remark or statement (often long forgotten or difficult to recall or explain) on which to found a claim, such as the present, to the existence of a collateral warranty. The entire agreement clause obviates the occasion for any such search, and the peril to the contracting parties posed by the need which may arise in its absence to conduct such a search. For such a clause constitutes a binding agreement between the parties that the full contractual terms are to be found in the document containing the clause and not elsewhere, and that, accordingly any promises or assurances made in the course of the negotiations (which, in the absence of such a clause might have effect as a collateral warranty) shall have no contractual force, save insofar as they are reflected and given effect in that document: *Inntrepreneur Pub Co (GL) v East Crown Ltd* [2000] 2 Lloyd's Rep 11. However, it must yield, like any written provision in a contract, to the dictates of commercial common sense: *North Eastern Properties Ltd v Coleman* [2010] EWCA Civ 277; [2010] BLR 579. Also known (particularly in the United States) as a **zipper clause**.

Entire completion Term used in some contracts to signify completion of all the contract works as opposed to **sectional completion**.

Entire contract A contract complete performance of which by a party supplying goods or services is a condition precedent to the other party's liability for the price. Such contracts are rare in the construction field because of the almost universal adoption of a system of interim or stage payments as provided for by s109 of the Housing Grants, Construction and Regeneration Act 1996 and their effect has in any event been mitigated by the courts' development of the doctrine of **substantial completion**.

Entresol An entresol is a mezzanine or an intermediate floor situated between the main floors of a building, and therefore typically not counted among the overall floors of a building. Commonly, a mezzanine is low-ceilinged and projects in the form of a balcony. The term is also used architecturally for the lowest balcony in a theatre, or for the first few rows of seats in that balcony.

Envelope The external containment of a building which protects against ingress of water. Also used as a planning term to define external appearance.

Environment Agency (EA) An executive non-departmental Public Body responsible to the Secretary of State for Environment, Food and Rural Affairs, the principal aims of which are to protect and improve the environment, and to promote sustainable development.

Environmental impact assessment (EIA) A written assessment of the likely effect of a design or a completed building upon the environment. Includes the output of heat, moisture, noise, vibration or other emissions, the effect on local fauna and flora, the effect on local residents and the impact on drainage and water courses. Sometimes required as a condition of planning permission, particularly in sensitive areas. Also a reference to an assessment of the effect of the process of construction on, for example, carbon balance.

E&OE Errors and omissions excepted or excluded. A legal disclaimer found, for example, on specifications or price lists which tries to limit liability for mistakes on those documents.

EOT See **Extension of time**.

EPC See **Engineering, Procurement, Construction**.

E-procurement Increasingly favoured by government bodies, the use of electronic methods in every stage of the tender or purchasing process.

Epoxy mortar Mortar with a resin-based additive often used for its adhesive strength as a filler in cracks.

Epoxy paint Paint combined with resin-based materials activated by hardener and used to coat metal surfaces. Also used as a powder coating.

EPS See **Emergency power systems**.

Equitable set-off Relied as a matter of defence upon matters of equity which formerly might have called for injunction or prohibition, namely cases in which a court of equity would have regarded the cross-claims as entitling the defendant to be protected in one way or another against the plaintiff's claim. That does not mean that all cross-claims may be relied on as defences to claims. Two factors are critical: it would be manifestly unjust for the claim to be enforced without regard to the cross-claim, and there is a close relationship between the dealings and transactions which gave rise to the respective claims: *Hanak v Green* (1958) 2 QB 9; 1 BLR 1. There have been a number of different formulations of the test to be applied, the most recent being that of whether the cross-claim is so closely connected with the claimant's demands that it would be manifestly unjust to allow him to enforce payment without taking into account the cross-claim: *Geldof Metaalconstructie NV v Simon Carves Ltd* [2010] EWCA Civ 667; [2010] BLR 401.

Equity A set of legal principles, originally developed by the Lord Chancellor and the Courts of Equity to prevent potential injustice arising from the strict application of the common law. A basic characteristic of equity is that relief will only be granted where it is fair to do so, embodied in the maxim: "he who comes to equity must come with clean hands".

Equity clause An arbitration clause which permits the arbitral tribunal to take a broader approach than that of the strict application of the law, also known as "honourable engagement" or *amiable compositeur* clauses. Such provisions are regularly used in other European jurisdictions but extremely rare in contracts governed by the law of England and Wales.

Equivalent temperature The temperature of air from which water vapour has been condensed and the latent heat thereby released has been used to heat the air. It is used as a measure of comfort.

Erection All Risks An insurance policy which typically protects a contractor against physical loss or damage to the contract works, construction plant and equipment or machinery.

Error ■ An error of law, which can be the subject of an appeal under certain legislation, such as the Arbitration Act 1996, is to be distinguished from an error of fact, which is often precluded from any right of appeal. This distinction is a difficult one to make, given that there can be mixed questions of fact and law, for example, where the issue is whether notice was given as required by a contract. The courts are hostile to the "dressing up" of findings of fact as errors of law. ■ See **Clerical error or mistake** and **Slip rule**.

ERs See **Employer's requirements**.

Escrow Something which is held conditionally; for example, a bank account or fund which is deposited to await the outcome of a dispute or a deed which is not to be released until payment has been made or some other condition has been fulfilled. In the construction context, the retention held by the employer can be required to be kept as a separate fund in escrow, so protecting it from the employer's possible insolvency.

Escutcheon An item of door furniture, often ornamented, which protects a key hole or lock cylinder from wear and tear or other damage. Word also used to describe plate used to conceal a functioning, non-architectural item.

ESD See **Electrostatic discharge**.

Estimate A price for the works provided by a contractor. Although an estimate is generally regarded within the construction industry as being of a more approximate nature than a quotation or tender, the description of a price as an "estimate" does not prevent it from amounting to a tender which can give rise to a binding contract if accepted by the employer: *Crowshaw v Pritchard* (1899) *Hudson's Law of Building, Engineering and Ship Building Contracts* 4th edn, Vol. 2, p. 274. ■ A projected costing of works provided by a construction professional. If the estimate is seriously in error, the professional may be unable to recover any fees for work on the project: see *Nye Saunders & Partners v Bristow* (1987)37 BLR 92 (CA). ■ To carry out the process of producing an estimate, quotation or tender. Estimating or pricing a job requires considerable experience and knowledge of the workings of the standard forms of contract.

Estoppel A principle of equity by which A is not allowed to alter his position if, to his knowledge, B has relied, to his detriment, on A's statement or representation as to facts or A's knowledge or belief. Promissory estoppel can arise where a party has given an assurance to another that they will not enforce their strict legal rights. Estoppel by convention may arise where the parties to a contract have acted on a common assumption that certain facts are true. Once they have acted in reliance of the truth, they cannot at a later stage deny the truth of those facts. ■ See **Estoppel by convention, Promissory estoppel** and, **Proprietary estoppel**.

Ethylene tetra fluoroethylene (ETFE) A plastic polymer compound used for roofing panels and plastic coating. A light weight but strong material which provides a good protection from corrosion.

Eurocode (EC) Technical codes which stipulate engineering design standards throughout the European Union and are intended to supersede British and other national standards. To date, they comprise (1) basis of structural design (2) actions on structures (3) design of concrete structures (4) design of steel structures (5) design of composite steel and concrete structures (6) design of timber structures (7) design of masonry structures (8) geotechnical design (9) design of structures for earthquake resistance and (10) design of aluminium structures.

European Commission The executive body of the European Union.

European Committee for Standardisation (CEN) The European Union body responsible for drawing up European Standards such as the **Eurocodes** and other standards.

European Standard, Euronorm (EN) The European technical standard for a wide variety of commercial and industrial activities.

Eurotunnel v TML [1993] 2 WLR 262: the House of Lords held that where parties had adopted in their contract a specific dispute resolution procedure then they were bound to follow that procedure irrespective of whether or not it was suited to the particular dispute in question.

Evaluative mediation A mediation process where the mediator takes a more active or interventionist role which can include putting forward views about the merits of a particular issue.

The Event Safety Guide ("The Purple Guide") A document published by the Health and Safety Executive that provides guidance for event organisers to help them comply with the Health and Safety at Work, etc. Act 1974 and other relevant regulations.

Evidence The means whereby a party proves his factual case, being relevant factual information concerning an issue. Evidence may be real evidence (the presentation of an object such as a fractured brick to demonstrate the mode of failure), documentary evidence, written evidence or oral evidence. It may be primary evidence which is first-hand information, such as an original document or evidence from a witness who was directly involved or secondary evidence (copy documents or hearsay evidence). It is a matter for the tribunal to decide what evidence to accept and what weight to give to it. ■ See **Extrinsic evidence and Hearsay**.

Evidence-in-chief The evidence of a witness given in response to questions by the advocate representing the party who has called the witness; the process is also known as examination-in-chief. Such evidence is now largely given in the form of a written **witness statement**, the contents of which the witness is asked to confirm in his oral testimony.

EVOH Ethylene Vinyl Alcohol Copolymer. A barrier resin which is widely used as a packaging application.

EWCA England and Wales Court of Appeal, which forms part of a short reference or citation for a reported case.

EWHC England and Wales High Court. Again, forms part of a short reference or citation for a reported case.

EWN See **Early Warning Notice**.

Ex aequo et bono Latin: "according to what is just and good". A rule that prevents one person being unjustifiably enriched at the expense of another. Illustrations of this doctrine are familiar in cases of money paid by mistake or deceit which ought to be returned. A quasi-legislative exercise in which, typically, a tribunal fashions the outcome to the equities involved, instead of strictly applying rules of law, thereby overriding the strict rule of law. The principle does not have general application; it is found mostly in arbitration and tribunal cases. Section 46(1)(b) **Arbitration Act 1996** recognises that parties may agree that their dispute should be settled in accordance with general principles of fairness. Such agreements are often interchangeably referred to as "equity clauses", arbitration "*ex aequo et bono*" or "amiable composition". The agreements effectively exclude rights of appeal to the court, because there is no question of law to appeal.

Ex gratia Latin: "out of grace", not as a result of any legal obligation.

Ex officio Latin: "from the office", indicating that the professional position or office which a person holds confers jurisdiction upon him; for example, the chairman of a panel who may be empowered to issue directions to the parties before a hearing takes place.

Ex parte Latin: "on one side only", indicating that only one party will be attending or has attended a court hearing, particularly in relation to the hearing of an application without notice (now the favoured description) to the other party: contrast **inter partes**. Such applications can be used in cases of urgency when there is no time to serve the responding party, but most often in circumstances where giving advance warning of the application may frustrate its purpose; for example, an injunction to prevent the respondent disposing of assets or goods. ■ See **Application, Freezing, Injunction.**

Examination-in-Chief See **Cross-Examination, Evidence-in-chief** and **Witness**.

Excavation The removal of soil, subsoil or other material below ground level in connection with works, such as the construction of foundations or laying of pipework.

Excepted Risk Any risk liability for loss or damage caused by or arising from which is excluded under the all-risks insurance required to be taken out under the **JCT** standard forms. The excepted risks are: ionising radiations or contamination by radioactivity from any nuclear fuel or from any nuclear waste from the combustion of nuclear fuel, radioactive toxic explosive or other hazardous properties of any explosive nuclear assembly or nuclear component thereof, pressure waves caused by aircraft or other aerial devices travelling at sonic or supersonic speeds.

Exceptionally adverse weather conditions A **relevant event** which can entitle the contractor to an extension of time for completion of the works under the **JCT** standard forms. The test to be applied in deciding whether or not an extension should be granted in respect of this **relevant event** is whether the weather itself was exceptionally adverse, not whether the amount of time lost by the adverse weather was exceptional: *Walter Lawrence & Son Ltd v Commercial Union Properties (UK) Ltd* [1984] 4 ConLR 37.

Excess Most insurance policies provide that the recoverable indemnity is to be only for "each and every claim" in excess of a particular sum, so that the insured will have to bear that sum. In the case of public liability policies, if more than one third party makes a claim for damages against the insured or there is more than one occurrence of damage, the question arises as to whether the excess will apply to each claim. Policies often contain "aggregation" provisions designed to limit the application of the excess where there is a "unifying factor" common to a number of claims. In *Trollope & Colls Ltd Haydon* [1977] 1 Lloyd's Rep. 244, an excess was held to apply to one comprehensive claim in respect of each house suffering defects and not to each claim in respect of each defect.

Excess spoil Surplus material arising from excavation works, usually because ground materials expand with air when excavated.

Exclusion clause A contractual provision, also known as an exemption clause, purporting to exclude liability wholly or in part, or a device having similar effect. This may be achieved by expressly stating that a party has no liability, or limited liability, for breach of a term or terms, or by defining a party's obligations in such a way as to prevent a liability from arising. Exclusion clauses are construed strictly at common law. ■ See also the Unfair Contract Terms Act 1978 and the **Test of reasonableness**.

Execution against goods The seizure (a bailiff or High Court sheriff) of the property of the defendant by a certified officer of the court on the instructions of a judgment creditor in order to secure and sell assets equal in value to the sum owed, following the issue of appropriate warrant from the court. ■ See **Judgment**.

Executory contract A contract under which something remains to be done by either party.

Exemplary damages Damages awarded to a claimant in circumstances where his or her loss has been caused or aggravated by malice or other wrongful conduct on the part of the defendant, to mark the court's disapproval of that conduct. Exemplary damages may exceed the actual loss sustained by the claimant but are only awarded in exceptional circumstances. This is unlikely to arise in a construction case.

Exemption clause See **Exclusion clause**.

Exhibit (1) A document referred to in an **affidavit** or **witness statement** and identified as such on its face. (2) A document or other evidence produced to and identified during the course of a hearing.

Expanded polystyrene (EPS) An air-expanded plastic material which is commonly used to wrap or protect goods from damage in transit and storage; it is also used in insulated plasterboards and extrusions.

Expanded PVC PVC (polyvinyl chloride) is a plastic compound most often in sheet form where it is used for piping and insulation. When used in foam form, it is used for packaging and moulding as it is extremely light yet strong.

Expansion joint (EJ) A small gap in construction (eg in a concrete floor or brick wall) to allow for thermal expansion without damage to the structure. Also found in pipework and ductwork.

Expedition Promptness, dispatch. Sometimes combined with "diligence" in a contractual term relating to progress, as in *GLC v Cleveland Bridge & Engineering Co Ltd* (1984) 34 BLR 50 (CA), where it was said that what is due diligence and expedition depends on the object which is sought to be achieved.

Expense Most commonly used in the phrase **direct loss and/or expense**. It is likely that "expense" on its own would be given a restricted meaning limited to costs actually incurred.

Expert See **Expert determination and Expert witness**.

Expert determination A long established form of **ADR** whereby the parties submit a technical dispute to be decided by an independent expert. It is most commonly used to settle disputes as to rent reviews under leases or the value of shares to be bought and sold. Until the decision of the House of Lords in *Arenson v Arenson* [1977] AC 405, it was thought that such experts were immune from any liability for negligence because they were performing a function of an arbitral or quasi-judicial character. In *Baber v Kenwood* [1978] 1 Lloyd's Rep 175, 179, where Megaw LJ said:

> "The parties desire a measure of certainty and by the words which they have used in their contract they seek to obtain it. They accept the risk, which applies equally either way, than expert may err; but they prefer to accept the risk rather than the alternative whereby either party would have the right to create the delay, the expense and, to be frank, the uncertainty of proceedings in Court, by the allegation that the expert has erred."

Knox J in *Nikko Hotels (UK) Ltd v MEPC plc* [1991] 2 EGLR 103, 108 said that if the expert had answered the right question in the wrong way, his decision would be binding, but that if he had answered the wrong question, his decision would be a nullity.

Expert witness In practically all construction cases, expert evidence will be required to assist the judge in understanding technical facts and providing opinion regarding matters about which he could not form a decision unaided. No party may call an expert or put in evidence an expert's report without the court's permission: CPR 35.5. The judge may also direct that evidence is to be given by a single joint expert in an appropriate case, where: the cost of adversarial expert evidence may be prohibitive; the technical topic is a separate and self-contained part of the case; there is a subsidiary issue requiring expertise of a relatively uncontroversial nature to be resolved; or testing or analysis is required and can conveniently be done by one laboratory or firm: CPR 35.7 and para 13.4.3 of the **TCC Guide**. See **Daubert Guidelines** and **Ikarian Reefer**.

Experts' joint statement Where permission has been given for expert evidence, the court will direct the preparation and service of statements showing those issues on which the experts agree and those issues on which they disagree and a summary of their reasons for disagreeing: CPR 35.12(3). Generally, legal advisors should not be involved in either negotiating or drafting the joint statement, although they may assist in identifying the issues which should be addressed or invite the experts to consider amending a draft statement in the exceptional circumstances of serious concerns where the court may misunderstand or be misled by its terms, when such concerns should be raised with all the relevant experts: para 13.6.3 of the **TCC Guide**.

Experts' meetings Where permission has been given for expert evidence, the court will order that experts in like fields hold meetings to identify issues and where possible reach agreement, in accordance with CPR 35.12, on all issues arising in their common fields or on specified issues: CPR 35.12(1), (2). Legal advisors should not attend experts' meetings or attempt to dictate what the experts should say, although it may be helpful for them to provide assistance as to the agenda and topics to be discussed, save in exceptional circumstances and with permission of the court: **TCC Guide** para 13.5.2. The contents of the discussions between the experts must not be referred to at trial unless the parties agree, and an agreement between experts is not binding unless the parties expressly agree to be bound by it: CPR 35.12(4), (5).

Experts protocol The CPR Protocol for the Instruction of Experts to Give Evidence in Civil Claims. Drafted by Mr Justice Bean and His Honour Judge Nic Madge, and introduced in June 2005, the Experts protocol was designed to give guidance to experts and those who instruct them when they work in the civil courts.

Experts' reports Where permission has been given for expert evidence, the court will usually order disclosure of experts' reports by exchange and filing on specific dates. The contents of an expert's report must comply with the relevant practice direction and end with a statement that the expert understands his or her duty to the court and that he or she has complied with that duty: CPR Practice Direction 35, CPR 35.10(1), (2). Although the detailed contents and format of his or her report is a matter for the expert, the instructing party may indicate that the report should: be as short as reasonably possible; not set out copious extracts from other documents; identify the source of any opinion or data relied upon and not to file any annex or exhibit more than is reasonably necessary to support the opinions expressed in the report: **TCC Guide** para 13.7.2, CPR 35.10(3). Legal advisors may also invite experts to consider amendments to their reports to ensure accuracy, internal consistency, completeness, relevance to the issues or clarity: **TCC Guide** para 13.7.2, CPR Expert protocol 15.2.

Exposed aggregate finish A surface finish (often on the face of walls or flooring) where small aggregate has been added to the mortar mix and exposed either by being applied to the surface while the concrete is wet (pebble dash being the classic example) or by the surface being rubbed or washed to expose the aggregate beneath.

Expressio eorum quae tacite instunt nihil operator Latin: "the express mention of those things which are implied operates nothing", a maxim of construction preventing an express term having a different effect to that had it simply been implied.

Expressio unius est exclusio alterius Latin: "the express mention of one thing implies the exclusion of another", a canon of construction which, although often criticised, is still frequently applied. In *London Borough of Dagenham & Barking v Terrapin Construction Ltd* [2000] BLR 479 (CA), it was held that the fact that one sub-clause in a clause dealing with the effect of the final certificate referred to "design" as a separate and additional category of contractual requirement (distinct from "works" and "materials") strongly suggested that a reference in another sub-clause to only the latter two contractual requirements and the omission of "design" was deliberate and reflected the intention of the parties.

Express terms Terms which have been specifically agreed, either orally or in writing, to be contrasted with **implied terms**.

Extended preliminaries The application of the time-based preliminary rates over a longer period of time than the contract originally intended, in cases of contract overrun or extension of time. ■ See **Preliminaries**.

Extended price The total price of work or goods calculated by multiplying the quantity by the unit price.

Extension of time (EOT) A formal increase under express provisions of a construction contract of the period within which a contractor is obliged to complete works. The provisions will usually require the employer or his architect or contract administrator to grant the extension. An extension

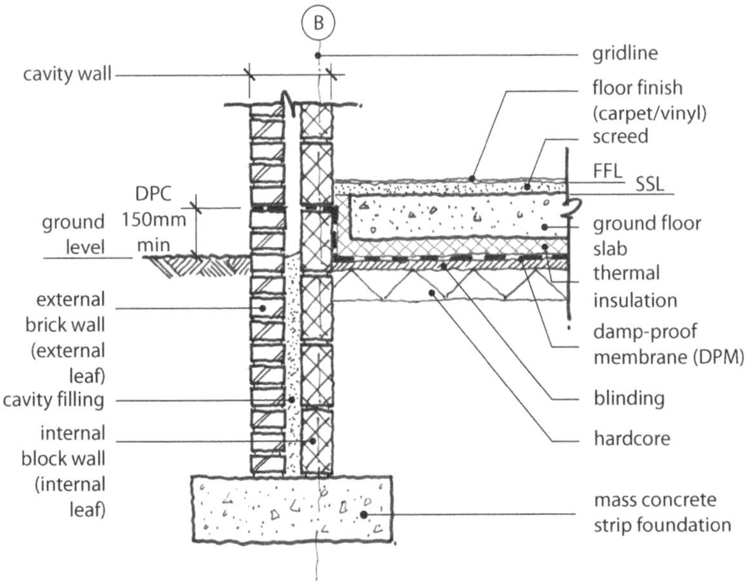

➤ **Figure E3.** External wall detail (section)

of time serves two purposes: first, that of relieving the contractor from the threat of a claim by the employer for damages (usually liquidated) for breach of contract in failing to complete by the original completion date and, secondly, that of preserving a contractual completion date by which the contractor will be bound to complete which might otherwise be lost (see **Time at large**). The grounds upon which an extension may be granted usually include matters beyond the control of either party, such as adverse weather conditions, and acts of prevention by the employer or his agents, such as a failure to provide design information timeously. The granting of an extension of time does not usually by itself entitle a contractor to recover loss and expense.

Exterior plywood Plywood that has been formed or treated specifically for outside use to resist the effects of damp and cold.

External insulation Thermal insulation installed in the cavity of an external wall. May be incorporated as the wall is constructed or injected subsequently through holes drilled into the brickwork.

External leaf The outer wall in cavity wall construction. Usually in brickwork but may also be blockwork and cladding. ➤ **Figure E3**.

External wall Wall which forms the vertical outer skin of a building, particularly of a cavity wall. May include cladding, vertical tiling or other external finishes. ➤ **Figure E3**

External works Works constructed outside the building but within the project site, including steps, driveways, paving lighting, landscaping and boundary walls and fences.

Extra contractual Outside the ambit of any contract between the parties.

Extra over An additional rate or item in a bill of quantities for a further aspect of work under other rates or items.

Extra work, extras Work not expressly or impliedly included in a lump sum price. Entitlement to payment for such work will depend on the circumstances, including express contractual terms permitting variations, any instructions for such work and compliance with any notice requirements. ■ See **Inclusive price principle** and **Variation**.

Extractor fan Fan for removing air smoke odours or vapour from a confined space. Often mounted through external walls, or as part of air extraction through ductwork system.

Extrinsic evidence Evidence relating to a contract or document but not contained within it. ■ See **Parol evidence rule**.

Extruded brick Brick formed by forcing clay and water mix through a shaping block to create a length which is then cut into individual bricks. This technique enables bricks with holes along their length to be made and is often used for structural bricks combining light weight with strength.

Extruded section Extrusion is a process by which construction material (eg concrete, plastics and aluminium) is forced through a shaping block to create a component with a cross-section which incorporates shaped perforations.

Eyebar A solid metal bar with holes at either end.

F

Fabric The main structure or framework of a building including the walls, floors and roof. Also known as the **carcass**.

Fabrication The process of constructing components, such as steel connections, before delivery to site.

Fabrication drawings Drawings showing details and dimensions for fabrication work, usually produced by a subcontractor.

Fabric reinforcement Welded mesh made from steel rods used to reinforce concrete construction. Usually manufactured, cut or bent to suit particular requirements identified by **engineer/designer**. ■ See **Rebar**.

Façade An architectural term for the external face of a building.

Façade retention Maintaining the outer walls of an existing building to preserve its external appearance. Can be a requirement of planning permission when the interior is to be demolished and rebuilt. Usually requires extensive propping or shoring with scaffolding and/or a steel framework.

Face bedding An arrangement in stone wall construction where the natural layers of the stone are laid vertically with the topmost bed forming the external surface of the wall. This tends to result in extensive flaking and scaling of the stone.

Face mark A mark to identify the external face of stonework or timber for the benefit of the craftsman installing it.

Facework Material on the external face of a constructed wall, sometimes decorative, for example, tiling, **Ashlar**.

Facilitative mediation An approach to mediation, where the mediator is there to assist the parties in reaching a mutually agreeable resolution. A facilitative mediator will not make recommendations to the parties, or give an opinion as to the outcome of the case.

Facilities management (FM) The organisation and maintenance of building services in large commercial and public buildings including building repairs, operation of heating, lighting, air conditioning and security systems and services such as gas and electricity. Sometimes these management services are outsourced to specialist companies.

Facility The end product to be provided in a project, such as an oil refinery.

Facing brick Brick which will be visible once construction is completed, and accordingly may be finished to a higher quality and may be textured or coloured. Sometimes only one face of the brick receives this treatment. Choice of facing brick frequently specified by **designer**. ■ See **Common brickwork**.

Fact An event which has taken place or a matter which has existed or does exist. Fact needs to be distinguished from law in relation to certain rights of appeal, such as that under the Arbitration Act 1996. In relation to misrepresentation, a statement of fact has a different consequence from that of a promise. ■ See **Misrepresentation** and **Point of law**.

Factor of safety (FS) An allowance made in a structural design, being the ratio between the ultimate stress in a member or structure and the safe permissible stress in it.

Factory Acceptance Test (FAT) Tests performed at a supplier's workshop or factory to confirm and verify the performance and functionality of equipment.

Fact sensitive Depending on the circumstances.

Factual matrix In *Prenn v Simmonds* [1971] 1 WLR 1381, 1384; [1971] 3 All ER 237, Lord Wilberforce coined the phrase "matrix of fact" to describe background which the court was entitled to take into account in undertaking the task of interpreting written contracts. In ***Investors Compensation Scheme v West Bromwich Building Society*** [1998] 1 WLR 896; [1998] 1 All ER 98, Lord Hoffman said:

> "... this phrase is, if anything, an understated description of what the background may include. Subject to the requirement that it should have been reasonably available to the parties and to the exception to be mentioned next, it includes absolutely anything which would have affected the way in which the language of the document would have been understood by a reasonable man."

He pointed out, however, in *BCCI v Ali* [2001] AC 251:

> "I did not think it necessary to emphasise that I meant anything which a reasonable man would have regarded as *relevant*. I was merely saying that there is no conceptual limit to what can be regarded as background. It is not, for example, confined to the factual background but can include the state of the law (as in cases in which one takes into account that the parties are unlikely to have intended to agree to something unlawful or legally ineffective) or proved common assumptions which were in fact quite mistaken. But the primary source for understanding what the parties meant is their language interpreted in accordance with conventional usage: 'we do not easily accept that people have made linguistic mistakes, particularly in formal documents'. I was certainly not encouraging a trawl through 'background' which could not have made a reasonable person think that the parties must have departed from conventional usage."

Failure to complete A failure by the contractor to complete the works or a section by the relevant completion date, resulting in the issue of a **certificate of non-completion**.

Fair-face(d) concrete Concrete specified in such a manner that its finish is usually acceptable once the formwork is struck. Often requires a more detailed specification to obtain a smooth textured or decorative finish. Used in engineering projects where large areas of concrete remain exposed as design features.

Fair valuation A basis for valuation often provided for in express contractual terms relating to varied work in circumstances where other contractual rates are inapplicable. In the absence of special circumstances, a fair valuation should include an element of profit and an element to cover the contribution the contractor makes towards fixed or running overheads: *Weldon Plant Ltd v Commission for New Towns* [2000] BLR 496; [2001] 1 All ER (Comm) 264. ■ See also ***Henry Boot Construction Ltd v Alstom Combined Cycles Ltd*** [2000] BLR 247 (CA).

Fall A downward slope or drop to allow water to run away.

Fall pipe See **Downpipe**.

Falsa demonstratio non nocet cum de corpore constat Latin: "A false description does not vitiate when the gist is evident", a canon of construction whereby an obviously incorrect part of a description will be dispensed with.

False attribution The public and wrongful crediting of a design to another person or organisation. A designer has a right not to have authorship falsely attributed to another under s84(1)(a) of the Copyright Act 1988. The designer may waive his rights in writing in an instrument signed by him.

False ceiling A ceiling constructed at a level lower than the underside of the floor above, often in commercial premises. Normally made from light weight tiles resting in metal gridwork suspended from wires or hangers fixed to the structure of the floor above. May be constructed at lower level to enhance appearance of room or to improve acoustics or insulation or to accommodate services above including lighting and air conditioning. Also known as a drop(ped) or suspended ceiling.

Fan coil unit A small element of mechanical plant typically installed in the ceiling which provides hot or cold air, produced by heated or chilled water passing through coils, to the ceiling diffusers. Allows the user to maintain control over the conditions localised area. In cooling mode may also dehumidify the air. Usually operated by thermostat.

Fascia, fascia board A board fixed to the eaves or edge of the roof rafters and fixed to them. Usually carries the gutter.

Fast track County Court procedure which directs the pre-trial stages for cases allocated to it. These are medium size cases where the sum claimed does not exceed £25,000, and the trial is not likely to last more than a day, but also includes non-monetary claims for injunctions or declarations which are too complex for the **Small claims track** but do not justify the extensive preparation allowed within the multi-track. This track is termed "fast" as the intention is that the trial date will be fixed for 30 weeks from the date the case is allocated, and generally only one case management conference is held. The costs recoverable in a fast track trial are limited. The procedure is not suitable for the vast majority of construction cases and Technology and Construction Court cases are automatically allocated to the **multi-track**. ■ See **Allocation Questionnaire**, **Multi-track** and **Small claims track**.

FAT See **Factory Acceptance Test**.

Feasibility study A study carried out at the very beginning of any project to establish the strengths and weaknesses of the proposed scheme and to determine whether or not to proceed. Analyses the brief against a proposed site. **RIBA work stage**.

Federated models A **Level 2 BIM** term which refers to several individual yet interlinked computer models, rather than one model which holds all of the project's information.

Federation Internationale des Ingenieurs-Conseils (FIDIC) The International Federation of Consulting Engineers, most noted for its preparation of the FIDIC standard forms of international engineering contract, favoured by the World Bank and Multilateral Development Banks.

Federation of Master Builders (FMB) Established in 1941 to protect the interests of small and medium-sized building firms. The FMB is now the largest trade organisation in the building sector in the United Kingdom.

FEED See **Front End Engineering Design.**

Feed In Tariff (FIT) An incentive to promote investment in renewable energy. The FIT is an amount of money (paid pursuant to a long-term) contract which is paid by a government or utility provider for renewable low-carbon energy produced by small-scale users.

Feedback loop The means by which readings from equipment controlled by a computerised system (eg temperature sensors recording the effects of a heating system) report back to the controller unit and modify its operation (eg by reducing the heat output).

Feltwork Material made of interwoven fibres, used for flat roofing when treated with asphalt.

Fenestration The arrangement of windows and other openings in a wall or building.

Ferroconcrete Concrete reinforced with iron or steel.

Ferrule Metal or plastic cap or ring fastened at end of a tube, cable or length of wood to seal or protect it, or hold the end together.

FFE Movable furniture, fixtures or other equipment that have no permanent connection to the structure of a building or utilities.

FFL See **Finished floor level.**

Fibreboard A lightweight composite material made of wood fibres compressed under heat and bound by formaldehyde resins or vegetable starch. Manufactured in sheets in a range of densities but can also easily be moulded during manufacture. Widely used in furniture and internal fittings with a covering veneer.

Fibre cement board Composite material made from cement and sand with cellulose fibres. Normally supplied in sheets and used in external cladding, acoustic protection and under tiling. It is water and fire resistant and can be painted or rendered but thinner sheets can be damaged by impact.

Fibreglass Material composed of glass formed into fine fibres by heating silica (usually with additives to provide specific characteristics) to high temperature and then drawing out into thin strands. Light weight and fire resistant and used in insulation, packaging and reinforcement of building materials, particularly glass reinforced plastic.

Fibre-reinforced concrete (FRC) Concrete with the addition of a small percentage of fibrous material (glass, plastic, steel or natural fibres). The effects on the concrete depend upon the fibre material, and more than one type may be added: steel provides additional tensile strength; glass reduces cracking due to shrinkage, added impact and abrasion strength and reduces damage caused by fire. Often used in cladding panels.

Fibre saturation point The point at which free water in timber has been removed in the process of drying or seasoning (generally where about 25–30 per cent of the water content remains) and the strength and dimensions of the timber now remain constant. Up to this point, shrinkage will have not occurred since the wood continues to hold water in its cell wall structure. The timber requires to be dried further in order to be classed as seasoned.

Fibrous plaster Plaster reinforced with the addition of fibres (often natural materials such as horsehair, hemp or textile mesh) to bind the material. Used for mouldings and castings, cornices, dados and other applications where strength is required.

FIDIC See **Federation Internationale des Ingenieurs-Conseils.**

FIDIC forms of contract The standard forms of international engineering contracts prepared and published by FIDIC, originally based on the English ICE standard forms, but subsequently revised and expanded. The "rainbow" suite of forms was introduced in 1999 comprising the **Red Book** for construction where the employer does the design, the **Yellow Book** for plant and design-build, the **Silver Book** for EPC/Turnkey projects and a short form of contract (the **Green Book**). These were followed in 2005 by the **Pink Book** for use on projects funded by the Multilateral Development Banks and by the **Gold Book** to design, build and operate projects in 2008.

Fiduciary interest An interest subject to a duty of good faith, as in the case of a trustee or a director of a company. The expression has been used for many years in JCT standard forms to describe the Employer's interest in **retention monies**. A number of decisions suggest that the contractual provisions create a trust of the monies in the hands of the Employer, although there is some doubt that it would be valid in the cases of the Employer's insolvency in the light of the decision in *British Eagle International Airlines Ltd v Compagnie Nationale Air France* [1975] 1 WLR 758 (HL); [1975] 2 All ER 390.

Fieri facias Latin: "that you cause to be made", a writ of execution being the mode of execution of a money judgment by the seizure and sale of the debtor's goods and chattels sufficient to satisfy the judgment debt and costs of the execution: see the *White Book Civil Procedure Service* 2011, para sc46.1.2.

Fi fa See **Fieri facias.**

Final account A final statement of the sum due to the contractor under a construction contract setting out the calculations by which the total sum has been arrived at. Subject to the express contractual provisions, a draft account will usually be prepared by the contractor, which will then be submitted to the employer's construction professionals, who will then produce the final account. The final account will then usually form the basis of a **final certificate** or **final statement**.

Final certificate A document issued by the employer's construction professional following the preparation of a **final account** stating out any final balance due to the contractor (or the employer) under a construction contract. Certain consequences can attach to the use of the words "final certificate". Express provisions, particularly in the JCT standard forms of contract, have for many years stated that a final certificate is to be "**conclusive evidence**" of various matters, including quality of workmanship and materials, extensions of time and **direct loss and/or expense**. Because the provisions have been revised from time to time, it is unwise to draw any general conclusions from the decisions, other than that the contractual procedures leading to the issue of a final certificate must be observed closely: *Cantrell v Wright & Fuller Ltd* [2003] EWHC 1545 (TCC); [2003] BLR 412.

Final completion A term used in the **NEC** form of contract to describe when the contractor has carried out all the work he is required to do including remedying defects about which he has been notified and handing over any as-built documentation, (eg any **operation and maintenance manuals**) that he is required to produce.

Final statement A document issued by the employer or his agent following the preparation of a **final account** stating out any final balance due to the contractor (or the employer) under a construction contract, usually in the case of a design and build contract where there is no provision for a **final certificate**.

Finance charges Loss of interest on working capital recoverable as **direct loss and/or expense** on a compound basis under the JCT forms: *Rees & Kirby Ltd v Swansea Corp* (1985) 30 BLR 1.

Fine aggregate A granular material (typically of crushed stone or gravel or natural sand) which forms one of the essential components of plaster, mortar and concrete in order to give it compression strength and cohesion. Fine is the designation given to the smaller aggregate sizes equal to or less than an upper (D) sieve size. See the European Standard BS EN 13139. ■ See **Aggregate**.

Finger plate A metal plate on a door, sometimes decorative. Also known as a door plate or **push plate**.

Finished floor level (FFL) The level of the finished floor surface, where a raised floor is installed, this includes the carpet or other floor finishes. ■ See **Structural slab level** and **Figure E3**.

Finishing coat The final layer of paint or plaster.

Finish-to-finish relationship See **Relationship**.

Finish-to-start relationship See **Relationship**.

Fire Although the general rule is that the destruction of works by fire would not excuse a contractor from performance on the grounds of frustration, construction contracts invariably provide for the insurance of the works and the effect of such provision is a question of construction. Under the current JCT standard forms, the employer has no claim for compensation against the contractor. All he can do is insist that the contractor must proceed with due diligence to carry out the reinstatement work and must authorise the release to him of the insurance monies. The contractor has no claim for compensation against the employer. All he can do is insist that the employer must use the insurance monies for payment of the cost of carrying out the reinstatement work. It makes no difference whether the fire was caused by the negligence of the contractor or one of his sub contractors or of the employer or of some third party for whose acts or omissions neither of the parties to the contract is responsible. The ordinary rules for the payment of compensation for negligence and for breach of contract have been eliminated. Whatever the cause of the fire, the obligation of the contractor is to carry out such work as is needed to put the matter right. His obligation is to restore the fire damage at his own cost, except in so far as the cost of doing so is met by sums recovered under the joint names insurance policy: *Co-operative Retail Services v Taylor Young Partnership* [2002] UKHL 17; [2002] Lloyd's Rep IR 555; [2002] 1 WLR 1419.

Fire damper Product used as passive fire protection aid, in ventilation and air conditioning (HVAC) ducts to inhibit the spread of fire inside the ductwork through fire-resistance rated walls and floors. Smoke dampers are similar to fire dampers and also prevent the spread of smoke inside the ducts. When there is an increase in temperature, the fire damper shuts, usually by a thermal element which melts at temperatures higher than ambient but low enough to indicate the presence of a fire, allowing springs to close the damper blades.

Fire protection A covering (cementious spray or board or intumescent paint) applied to structural steelwork to prevent rapid catastrophic failure during a fire.

Fire stopping Fire barriers installed within the construction of a building, such as brick walls across roof spaces.

Firm price A synonym for **fixed price**.

Firring piece A long thin strip of timber or metal used to support something else. One example: a long wedge often made of timber, tapered at one end and fixed on top of roof joists to create the fall on a flat roof. Used to pack out or support another material or building component.

First fix or fixing The first part of an M&E installation which involves the fixing of conduit back boxes and other similar M&E products in the ceiling voids and on wall partitions. Partitions are then installed, following which the **Second fix** occurs.

Fishing expedition Term used to describe the attempt by one party to seek disclosure in a particularly wide manner in the hope that something useful may emerge to assist the case. See *Gwelhayl Ltd v Midas Construction Ltd* [2008] EWHC 2316 (TCC); 123 ConLR 91.

Fitness for habitation A standard of quality applicable to works to be used as a dwelling by virtue of express or implied terms of a contract or statutory duty. A promise to construct a dwelling carries with it a threefold implication that the builder will do his work in a good and workmanlike manner; that he will supply good and proper materials; and that it will be reasonably fit for human habitation. The implication arises in law and is most notably summarised in *Hancock v Brazier* [1966] 1 WLR 1317 (CA); [1966] 2 All ER 901. A person who takes on work for, or in connection with, the provision of a dwelling owes a statutory duty to ensure that the work is done in a workmanlike or, as the case may be, professional manner, with proper materials and so that, as regards to that work, the dwelling, when completed, will be fit for human habitation: Defective Premises Act 1972, s1. General guidance was given in *Bole v Huntsbuild Ltd* [2009] EWCA Civ 1146; 127 ConLR 154 as follows: (1) The finding of unfitness for habitation when built is a matter of fact in each case. (2) Unfitness for habitation extends to "defects of quality" rendering the dwelling unsuitable for its purpose as well as to "dangerous defects". (3) Unfitness for habitation relates to defects rendering the dwelling dangerous or unsuitable for its purpose and not to minor defects. (4) Such a defect in one part of the dwelling may render the dwelling unsuitable for its purpose and therefore unfit for habitation as a dwelling house even if the defect does not apply to other parts of the dwelling. (5) The Act will apply to such defects even if the effects of the defect were not evident at the time when the dwelling was completed. (6) In considering whether or not a dwelling is unfit for habitation as built, one must consider the effect of the defects as a whole.

Fitness for purpose A standard of quality of goods and materials and the completed works themselves which can be the subject of express or implied terms in construction contracts. Where the employer expressly or by implication makes known to the contractor any particular purpose for which goods the property in which is being transferred to the employer under the construction contract, there is an implied condition that the goods are reasonably fit for that purpose: Supply of Goods and Services Act 1982, s4. There is no implied term in a construction contract that the site is fit for the works: *Appleby v Myers* [1867] LR 2 CP 651. Fitness for purpose is not usually implied into a contract under which a design is to be prepared by a construction professional, although it can arise from the particular facts: *Greaves v Baynham Meikle* [1975] 2 Lloyd's Rep 325; [1975] 1 WLR 1095 (CA); [1975] 3 All ER 99.

Fixed charge A form of security over specific assets which can only be sold, transferred or otherwise dealt with, with the consent of the creditor.

Fixed light A window which cannot be opened.

Fixed overheads See **Head office overheads**.

Fixed price Usually, a contract price which will not vary as a result in fluctuations in the costs of materials or labour. Also used as a synonym for **lump sum**.

Fixing strip Usually a metal or plastic strip used for fitting coverings to walls.

Flange (1) A projecting steel plate to simplify the bolting of steelwork or pipework. (2) The bottom and top plates of a structural beam or column. ➤ **Figure U1**.

Flank wall A side wall of a building.

Flashing Copper, lead or tin in sheet form dressed over joints between roof coverings and other surfaces to prevent water penetration.

Flat roof A roof with a slope of less than 10° but a fall of at least 1 in 60.

Flaunching Cement mortar fillet on top of a chimney stack at the base of the pot to hold the chimney in place.

Flemish Bond A pattern of bricklaying where stretcher and header bricks alternate in each course. The bond can be built in bricks of two colours to provide a decorative pattern. To be contrasted with **English bond**. ➤ **Figure B3.**

Fletton The most common and cheapest type of brick made of Oxford clay originally from a residential area of Peterborough. The area gave its name to the Fletton Brick Company and to Fletton Brick in the nineteenth century. Fletton bricks are a fairly soft brick and porous to a certain extent. This means they are not frost resistant and cannot be used as a finishing brick.

Float A period or periods include within a contractor's tender programme to cover any additional time available for a particular activity or the whole project. The question naturally arises as to whether the contractor is entitled to an extension of time which preserves this "float". Under the JCT conditions if an architect is required to form an opinion then, if there is then unused float for the benefit of the contractor (and not for another reason such as to deal with **prime cost** or **provisional sums** or items), then the architect is bound to take it into account since an extension is only to be granted if completion would otherwise be delayed beyond the then current completion date. This may seem hard to a contractor but the objects of an extension of time clause are to avoid the contractor being liable for liquidated damages where there has been delay for which he is not responsible, and still to establish a new completion date to which the contractor should work so that both the employer and the contractor know where they stand. The architect should in such circumstances inform the contractor that, if thereafter events occur for which an extension of time cannot be granted, and if, as a result, the contractor would be liable for liquidated damages then an appropriate extension, not exceeding the float, would be given. In that way the purposes of the clause can be met: the date for completion is always known; the position on liquidated damages is clear; yet the contractor is not deprived permanently of "his" float: *Royal Brompton Hospital NHS Trust v Hammond* [2002] EWHC 2037 (TCC).

Floating charge A form of security over general assets, such as stock, finished or raw material, work in progress or fixtures and fittings, that may change over time or be converted into a **fixed charge**.

Floating floor An acoustic floor. A floor constructed or laid above the structural floor with an energy absorbing material to reduce sound transmission.

Floor box A terminal in the floor with sockets for power, data and telephone connections.

Fluctuations clause A contractual provision to reflect changes in the costs of materials or labour by varying the contract price, also known as a "variation of price", "variation in cost", "rise and fall" or "cost adjustment" clause. UK standard forms tend to use formulae based on indices of prices: see **JCT 2011**, Schedule 7 and ICE Special Condition 72.

Flush A surface in one plane, as in a flush door with no indented panels.

FOIA The Freedom of Information Act 2000

Footing A foundation to a wall.

Forbearance The abstention from or postponement of the enforcement of a legal right, particularly a debt, which can provide consideration for an agreement to pay a lesser sum.

Force majeure A term from the *Code Napoléon* and used in construction contracts, particularly the JCT forms, as a ground for an extension of time. In *Atlantic Paper Stock Ltd v St Anne-Nackawic Pulp and Paper Co Ltd* [1976] 1 SCR 580, Dickson J in the Supreme Court of Canada said that: "An act of God or force majeure clause generally operates to discharge a contracting party when a supervening, sometimes supernatural, event, beyond the control of either party, makes performance impossible. The common thread is that of the unexpected, something beyond reasonable human foresight and skill." It appears to be designed to protect a contractor from liability for (liquidated) damages for delay in the event of his being prevented from performing the contract by circumstances beyond his control: *Hong Guan and Co Ltd v R Jumabhoy and Sons Ltd* [1960] AC 684; [1960] 2 All ER 100. The exact ambit of those circumstances would depend on the other provisions of the contract entitling the contractor to an extension of time.

Foreseeability (1) A test for the recoverability of damages in actions for breach of contract. (2) A test for liability in actions in tort. ■ See **Negligence** and **Remoteness of damage**.

Forfeiture clause A clause expressly providing for **Determination**.

Formalities Any relevant requirements as to the form of a contract, such as that of it being in writing.

Form of tender The documents sent out by an employer for completion by a contractor wishing to tender for a contract.

Formula price adjustment See **Fluctuations clause**.

Formwork Boarding erected, in the manner of a mould into which concrete is poured, to improve its finish. Also known as **shuttering**.

Forum shopping The practice of seeking to make claims in alternative jurisdictions or before alternative tribunals on the basis of perceived tactical advantage. It is highly discouraged by the courts, see *Lanes Group plc v Galliford Try Infrastructure Ltd* [2011] EWCA Civ 1617, although there is nothing to prevent adjudication taking place at the same time as litigation between the same parties in respect of the same issues: *Herschel Engineering Ltd v Breen Pty Ltd* [2000] BLR 272.

Fossils A mineralised relic of an animal or plant, the discovery of which on a construction site can lead to delay while the appropriate authorities are informed and a decision made as to how to proceed. Most standard form contract make express provision in respect of such matters, such as clause 3.22–3.24 of the 2011 JCT forms, which refers to "fossils, antiquities and other objects of interest or value".

Foundation An object placed in position on or in the ground in the course of constructing a building, or for the purpose of a building which is being constructed, the function of which is to provide support for that building so that it in fact transmits load to the material beneath: *Worlock v SAWS* (1981) 20 BLR 94. The main types of foundations are shallow strip or pads, raft and piled.

Fragnets Fragments of a **CPM** network. Individual delay events are identified retrospectively and a fragnet is created to represent those events. The fragnet will then show the original planned programme intended f or that element of the work. By preparing a similar fragnet setting out the actual as-built progress in respect of the same element of the work, the affect of the chosen delay event on the work can be demonstrated. See *ERDC Group Ltd v Brunel University* [2006] EWHC 687 (TCC); [2006] BLR 255.

Framework Agreement An agreement with suppliers of goods or services which establishes the terms governing any contract for the supply of goods and services that may be awarded in the period during which the framework agreement applies. ■ See **Call off contract**.

Fraudulent Misrepresentation A false representation made knowingly or without belief in its truth or recklessly, careless whether it be true or false: *Derry v Peek* [1889] 14 AC 337.

Freeboard bridge Often used to cross rivers. The bridge deck or surface will need to be constructed at a height above the potential flood level.

Free float The amount of time an activity can be delayed before affecting a successor activity and thereby possibly reducing the **Total float**.

Freezing injunction An interim court remedy in the form of an injunction restraining a party from removing from the jurisdiction assets located there, or restraining a party from dealing with any assets, whether located within the jurisdiction or not. See r25.1 of the CPR. Such an injunction was previously known as a **Mareva injunction**.

Frieze (1) Part of the entablature between the architrave and cornice. See **Figure A5**; (2) Any ornamented horizontal band in a building.

Frog An indentation, traditionally v-shaped, on one side of a brick. The frog reduces the weight of the brick. The frog should be laid uppermost to ensure that the loading of the wall is evenly spread across its width, rather than being concentrated onto the edges.

Front End Engineering Design (FEED) Basic engineering design which is conducted at the outset of a project, usually after completion of the **feasibility study**. The idea is to define and/or develop the management systems and specific project plans to be employed during the execution of the project. This can include consideration of technical concepts, project standards, common functional design criteria and generic equipment specifications.

Front loading The practice of pricing a tender in such a way that the contractor's return will be greater on those items of work carried out early in the project, so as to ensure an optimum cash flow at that point.

Frustration A doctrine whereby the law recognises that without default of either party a contractual obligation has become incapable of being performed because of the circumstances in which performance is called for would render a thing radically different from that which was undertaken by the contract: "It was not this that I promised to do": *Davis Contractors Ltd v Fareham UDC* [1956] AC 696. An example in the construction field is the debris of a 13-storey block being carried onto a construction site by a landslip, obliterating partly completed works and causing 67 deaths: *Wong Lai Ying v Chinachem Investment Ltd* (1979) 13 BLR 86 (PC).

Full planning permission An application for full or detailed planning permission must be made under s62 of the Town and Country Planning Act 1990 (as amended), for any development which includes building, engineering or other works, in, on, over or under land, or the making of any material change in the use of any buildings or other land. Full planning permission is not usually required for works which can be classed as maintenance, improvements or other alterations inside the building, or which do not "materially affect" the way the outside of the building looks.

Functus officio Latin: "discharged from the office or duty", and therefore unable to act further in that capacity. It has been held that an architect under a JCT 1963 standard form is functus officio after issuing the final certificate: *H Fairweather Ltd v Asden Securities Ltd* (1979) 12 BLR 40.

Fundamental breach A doctrine developed in particular by Lord Denning whereby it was said that a breach that went to the root of a contract would have the effect of discharging the contract in such a way as to prevent a party from relying on an exclusion clause. It was disapproved of by the House of Lords in *Photo Productions Ltd v Securicor Transport Ltd*

[1980] AC 827; [1980] 2 WLR 283; [1980] 1 All ER 556. The phrase is now limited to meaning a breach of contract which would entitle the innocent party to treat himself as discharged from further performance, a repudiatory breach.

Furring strip See **Firring piece**.

G

GA General arrangement (drawing). ➤ **Figure G3**

Gabion Container (usually in the form of wire mesh) which is filled with stone or other material used to retain ground, support embankments and prevent soil erosion.

Gable Upper part of (external) wall of building between edges of sloping roof from eaves level to ridge, usually triangular in shape.

Gable board Length of timber fixed to end of roof rafters where they extend over the gable: sometimes carved or decorated. Also known as a **bargeboard**.

Gable post Short timber post at apex of gable to provide fixing for the upper end of gable boards.

Gable roof Roof sloping on two sides extending from ridge to eaves and creating a gable at one or both ends.

Gable springer Triangular shaped brick(s) or stone(s) positioned at the top of wall as a transition from the vertical wall to the roof construction.

Gable wall That part of an external wall which forms or includes a gable.

Gaffer Foreman.

Galvanising Process of coating metal (usually steel or iron) by electroplating or hot dip with thin layer of protective metal (commonly zinc) to prevent corrosion.

Gang Group of workmen working under foreman (ganger or gaffer).

Gang form Several units of formwork fixed together (or a single large unit) to allow rapid construction of concrete elements, usually placed by crane because of weight, and are reuseable.

Gantt chart A type of bar chart developed by Henry Gantt, an American mechanical engineer and management consultant, before the First World War upon which most diagrammatic programmes for construction projects are based. See ➤ **Figure G1**.

Garnishee proceedings See **Third Party Debt Orders**.

Gas concrete Lightweight concrete produced by action of gas on concrete mixture before it hardens, usually by addition of powdered aluminium sulphate which reacts with alkaline content of cement. ■ See **Aerated concrete**.

Gas Safe Register The official list of gas engineers who are registered to work safely and legally on boilers, cookers, fires and all other gas appliances.

Gauged mortar Mortar mixed with lime to produce a softer mix with lower strength for use where some movement may occur and hard mortar would lead to cracking.

GBG See **Good Building Guides.**

GC/Works Government standard forms of contract for major government projects for both building and civil engineering, comprising ten forms of contract GC/Works/1 to 10.

GEA See **Gross external area.**

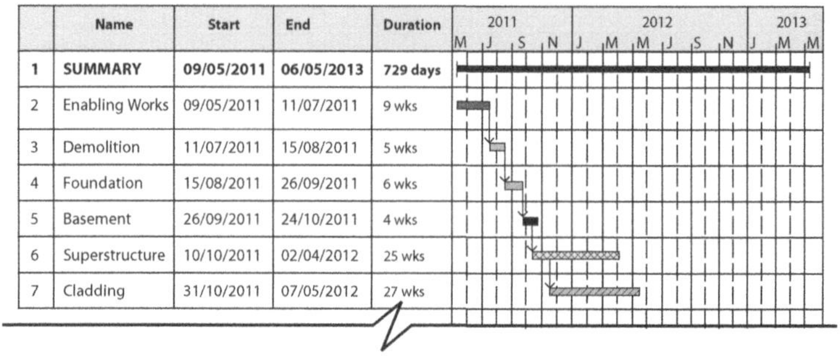

➤ **Figure G1.** Gantt Chart

General conditions Standard provisions contained in conditions of contract, bills of quantities or specifications.

General contractor A building contractor undertaking a variety of work, being a non-specialist and often employed as main contractor. The latter term is generally employed in UK standard forms of contract.

General damages Compensation awarded by a court or other tribunal for losses other than purely financial: for example, for personal injury or loss of use of a chattel. Such damages are assessed by the tribunal according to established scales or the value of property affected. ■ See **Distress and inconvenience** and **Special damages**.

General Permitted Development Order (GPDO) Statutory Order made under Planning Acts permitting defined types of development without the need to apply for planning consent: examples are modest extensions of houses (limited by volume) and addition of porches. The current Order is the Town and Country Planning (General Permitted Development) Order 1995, SI 1995/418, as amended in 2008 and 2011. The 2008 amendments take greater account of the visual impact of permitted developments and limit their dimensions. The 2011 amendments allow for the installation of a wind turbine mounted on a building.

Georgian wired glass Annealed glass containing a wire mesh usually 12.5 mm^2. In the event of breakage, the wire mesh helps to hold glass fragments together and provides limited additional security and fire resistance.

Geotechnical report A site investigation report to establish the ground conditions likely to be encountered during the course of a project, based upon borehole results, trial pits and laboratory testing.

GHG Greenhouse gas. Name given to gasses which absorb and emit infrared radiation, something which leads to the **greenhouse effect**, that is, an increased temperature.

Girder A beam made of wood, metal or reinforced concrete to provide support to a building or other structure. Cross sections include I-forms and box sections.

Girder truss A strengthened roof truss (sometimes formed by doubling a timber truss) used to support heavy loads such as perpendicular framing in hip roofs.

Glassfibre-reinforced gypsum (GRG) A composite of high density gypsum reinforced with glass fibre used for internal mouldings for ceilings and decorative elements such as columns: the use of reinforcement makes them stronger and lighter than traditional plaster mouldings.

Glassfibre-reinforced plastic, fibreglass (GRP) A plastic material such as polyester or epoxy resin combined with fine fibres of glass to produce strong lightweight panels which can easily be moulded. Fibreglass is used for boat building, septic and water storage tanks, flat roofing, pipework, insulation panels and containers.

Glass(fibre)-reinforced concrete (GRC) Concrete incorporating glass fibre as reinforcement often fabricated in laminated form. Much lighter than steel-reinforced concrete, resists corrosion and can be moulded and shaped to many applications. Used for panels for external facades.

Glazing (1) the insertion of glass into frames and hence a general term for windows or other glass panels admitting light; (2) the application of a thin colour coat or varnish to change the appearance of the substrate. Makes the surface less porous and therefore also provides protection.

Glazing bead A piece of wood plastic or metal which holds the glass in position in a window.

Glazing fillet A small piece of wood fixed to the rebate to hold glass in position.

Global claim A contractor's claim based on the inference that the difference between the contract allowance for and the actual cost of the works results from matters for which the employer is responsible, also known as a "total cost" claim. The causal connection between the matters relied upon and their consequences are thus not fully spelt out, and the term is also often used somewhat loosely to describe claims which do not identify that connection clearly. It seems likely that a true global claim could only succeed in exceptional circumstances. However, in cases where the full extent of extra costs incurred through delay depend upon a complex interaction between the consequences of various events (so that it may be difficult to make an accurate apportionment of the total extra costs), it may be proper to make individual financial awards, in respect of claims which can conveniently be dealt with in isolation, and a supplementary award in respect of the financial consequences of the remainder as a composite whole: *J Crosby & Sons Ltd v Portland UDC* (1967) 5 BLR 121; *Walter Lilly & Co Ltd v Mackay & Others* [2012] EWHC 1773 (TCC).

Glued-laminated timber Timber formed of thin sections of wood glued together under pressure to create a solid piece, often as a beam: this may have greater strength than a natural length of timber and uses timber products economically and sustainably.

Glulam An abbreviated term for **glued-laminated timber**.

GMP See **Guaranteed maximum price.**

GOCO See **Government owned, contractor operated.**

Going The depth of the tread of a staircase: ■ See **Riser**. ➤ **Figure G2**

Gold Book FIDIC conditions of contract for Design, Build and Operate Projects.

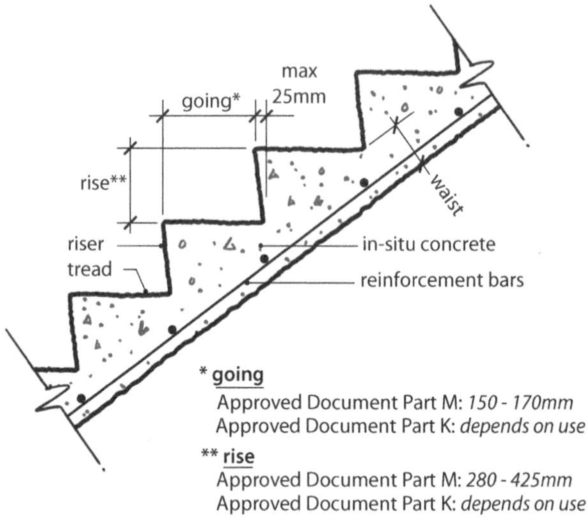

➤ **Figure G2.** Stair Detail

Golden rule The golden rule of construction of written instruments, which is that the grammatical and ordinary sense of the words is to be adhered to unless that would lead to some absurdity or some repugnance or inconsistency with the rest of the instrument, in which case the grammatical and ordinary sense of the words may be modified, so as to avoid that absurdity and inconsistency, but no further: *Grey v Pearson* 6 HLCas 61.

Good Building Guides (GBG) Guides to good building practice published by **Building Research Establishment (BRE)**.

Good faith Fair and open dealing. The law imposes a duty to act in good faith in restricted contexts, such as in the case of a party subject to a Fiduciary duty. In the field of construction contracts, an implied duty to act in good faith may arise where there is a contract to consider tenders, an express termination provision is being exercised or where a certifier or employer's representative has a discretion. An express contractual provisions requiring the parties to act in good faith has been held to impose on one of them a contractual obligation to observe reasonable commercial standards of fair dealing in accordance with his actions which related to the contract and also requiring faithfulness to the agreed common purpose and consistency with the justified expectations of the other party: *Berkeley CommunityVillages Ltd v Pullen* [2007] EWHC 1330 (Ch); [2007] 3 EGLR 101. In English law, there is no general duty of good faith, although one has been recognised in Australia, but with some caution. In contrast, most Civil Codes do impose an obligation that contracts must be performed in accordance with both the requirements of the contract and in a manner that is consistent with the requirements of good faith. See, for example, Article 246(1) of UAE Civil Code which states that: "The contract must be performed in accordance with its contents, and in a manner consistent with the requirements of good faith".

Good Practice in Selection of Construction Materials Published by the British Council for Offices and drafted by Ove Arup & Partners (Co they were then called), it provides guidance on positive practice for the selection of building materials in specifications and tenders, rather than negatively listing the exclusion of deleterious materials.

Good and workmanlike manner The traditional description of the standard of workmanship to be achieved as part of a contractor's implied obligations under a construction contract at common law. The position is now covered by s13 of the **Supply of Goods and Services Act 1982** which implies a term that the contractor will carry out the works with reasonable care and skill. A person who takes on work for, or in connection with, the provision of a dwelling owes a statutory duty to ensure that the work is done in a workmanlike or, as the case may be, professional manner, with proper materials and so that, as regards that work, the dwelling, when completed, will be fit for human habitation: Defective Premises Act 1972, s1.

Goods and materials Personal property (as opposed to real property) brought onto site for incorporation into the works. A traditional term used in standard forms, although there is no distinction in law between goods and materials: they would both be regarded as "goods".

Governing law The law chosen by the parties to an agreement to interpret the agreement and to govern disputes in relation to it. The governing law does not have to be the law of the country in which the document is signed or where the parties reside or the contract is performed, but in the absence of an express or implied stipulation otherwise it is likely to be the relevant law of the country where the contract was made.

Government owned, contractor operated (GOCO) A form of **Public Private Partnership (PPP)** procurement whereby the host government retains ownership of the site upon which the private sector contractor has constructed and operates the **Facility**.

GPDO See **General Permitted Development Order.**

Grade (1) The levelling of land or reduction to a gradient and/or the distribution of materials in this process according to their characteristics such as size (for construction of embankments or the substructure of roads). (2) The American term for a ground level at a given point. (3) The level of quality or other characteristic of a particular construction material. For example, there are different grades of concrete (now known as strength classes) such as C32/40 and C40/50, which indicate its compressive strength. Similarly, there are different grades of reinforcement bars which indicate its yield strength and ductility class. ■ See **Concrete** and **Reinforcement bar**.

GRC See **Glass fibre reinforced concrete.**

Grandfather clause A provision exempting a party from legislative changes, originating from discriminatory legislation passed in the southern United States after the Civil War, which enabled illiterate whites ("grandfathers") who had previously enjoyed the right to vote to continue to do so despite the introduction of a literacy requirement.

Grand master key A key that opens every lock within the key system. For example, a property manager may have a grand master key to access all buildings.

Granular fill Material comprising gravel, crushed concrete or stone used as fill between structures or in layers for foundations. ➤ **Figure R2.**

Graphic work Drawings diagrams and plans entitled to protection under the Copyright Act 1988 s4(1) (a).

Grass concrete Concrete blocks used for paving and walling constructed in cellular form which permits natural growth of grass in the interstices to lessen environmental impact: also used for green roofing.

Green Book (1) **FIDIC** short form of contract for engineering and building contracts of relatively small capital value. (2) **IChemE** handbook containing General Conditions of Contract for cost reimbursable contract.

Green concrete (1) Concrete that has dried but not set. (2) Pervious concrete which allows water to pass.

Greenfield site A site for building activity which has not previously been developed and remains in its natural state.

Green form The JCT nominated standard form of subcontract.

Green Guide See **Guide to Safety at Sports Grounds**.

Greenhouse effect The absorption of heat by gasses in the upper atmosphere and their radiation towards the earth leading to a rise in temperature. Solar energy heats the atmosphere and the earth's surface and is then radiated back as infra-red heat which is absorbed and returned to the earth by the greenhouse gases (chiefly water vapour and carbon dioxide). This is a natural process but its heating effects have been enhanced by increasing levels of carbon dioxide, methane and fluorocarbons in the atmosphere.

Green timber Timber which has not been seasoned.

Grid A layout of crossing lines on a plan or drawing which is used to help identify specific points and/or dimensions of, for example, either the ground just surveyed or the building to be built.

Grid line The vertical and horizontal lines of a grid. Used in plans, sections and elevations to enable building elements/components to be precisely located and set out. ➤ **Figure E3**

Gripper strip A wood or metal strip fixed to the floor around the perimeter of a room to be carpeted. It has short projecting metal teeth on the upper side which fix into the backing of the carpet and hold it stretched in position.

Groin vault Produced by the intersection of two **barrel vaults**. A "groin" or edge is formed at the intersection of the two vaults.

Gross external area (GEA) The aggregate superficial area of a building, previously known as "reduced covered area" or "gross floorspace".

Gross features Characteristics, such as knots and splits, taken into account in deciding the stress to which timber may be subjected.

Gross floor area The area of a floor measured from the inside face of the perimeter wall of the building: no deduction is made for area occupied by structure, internal walls, service risers, corridors or other non-useable space. ■ See **Net floor area**.

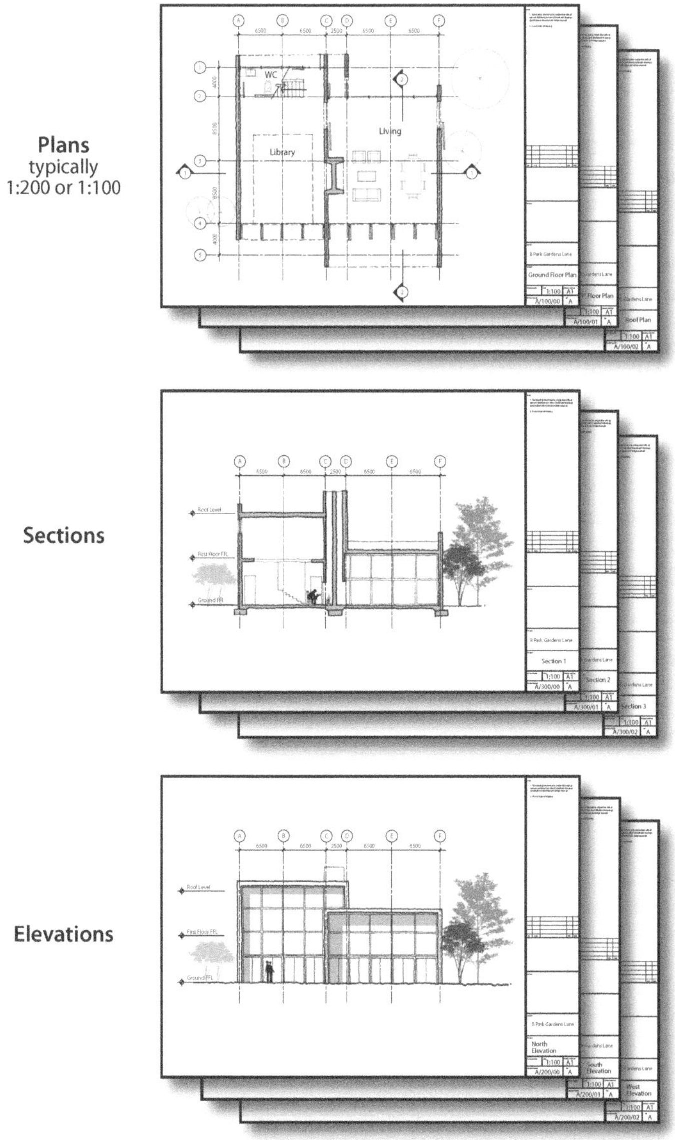

➤ **Figure G3.** General Arrangements (GAs)

Ground conditions The state of the ground at a site, particularly in relation to **Adverse physical conditions**.

Ground investigation A site investigation, often carried out at the feasibility stage of any project, to identify the **ground conditions** and any risks which either the employer or potential tenderer need to be aware of.

Ground level The natural level of the land at a specific location: its height measured by a datum such as mean sea level: the level of the ground where a building stands and a description of the floor at or about that level. ➤ **Figure R2.**

Ground plate A beam forming the lowest level of a timber frame, onto which the uprights are attached. Also known as a ground sill or sole plate. Also a metal plate placed in the ground as an earthing device.

Ground sill See **Ground plate**.

Ground slab A flat concrete construction containing steel reinforcement resting on hardcore and off which the walls of a building may be constructed. ➤ **Figure E3.**

Groundwork Excavation and construction work carried out below ground level, such as preparation for foundations and drainage trenching. Also civil engineering work such as excavation and removal of ground materials, changing ground levels and profiling ground. Often carried out by specialist contractors using heavy machinery.

Grout, grouting A mortar mix (sometimes with chemical additives or epoxy resin) with added water to enable it to fill cracks in concrete or stonework. May be pumped to fill voids around structures or to reinforce foundations. Also a plaster-based mix with added water to seal gaps around tiling or plasterwork.

Groyne Wall or jetty built on coastline or river estuary to limit erosion and encourage deposition of sand and gravel through longshore drift, but may accelerate erosion in areas not protected. Traditionally made of solid timber fencing at right angles to beach but increasingly built of imported rock and parallel to coastline. ■ See **Reef**.

GRP Glass reinforced plastic, Glass fibre-reinforced polyester

Guarantee (1) A contract of suretyship under which the surety or guarantor undertakes a secondary liability to answer for a debtor, governed by the **Statute of Frauds 1677**, s4, which requires the agreement or some memorandum or note of it to be in writing and signed by the guarantor. If, however, the surety assumes a primary liability which is not dependent on the principal debtor's failure to meet his liability, the contract will be one of indemnity, which is not covered by s4. (2) A direct contractual undertaking by a contractor or supplier to the subsequent owner of goods or works to replace or repair defects arising within a limited period after purchase or completion. ■ See **Indemnity, Parent company guarantee, Subrogation, Surety**.

Guaranteed costs contract A contract where the contractor's actual costs of labour, materials and overheads are reimbursed by the employer, usually up to a stated maximum sum. A fixed or percentage fee to provide a profit and indirect costs for the contractor is sometimes added. The open ended nature of the employer's obligation means that such contracts are only used where it is difficult to price the work in advance or the work is urgent.

Guaranteed maximum price (GMP) A contractual provision by which the contractor acknowledges that the contract price includes the full cost to him of all risks and responsibilities and that he shall not be entitled to make any claim except for certain identified exceptions such as employer's changes: see *Mowlem plc v Newton Street Ltd* [2003] EWHC 737 (TCC); 89 ConLR 153, by way of example.

Guidance notes Notes issued with standard forms of contract explaining any changes made from previous editions, the circumstances in which the form is recommended for use and the options available under the terms. Although such notes can be helpful in understanding the thinking behind the form, it is doubtful that they could be taken into account as an aid to construction of the terms.

Guide rails Metal rails fixed to building to guide and control movement of equipment such as cradles for external window cleaning and maintenance or (when fixed to floor) forklift trucks in warehouse.

Guide to Safety at Sports Grounds ("Green Guide") A guide produced by the Football Licensing Authority (FLA) for the Department of Culture Media and Sport which provides detailed design and safety management guidance for both existing and new sports grounds for architects, engineers and public authorities. The guidance is not mandatory but it sets out best practice, and UK building control departments will require compliance with its principles.

Gully, gulley A container constructed at ground level to receive water from a downpipe or surface drain and direct it into an underground drain. Also refers to channel (laid to a fall) curved or square in section to conduct water or fluids to a drain: usually made of plastic, metal, earthenware or formed in concrete: may be open or covered with a grille to permit entry of water along its length.

Gunmetal An alloy of copper, tin and zinc forming a type of bronze formerly used for making cannon and still used for castings and statues, bearings and pumps.

Gusset plate or piece A plate typically made of metal used to strengthen or connect beams to columns or other load bearing structures. Can be bolted, welded or screwed depending on the materials.

Gypsum A naturally occurring mineral (calcium sulphate) used widely for plaster and as an additive for cement. Varieties include plaster of Paris (burned gypsum) for making models and alabaster (a fine grained white gypsum) used for carvings.

Gypsum plasterboard Thin board manufactured from gypsum and widely used for internal lining of walls and ceilings. Lightweight and easily cut but damaged by damp. Glass fibres may be added to promote fire resistance. Its disposal as waste is now controlled and recycling is encouraged.

Gypsum wallboard Plasterboard made with gypsum core and reinforced paper covering on both sides treated to receive decoration: also known as drywall. Has replaced traditional lath and plaster construction for internal walls.

H

HA Highways Agency

Ha Hectare

Ha-ha A broad ditch with a brick wall on one side separating formal gardens from parkland. It provides a barrier against animals encroaching without interrupting the view.

Habitation See **Fitness for habitation**.

Hadley v Baxendale *Hadley v Baxendale* [1854] 156 ER 145, the authority establishing the underlying rule as to the recoverability of damage on the basis of a foreseeability test. Under the first limb of the rule, a claimant can recover damages for loss likely to arise in the usual course of things from the breach and under the second, he can also recover such other loss as was in the contemplation of the parties at the time of the contract as the likely result of breach. ■ See **Remoteness of damage**.

Half landing A platform within a flight of stairs at which point the stairs may change direction (usually through 90°).

Half-hour fire door A door constructed to resist the passage of fire for at least 30 minutes.

Halsey Guidelines Guidelines set out by the Court of Appeal in *Halsey v Milton Keynes General NHS Trust* [2004] EWCA Civ 576; [2004] 1 WLR 3002; [2004] 4 All ER 920, which are to be considered when considering whether or not to penalise a party in costs for refusing to mediate. ■ See **Mediation**.

Hammerhead crane A crane with a large fixed cantilevered jib which is able to revolve and is used to raise heavy loads and move them horizontally; it is constructed particularly in dockyards.

***Hancock v Brazier* terms** The three terms usually implied into a contract for the sale of a house to be erected: that the builder will do his work in a good and workmanlike manner; that he will supply good and proper materials; and that it will be reasonably fit for human habitation. See *Hancock v BW Brazier (Anerley) Ltd* [1966] 1 WLR 1317; [1966] 2 All ER 901.

Handover, handing over The passing of possession of works or a section from the contractor to the employer. Not a formal term used in contractual documents, which tend to refer to the employer "taking possession" of the works after **practical completion** or **partial possession** before that date. It is also known as **take over** or **taking over**.

Hangar A wide-span building, often used for aircraft, usually fronted by hangar doors which are mounted on rolling wheeled tracks.

Hanger A built-in or fixed steel strap holding up a horizontal member, such as a beam.

Hansard The Official Report of Debates in Parliament, which may be referred to as an aid to the construction of legislation which is ambiguous or obscure or the literal meaning of which leads to an absurdity, under the rule in *Pepper v Hart* [1993] AC 593 (HL). Even in such cases, references to Parliamentary material should only be permitted where such material clearly discloses the mischief aimed at or the legislative intention lying behind the ambiguous or obscure words.

Hard landscaping External features such as walls, paving and parking areas constructed of hard, durable materials intended to be permanent features. ■ See **Soft landscaping**.

Hardboard Flexible sheet material made from compressed wood chips and sawdust and glue.

Hardcore Material, such as stone, imported to site to be placed on soft ground to provide a base for foundations or roads. The constitution of this material is of some importance and is usually the subject of strict specification to avoid structural failure through subsidence or as a result of contamination leading to **sulphate attack**. See **Figures E3 & R2**.

Hardwood Timber, characterised by close grain and high density. Hardwood comes from a variety of trees, including Birch, Maple and Oak. Some species, such as mahogany and teak, are now scarce due to over exploitation. ■ See **Softwood**.

Haunching The concrete applied around (underground) drainage pipes. Also used to refer to the cement mortar fillet used in place of a flashing for weathering the joint between the chimney stack or a projecting wall and pitched roof.

HAZID Hazard Identification Studies. Used for projects in the early stages of design when insufficient information is available for the full-scale HAZOP.

HAZOP Hazard and Operability Studies. First used by ICI in the 1960s, HAZOP studies started to be more widely used within the chemical process industry after the Flixborough disaster in 1974. HAZOP studies are carried out by reviewing the design to identify potential hazards and operability problems usually in new (but can be in existing) process plants and similar facilities.

Head contract A synonym for main contract.

Head office overheads A contractor's general costs of running his business, such as rent, heating, lighting and the wages of support staff, which he will continue to incur during periods of delay in works which prevents him from earning profits on other projects. It is thus a recognised head of damage or **direct loss and/or expense** recoverable by a contractor who has been delayed by matters for which the employer is responsible under the terms of a construction contract. The difficulty of proving such a loss led to the proposition that a formula could be an appropriate method of assessing this damage. The first in time was the **Eichlay formula** adopted for claims under US government contracts,

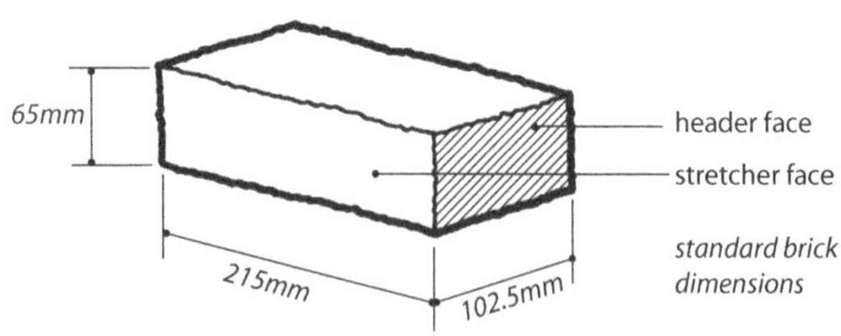

➤ **Figure H1.** Header and Stretcher

followed by the **Hudson formula** and the **Emden formula** for general application in the United Kingdom. Each approach has been subject to criticism and the current trend towards increased recoverability of management time as a head of damage may reduce their importance in the future: see *Aerospace Publishing Ltd v Thames Water Utilities Ltd* [2007] EWCA Civ 3; [2007] BLR 726 (CA); 110 ConLR 1.

Header A brick laid across a wall so that its end is visible on the elevation. See ➤ **Figure H1**

Heading bond A brickwork pattern in which all the bricks are laid such that their header face is visible.

Heading course A **course** of brickwork consisting of headers. See **English bond** and **Flemish bond** and **Figure B3**.

Headroom The ceiling clearance of a staircase, also known as stair clearance or headway.

Health and Safety at Work, etc. Act 1974 The primary legislation covering occupational health and safety in the United Kingdom. It imposes criminal liability for breaches of the legislation.

Health and Safety Executive (HSE) Whilst it places emphasis on preventing death, injury and ill-health in the workplace, the HSE is also the statutory body responsible for enforcing workplace-related health and safety law.

Health and safety file The health and safety file is prepared or revised by the **CDM co-ordinator** for **notifiable projects**. The file should contain information necessary for future construction, maintenance, refurbishment or demolition to be carried out safely and is retained by the client or any future owner of the property. ■ See **Construction (Design and Management) Regulations 2007, SI 2007/320**.

Health and safety plan The plan prepared by the **principal contractor,** for **notifiable projects**, which sets out the arrangements for managing health and safety on site during construction work. Now known as the Construction Phase Plan under the CDM regulations. ■ See **Construction (Design and Management) Regulations 2007, SI 2007/320**.

Hearsay A statement by a person giving evidence or in a document produced in evidence which refers to another statement made on another occasion and is intended to be evidence of the truth of that other statement. Generally, the statement given in evidence or in the document was not admissible as to the truth of that other statement at common law. Reforms introduced by the Civil Evidence Act 1972 and 1995 have given the tribunal, bound by the strict rules of evidence, a discretion to admit hearsay evidence. ■ See **Weight of evidence** and **Witness**.

Heat detector A type of thermostat for appliances operating at high temperatures, operating in conjunction with a gas-flow control valve.

Heat exchanger Any device which exchanges heat between two substances without intermixing them. Used in heat recovery systems.

Heating coil A device that turns electric current into heat energy found in equipment that needs to produce its own heat.

Heat loss The heat transferred through the fabric of a building, the extent of which is determined by the building's air tightness and efficiency of its insulation. ■ See **U-value**.

Heat of hydration The product of a chemical reaction when cement is mixed with water. Heat generated during the setting of concrete, mortar or plaster. Typically dissipated into the ground or air, though if not taken into account during the design and passing of the concrete, can cause cracking.

Heat pump A machine in which a fluid absorbs energy from a natural source at a low temperature and is compressed to cause a temperature increase which is in turn transferred in a **heat exchanger**.

Heat recovery/MVRH Mechanical ventilation with heat recovery (MVHR) are heat recovery ventilation systems that work by both supplying and extracting air throughout building to provide continuously good air quality. Air is extracted constantly from the wet rooms (i.e. the kitchen, bathrooms, and utility rooms). This air passes into the ventilation device and over the heat exchanger unit, which can recover up to 90+% of the heat in the air that would otherwise be lost. At the same time, air is continuously drawn in from the atmosphere and ducted to habitable rooms (living rooms and bedrooms) to provide a balanced ventilation system.

Heat-transmission value See **U-value**.

Hedley Byrne duty A duty of care not to cause economic loss, as opposed to physical damage, to another, first recognised in *Hedley Byrne & Co Ltd v Heller & Partners Ltd* [1964] AC 465 (HL), a case concerning negligent misstatement. ■ See **Economic loss**.

Heel That part of a beam which rests on a support.

Helibar ties Often known by the proprietary name – "HeliBar" – these are stainless steel reinforcing bars which are inserted into mortar and are used to tie masonry and brickwork together, stitch cracks in brickwork and otherwise spread the load and reinforce structures.

***Henry Boot Construction v Alstom Combined Cycles* Ltd** [2000] BLR 247 (CA): the court defined a "fair valuation" as one which does not give the contractors more than their actual costs reasonably and necessarily incurred plus similar allowances for **overheads and profit**.

Heras fencing Proprietary brand of movable rigid fencing made from wire mesh.

Herring-bone strutting Timber or mild steel supports beneath floor joists placed in X formation to distribute load.

H-frame tower As the name would suggest, a structure where two vertical members are joined together at approximately mid-level by a horizontal beam.

HGCRA See **Housing Grants, Construction and Regeneration Act 1996**.

Hickman & Co v Roberts [1913] AC 229; 82 LJKB 678: in carrying out his role as a certifier, the architect/engineer must act fairly, reasonably and impartially as between the employer and contractor, in exercising his discretion and forming his opinion. In this case, the contractor was entitled to payment in the absence of a certificate because the architect had allowed himself to be influenced by the employer.

High Court A superior court consisting of the Chancery, Queen's Bench and Family Divisions, the principal registry of which is located at the

Royal Courts of Justice in the Strand in London. It was previously known as the Supreme Court of Judicature, the name being changed upon the creation of the Supreme Court in 2009. ➤ **Figure C3**

High-pressure hot water (HPHW) A system for producing hot water above boiling point and at mains pressure by unvented cylinder: the system is fully enclosed which increases pressure when water is heated. It provides greater thermal efficiency but this pressurised system requires safety features.

Highways Agency An executive agency of the Department for Transport (DfT), responsible for operating, maintaining and improving the strategic road network in England on behalf of the Secretary of State for Transport. It frequently enters into construction contracts for the carrying out works relating to the road network.

Hindrance A synonym for prevention. ■ See **Prevention principle**.

Hip rafter Rafter to construct the slope of a hipped roof.

Hip truss A trussed rafter used in the construction of a hipped roof.

Hip, hip ridge The sloping edge (hip) or level edge (ridge) where the sides of a hipped roof meet.

Hip(ped) roof A form of roof construction where all sides of the roof slope down to eaves level (compare with gable where wall rises to create vertical end to roof). The eaves on a hipped roof are usually at same level and construction of such roof offers better wind resistance being self bracing, but the framework is more complex to construct.

Hit and miss (1) Fencing panels where individual slats of timber are fixed alternately on the front and rear face of frame to reduce wind resistance: it is also known as ventilation panels. (2) Ventilators for doors and walls where slots are cut alternating with solid metal. (3) In underpinning, the excavation of alternate sections beneath the structure in a hit and miss sequence so that the ground is disturbed only in a limited way, reducing the risk of collapse but enhancing the support to the structure in the areas where underpinning support is introduced.

HMRC HM Revenue & Customs. Formed in April 2005 following the merger of the Inland Revenue and HM Customs and Excise Departments. It is responsible for ensuring that the correct tax is paid at the right time.

Hoarding It is a temporary fencing around the perimeter of a construction site partly to protect against trespass and to keep stray animals off the works and as a delineation of a temporary boundary to zone construction activity. Often sheet plywood or particle-oriented strand board (OSB) material of 2 m, painted, with skirting, and work lights is used. Wire mesh versions are used in more transient situations.

Hoist A mechanical means of lifting heavy objects, usually by a pulley system powered by an electric motor. Hoists may also be similar in appearance and function to small cranes, or like lifts when fixed to the side of a building to raise building materials.

Holdback A North-American term for the retention of money from a contractor's account: unlike the position in English law, claims may be made against holdback by unpaid subcontractors. ■ See **Retention**.

Holding-down bolt A heavy steel bolt used to fix base plates of steel or concrete stanchions/columns to reinforced concrete platform or foundation.

Hollow block Concrete block manufactured with internal holes in various sizes and shapes. Lighter and providing better insulation than solid blocks, steel reinforcement and concrete can be placed through the holes in order to add strength. It is sometimes made with aerated concrete.

Hollow brick Clay brick manufactured with internal holes: advantages are similar to hollow concrete blocks.

Hollow tile Clay tiles used for structural purposes in construction of floor slab/vaulting, particularly where resistance to passage of fire is important: the concrete which fills the holes provides additional structural strength and fire protection.

Hollow wall A cavity wall built with inner and outer leaf off of the same foundation, leaving air space in between. The two leaves are held together by metal ties. The air space insulates the building and protects against damp/water penetration. The cavity is often partially filled with insulating material either during construction or injected subsequently.

Hollow-core door A door manufactured with panels on either side of frame but with a void centre or a centre filled with insulation or other material to preserve integrity: usually timber doors for internal locations only, as they are much lighter and cheaper than solid timber doors but less robust.

Honeycomb bond A bond with gaps left in each course below and above the stretcher to create a chequer board appearance. Used decoratively on garden walls in particular, it lessens wind resistance and allows some view through the wall.

Honeycomb core door An internal door with a core made of resin impregnated paper honeycomb and also refers to metal doors with aluminium honeycomb core. The design offers resistance to fire and impact damage.

Honeycomb fire damper A fire damper used in air conditioning and ventilation ductwork made of a strong paper honeycomb coated with intumescent coating. Heat causes the paint to swell and block the duct against the passage of heat and fire.

Honeycombing The presence of air voids in concrete caused by poorly graded concrete mix, inadequate vibration or compaction, or gaps in formwork. It weakens concrete since water may fill voids and freeze. Honeycombing can be remedied by grouting to fill the voids.

Hopper An architectural feature on buildings which serves as a collection point for rain water collected by gutters. ■ See **Rainwater outlet**.

Hostilities Hostile acts by persons acting as the agents of sovereign powers, or of such organised and considerable forces as are entitled to the name of rebels as contrasted with mobs or rioters, and does not cover the act of a mere private individual acting entirely on his own initiative, however hostile his action may be: *Atlantic Mutual Insurance Co v King* [1919] 1 KB 307. It is part of the definition of All Risks Insurance against the Specified Perils under the JCT standard forms of contract. The full phrase is: “any consequence of war, invasion, act of foreign enemy, hostilities (whether war be declared or not) civil war, rebellion, revolution, insurrection, military or usurped power, confiscation, commandeering, nationalisation or requisition or loss and destruction of or damage to any property by or under the order of any government *de juris* or *de facto* or public, municipal or local authority”. Loss or damage occasioned by any of the specified perils is a **relevant event** which can entitle the contractor to an extension of time.

Hot tubbing It is also known as **witness conferencing**. Evidence being given by experts concurrently and dealing with particular issues at the same time. There is no set procedure: one party may ask its expert for his or her view on an issue, then ask the other parties' experts for their views, and then return to its own expert for any comment, or the judge or the experts may ask questions. It enables the court to have the evidence on each of a large number of items on the same occasion rather than having it divided and can allow the extent of agreement and reason for disagreement to be seen more clearly: see para 13.8.2 of the **TCC Guide**. Despite the wide provisions of CPR 31.2, it is not clear that such a procedure could be imposed on parties in the absence of their consent.

Hot work Building work requiring the application of direct heat from flame or hot air, such as welding, cutting, brazing and soldering. Such work carries risk of fire damage to property and often requires permit from employer, local authority or insurers.

House of Lords Previously the court hearing appeals from the **Court of Appeal**, now replaced by the **Supreme Court**. ➤ **Figure C3**

House wrapping The application of protective sheet material to the exterior of a building (breather membrane) prior to cladding which prevents water penetration and limits air penetration to insulate the interior but allows water vapour to escape.

Housing Association As defined by the Housing Associations Act 1985, s1(1), a society, body of trustees or company—

> (a) which is established for the purpose of, or amongst whose objects or powers are included those of, providing, constructing, improving or managing, or facilitating or encouraging the construction or improvement of, housing accommodation, and (b) which does not trade for profit or whose constitution or rules prohibit the issue of capital with interest or dividend exceeding such rate as may be prescribed by the Treasury, whether with or without differentiation as between share and loan capital.

Housing Corporation The body established in 1964 to promote voluntary non-profit-making housing associations and local housing companies. It was dissolved under the Housing and Regeneration Act 2008, s64, and its main regulatory functions were transferred to the Regulator of

$$\frac{\text{head office overhead costs and profit*}}{100} \times \frac{\text{the contract sum}}{\text{the contract period}} \times \text{the period of delay} = \text{head office overhead damages attributable to the specific project}$$

* Allowance for head office overheads and profit <u>included in tender</u>

➤ **Figure H2.** Hudson Formula: Calculation of head office overheads attributable to a project

Social Housing by the Transfer of Housing Corporation Functions (Modifications and Transitional Provisions) Order 2008, SI 2008/2839.

Housing Grants, Construction and Regeneration Act (HGCRA) The Housing Grants, Construction and Regeneration Act 1996, Part II introduced various amendments of or additions to terms in "construction contracts" as defined by the Act. Amended by the **Local Democracy, Economic Development and Construction Act (LDEDCA)**, it gives the parties the right to resolve their disputes on a temporary basis by adjudication, imposes a stage payment regime and regulates the exercise of the right of set-off in the absence of written notice which must be given not later than the prescribed period before the final date for payment. The parties are free to agree what the prescribed period should be. In the absence of such agreement, a statutory scheme provides that the period shall be not later than seven days before the final date for payment. It also confers a right to suspend performance for non-payment, and prohibits conditional payment ("pay-when-paid") provisions. Similar legislation has subsequently been introduced in all Australian jurisdictions, New Zealand and Singapore. ■ See **Adjudication**, **Construction Act Withholding Notice, Default Payment Notice** and **Payless notice**.

HPHW High-pressure hot water

HRSG Heat Recovery Steam Generator

HSE See **Health and Safety Executive.**

Hudson formula A method of calculating **Head office overhead**s attributable to a contract overrun as part of a loss and expense claim. The overhead costs allowed in the tender for the original contract period are calculated and the weekly rate is applied to the number of weeks overrun. Received judicial approval in the case of *J F Finnegan Ltd v Sheffield City Council* (1988) 43 B.L.R. 124. This calculation can be criticised on the basis that it takes no account of whether the contractor has been able to recover the overheads from other contracts or has been precluded from doing so: see **Eichlay formula**, **Emden formula** and **Head office overheads**. ➤ **Figure H2**

Hudson or Hudson's Building and Engineering Contracts A leading construction law text book previously edited by the late I.N. Duncan Wallace. The latest 12th edn was published in 2010, edited by members of Atkin Chambers.

Human Rights Act The Human Rights Act (HRA) 1998, under which the articles set out in Schedule1 are to have effect for the purposes of that Act subject to any designated derogation or reservation. The articles consist of articles of the European Convention on Human Rights and subsequent protocols, collectively known as "Convention rights". So far as it is possible to do so, primary legislation and subordinate legislation must be read and given effect in a way which is compatible with the Convention rights. If the court is satisfied that the provision is incompatible with a Convention right, it may make a declaration of that incompatibility, but a declaration of incompatibility does not affect the validity, continuing operation or enforcement of the provision in respect of which it is given, and it is not binding on the parties to the proceedings in which it is made. It is unlawful for a public authority to act in a way which is incompatible with a Convention right. A person who claims that a public authority has acted (or proposes to act) in a way which is made unlawful by the HRA may bring proceedings against the authority under this Act in the appropriate court or tribunal, or rely on the Convention right or rights concerned in any legal proceedings, but only if he or she is (or would be) a victim of the unlawful act. An adjudicator exercising functions of the sort required by the 1996 Act is not a public authority and is not bound by the HRA not to act in a way incompatible with a Convention right, and proceedings before an adjudicator are not legal proceedings: *Austin Hall Building Ltd v Buckland Securities Ltd* [2001] EWHC 434 (TCC); [2001] BLR 272; 80 ConLR 115.

Hurry-up notice A notice served pursuant to the contract that a party is failing to proceed **regularly and diligently**. See *Leander Construction Ltd v Mulalley & Co Ltd* [2011] EWHC 3499 (TCC).

HVAC Heating, ventilation and air conditioning

HVOTL High voltage overhead transmission line

Hydration The addition of water to a dry mixture such as cement or plaster. Results in a chemical reaction creating a new molecular structure. ■ See **Heat of hydration**.

Hydraulic lift Lift for goods or passengers, often used to provide disabled access and in the car industry. Applying the principles of Pascal's law, hydraulic systems use a incompressible fluid, such as oil and water, to transmit forces from one location to another within the fluid.

Hygroscopic salts Chemical substances which attract and absorb moisture from the atmosphere, particularly some elements in plaster which absorb water and may lead to **Efflorescence**.

Hypalon (cspe) A synthetic rubber product sometimes used in roofing.

Hyperbolic paraboloid Geometrical shape convex on one axis and concave on the other rarely used in roof design (saddle roof) of modern buildings.

I

IBC See **Intermediate Building Contract.**

iBIM See **Integrated BIM.**

ICC See **International Chamber of Commerce.**

ICD JCT Intermediate Building Contract with contractor's design

ICE See **Institution of Civil Engineers.**

ICE 6 A common abbreviation for the 6th edition of the Measurement Contract published by the ICE.

ICE 7 A common abbreviation for the 7th edition of the Measurement Contract published by the ICE.

ICE conditions Standard forms of contracts published by the ICE the most well known of which is the Measurement Version (currently in its 7th edn).

IChemE Institution of Chemical Engineers

IChemE Burgundy Book The target cost contract produced by IChemE. ■ See **Target Cost.**

IChemE Green Book The cost reimbursable contract produced by IChemE. ■ See **Cost contract.**

IChemE Red Book The lump-sum contract produced by IChemE. ■ See **Cost contract.**

IEE See **Institution of Electrical Engineers.**

IEE wiring regulations The Wiring Regulations BS: 7671: Currently 17th edition produced by the Institution of Electrical Engineers, a non-statutory document, which plays a key role in the electrical industry in terms of standards and safety of electrical installations in buildings. The regulations provide guidance of the standards and the latest 17th edition was released In January 2008 and amended in 2011. The regulations can be used in a court of law as evidence of working to the standards.

IFC Intermediate Form of Contract (JCT); **Issued for construction**; **Industry Foundation Classes.**

IFC 84 The JCT standard Intermediate Form of Contract 1984 version

If contract A contract, conventionally known as a unilateral contract, under which A requests B to carry out a certain performance and promises B that, if he does so, he will receive a certain performance in return, usually as remuneration for his performance. A standing offer which, if acted upon before it lapses or is lawfully withdrawn, will result in a binding contract: see *British Steel Corp v Cleveland Bridge & Engineering Co Ltd* (1981) 24 BLR 94; [1984] 1 All ER 504.

Ikarian Reefer Seminal case on expert evidence in which Mr Justice Cresswell set out the seven key duties and responsibilities of expert witnesses in civil cases. These principles, which include that the expert should provide independent assistance to the court by way of objective unbiased opinion in relation solely to matters within his expertise, are now enshrined within CPR 35; *National Justice Compania Naviera SA v Prudential Assurance Company Ltd* ("The Ikarian Reefer") [1993] 2 Lloyd's Rep 68. ■ See **Expert witness.**

Illegality The quality of being contrary to the law and a ground upon which a contract may become void and unenforceable. Examples are contracts to carry out works prohibited by statute or entered into with the intention of defrauding a third party.

Impacted as-planned With an impacted as-planned analysis, the effect of only the employer risk events is imposed on the contract programme, such that the whole of the difference between the original contract completion date and the calculated completion date represents the contractor's entitlement. This method does not take account of other events that may have rendered the employer risk events non-critical and the approach was disapproved in *Henry Boot Construction (UK) Ltd v Malmaison Hotel* [2000] EWCA Civ 175; 70 ConLR 32.

Impartiality Fairness, the quality of being without bias. A certifier under a construction contract must be and act impartially in relation to his functions but an interest known to the contractor will not disqualify him form acting. Section 108(2) of the **Construction Act** requires that a construction contract shall impose a duty on the adjudicator to act impartially. If the contract is subject to the **Scheme for Construction Contracts**, para 12 of that scheme states that the adjudicator shall act impartially in carrying out his duties. ■ See **Bias**.

Implied contract A contract made by the conduct of the parties.

Implied term A term that forms a part of a contract which has not been expressly agreed by the parties; the common law implied terms relating to the quality of workmanship and materials into all construction contracts which did not deal with such matters expressly. The position is now covered by the **Supply of Goods and Services Act 1982**, which implies terms that goods supplied under the contract are of satisfactory quality and are reasonably fit for any particular purpose for which the goods are being acquired, and to carry out the service which he is supplying with reasonable care and skill, within a reasonable time and, where the consideration is not determined by the contract, is left to be determined in a manner agreed by the contract, or is to be determined by the course of dealing between the parties, there is a term implied by statute that the employer will pay a reasonable charge. The **Construction Act** implies terms giving the parties the right to adjudicate, imposing a stage payment regime, limiting the exercise of the right of set-off to matters subject to prior written notice, conferring a right to suspend performance, and prohibiting conditional payment provisions. There is no term implied in law that the site is fit for the works, or that the works are practicable.

In addition to terms implied in law or by statute, terms can be implied in fact on an ad hoc basis. Here the central test is that the proposed term must spell out what the contract actually means: *see* ***Attorney General of Belize v Belize Telecom Ltd*** [2009] UKPC 10; [2009] 1 WLR 1988; [2009] 2 All ER 1127.

Impossibility Incapability of being done. In the absence of express provision in a construction contract, physical impossibility is not an excuse for failing to complete the works. The employer does not warrant that the design is practicable and the contractor impliedly warrants his ability to complete according to the design: see **inclusive price principle**. This position at common law can be mitigated by express contractual provision, as in the case of the ICE conditions under which the contractor undertakes to complete the works "save in so far as it is legally or physically possible" (clause 13). If the subject matter never existed, then the contract may be void for mistake; if the subject matter disappears or is destroyed or changes to an extent that contractual performance is impossible, the contract may be discharged in accordance with the doctrine of frustration. ■ See **Mistake** and **Frustration**.

Impost The springing point of an arch.

Incertum Random rubble masonry made of small stones bonded in mortar to irregular courses. It is sometimes known as rubblework. In ancient times, it consisted of more careful placement of the *coementa* (rock fragments and small stones mixed with concrete), making the external surface as plain as possible.

Inclement weather A previous ground for an extension of time under the JCT standard forms of contract. The phrase now used is "exceptionally adverse weather conditions".

Inclusive price principle The term originated in the 11th edition of **Hudson**. The principle that a contractor under a construction contract, in the absence of express terms to the contrary, is obliged to complete the works, whatever the difficulties may be, for the price: see *Thorn v Mayor and Commonality of London* (1876) 1 App Cas 120 (HL). The alternative way of viewing this principle is that the contractor is entitled to be paid the contractual price for the work defined in the contract as constituting the entirety of its contractual obligations.

Inconvenience A head of damages for breach of contract, when combined with distress. ■ See **Distress and inconvenience**.

Incorporation of documents or terms The inclusion of documents or terms as part of a contract, which gives rise to particular problems in relation to construction contracts. Incorporation is most effectively achieved by listing the documents intended to form part of the contract signed by the parties. In other cases, incorporation can take place as a result of reference in a contract document and evidence will be admissible to identify a standard form incorrectly described. An arbitration clause contained in another document will only be achieved if it can be clearly shown that that was the intention of the parties.

Incoterms International Commercial Terms (Incoterms) are standard definitions of commonly used shipping and trade terms which are adopted worldwide in international and domestic contracts for the sale of goods.

Indemnitee The party receiving an indemnity.

Indemnitor The party giving an indemnity.

Indemnity The reimbursement by one party, the indemnitor, of another, the indemnitee, under an agreement to do so, or arising from principle of law or statute. Construction contracts are primarily concerned with agreements to indemnify, the most important being those given by the main contractor to the employer and by sub contractors to the main contractor. The other important category is that of indemnities ordered under the Civil Liability (Contribution) Act 1978 in respect of the same damage.

Indemnity basis A basis of assessment of legal costs recoverable by a successful party in litigation. The beneficiary of an order for costs to be paid on the indemnity basis will still be paid only the costs which he has incurred reasonably. However, there is no requirement of proportionality and in cases of doubt it is for the payer to show that the costs were *not* incurred reasonably. This contrasts with the standard basis where there is a requirement of proportionality and it is for the beneficiary to show that the costs were incurred reasonably: see *Home Office v Lownds* [2002] EWCA Civ 365; [2002] 1 WLR 2450; [2002] 4 All ER 775 and *Sinclair Roche and Temperley v Somatra* [2003] EWCA Civ 1474; [2003] 2 Lloyd's Rep 855.

Independent contractor A party for whom the party employing him is not vicariously liable in tort, subject to exceptions. Thus, a main contractor may be able to defend a claim against him for negligence on the basis that he employed an independent contractor and was not negligent.

Indirect or consequential loss Loss and damage not flowing naturally in the usual course of things within the first limb of the rule in *Hadley v Baxendale* [1854] 9 Ex 341; [1854] 23 LJ Ex 179, but such other loss outside the usual course of things as is in the contemplation of the parties at the time of the contract as the likely result of the breach of it, under the second limb. Such loss is often the subject of exclusion clauses in contracts. ■ See **Remoteness of damage**.

Individual Voluntary Arrangement (IVA) A formal, legally binding agreement between and individual and his or her unsecured creditors. An IVA must be approved by the court.

Industry Foundation Classes (IFC) A neutral and standardised specification for data representation and file formats in BIM developed by the International Alliance for Interoperability (IAI), now building SMART. As it is an open format, not belonging to a particular vendor, greater interoperability between software platforms is achievable.

Ineffectiveness A declaration by the court, under the **remedies directive** that a concluded contract is ineffective where certain serious breaches are found to have occurred.

Infill A material inserted within the frame of a building (such as brick-work), a panel or a partition.

Information exchange A **BIM** term used to denote the point at which information on a project is shared or downloaded from a model. It is somewhat equivalent to a "design freeze" or a stage report. Previously known as a "data drop."

Infra Latin: "below".

Inglenook A recessed seat built into a chimney breast or beside a fireplace. The Inglenook (which means "corner chimney") fireplace generally came into use in the mid-to-late 16th century.

Initial notice Notice an approved inspector is required to give.

Injection damp course Protection from rising damp in older buildings by the injection of a water repellent silicone.

Injunction A court order prohibiting a person from doing something or requiring a person to do something. An injunction can be either interim or permanent and, being a discretionary remedy, will not be granted where the party seeking the remedy has delayed applying for it. Arbitrators and adjudicators cannot grant injunctions.

Inner House The Inner House of the **Court of Session** in Scotland, which acts as the Court of Appeal in civil matters.

Innocent misrepresentation A misrepresentation which is not fraudulent. Under the Misrepresentation Act 1967, a party who has entered into a contract in reliance on such a misrepresentation may avoid the contract or claim damages. ■ See **Fraudulent** and **Negligent misrepresentation**.

Innominate term An intermediate contractual term which falls between the conventional categories of conditions and warranties, the breach of which might entitle the innocent party to regard himself as discharged from further performance if the breach is sufficiently serious.

In re Latin: "in the matter of".

In-situ concrete Concrete poured on site, as opposed to precast and delivered to site.

Insolvency An inability to pay debts. Legal consequences occur after a formal proceeding such as a winding up. The JCT standard forms of contract identify circumstances in which a party is deemed to be insolvent for the purposes of the termination provisions.

Inspection Examination. In the case of a certifier of the value of the works under a construction contract who has undertaken an inspection obligation, the following propositions apply: (1) The frequency and duration of inspections should be tailored to the nature of the works going on at site from time to time; (2) Depending on the importance of the particular element or stage of the works, the inspecting professional can instruct the contractor not to cover up the relevant elements of the work until they have been inspected; (3) The mere fact that defective work is carried out and covered up between inspections will not, therefore, automatically amount to a defence to an alleged failure on the part of the architect to carry out proper inspections; (4) If the element of the work is important because it is going to be repeated throughout one significant part of the building, such as the construction of a proprietary product or the achievement of a particular standard of finish to one element of the work common to every room, then the inspecting professional should ensure that he has seen that element of the work in the early course of construction/assembly so as to form a view as to the contractor's ability to carry out that particular task; (5) However, even then, reasonable examination of the works does not require the inspector to go into every matter in detail; indeed, it is almost inevitable that some defects will escape his notice and (6) It is a misconceived approach for an employer with a claim for bad workmanship against a contractor to make the same claim automatically against the inspecting officer, on the assumption that, if there is a defect, then the inspector must have been negligent or in breach of contract for missing the defect during construction. See *McGlinn v Waltham Contractors Ltd* [2007] EWHC 149 (TCC); [2008] BLR 233; 111 ConLR 1.

Inspection chamber The purpose of an inspection chamber is to provide access for maintenance equipment, such as drain rods, to enable a drain or sewer to be inspected and cleaned.

Institution of Chemical Engineers (IChemE) A professional body for chemical, biochemical and process engineering professionals which also produces a range of standard form engineering contracts. ■ See **IChemE Burgundy Book, IChemE Green Book** and **IChemE Red Book**.

Institution of Civil Engineers (ICE) The professional body for civil engineers which publishes standard forms of civil engineering contracts. ■ See **ICE 6** and **ICE 7**

Institution of Electrical Engineers (IEE) A professional body for electrical engineers which produces wiring regulations. ■ See **IEE wiring regulations**.

Institution of Engineering and Technology (IET) A professional society for engineering and technology industries. Formed in 2006 by the Institution of Electrical Engineers (IEE) and the Institution of Incorporated Engineers (IIE).

Institution of Structural Engineers A professional body for engineers specialising in structural design.

Instruction A direction, usually issued by a construction professional on behalf of the employer under a construction contract. Instructions may vary the works or simply give further detail about the design. Although standard forms contain requirements that instructions should be issued in writing, there is usually also a term permitting recovery for a variation ordered "otherwise than in writing" and the employer may be held to have waived the requirement in an appropriate case.

Instructions to tenderers A set of instructions prepared by the employer which accompany an invitation to tender. These will typically include details of how the contractor should prepare his tender and when, where and how it should be returned to the employer.

Instrument A document intended to have legal effect.

Insurable interest An interest in property or some transaction which entitles the party holding it to insure against loss in relation to that property or transaction. This is an unfortunately vague area of law, although it is clear that a contractor has an insurable interest in the works, plant and goods and materials in his possession, as the employer has an interest in the works and goods and materials on site.

Insurance The indemnity to be provided under a contract, the policy, whereby one party, the insurer, agrees to indemnify another party, the insured, against loss or to pay a specified sum on the occurrence of a particular event, in return for the payment of a premium. Construction contracts almost invariably require the contractor to insure against the risk of damage occurring to the works themselves during construction ("property damage" insurance), and the risk of claims by third parties for personal injuries or damage to their property resulting from the carrying out of the work in the contract ("liability" insurance policies). Contracts for the engagement of construction professionals require the professional to insure against the risk of damage resulting from professional negligence.

Integrated BIM (iBIM) Also known as "Collaborative BIM". Used to refer to the project environment when all parties are utilising BIM – opposite of **Lonely BIM**.

Integrated project team (IPT) Used in **Prime Contracting**, and other forms of collaborative working, the IPT brings together design and construction activities and is made up of client's project team and the supply team of consultants, constructors and specialist suppliers working together as a team to maximise the benefits of collaborative working and thereby, in theory, reducing the total costs and improving the quality.

Intelligent building, smart building A building in which advanced information and communication technology has been installed.

Intention to create legal relations The parties' intention to create a legally binding contract. If the parties do not have this intention, then the promise or obligation between the parties is a social or moral one and will not be enforced by the courts.

Intention to rebuild A claimant's future course of action in respect of defective works. Although the claimant's subjective intentions may be irrelevant once the correct measure of damage has been established, intention may be a ground for deciding that the cost of repair is unreasonable where the claimant intends to sell without repairing, the defects do not reduce the structure's value, or no work has been carried out and the defendant claims that none will be carried out.

Inter alia Latin: "among other things".

Intercepting trap, interceptor A trap to disconnect the air in a sewer from that in a domestic drain.

Interdict The Scottish equivalent of an injunction.

Interest A charge made by a lender of money, usually calculated as an annual percentage rate (APR) which may or may not be compounded at intervals. A contractor will lose interest arising from the use of money not paid promptly either because he is borrowing or unable to earn a return on it and most construction contracts provide for the recovery of interest for late payment of sums due. If they do, the contractual rate may not provide a **substantial remedy** within the meaning of s9 of the Late Payment of Commercial Debts (Interest) Act 1998 and could be replaced by the rate provided for by that Act, which is also awardable by the court where no contractual rate applies. The court can award simple interest under s35A of the Senior Courts Act 1981 on both debt and damages. An arbitrator can award simple or compound interest under s49 of the Arbitration Act 1996. An adjudicator has no "freestanding" power to award interest, but can award interest at a contractual rate under the statutory scheme. Interest may also be recoverable by way of damages on a simple or compound basis: see *Sempra Metals Ltd v Revenue* [2007] UKHL 34; [2008] AC 561 (HL); [2007] 3 WLR 354, or as direct loss and/or expense: see **Direct loss and/or expense**.

Interface documents Cooperation agreements between parties involved in a public–private partnership (PPP) project.

Interference Improper intervention by an employer in the certification process and a ground for disregarding a certificate or its absence. ■ See **Prevention principle**.

Interim award An arbitrator's award dealing with only some of the issues between the parties. It is common practice for an arbitrator to deal with all issues other than costs by way of interim award before considering costs in the final award which might require taking sealed offers into account.

Interim certificate One of a series of certificates issued on a regular basis under traditional forms of construction contract recording the certifier's valuation of the works to date and any further amount due to the contractor as part of the contract price after deduction of sums previously certified. In the case of contracts subject to Part II of the Housing Grants, Construction and Regeneration Act 1996, the employer cannot set-off the sums against an amount due under an interim certificate unless he has first served a payless notice (or withholding notice under contracts entered into prior to 1 October 2011). ■ See **Payless Notice and Withholding notice**.

Interim payment One of a series of payments made at intervals during the currency of a construction contract. In the absence on an express right to periodic payments, that term will be implied into construction contracts by virtue of s110(1) of the Housing Grants, Construction and Regeneration Act 1996.

Interim remedy A remedy, as specified by the Civil Procedure Rules which is ordered by the court during proceedings but before final determination of the matter.

Interlocutory Interim, in relation to court proceedings before trial.

Intermediate Building Contract (IC and ICD) A contract first produced by JCT in 2005 to replace the intermediate form of contract (IFC). The intermediate building contract (IC) is a traditional contract and the intermediate building contract with contractor's design (ICD) allows for some contractor design. The contract is less detailed than the standard building contract but more detailed than the minor works contract. ■ See **Intermediate Building Contract** and **Minor Works Contract**.

Intermediate Form of Contract (IFC) A contract first produced by JCT in 1984 and now replaced by the intermediate building contract (IC) and intermediate building contract with contractor's design (ICD).

Intermediate rafter A sloping timber laid on the purlins above the principal rafters forming a roof.

International Chamber of Commerce (ICC) An international body created by national chambers of commerce in 1920 which includes amongst functions that of the conduct of international arbitration through its Court of Arbitration. The court provides an administrative framework within which arbitrations can be conducted and its participation is in the main limited to the early and concluding stages of dispute resolution, leaving the decision-making function to the arbitrators appointed pursuant to the ICC rules of arbitration: see *Copée-Lavalin SA/NV v Ken-Ren Chemicals and Fertilizers Ltd* [1994] 2 All ER 449. A new set of Arbitration and ADR Rules was introduced by the ICC in January 2012.

International Federation of Consulting Engineers The English name for FIDIC. ■ See **Federation Internationale des Ingenieurs-Conseils**.

International Institute for the Unification of Private Law A body most noted for issuing the UNIDROIT Principles of International Commercial Contracts which are intended to be used by agreement where parties to a contract cannot agree a governing law.

International Organization for Standardization (ISO) An international body to coordinate units of measurement of which the British Standards Institution is a member.

International SfB Swedish: Samarbetskommitten för Byggnadsfrågor, an international classification of building subjects.

In terrorem Latin "in terror", a ground of objection to a liquidated damages provision, which on analysis is a penalty, and threatens the contractor with greater loss if he were to breach the contract.

Interstitial condensation Occurs when relatively warm moisture-laden air diffuses into a vapour-permeable material or structure such as fibrous insulation or a porous brick wall. If it is relatively warm on one side and below the dew point temperature on the other, this can result in the moisture-laden air reaching "dew point" within the material and depositing liquid water at this point between two media.

Intrados The soffit and lower curve of an arch. An extrados being the exterior face of an arch.

Intramural Within the walls of a building or cavity.

Intumescence The attribute of a material to swell when heated; intumescent materials like paints and door strips in bulk and sheet form are used as fireproofing agents.

Inverted roof A **warm roof**, whereby the waterproof membrane is installed below the insulation.

Investors Compensation Scheme Ltd v West Bromwich Building Society [1997] UKHL 28; [1998] 1 WLR 896; [1998] 1 All ER 98: Lord Hoffman restated the governing principles of contractual interpretation, emphasising that interpretation is the task of ascertaining the meaning that a contractual document would convey to a reasonable person. The case also adopted a broad test for admissible background.

Invitation to negotiate A procedure whereby an employer invites a contractor to negotiate in respect of work rather than adopt a formal tender procedure.

Invitation to tender A procedure by which an employer invites contractors to submit their tender to carry out work. If a contractor submits a conforming tender, there may be an implied contract obliging the employer to consider that tender in conjunction with other conforming ones: see *Pratt Contractors Ltd v Transit New Zealand* [2003] UKPC 83; [2004] BLR 143.

Invitation to treat An invitation by one party to other(s) to make an offer (usually by display of goods in a shop window or by some other advertisement) which if accepted becomes the basis of a binding contract.

Ipso facto Latin: "by the fact itself".

Ipso jure Latin: "from the law itself".

IPT Integrated project team

Iroko A durable hardwood timber which originates from West Africa. It is often used externally as a cladding system or garden furniture, or internally for flooring, bespoke joinery or wall coverings. The use of iroko is controversial as it is questionable whether or not it can be sustainably sourced.

ISO See **International Organization for Standardization.**

ISO 216 An internationally recognised standard paper size system. It is based on the German standard DIN 476, established in 1922. ISO 216 is comprised of three categories: "A Series", "B Series" and "C Series" formats. The main principle behind the paper sizes in the "A Series" is that the height-to-width ratio of each size is √2:1. Furthermore, each sheet size is defined by halving the next larger sheet in the series. For example, two A1 sheets are made by cutting an A0 in half. Two A2 sheets are created by halving an A1 sheet. The "B Series" sizes provide a wider range of paper sizes. The dimensions of a B Series sheet are the geometric means of the dimensions in the "A Series". For example, the dimensions of B1 are the geometric means between A0 and A1. "C Series" formats have been developed for envelopes. For technical construction drawings, "A Series" formats are generally used. Standard sheet sizes include: A0, A1, A2, A3, A4 and A5.

ISO 9001:2008 An international standard produced by the **International Organization for Standardization** which specifies requirements for a quality management system. The requirements are generic and are intended for all orgnizations, regardless of type or size.

ISO 14001 An international standard produced by the **ISO** that specifies requirements for an environmental management system to enable an organization to develop and implement a policy and objectives taking into account legal and other requirements to which the organization subscribes, as well as information about significant environmental aspects.

Isolator Known as a disconnector in the USA. An isolator or isolator switch is used to break (or isolate) a section of an electrical circuit.

Isometric drawing A drawing based on an apparently perspective view.

Isotropic Properties of a material are identical in all directions. ■ See **Anisotropic**.

Issued for Construction (IFC) Information, including drawings, issued for the purpose of constructing a building or engineering project, having been produced by the professional design team or specialist contractors with design obligations.

ITB Invitation to bid

ITN See **Invitation to Negotiate.**

ITT See **Invitation to Tender.**

IVA See **Individual Voluntary Arrangement.**

J

J (after a surname) indicating a High Court Judge as in Mr, Ms or Mrs Justice ....

Jackleg cabin Portable buildings built in timber or lightweight materials within a metal frame enabling them to be raised off the ground, lifted by crane and double stacked: often used as site accommodation.

Jack rafter A short rafter used in constructing a hip or valley roof.

Jamb The vertical sides of the frame of a door or window or other opening.

Japanese knotweed An invasive and fast growing plant possessing considerable strength whose roots can grow through concrete. It is difficult to eradicate since its root system is extensive and deep. It is classified as controlled waste and can only be disposed at licensed sites: see the Knotweed Code of Practice.

JCT See **Joint Contracts Tribunal**.

JCT form of contract The standard form of building contract based on a form originally agreed in 1931 between the RIBA and the Builders' Society and adopted by the Central Association of master builders of London: see *Clemence v Clarke* (1879) *Hudson's Law of Building, Engineering & Ship Building Contracts* 4th edn, Vol. 2, p. 54. The form was subsequently the subject of agreement between the constituent members of the **Joint Contracts Tribunal**.

JCT suite of contracts The current suite of JCT building contracts are the 2011 edition which include **Standard**, **Intermediate**, **Minor Works, Design and Build**, **Major Project Construction**, and sub-contracts for all these standard forms (save for Minor Works), **Prime Cost**, Management Building, Repair and Maintenance, Measured Term Contracts, Adjudication Agreement, **Framework Agreement**, Pre-Construction Services Agreement, **Consultancy Agreement**.

JCT 63 The first major revision of the JCT standard forms of contract since their introduction in 1931. It remained widely used even after the production of JCT 80 and many court decisions have been reported on its terms

JCT 80 A major revision of the JCT Standard Contracts undertaken in 1980: subject to many amendments which were incorporated in JCT 98

JCT 98 A further substantial revision of the JCT Standard Form suite of Building Contracts.

JCT 05 A further revision of the JCT Contracts and the current suite (with revisions). The name was changed from JCT Form of Contract to Standard Building Contract and the number of contracts was consolidated.

JCT 2011 This current edition of the JCT Contract suite which incorporates the changes made to the Construction Act which came into force on 1 October 2011.

Jib A type of crane which can be post or wall mounted: in particular the horizontal arm along which the hoist travels: some cranes have fixed jibs but most jibs can rotate through an arc and may be cantilevered.

John Doyle Construction Ltd v Laing Management 2002 Scot (CS) 110; [2002] BLR 393; 85 ConLR 98 and (2004 Scot (CS) 141; [2004]

BLR 295; 2004 SCLR 872): Scottish case where the courts held that apportionment of loss between different causes is possible where the causes of the loss are truly concurrent, in the sense that both operate together at the same time to produce a single consequence, for example, late provision of information during a period of bad weather might have prevented work for a part of the time. In such a case, responsibility for the loss can be apportioned between the two causes, according to their relative significance. See also *City Inn Ltd v Shepherd Construction Ltd* [2010] CSIH 68; [2010] BLR 473 and *Walter Lilly & Co v Mackay & another* [2012] EWHC 1773 (TCC). ■ See **Apportionment**.

Joinder The process by which further parties become formally involved in existing proceedings, as in the addition of a further defendant. In litigation this can be achieved by an order of the court, but in adjudication and arbitration it will not be possible without the agreement of both the existing parties to the proceedings and that of the party to be joined. In the case of construction contracts, the agreement is sometimes contained in both a main contract and the subcontracts made under it.

Joiner A worker in wood, in a workshop rather than on site: traditionally distinguished from a carpenter as joinery was considered more skilled, involving the making of furniture, fittings, doors and staircases, but these trade distinctions are now less important.

Joinery Products in wood such as furniture assembled by skilled jointing rather than nailing: nowadays it refers to the prefabrication and installation of fittings, such as kitchens and bathrooms, windows and doors, conservatories and roofs in wood and products used in fitted units.

Joint Contracts Tribunal (JCT) A committee (now JCT limited a company limited by guarantee) first established in 1931, whose main function is to produce standard forms of building contract which balance the interests of employers, contractors and professionals and to promote clarity and certainty in contract terms and to foster construction activity. As on 2011, its members were the RIBA, the RICS, British Property Federation, Local Government Association, Contractors' Legal Group Ltd and National Specialist Contractors' Council and the Scottish Building Contract Committee Ltd. The members jointly approve publications through their working groups. It also published tender documentation and practice notes and frequently updates its standard forms by amendment. ■ See **JCT Suite of Documents**.

Joint Fire Code *Fire Prevention on Construction Sites: The Joint Code of Practice on the Protection from Fire of Construction Sites and Buildings Undergoing Renovation*, published jointly by the *RICS, Construction Confederation* and the *Fire Protection Association* (FPA), containing a series of procedures to be followed and standards to be met to minimise the risk of accidental or malicious fires. Several JCT standard forms refer to the code and many insurers require compliance with it.

Joint liability The liability which arises in contract when two or more parties promise to do the same thing. There is only one obligation, so that performance by one party will discharge the other party or parties. Generally, all joint contractors should be made defendants to a claim under the contract.

Joint reinforcement Prefabricated steel wire reinforcement laid in cement of horizontal beds in brickwork, blockwork or masonry walls in order to strengthen them to carry increased loads and to reduce the appearance of cracking.

Joint runner Asbestos or metal tape secured around a joint, for example, between pipe sections in order to contain molten lead when it is poured to seal the joint.

Joint and several liability (1) The liability which arise in contract when two or more parties jointly promise to do the same thing and also each make a separate promise to do it. Performance by one will discharge the other or others, but not all need be joined as defendants to a claim under the contract. (2) The liability of wrongdoers acting independently to cause the same damage in tort, in contract or a mixture of the two. Each is liable to the claimant for the whole loss, but may claim a contribution from the other or others under the **Civil Liability (Contribution) Act 1978**.

Joint tape A paper or polypropylene adhesive tape used to cover joints to plasterboard including internal angle joints, with the application of drywall compound to make paper tape adhere and to cover both types of tape once in place.

Joint tortfeasors Two or more parties jointly liable for a tort which they both commit or are responsible for the commission of the tort.

Joint venture A business agreement between two or more companies or persons to carry out a specific project, often through a special purpose vehicle. Often used in respect of large developments where members of the joint venture would not have sufficient resources and expertise on their own to carry out the project, or to work in combination with a foreign company. The JV agreement will specify the contribution which each party makes to the project, including their share in the cost and any profit, but it does not normally create a partnership: each venturer retains its independence and is not committed beyond the duration of the agreement.

Joist A beam of timber, steel or reinforced concrete (or composite) to support a floor or ceiling or other part of a roof or floor structure.

Joist hanger Usually an engineered galvanised metal fixing for supporting a joist:nailed or screwed to the sides of a wall, or bottom of a timber or steel and secured to the wall plate which the joist abuts in order to support the weight of the joist and the load it bears and hold it in position.

Joist trimmer See **trimmer beam**.

Judge Judges of the Technology and Construction Court (TCC) are responsible for resolving technology and construction disputes. TCC business in the High Court is conducted by TCC judges who include High Court judges, senior circuit judges and recorders. Circuit judges and recorders only have jurisdiction to manage and try TCC cases if they have been nominated by the Lord Chancellor pursuant to section 68(1)(a) of the Senior Courts Act 1981 or are authorised to sit in the TCC as High Court judges under section 9 of that Act. TCC business in the

County Court is conducted by TCC judges who include circuit judges and recorders. TCC business may also be conducted by certain district judges ("TCC liaison district judges").

Judgment The final determination made by a Judge of the claims and issues in an action or application: the term is used to describe both the reasons for the decision given and the order which embodies and gives effect to the court's decision by providing remedies or dismissing the claim. Judgments may be delivered orally immediately after the hearing is concluded (*ex tempore*) or may be reserved (deferred) for further consideration and the drafting of a written decision. A judgment is binding on the parties to the proceedings and they may not re-litigate the same issues but (with few exceptions) they may appeal to a higher court provided they obtain permission to do so either from the trial judge or the higher court.

Judgment creditor A party entitled to be paid as a result of a judgment.

Judgment debt The sum of money (together with interest) ordered to be paid to the successful party following judgment. Normally payable within 14 days unless the court orders otherwise. If the sum ordered is not paid, the successful party may enforce the debt in a number of ways including the execution against goods or third-party debt orders. In the County Court, the debt will also be included in the Register of County Court Judgments if not paid within one month. ■ See **Execution against goods** and **Third party debt orders**.

Judgment debtor A party obliged to make payment as a result of a judgement.

Judgment in default If the defendant fails to serve a defence within 14 days of service of the particulars of claim or having served an acknowledgement of service fails to serve a defence within 28 days of the service of the particulars of claim CPR Part 12 allows the claimant to enter judgment in default. This is an administrative process in which the merits of the claim are not investigated and the judgment may be set aside, but an application to do so must be made promptly and show the merits of the defence. Judgment in default may also be ordered to be entered if a party fails to comply with procedural orders: for example, a claim may be struck out if the claimant persistently fails to disclose documents. ■ See **Setting aside** judgment in default.

Judicial Committee See **Privy Council**.

Judicial notice The convention that the court will accept some facts as correct from general knowledge rather than requiring them to be strictly proved by evidence; for example, that London is the capital city of England. A specialist tribunal such as a **TCC** judge or an engineer arbitrator may take judicial knowledge of technical facts but should disclose his understanding to the parties if he intends to apply his own knowledge and experience to contentious issues in the case.

Judicial precedent See **Precedent**.

Judicial review The process of dealing with a claim in the High Court under CPR Part 54 to review the lawfulness of an enactment or a decision action or failure to act in relation to the exercise of a public function. Its most common use in relation to construction disputes is to challenge public procurement decisions.

Jump form Formwork used to construct the concrete core of high rise buildings and other high structures. Supported by the concrete structure already cast, the formwork is lifted by crane or by hydraulic jacks guided by rails running up the completed sections.

Jurat Latin: "one who has been sworn" (juratus), a statement set out at the end of an affidavit which authenticates the document. It must be: signed by all the deponents; completed and signed by the person before whom the affidavit was sworn or affirmed whose name and qualifications must be printed beneath his signature; contain the full address of the person before whom the affidavit was sworn and follow immediately on from the text and not be put on a separate page. See CPR 32 Practice Direction 5.

Jurisdiction The authority of a court or other tribunal to decide disputes and legal issues and the scope of that power: also refers to the geographical extent over which the courts' power runs, for example, England and Wales. The jurisdiction of the High Court is unlimited regarding the value and subject matter of claims but may be limited by an arbitration clause or a contractual provision submitting disputes to another jurisdiction such as a foreign court. Following *West Country Renovations Ltd v McDowell and another* [2012] EWHC 307 (TCC), most **TCC** claims valued at less than £250,000 should be issued in County Courts or High Courts outside of London that have designated TCC judges, rather than in the TCC in London. The County Court may not issue **Anton Piller** and **Mareva** injunctions. The jurisdiction of arbitrators and adjudicators is limited to the scope of the matters referred to them for decision, and they have no power to decide issues beyond the reference. In addition, they do not possess the full range of powers available to the court in relation to enforcement such as granting injunctions or charging orders.

Jurisdictional challenge An objection, particularly in adjudication, to the validity of the entire proceedings or an element of them. If a party challenges the entire jurisdiction of the adjudicator, it has four options. Firstly, it can agree to widen the jurisdiction of the adjudicator so as to refer the dispute as to the adjudicator's jurisdiction to the same adjudicator. If the referring party agrees to that course, and the appointed adjudicator accepts the reference to him of this second dispute, the jurisdiction of the adjudicator could then be resolved as part of the reference. The challenging party could, secondly, refer the dispute as to jurisdiction to a second adjudicator. This would not put a halt to the first adjudication, if that had already led to an appointment, since the adjudicator has a statutory duty, unless both parties agree otherwise, to decide the reference in a very short timescale. The challenging party could, thirdly, seek a declaration from the court that the proposed adjudication lacked jurisdiction. This option is of little utility unless the adjudicator has yet to be appointed or the parties agree to put the adjudication into abeyance pending the speedy determination of the jurisdiction question by the court. The **TCC** can, for example, resolve questions of that kind within days of them being referred to it. Fourthly, the challenging party could reserve its position, participate in the adjudication and then challenge any attempt to enforce the adjudicator's decision on jurisdictional grounds: *Fastrack Contractors Ltd v Morrison Construction Ltd* [2000] BLR 168; 75 ConLR 33. The right to maintain a jurisdictional challenge may be lost by waiver in the form of submitting to the jurisdiction by participating in the proceedings without reservation of position. In the case of arbitration, the loss of a right to object is the subject of express statutory provision: see the Arbitration Act 1996, s73. ■ See **Reservation of position**.

Jurisdictional error An error as to jurisdiction, particularly in the case of adjudication, which might invalidate the entire proceedings. A "threshold" jurisdictional error occurs when an adjudicator embarks on a reference where: (1) There was no relevant construction contract or construction operation. (2) There was no construction contract in writing. (3) The claiming party has purported to refer a dispute when the subject matter of that purported dispute has yet to crystallise into a dispute between the parties. A "procedural" jurisdictional error will occur during the adjudication process itself and concerns whether the question considered by the adjudicator was the one referred to adjudication and whether the error was one which changed the nature of the question referred sufficiently or so profoundly that it turned itself into a different question. See *Joinery Plus Ltd v Laing Ltd* [2003] EWHC 3513 (TCC); [2003] BLR 184; 87 ConLR 87.

JV See **Joint Venture.**

K

Keating on Construction Contracts A leading construction law text book originally written by Donald Keating QC (under the title *Building Contracts*) and now edited by Stephen Furst QC and Mr Justice Ramsey. The ninth edition was published in February 2012.

Key performance indicator A tool to measure performance against standards or indicators usually defined in the contract specification.

Key plan A plan showing the location and main features of a development site, sometimes included in a more detailed plan to make clear how the large-scale plan relates to the development as a whole. ➤ **Figure T3**.

Key plate A metal piece, often ornamented, fixed to the wood surrounding a key hole to prevent scratches to the surface of the door/window. ■ See **Escutcheon**.

Keyed joints An expansion joint between concrete slabs similar to tongue and groove joints in timber but without direct contact between these edges. This is usually created by preformed metal edge strips.

Keying Making smooth surfaces rough in order to create a bond for plaster coating or a concrete screed: see **scabbling**.

Keystone The wedge-shaped stone at the top of a curved arch which secures it in position. ■ See **Voussoir**.

Kick plate Metal plate fixed to protect the bottom of a door.

Kicker (1) A raised concrete section (usually about 75 mm high) cast integrally with the floor slab in the location of where walls and columns will be placed. Its purpose is to assist with the subsequent positioning of the formwork for the walls and columns. (2) Also used as a diagonal brace to a stud wall.

Kicker frame Formwork fixed above slab level for the construction of a kicker.

Kiln-dried timber Timber dried in a kiln to reduce its moisture content uniformly and to avoid uneven shrinkage and warping. Kilns generally operate with steam heat exchangers and air is forced over the timber by fans: this process can be closely controlled and adapted for different types and quality of wood. Most commercial timber is seasoned in this way, since it is quicker and better controlled than stacking timber in the open air. ■ See **Air-dried timber**.

Kiss mark A blemish on the face of a clay brick produced during firing where two bricks have touched.

Kitemark The certification mark awarded by the British Standards Institution (BSI) to a wide range of products and services to show their conformity to a BSI standard in respect of quality and performance: the Kitemark is a registered trademark. ■ See **BSI**.

Knee brace A wood or metal strut fixed from the underside of a horizontal beam or truss to the vertical face of the structure supporting it to strengthen the joint: see **corbel**.

Knee, elbow This usually refers to a pipe bend fitting that allows a pipe to perform a turn of any angle, but commonly 90°.

Knock-on effects Consequential effects (or impacts) of delay or disruption to one or more activities on subsequent activities in the same construction project.

Knowledge (1) In cases of breach of contract, the aggrieved party is only entitled to recover such part of the loss reasonably foreseeable to result from the breach, and what was reasonably foreseeable depends on the knowledge possessed by the parties. For this purpose, knowledge possessed is of two kinds, one imputed and the other actual. Everyone, as a reasonable person, is assumed to know the ordinary course of things and consequently what loss is liable to result from a breach in that ordinary course. But to this knowledge there may have to be added, in a particular case, knowledge which the contract-breaker actually possesses of special circumstances outside the ordinary course of things of such a kind that breach in those special circumstances would be liable to cause more loss: *Victoria Laundry (Windsor) Ltd v Newman Industries Ltd* [1949] 2 KB 528 (CA) (later considered in *The Heron II (C Czarnikow Ltd v Koufos* [1976] 2 Lloyd's Rep 555; [1967] 3 WLR 1491; [1967] 3 All ER 686 [1969] 1 AC 350 (HL))). (2) The knowledge required for bringing an action for damages for negligence under the Limitation Act 1980, s14A is knowledge both (i) of the material facts about the damage in respect of which damages are claimed and (ii) of the other facts relevant to the current action. See *Harris Springs Ltd v Howes* [2007] EWHC 3271 (TCC); [2008] BLR 229.

Kompetenz-kompetenz German: "competence-competence", a principle entitling arbitrators to decide for themselves whether they have jurisdiction to determine the validity or applicability of an arbitration clause on a provisional basis, the parties being entitled to apply to court to have the issue reconsidered. ■ See the **Arbitration Act 1996**, s30.

KPI See **Key Performance Indicator.**

Kraft paper Strong brown paper produced from wood pulp chemically treated to retain only cellulose fibres: used for packaging, including wrapping paper, and multi-wall sacks to supply building materials: can also be treated with bitumen or wax or bleached white for special uses.

K-value The measure of the thermal conductivity of a building material. It is measured by the rate of transfer of heat over a period of time, in watts per square metre per degree Celsius. The lower the value, the better the insulation provided by the material since it limits the transfer and loss of heat. The K-value of an entire building can also be ascertained. ■ See also **R-value** and **U-value**.

L

Labour In bills of quantities, an item for work to be done with materials itemised separately.

Labour constant The rate of production for repetitious construction activities such as bricklaying plastering and tiling: standard labour constants are given in pricing books and are used by quantity surveyors to price work before tenders are obtained and to check tenders.

Labour-only subcontractor A subcontractor who provides the tradesmen to work on site but the main contractor has to provide the tools and equipment and supervision of the work. The main contractor may be held responsible for the employment and tax status of each tradesman.

Laches Fourteenth century English (from the Latin *lax* and the Old French *lasche*): negligent or unreasonable delay in prosecuting a claim for an equitable remedy. The principle of the doctrine is that it would be unjust to give a remedy to a party who either by his conduct has done that which might fairly be regarded as equivalent to a waiver of it or by his conduct and neglect has put the other party in a situation in which it would not be reasonable to place him if the remedy were afterwards to be asserted: *Lindsay Petroleum Co v Hurd* [1874] LR 5 PC 221. Its most common application is in the case of injunctions, where a party who stands by and allows another party to proceed with an undertaking is not entitled to seek an injunction at a later date.

Lack of cover (1) The absence of relevant or adequate insurance cover: a **Contract administrator (CA)** will require the main contractor to produce evidence of cover for public liability, all risks and third-party insurance to the limits stated in the tender documents. (2) Insufficient concrete cover to the steel reinforcement bars in reinforced concrete.

Lacquer A clear or coloured varnish which dries by the evaporation of its solvent base. Some lacquers are now usually sprayed onto metal surfaces.

LADs Liquidated and ascertained damages. ■ See **Liquidated damages**.

Lady Justice A female member of the Court of Appeal.

Lagging Insulation material surrounding pipes and boilers to prevent heat loss from heating pipes or freezing of pipes exposed to cold conditions, for example, in roof space. Asbestos fibre was often used in the past to lag boilers and hot pipes but its use has been banned for many years. Modern pipe lagging usually comprises foam and rubber compounds formed in a circular sleeve. Lagging may also refer to insulation in a roof space in the form of blankets of cellulose glass or mineral fibre.

Laid to fall The regular slight slope to which external hard surfaces are laid (particularly roads, pathways and hardstandings) to facilitate drainage into the ground or to a drainage channel to avoid ponding of water and formation of ice.

Laitance A layer on the surface of newly laid concrete consisting of cement and fine aggregate which forms a thin weak crust. It is caused by the concrete being too wet or being overworked: the excess water migrates to the surface carrying the fines. Laitance has to be removed to expose a solid concrete surface: this is done by acid etching or mechanical means such as grit blasting, scabbling or mechanical planing.

Laminate Process by which thin sheets of material (glass, plastic, wood, fabric) are bonded together under pressure with an adhesive material. In some products (eg plywood and **Glulam**), the same material is used throughout, while in others, layers of plastic are incorporated.

Laminated glass Safety glass formed by a layer of thermoplastic material **PVB** bonded between two sheets of annealed glass. If shattered, the glass fragments into small pieces and the plastic layer holds it together. It also blocks ultra violet light and reduces sound transmission. It is used in car windscreens, shop fronts, roof lights and windows which might cause injury if damaged particularly when external glazing at height.

Laminated plasterboard Plasterboard backed by a vapour barrier and a sheet of thermal insulation material, often phenolic foam.

Laminated wood Formed by thin sheets of timber glued together with resin under pressure. Plywood has the wood grain running crosswise in successive layers: in other types of laminated wood (eg for furniture) the grain runs in the same direction. It is widely used for flooring where the veneer surface is backed by laminated layers for strength.

Lands Tribunal A tribunal established under the Lands Tribunal Act 1949 to deal with various compensation claims relating to land. It was abolished in 2009, its functions being transferred to the **Upper Tribunal (Lands Chamber)**.

Lap joint Joint between two pieces of timber where one partially overlays the other: normally a half lap joint where half the thickness is chiselled away on each piece where they overlap. In a cross joint, the timbers meet at right angles, for example, at the corner of a frame: in a mitred joint, the timber is cut at an angle and in a dovetail joint the joining sections are cut at an angle in two planes to strengthen the joint. A lap joint may be strengthened by wooden dowels through the joint or by a metal fastener.

Lapse of offer The expiry of the period for the acceptance of an offer to enter into a contract.

Latent damage Damage caused by tortious negligence of which the victim does not have the knowledge required for bringing an action for damages, identified in the Limitation Act 1980, s14A(6) as inserted by the **Latent Damage Act** 1988. ■ See **Limitation**.

Latent Damage Act The Latent Damage Act 1988, which reformed the law relating to limitation concerning claims in tort for negligence other than those causing personal injuries. Its importance has been minimised by subsequent decisions limiting a builder's duty of care: see **Economic loss**.

Latent defect A defect that is not obvious or easily discovered, as opposed to a **Patent defect**, which is obvious. ■ See **Defect**.

Latham Report An influential report and review of the procurement and contractual arrangements in the UK construction industry, entitled *Constructing the Team*, written by Sir Michael Latham and published in July 1994.

Law Lord Previously, an informal description of a member of the House of Lords exercising a judicial capacity in deciding appeals.

Law Report A record of a judgment prefaced by a summary, known as a headnote and sometimes accompanied by a brief commentary. The most widely cited series of law reports are those published by the Incorporated Council of Law Reporting, being the Appeal Cases (AC), the Chancery Division (Ch), the Queen's Bench Division (QB), Family (Fam) and the Weekly Law Reports (WLR). The All England Reports (All ER) are also often cited. Specialist series relating to construction cases are the Building Law Reports (BLR), the Construction Law Reports (ConLR) and the Technology and Construction Law Reports (TCLR).

Laxton's Building Price Book A commercial guide that provides detailed information on the price of building works broken down into constituent elements such as the cost of materials and labour. The rates and prices given are derived from recent contracts and suppliers' price lists and are used by quantity surveyors to price tenders or estimates and to value variations. ■ See also **Spon's Price Books**.

Layout The spatial arrangement of a structure(s) or a plan or drawing showing such an arrangement.

LCIA London Court of International Arbitration

LCJ See **Lord Chief Justice**.

LDEDC or LDEDCA Local Democracy, Economic Development and Construction Act 2009.

LDF See **Local Development Framework**.

Lead flashing See **Flashing**.

Leaded light A window consisting of diamond-shaped panels of glass held in lead.

Leading question A question which assumes a fact not proved, the most famous example being "When did you stop beating your wife?". A leading question may not be put to a witness during either his examination-in-chief or his re-examination because he will be questioned on behalf of the party who has called him to give evidence, who cannot suggest the answer he should give. There can be no objection to a leading question being asked in cross-examination.

Leads and lags A lead is period of time which must elapse between the beginning of one activity in a construction programme and the beginning of another and a lag is the period of time which must elapse between the end of one activity and the beginning of another.

Leaf Part of a **Cavity wall.** ➤ **Figure E3**

Lean mix Mortar or concrete containing little cement.

Lean to roof Rafters inclined at 30° against a wall.

Learning curve A graphical representation of the rate of learning an activity, taken into account in planning a construction project by reference to the resources, particularly labour, likely to be needed. Delay and disruption claims often cite interruption of the learning curve, particularly during the early stages of an activity, as a cause of loss of productivity.

Legal set-off A common law right to claim a credit for one liquidated debt or money demand against another, even if unrelated, provided that the amounts can be ascertained readily and without difficulty.

Legal time See **Time immemorial**.

Letter of acceptance A letter from one party (usually a contracting authority) to another (usually a contractor or supplier) which creates a binding contractual relationship between the parties prior to the entering of a formal contract.

Letter of intent A letter from one party (usually an employer or main contractor) to another (usually a contractor or subcontractor) indicating an intention to enter into a formal contract with that other party. The effect of such a letter depends entirely on its terms and the surrounding circumstances and there is no generally accepted understanding of the consequences of using the term, unlike "without prejudice". As contractors frequently begin mobilisation and even work on site after receipt of letters of intent, difficult question can arise as to any entitlement to payment and its basis of calculation. The letter may be no more than expression of current intention and of no binding effect (***Turriff Construction Ltd v Regalia Knitting Mills*** (1971) 9 BLR 20), or it may give rise to a binding contract to pay for part or the whole of the works (*Monk Construction Ltd v Norwich Union Life Assurance Society* (1992) 62 BLR 107 (CA)).

Level 2 BIM The second level of the Bew/Richards BIM Maturity Model. It requires that all design team members utilise 3D models, but not necessarily one single, shared model.

Level 3 BIM The third level of the Bew/Richards BIM Maturity Model. Currently not widely employed on projects, but is envisaged that all designers will contribute to one single 3D model with the model's embedded information harnessed for purposes not yet fully defined. Technological advances in software will inform the direction of Level 3 BIM.

Lex arbitri Latin: "law of the arbitration", the **Curial law** or law governing the arbitration.

Lex fori Latin: "the law of the forum", the law of the place where a hearing is taking place.

Liability The issue of one party's entitlement against another in principle, as opposed to the issue of the **Quantum** of any damages or debt involved. The distinction is sometimes a difficult one to make, particularly where there may be separate trials on the two issues.

LIBID The London interbank bid rate, being the rate of interest a bank will receive for overnight deposit in the market.

LIBOR The London interbank offered rate, being the rate of interest at which leading London banks lend to each other in the open market.

Lien A right to retain the property of another until a claim has been satisfied. In the absence of express contractual provisions, liens can only arise from certain relationships which do not include that between an employer and a contractor or a main contractor and a subcontractor. An architect, engineer or surveyor, however, has a lien upon plans and documents prepared on his client's instructions until payment. A lien can arise by express contractual provision: *Hawthorn v Newcastle-on-Tyne & Hallway Co* [1840] 3 QB 734. In other common law jurisdictions, legislation has provided for charges similar to liens on completed works in favour of those who have carried them out. Apart from United States and Canada, these have largely been superseded by security of payment legislation similar to the Housing Grants, Construction and Regeneration Act 1996.

Life cycle The expected economic life of works after completion.

Life cycle cost analysis A method of assessing the total costs of a building throughout its useful life.

LIFT Local Improvement Finance Trust. A form of PPP designed to build and refurbish primary care premises.

Lifting the corporate veil See **Corporate veil**.

Light A window.

Lightweight aggregate Materials, such as perlite or vermiculite, used in plaster or concrete.

Limitation Limitation of actions, the law relating to statutory provision for the time within which claims may be brought. An essential feature of the English law of limitation is that it bars the remedy of bringing a claim but does not extinguish the right underlying it. A claimant is thus not prevented from bringing a claim after the relevant period unless the defendant relies on the legislation, now the Limitation Act 1980. The relevant periods are six years from the date of damage for a claim in negligence or, if later, three years from the date a claimant could have known, that is, the "date of knowledge", six years from the date of breach of a contract not made as a deed or 12 years for breach of one made as a deed, and six years from the date of a debt falling due. A failure to include a sum in an interim certificate gives rise to a different cause of action from the failure to include a sum in a final certificate (even if it happens to be the same sum), so that there can be two different limitation periods in respect of the same sum: *Henry Boot Construction Ltd v Alstom Combined Cycles Ltd* [2005] EWCA Civ 814; [2005] BLR 437 (CA); [2005] 1 WLR 3850.

Limited company A company the liability of which is limited by its shares or a guarantee. The essential characteristic of a limited company is that it is a separate legal personality from that of the shareholders or guarantors, who will not be directly liable for the company's debts. ■ See **Corporate veil**.

Limited liability partnership (LLP) An entity formed under the provisions of the Limited Liability Partnership Act 2000, the members of which have limited liability. An LLP has a legal personality independent of its members and resembles a limited company in its relationship with others. An LLP should not be confused with a limited partnership formed under the provisions of the Limited Partnerships Act 1907, some members of which will have limited liability.

Line of balance A type of programme which allows the different rates of productivity to be modelled and the interrelationship between different trades in an area to be compared. It is a management control process for collecting and measuring facts relating to time, cost and accomplishment. Typically used in road projects or high-rise construction where there are repeated blocks of activities. It is also known as the **Vertical Production Method**.

Linear thermal bridge Additional heat loss through the fabric or joints of a building, for example, where a wall meets a floor.

Lintel, lintol A beam above a door, window or other opening which carries and transmits the load from above.

Liquidated and ascertained damages (LADs) A synonym for liquidated damages; sometimes used in construction contracts.

Liquidated damages Also known as **Delay Damages**. A sum agreed in a contract as the damages for a breach of the contract. Construction contracts usually contain such a provision relating to delay for which the contractor is responsible and calculated at a weekly rate. If the sum is greater than that which the employer could possibly suffer as a result of the breach, the provision will amount to a **Penalty** and so will not be enforceable. Whether a clause is a penalty clause or a liquidated damages clause depends principally upon its amount; the test was formulated by the House of Lords in *Dunlop Pneumatic Tyre Co Ltd v New Garage & Motor Co Ltd* [1915] AC 79:

"(1) Though the parties to a contract who use the words 'penalty' or 'liquidated damages' may prima facie be supposed to mean what they say, yet the expression used is not conclusive. The court must find out whether the payment stipulated is in truth a penalty or liquidated damages …

(2) The essence of a penalty is a payment of money stipulated as *in terrorem* of the offending party; the essence of liquidated damages is a genuine pre-estimate of damage …

(3) The question whether a sum stipulated is a penalty or liquidated damages is a question of construction to be decided upon the terms and inherent circumstances of each particular contract judged of at the time of the making of the contract, not as at the time of the breach …

(4) To assist this task of construction various tests have been suggested, which if applicable to the case under consideration, may prove helpful, or even conclusive. Such are: (i) It will be held to be a penalty if the sum stipulated for is extravagant and unconscionable in amount in comparison with the greatest loss which could conceivably be proved to have followed from the breach …; (ii) It will be held to be a penalty if the breach consists only in not paying a sum of money, and the sum stipulated is a sum greater than the sum which ought to have been paid …; (iii) There is presumption (but no more) that it is a penalty when 'a single lump sum is made payable by way of compensation, on the occurrence of one or more or all of several events, some of which may occasion serious and others but trifling damage'….; On the other hand: (iv) It is no obstacle to the sum stipulated being a genuine pre-estimate of damage, that the consequences of the breach are such as to make precise pre-estimation almost an impossibility. On the contrary, that is just the situation when it is probable that pre-estimated damage was the true bargain between the parties…."

See also *Philips Hong Kong Ltd v Attorney-General of Hong Kong* (1993) 61 BLR 41 and *Alfred McAlpine Capital Projects Ltd v Tilebox* [2005] EWHC 281 (TCC); [2005] BLR 271; 104 ConLR 39.

Liquidated demand A demand for a sum capable of arithmetical calculation without further investigation.

Liquidation The insolvency process, also known as winding up, leading to a company's dissolution, involving the collection and realisation of its assets, followed by their distribution in accordance with established rules.

Liquidator An authorised insolvency practitioner whose function is to carry out the insolvency process of **Liquidation**. He may be appointed by creditors, the company itself, the court or, on the application of the official receiver, by the Secretary of State. A liquidator can bring proceedings in the name of the company.

Lis Latin: "an action", coming to mean an issue.

Listed building A building noted as being of special architectural or historic interest which has been placed on the Statutory List of Buildings of Special Architectural or Historic Interest. Grade I buildings are those of exceptional interest. Grade II* are particularly important buildings of more than special interest, whilst Grade II are of special interest, justifying every effort to preserve them. There are approximately 374,000 list entries. 92% are Grade II.

LJ Lord Justice or Lady Justice, a member of the Court of Appeal.

LJJ Lords Justices or Ladies Justices.

Lloyd's Rep Lloyd's Law Reports, a series containing commercial cases.

LLP See **Limited liability partnership**.

Load-bearing wall A wall carrying a load as well as its own weight and wind force.

Load factor The ratio of a load which would cause failure to the design load of a structure or member.

Local Democracy, Economic Development and Construction Act 2009 (LDEDC or LDEDCA) Came into force on 1 October 2011. Part 8 included a number of amendments to the adjudication and payment provisions of the **Housing Grants Construction and Regeneration Act** 1996. ■ See **Adjudication** and **Construction Act**.

Location plan A plan showing the position of a site in relation to the surrounding area.

Local Development Framework (LDF) As a consequence of the Planning and Compulsory Purchase Act 2004, local authorities are required to produce a Local Development Framework (LDF) which will set out guidelines for spatial planning and development. The LDF, together with the **Regional Spatial Strategy (RSS)**, forms the development plan that will determine how the planning system will shape particular areas in the future. In determining planning applications, local planning authorities must have regard to their LDF.

Lock out The closure of or the suspension of work at a workplace or a refusal by an employer to continue to employ part of his workforce. One of the relevant events under the JCT forms of contract which can justify an extension of time.

Lockshield valve A valve on a radiator which allows it to be disconnected without draining the heating system.

Locus sigilli (LS) Latin: "the place of the seal": it indicates where a seal should be fixed to a deed.

LOI See **Letter of Intent**.

London stock A yellow, hand-made, brick from Kent used for the majority of building work in London and the South East in the early 19th to 20th centuries.

Lonely BIM A **BIM** term used to refer to a project environment where only one party is using a 3D model (typically for visualisation purposes) with all other parties using 2D files. Synonymous with Level 1 BIM.

Lord Chancellor Until 2005, the head of the judiciary in England and Wales.

Lord Chief Justice The head of the judiciary and president of the Courts of England and Wales.

Lord Justice A male member of the Court of Appeal.

Lord Ordinary A Scottish judge normally sitting as a judge of first instance in the **Court of Session**.

Loss and/or expense See **Direct loss and/or expense**.

Loss of productivity A head of contractor's claim arising from the fact that the amount of labour or equipment required for a particular task is greater than that allowed for in the contractor's tender. The implication of the phrase is that the contractor has "lost" the productivity which he would otherwise have achieved but for an event or events entitling him to loss and expense under the express terms of his contract with the employer or amounting to a breach of that contract by the employer. The proof of such a claim will be dependent on the reasonableness of the allowances included in the tender sum and establishing causation, particularly where the contractor or his subcontractors may have been inefficient.

Loss of profit A head of damage arising from the claimant being deprived of an opportunity to make a profit. In the case of a contractor, this could be the profit to be made on the balance of works where there has been a repudiation or wrongful termination by the employer, or a profit to be made on another contract where the employer has been responsible for delay. An employer can rarely claim loss of profit arising from delays during the course of the works because of the parties' agreement of **liquidated damages**, although the claims concerning business interruption due to defects and remedial work are not unusual. Construction contracts often provide for the recovery of loss of profit by the contractor where an item is omitted by instruction.

Louvers, Louvres A blind or shutter with horizontal slats that can be angled and which is used, in commercial and residential buildings, to provide ventilation or admit and control light entry whilst maintaining protection against rain and other elements. It is also used to provide screening or simply for aesthetic effect.

Lowest price One of the two systems of procurement under the EU Procurement Regulations that allows for selection on the grounds of price alone. ■ See **Most Economically Advantageous Tender** (**MEAT**).

Luminaire An electric light fitting, lamp or similar device used to create artificial light and/or illumination, by use of an electric lamp.

Lump sum contract A lump sum price is a price for a given amount of work which is not subject to remeasurement. The traditional building contract based on bills of quantities which represent the amount of work to be undertaken is a lump sum contract. By way of contrast, a traditional civil engineering contract is based on a schedule of rates: see **Measurement and value**.

M

M&E Mechanical and electrical

M&O Management and operations, a form of contractual arrangement primarily used in the nuclear industry.

Macob Civil Engineering Ltd v Morrison Construction Ltd [1999] BLR 93; 75 ConLR 101: Seminal decision which provided a clear route for the enforcement of adjudicator's decisions. It was held that although the timetable for adjudication was very tight and was sometimes likely to result in injustice, Parliament must be taken to have been aware of this. It was clear that Parliament had intended that the adjudication should be conducted in a manner which those familiar with the grinding detail of the traditional approach to the resolution of construction disputes found difficult to accept. The intention of Parliament was to introduce a speedy mechanism for settling disputes in construction contracts on a provisional interim basis. This required the decision of adjudicators to be enforced pending the final determination of the disputes by arbitration, litigation or agreement.

Made ground Site which has been filled or raised with imported material such as excavated sub-soil or building debris such as bricks or concrete. Unless this artificial fill has been laid and consolidated under controlled conditions, it may need to be excavated to undisturbed ground level for sound foundations to be constructed.

Main contract A contract between a **main contractor** and an employer, site owner or client, as opposed to a subcontract between a main contractor and subcontractor.

Main contractor The contractor directly employed by the site owner or client, usually a general contractor experienced in a wide range of construction work, who employs subcontractors who may be domestic or named by the employer. A main contractor is likely to be the **principal contractor** under the **Construction (Design and Management) Regulations 2007, SI 2007/320** responsible for planning, managing and co-ordinating work on site during the construction phase to ensure that health and safety requirements are met. Increasingly, main contractors are taking on some degree of responsibility for design.

Main Contractor's Discount (MCD) Main Contractors Discount is a trade discount that applies to the value of the works undertaken by any party. The value of this discount is typically 1/39th or 2½% of the tendered figure and is usually deducted from any application for payment and should be clearly stated on all invoices, applications and accounts. It is sometimes linked to prompt payment.

Main services duct An underground pipe or channel carrying main services such as water gas and electricity into a building.

Main stop valve Manual control which allows the flow of mains water to a building to be cut at the rising main if internal pipework is damaged: the valve is often located immediately outside the building. Also safety valve to cut supply of high pressure water or steam to a boiler or similar apparatus.

Mains supply The pipe or cable through which water or electrical power is supplied to a site or building.

Mains voltage The measurement of electrical power: the consumer supply in the United Kingdom operates at 240 V (nominally at 230 V ± 10%) with a frequency of 50 Hz. The voltage from the generating plant is dropped by a series of transformers controlled by the supply company.

Maintenance period The traditional description in civil engineering contracts for a period of several months after practical or substantial completion of the works the appearance of defects during which the contractor will be responsible for remedying at his own expense. Usually, a contractual provision for a maintenance period provides an additional right and the contractor will remain liable to rectify defects resulting from defects in materials or workmanship during the limitation period. ■ See **Defects Liability period**.

Major Project Construction Contract A JCT 2011 form of contract for use in substantial projects by experienced employers and contractors. It provides only core terms and omits some terms from the standard building contract such as insurance provisions on the basis that the parties will draft their own detailed terms for matters such as insurance and variations. The contract includes a Third Party Rights Schedule to avoid the need for separate collateral warranties, and a Pricing Document. The employer states his requirements and the contractor provides his proposals. A sub-contract form and a contract guide are also produced.

Make-up The composition of a tender or a price for an item of work.

Mala fides Latin: "bad faith".

Management contract A contract by which an employer or developer engages a management contractor to carry out the management function for a project, such as the JCT Management Building Contract (MC) 2011. In the first phase the manager carries out specified duties, and in particular helps the employer to assemble works packages for tender, for which he is paid a fee. In the second phase, the manager or management contractor enters into the works contracts and manages them: he is paid the prime cost of the building works, but the manager's powers in relation to **works** or **trade contractors** are subject to co-operation with the employer's architect, so he is in an intermediate position between a traditional main contractor and management contractor, who has no contractual obligation to carry out the works: see **Construction management**. See **Appendix 4**.

Management time A head of damage recoverable in principle for breach of contract. The current trend is towards increased recoverability of management time: see *Aerospace Publishing Ltd v Thames Water Utilities Ltd* [2007] EWCA Civ 3; [2007] BLR 726 (CA); 110 ConLR 1.

Mandatory provision A provision in a statute, contract or rule which must be complied with, as opposed to a permissive provision which enables a course to be adopted. A mandatory provision is usually, although not invariably, indicated by the use of the word "shall" as opposed to "may".

Manhole Access point at or about ground level for inspection, unblocking and repair of underground services, particularly drainage: often at junctions of drain and sewer runs. Circular or rectangular in shape with a metal or concrete cover.

Manifest error One of the grounds upon which an **expert determination** may be challenged. The following principles will be applied: (1) It is important for the operation of commerce that commercial men and bankers can rely upon the finality of a certificate: in *Toepfer v Continental Grain Co* [1974] 1 Lloyd's Rep 11 (CA). Lord Denning put the position in the following terms: (2) "Apart altogether from authority, I am clearly of the opinion that a mistake by the certifier, even when afterwards admitted by him to be a mistake, does not invalidate the certificate. It remains binding as between seller and buyer all down the chain... it must be remembered that numerous persons act on the faith of the certificate, such as buyer, sub-buyers, bankers lending money and so forth. Good sense requires that the finality of the clause should be upheld by arbitrators and the Courts in full." (3) Even if the certifier admits that he has made a mistake, the court should uphold the finality of the certificate (see the passage quoted above). (4) The exception of manifest error should be construed in this commercial context. (5) "Manifest" meant in ordinary language "plain and obvious". (6) The manifest error must relate to the certificate or the procedure that led to the making of the certificate; for example, it would be a manifest error if a plain and obvious mistake of transcription had been made or a plain and obvious error had been made in testing or in sampling or in mixing the samples. (7) In deciding whether there was a manifest error the court should take into account the technical knowledge that parties would have about the testing procedure. See *Galaxy Energy International Ltd v Eurobunker Spa* [2001] EWHC 502 (Comm); [2001] 2 Lloyd's Rep 725; [2001] 2 All ER (Comm) 912. Manifest error is not a ground upon which the enforcement of an adjudicator's decision can be resisted: *Bouygues (UK) Ltd v Dahl-Jensen Ltd* [2000] BLR 522 (CA).

Manifestation Markings on glass as a decorative feature and in particular to warn against risk of collision into glazed door screens and windows, in order to comply with Building Regulation Requirements N1/N2. Made by etching or sand blasting glass or adhesion of translucent vinyl strips.

Manipulative interpretation The rejection as repugnant to the main purpose of the contract, or cutting down to size in order to produce a reasonable result, of wide words in a contract which in their natural meaning would give rise to an unreasonable result. Its use in relation to exclusion clauses was disapproved of by the House of Lords in *Photo Productions Ltd v Securicor Transport Ltd* [1980] AC 827.

Mansard roof Roof construction with sloping roof on two or four sides: the slope on each side changes, at a steeper (near vertical) pitch on the lower section and a shallower pitch towards the top, with the effect that greater headroom is created within the roof, which can more easily be used as a habitable space in the attic. Dormer windows are often inserted to give light. ■ See also **Dormer window**.

Mareva injunction The previous name for a **freezing injunction**, after *Mareva Compania Naveira SA v International Bulkcarriers SA* [1975] 2 Lloyd's Rep 509. See r25 of the CPR.

Masonry Generic term for blocks of natural stone, artificial stone products, bricks and similar materials, usually in its constructed form with mortar or render.

Master An officer of the High Court who exercises many important judicial functions, particularly the giving of directions before trial. Masters do not deal with cases in the **TCC** list.

Master key A key capable of opening several locks in a building.

Master programme A programme for a construction project showing all activities.

Mastic A plastic waterproof compound with adhesive qualities which becomes firm when exposed to air over time but retains some flexibility. Used extensively for sealing adjoining hard surfaces where little movement is expected, such as glass in window frames and around bathroom and kitchen fittings to prevent water penetration.

Material change See ***Pressetext Nachrichtenagentur v Republik Oesterreich (Bund)***.

Material circumstances Under the JCT forms, if and whenever it becomes reasonably apparent that the progress of the Works or any Section is being or is likely to be delayed, the contractor should forthwith give written notice of the material circumstances, including the cause or causes of the delay, and should identify any event which in his opinion is a Relevant Event. Thus notice must be given of material circumstances even where there is no Relevant Event.

Materials Personal property (as opposed to real property) brought onto site for incorporation into the works. ■ See **Goods and materials**.

Materials available Evidence to be taken into account in construing a written contract, the primary material being the document itself. ■ See **Factual matrix and Parole evidence rule**.

Matrix That part of a composite material holding together larger grains, as in concrete, where the mortar is the matrix.

Matrix of fact See **Factual matrix**.

MCD See **Main Contractor's Discount**.

MDB Multilateral Development Banks. ■ See **Pink Book**.

MDF Medium-density fibreboard

MDP See **Multi-Disciplinary Practice**.

Mean radiant temperature (MRT) The temperature within a room from all sources of radiant heat such as radiators and monitors, weighted according to their surface temperature and area. This may be important in terms of design for comfort for occupants since humans are sensitive to the effects of radiant heat, which is measured by a black bulb thermometer. The MRT may have a positive or a negative value since it is compared with the radiant heat transfer from a person in the room.

Meaning of words A written instrument is to be construed according to its sense and meaning as collected in the first place from the terms used in it, which terms are themselves to be understood in their plain, ordinary and popular sense, unless they have generally in respect to the subject matter, as by known usage of a trade, or the like, acquired a peculiar sense of the same words; or unless the context evidently points out that they must in the particular instance, and in order to effectuate the intention of the parties to that contract, be understood in some other special and peculiar sense: *Robertson v French* [1803] 7 East 130.

Measured mile Used by contractors to quantify direct labour productivity losses. The method works by comparing the cost of the delayed or impacted work against the cost incurred to carry out the same or similar work which was not so-impacted. Works best with roads – hence the name – or other transport links but can equally be used on any repetitive form of construction, for example, hotel rooms or floors of a building.

Measurement The ascertainment of quantities in accordance with criteria relevant to the product: for example, linear measurement for pipework, square metres for flooring, cubic metres for ready mix concrete. In particular, the ascertainment by a quantity surveyor of the amount of work to be undertaken (in bills of quantities) or actually carried out on site (interim and final valuations). Some contracts are subject to remeasurement where payment depends on precise quantity of work undertaken or there are variations to be valued.

Measurement and value contract A contract where the works are measured in order to ascertain the sum payable to the contractor on the basis of an agreed schedule of rates. This may apply in particular to work of a repetitive nature and/or where the volume of work is not easy to predict, for example, in repair and maintenance contracts. A significant change in the measure of an item of work may justify a variation order with regard to the rate. ■ See **Remeasurement contract**.

MEAT Most Economically Advantageous Tender

Mechanical completion Term typically used in engineering projects to refer to the planned completion of the work in order that commissioning can commence. The term can be used to refer to the checking and testing of equipment and construction to confirm that it has been built and constructed in accordance with the design and specification requirements.

Mechanical engineer An engineer qualified and experienced in the design, function, construction and operation of mechanical services such as heating, air-conditioning, ventilation, gas and water supply.

Mechanical ventilation The movement of fresh air into a room and the extraction of stale air by means of a fan or other mechanical means (in contrast to natural currents of air) usually associated with the plenum and ductwork of an air conditioning system.

Mechanics' lien A charge, more typically used in the USA and Canada, that contractors or others can place against property for the value of the services and/or materials if not paid. ■ See **Lien**.

Med-Arb A process of dispute resolution by which the parties agree to mediate their dispute and if this fails to arbitrate all (or the contentious parts) of their dispute in order to achieve a binding result. It is possible to appoint the same person to both roles but difficulties arise regarding confidential information disclosed in the mediation and therefore separate appointments are usually desirable.

Mediation A procedure whereby the parties seek to resolve their dispute by agreement with the assistance of a mediator. Usually, mediation is facilitative and operates as a joint problem-solving process involving a discussion of each party's interests, "brainstorming" options, determining acceptable options by reference to objective criteria, and committing to a settlement if one can be attained. However, it is not for one party to impose a process: rather, both parties should negotiate the process. Mediation can also be evaluative in the sense that the mediator expresses a view as to the relative strengths of the parties' cases, although this is not common. As pointed out in *Nigel Witham Ltd v Smith No.2* [2008] EWHC 12 (TCC); [2008] TCLR 3; 117 ConLR 117, the courts attach importance to the willingness of parties to mediate. A common complaint from the party at risk of paying some or all of the successful party's costs is that the eventual winner failed to mediate or engage in some other form of ADR and so should not be rewarded by the court for his failure to explore ways in which the costs of the case might have been significantly reduced, if not avoided altogether. The leading case on this issue is *Halsey v Milton Keynes General NHS Trust* [2004] EWCA Civ 576; [2004] 1 WLR 3002; [2004] 4 All ER 920. In giving the principal judgment in the Court of Appeal, Dyson LJ stressed that a departure from the general rule on costs was not justified unless it had been shown that the successful party had acted unreasonably in refusing to agree to ADR. In deciding whether a party had acted unreasonably, the court should bear in mind the advantages of ADR over the court process and have regard to all the circumstances of the particular case, including the nature and merits of the dispute, the extent to which other settlements had been attempted and whether the ADR had a reasonable prospect of success.

Mediator An independent and impartial person appointed by the parties to conduct a mediation. Drawn from a wide spectrum of professional backgrounds including quantity surveyors, architects, engineers, lawyers and even retired diplomats and judges. There is no generally recognised qualification to be a mediator, but many are members of bodies such as CEDR, who provide training and will nominate a mediator on the application of the parties.

Medium-density fibreboard (MDF) A manufactured type of hardboard made from wood fibres bound together by resin and wax and formed under high pressure and temperature into boards with a typical density of 600–800 kg/m^3. It is able to be sawn and curved and is typically used for storage units: it can also be veneered. It is denser than plywood, and it is liable to be damaged by water: it also gives off urea f ormaldehyde when cut or broken. Fire retardant MDF may be coloured red or blue.

Membrane See **DPM**.

Memorandum of understanding A document recording a measure of common ground between negotiating parties but, usually, not committing either party to a binding agreement.

Memorial Term used in arbitration to describe a party's **pleading** or **statement of case**.

Merchantable quality The standard of quality to be implied into a contract for the supply of goods under common law. The position is now covered by the Supply of Goods and Services Act 1982 s4, which implies a condition that the goods supplied under the contract are of satisfactory quality. ■ See **Satisfactory quality**.

MEP Mechanical, electrical and plumbing

Metal conduit Metal pipework or circular tubing used to protect electrical cable run: usually galvanised steel or aluminium which can be bent: a number of cables can be run through the same conduit, and it may be buried in concrete.

Metal decking Profiled steel interlinked panels used for floor construction (often of composite beam design), structural roof decking, and walkways and platforms for permanent access to roofs.

Method statement A written account produced by the contractor describing the steps by which a particular activity is to be carried out or work performed. It is an important ingredient for fulfilling health and safety requirements to ensure that the risks inherent in many construction activities are analysed and guarded against. A method statement may be required by the employer for dangerous or unusual operations and particularly in complex engineering projects or where third parties may be affected. If he approves the method statement, however, the employer may run the risk that it becomes a contract document and any changes may constitute a variation in the method of working. A method statement is likely to contain a description of the work, who is to carry out the work, a risk assessment for each operation, the control measures to be employed, when each activity is to take place, the duration of the activity, where activity is to take place showing access and safe areas, and special considerations such as possession working, permits, protection for the public, security systems, number of resources (operatives, plant materials), temporary amended systems, for example, fire evacuation.

Methods of Assessment and Testing (MOAT) Range of tests of products by the British Board of Agrément for the Agrément Certificate.

MEWP Mobile elevating work platform, that is, a cherry picker or scissor lift. Designed to provide a safe way of working at height, they allow the worker to reach the task quickly and easily and have guard rails and toe boards which prevent a person from falling. It is also known as "Pop Ups".

MEWPs Mobile elevating work platforms (MEWPs) used as access equipment by ceiling fixers and electricians and MEP trades. MEWPs include cherry pickers, scissor lifts and vehicle-mounted booms. Mobile elevating work platforms (MEWPs) can provide a safe way of working at height. They allow the worker to reach the task quickly and easily, have guard rails and toe boards which prevent a person from falling and can be used in-doors or out.

MF/1 Model Form of General Conditions of Contract for the Supply of Electrical, Electronic or Mechanical Plant with Erection. A standard form of contract published by the Institutions of Mechanical Engineers (IMechE) and Electrical Engineers (IEE) now in Revision 5.

MF/2 Model Form of General Conditions of Contract for the Supply of Electrical, Electronic or Mechanical Plant. A "supply only" version of the MF/1 contract. Revision 1. ■ See **MF/1**.

MH Manhole

MicroStation Computer software developed by Bentley Systems for computer-aided design in both two- and three- dimensions. This is one of several standard computer programmes used in the construction industry by designers and manufacturers to draw and develop both schematic and technical designs. Electronic files created using MicroStation tend to have the file extension ".dgn".

Midspan Halfway between the supports of a beam.

Mild steel Steel with a low carbon content used for reinforced concrete, pipes and joints.

Milestone A completed stage in a project defined in the contract as a marker point, for example, triggering an entitlement to payment when the foundations are installed or the roof is complete.

Mineral wool Insulation made from mineral fibres such as rock wool, furnace slag or other man made materials.

Mini-trial A form of alternative dispute resolution where each party presents their case in a concise form and subject to a fixed time limit (usually one day for the whole process) including evidence and argument. The function of the independent chairman may vary, but usually he acts in a role similar to a mediator to encourage the parties to reach their own solution. The opportunity to present evidence and to question witnesses and make submissions may bring out more clearly the strength and weaknesses of each party's case. In some versions of the mini trial, a nominee of each party may be a member of the tribunal (as with some arbitrations) and the panel may be empowered to give a binding decision having heard the case

Minor Works Building Contract (MW) A simplified form of contract published by the JCT intended for work which is simple in character and lower in value. The contract terms are therefore less comprehensive than the Intermediate Building Contract and the Standard Building Contract, but still require an Architect/CA to administer the contract. There is a separate minor works building contract with contractors design (MWD) and a sub-contract with subcontractor's design (MWSUB/D). ■ See **Intermediate Building Contract** and **Standard Building Contract**.

Misconduct Such a mishandling of an arbitration as is likely to amount to some substantial miscarriage of justice: *Williams v Wallis & Cox* [1914] 2 KB 478. Misconduct was previously a ground for the removal of an arbitrator under the Arbitration Act 1950 s23(1). It did not imply impropriety, but it came to be resented as doing so by arbitrators and was replaced by the expression "serious irregularity" in s68(2) of the **Arbitration Act 1996**.

Misfeasance in public office A tort consisting of the deliberate and dishonest wrongful abuse of the powers given to a public officer, to compensate those who have suffered loss as a result of improper abuse of power. It can be established in two alternative ways: (1) Where a public officer has performed or omitted to perform an act with the object of injuring the plaintiff, known as targeted malice; and (2) Where a public officer has performed an act which he knew he had no power to perform and which he knew would injure the plaintiff. Malice, in the sense of an intention to injure the claimant or a person in a class of which he is a member, and knowledge by the officer both that he had no power to do the act complained of and that the act or omission would probably (but not that it would necessarily or inevitably) injure the claimant or such a person, are alternative, not cumulative, ingredients of the tort. To act with such knowledge is to act in a sufficient sense maliciously. This can occur when a public contract is awarded in breach of the European procurement regime: *Harmon CFEM Facades (UK) Ltd v House of Commons* [1999] 67 ConLR 1.

Misnomer The correction as a matter of construction by the court of a name in a contract. The doctrine of misnomer is of uncertain width. It is clearly a doctrine of construction, but it is not plain to what extent it permits the reference to extrinsic evidence. *Davies v Elsby Brothers Ltd* [1961] 1 WLR 170 (CA) would suggest that where there are two possible entities, the rule is a strict one: unless one can say from the four corners of the document that the parties must have intended to refer to one rather than the other entity, then the doctrine does not apply. If, however, there is only one possible entity, then it is possible to use extrinsic evidence to identify a misdescribed party. It is arguable that *Nittan (UK) Ltd v Solent Steel* [1981] 1 Lloyd's Rep 633 (CA) falls into this latter category. Moreover, the cases, as does the common sense, suggest that a case of mere misnomer is not easily (query if ever?) concluded to be such without the mistake being explicable: *Dumford Trading AG v Oao Atlantrybflot* [2005] EWCA Civ 24.

Misrepresentation An inaccurate statement of fact or law by a party which, if acted upon by another party to whom the statement was made, may give rise to a cause of action in a number of different ways as follows: (1) In the tort of deceit, where the statement is made knowingly or without belief in its truth or recklessly, careless whether it be true or false: *Derry v Peek* [1889] 14 App Cas 337. (2) In the tort of negligence, where the statement is made without reasonable skill and care which causes damage to another where the representor is under a duty of care in tort to that other. The representation can be made to the person suffering loss or to a third party. The duty was first recognised in *Hedley Byrne & Co Ltd v Heller & Partners Ltd* [1964] AC 465 (HL); [1963] 3 WLR 101; [1963] 2 All ER 575. (3) Under the **Misrepresentation Act 1967**, which confers a discretion on the court or an arbitrator to award damages for innocent misrepresentation. (4) For breach of a warranty collateral to any contract into which the parties subsequently enter.

Misrepresentation Act 1967 A statute reforming the law relating to misrepresentation, particularly by providing a remedy of damages for an "innocent" misrepresentation which induces a party to enter into a contract with the representor. It imposes an absolute obligation not to state facts which the representor cannot prove he had reasonable grounds to believe. It thus provides a potentially more effective ground of claim than one in negligence.

Mistake In relation to contracts, mistakes which may entitle a party to relief fall into two broad categories: (1) Mistakes that prevent there being consent to the particular transaction, and (2) Mistakes that consist of a failure to express correctly in a written document the intention of the parties. The law on common mistake was reviewed by the Court of Appeal in *Great Peace Shipping Ltd v Tsavliris Salvage International Ltd*

("The Great Peace") [2002] EWCA 1407; [2003] QB 679, where it was held that the doctrine was a rule of law not based on an implied term, and that the following five elements must be present if the mistake is to avoid the contract: (1) A common assumption as to the existence of a state of affairs; (2) No warranty by either party that state of affairs exists; (3) The non-existence of the state of affairs is not attributable to the fault of either party; (4) The non-existence of the state of affairs renders contractual performance impossible; (5) The state of affairs can be the existence, or a vital attribute, of the consideration to be provided, or circumstances which must subsist if performance of the contractual adventure is to be possible. Where the parties are genuinely at cross-purposes ("mutual mistake") no contract will come into existence. The fact that the parties disagree as to the meaning of the contract does not prevent them from being bound by it: *LCC v Henry Boot & Sons Ltd* [1959] 1 WLR 1069; [1959] 3 All ER 636. A contract will be set aside as void where one party's mistake ("unilateral") as to the terms is known to the other party, or possibly ought to have been known to the other party. Specific performance of a contract may be refused where the other party did not know of the first party's mistake where it would cause a hardship amounting to injustice.

Mitigation The avoidance of loss, sometimes said to give rise to a duty, but more in the nature of a rule that a claimant cannot recover damages for a loss which he could reasonably be expected to avoid. Questions of mitigation in relation to construction contracts usually concern: (1) An offer by the contractor to remedy defects; (2) The extent and cost of a remedial scheme; and (3) Potential recovery from another party. The burden is upon the defendant to prove a failure to mitigate and the question of whether there has been such a failure is one of the facts. ■ See **Betterment** and **the Three Rules of Mitigation**.

Mix The proportions of each material in concrete, mortar or plaster.

Mobilisation Work preparatory to the start of construction on site.

Mock-up A full-scale model of part of works to be constructed to enable a final decision to be taken as to appearance and functionality.

Model A scale model of proposed works to demonstrate their appearance upon completion.

Model Law The Model Law on International Commercial Arbitration adopted by the United Nations Commission on International Trade Law (**UNCITRAL**).

Modular construction The off-site manufacture and fit out of building elements which can be delivered to site and positioned to form a structure. It is often used for buildings such a hotels, flats or university accommodation.

Modular control Control of a heating system by automatic means increasing or reducing the heat gradually.

Modular ratio The ratio of the modulus of elasticity of reinforcement to that of the masonry in reinforced concrete or brickwork.

Module A fixed dimension used in a grid on the basis of which the design of works is developed, a method known as modular design, which reduces the number of dimensions needed to be shown on drawings and assists in the preparation of specifications, bills of quantities and the production of prefabricated parts.

Modulus of elasticity The ration of the tensile stress to the tensile strain in a linear elastic material at loads less than the elastic limits of the material. Widely known as Young's modulus.

Moiety A half, usually used in relation to the **Retention monies** under a building contract.

Moisture barrier Any barrier, such as a damp proof course, intended to prevent the transmission of moisture from one part of a structure to another.

Moisture content The weight of water in a soil mass divided by the weight of the solids and multiplied by 100.

Moisture expansion An increase in volume of a material due to absorption of moisture. Bricks expand, particularly, during the first week after firing.

Moisture meter An electrical device used to detect the presence of moisture, particularly in surveys of buildings. Their accuracy is usually limited to detecting water on the surface of materials.

Moisture movement An increase in the length of a material due to an increase in its **moisture content**.

Moment distribution Analysis of the forces in a continuous structure by adjusting between the imposed loads, spans and sectional properties of the members.

Month In all deeds, contracts and other instruments executed, made or coming into operation after 1 January 1926, unless the context otherwise requires, "month" means calendar month: Law of Property Act 1925, s61. In statutes, "month" also means calendar month unless the contrary intention appears: Interpretation Act 1978, s3, Schedule 1.

Mortar The workable paste used throughout the construction industry for a variety of purposes including separating and binding brickwork, blockwork or masonry, consisting of cement, sand and water. On site, it may be referred to as "Gobbo", "Compo", "Wallop" or "Muck".

Mortise and tenon joint Traditional form of interlocking joint where the mortise is a hole into which the tenon slots. The joint can take many forms but is most frequently used in tables and doors.

Most Economically Advantageous Tender (MEAT) One of two systems of procurement under the EU Procurement Regulations, allows for selection of the tender which will bring the greatest benefit to the contracting authority taking all elements of the bid, and not just price, into account. ■ See **Lowest Price**.

Movement joints Joints deliberately formed during construction, particularly in concrete and brickwork, to accommodate movement in the completed work due to a number of causes such as thermal expansion and contraction, shrinkage, creep and subsidence.

Mullion A vertical bar dividing the lights of a window.

Multi-disciplinary practice An organisation which will provide both legal services and non-legal services under the provisions of the Legal Services Act 2007.

Murphy v Brentwood [1991] 1 AC 398, overruled the decision in *Anns v Merton London Borough Council* [1978] AC 728. Case decided on the same day and principles as *Department of Environment v Thomas Bates* [1991] 1 AC 499 (CA). Both cases involved claims for economic loss in negligence and both claims failed. In *Murphy*, a claim by subsequent purchaser against local authority for negligent approval of plans for foundations Lord Oliver stated:

> "I have found it impossible to reconcile the liability of the builder propounded in Anns with any previously accepted principles of the tort of negligence and I am able to see no circumstances from which there can be deduced a relationship of proximity such as to render the builder liable in tort for pure pecuniary damage sustained by a derivative owner with whom he has no contractual or other relationship."

However, the House of Lords did make it clear that pure economic loss may be recoverable against a party, where there is a "special relationship of proximity" which imposes "a duty of care to safeguard the plaintiff from economic loss".

Mutatis mutandis Latin: "that to be changed having been changed", the necessary changes having been made. Used for brevity when repeating a proposition in relation to a different topic or set of facts.

Mutual dealings Where, before a company goes into liquidation there have been mutual credits, mutual debts or other mutual dealings between the company and any creditor of the company proving or claiming to prove for a debt in the liquidation, an account is taken of what is due from each party to the other in respect of the mutual dealings and the sums due from one party are be set off against the sums due from the other. Only the balance (if any) of the account is provable in the liquidation. Alternatively (as the case may be), the amount is paid to the liquidator as part of the assets: Insolvency Rules 1986, r4.90. Insolvency set-off affects the substantive rights of the parties by enabling the insolvent's creditor to use his indebtedness to the insolvent as a form of security. Instead of having to prove with other creditors for the whole of his debt in the insolvency, he can set off pound for pound what he owes the insolvent and prove for or pay only the balance: *Stein v Blake* [1996] AC 243 (HL); [1995] BCC 543; [1995] 2 WLR 710.

Mutual mistake The occurrence of the parties being at cross purposes when entering into a contract: see **Mistake**.

Mutually explanatory Giving equal weight to a number of different contractual documents, as opposed to construction by reference to a specified **priority of documents**. A term is often included in construction contracts providing that the various documents forming the contract shall be taken as mutually explanatory of one another, as in the ICE Conditions.

N

NAECI the National Agreement for the Engineering Construction Industry.

Nail sickness Weakened wood caused by rusty nails. The moisture content of the wood or a preservative may have caused the nails to rust.

Nailing strip Material built into brick or blockwork that will hold nails.

Nailplate Galvanised steel plate incorporating nails designed to connect timber. It is often used in the construction of trussed rafters.

Name borrowing A process whereby a party pursues a claim in the name of another by agreement, to be distinguished from a claim vested in the first party by assignment and pursued in its own name. Name-borrowing provisions have been a feature of standard forms of subcontract for many years as a device to limit the subcontractor's recovery to the amount recoverable at his own expense in the name of the main contractor from the employer. Despite some procedural difficulties, the courts have given effect to such provisions, and the device can be used as part of a compromise: see *A Monk & Co Ltd v Devon County Council* (1978) 10 BLR 9 (CA).

Named subcontractor A subcontractor or supplier named in the main contract documents who, depending upon the terms, the main contractor must appoint or negotiate terms with for a particular task. Once appointed, the subcontractor or supplier will become a domestic subcontractor for which the main contractor is usually, entirely responsible for. Depending upon the contract the employer may assume some responsibility for named design subcontractors and termination. To be contrasted with the former procedure of nomination of subcontractors and suppliers. ■ See **Nominated subcontractor**.

National Agreement for the Engineering Construction Industry (NAECI) The NAECI or "**Blue Book**" sets the terms and conditions of employment for hourly paid engineering construction workers on major engineering construction projects and repair and maintenance sites throughout the United Kingdom.

National Building Specification (NBS) A set of standard form specifications published under the trading name of NBS by RIBA Enterprises Ltd, a company owned by the RIBA.

National House Building Council (NHBC) An organisation that began life as a self-improvement builders' organisation in 1936 and in 1965 introduced a 10-year warranty underwritten by the insurance market. The effects of the dry summers of 1975 and 1976, together with the rapid inflation of the 1970s, led to the original insurers' withdrawal and replacement by a consortium, which had no greater success. In 1978, the council became an official insurance company. The Buildmark warranty and insurance cover has been available since 1988. Mandatory arbitration under the scheme was held to contravene the Unfair Terms in Consumer Contracts Regulations 1994, SI 1994/3159 in *Zealander & Zealander v Laing Homes Ltd* [2000] 2 TCLR 724 and the effect of the current scheme is that of an agreement to agree whereby the parties can decide and agree upon what is the most suitable dispute resolution process for a particular case: see *Crest Nicholson (Eastern) Ltd v Western* [2008] EWHC 1325 (TCC); [2008] BLR 426; [2008] TCLR 9. The NHBC also undertakes building control functions.

National Joint Consultative Committee for Building (NJCC) Organisation of construction bodies and publisher of technical codes of procedure disbanded in 1996 but much of the literature is still in use with particular regard to tendering.

National Specialist Contractor's Council (NSCC) Representative body of specialist trade organisations within the construction industry.

Natural ground levels Agreed level of natural ground before ground works start.

Natural Justice The principle that a judicial or administrative decision must be made fairly is embodied in two rules: (1) No man can be a judge in his own cause, and (2) No man shall be condemned unheard. Although certifiers under construction contracts are obliged to act impartially, the rules of natural justice do not apply: see *Hounslow London Borough Council* v *Twickenham Garden Developments Ltd* [1971] Ch 233. In adjudication, any breaches of the rules must be more than peripheral; they must be material breaches. Breaches of the rules will be material in cases where the adjudicator has failed to bring to the attention of the parties a point or issue which they ought to be given the opportunity to comment upon if it is one which is either decisive or of considerable potential importance to the outcome of the resolution of the dispute and is not peripheral or irrelevant: see *Cantillon Ltd v Urvasco Ltd* [2008] EWHC 282 (TCC), [2008] BLR 250; 117 ConLR 1.

Natural ventilation Movement of air without a fan, for example, by air vents and flues.

NBS See **National Building Specification**.

NDA Non-Disclosure Agreement;Nuclear Decommissioning Authority

Neat cement grout A mixture of cement and water (not sand) to fix something (eg tiling) in place.

NEC See **New Engineering Contract**.

Negative pressure A situation in which an enclosed area has lower pressure than the area around it. Anything affecting the divide between the area of negative pressure and the more highly pressurised area around it would cause substances to flow into the area of negative pressure. Negative pressure is used in the prevention of oil spills, clearing blockages and the vacuum cleaner.

Negative rate A rate in a tender or contract that credits the employer. It is used where the contractor is able to sell on material to be removed from site.

Negligence A failure to exercise reasonable skill and care, either in breach of a contractual term or a duty of care in tort. The three elements to the tort of negligence are: (1) a duty of care; (2) breach of that duty and (3) damage as a result of the breach.

Negligent Misrepresentation An inaccurate statement of fact or law made without reasonable skill and care by one contracting party to the other before the contract has come into being which has the effect of inducing that other party to enter into the contract, which qualifies as an innocent misrepresentation under the Misrepresentation Act 1967: see **Innocent misrepresentation**. It is also used to mean a negligent misstatement in breach of a duty of care in tort: see **Negligent misstatement**.

Negligent misstatement An inaccurate representation of fact or law made without reasonable skill and care, which causes damage to another where the representor is under a duty of care in tort to that other. The representation can be made to the person suffering loss or to a third party. The duty was first recognised in *Hedley Byrne & Co Ltd v Heller & Partners Ltd* [1964] AC 465 (HL).

Negotiated procedure Form of public procurement that allows contracting authorities to negotiate with selected bidders. It is only available in limited circumstances, for example, in matters of urgency.

Negotiations Communications between parties before they enter into a contract. The parole evidence rule excludes evidence of what was said or done during the course of negotiating the agreement for drawing inferences about what the contract meant. It does not exclude the use of such evidence for other purposes: for example, to establish that a fact which may be relevant as background was known to the parties or to support a claim for rectification or estoppel. These are not exceptions to the rule. They operate outside it. See *Chartbrook Ltd v Persimmon Homes Ltd* [2009] UKHL 38; [2009] AC 1101; [2009] BLR 551; [2009] 3 WLR 267.

Nemo dat quod non habet Latin: "nobody gives what he does not have". A common law rule that prevents a person who does not own goods from passing ownership of the goods to another, there are exceptions. ■ See **Retention of title**.

Nemo debet esse judex in propria sua causa Latin: "no man can be a judge in his own cause": ■ See **Natural justice**.

Net contribution An arrangement limiting the damages payable by a construction professional where another party or parties contributed to the same damage on the basis of a deemed recovery by the employer against that or those other party or parties. A clause providing for such an arrangement will limit the professional's indemnity insurer's exposure to risk, because in its absence, the professional would be liable to pay all the damages subject to recovery of a contribution from the other party or parties. The risk of failure to recover the balance of the damages is thus passed to the employer. Net contribution clauses are common in construction professionals' standard terms of engagement, for example, clause 7.3 of the RIBA Standard Conditions of Appointment for an Architect 2010. Such a term has been held to be fair and reasonable under the Unfair Contract Terms Act 1977: see *Langstane Housing Association Ltd v Riverside Construction (Aberdeen) Ltd* [2009] CSOH 52; 124 ConLR 211.

Net floor area The internal area contained within the external walls, not including the area occupied by the structure, service risers, walls and other non-useable space.

Net lettable area Sometimes referred to as the net office or net usable area. The fraction of the net floor area for the intended occupation of the building, that is, net floor area reduced by secondary circulation areas such as route to work station.

Network A diagram showing the relationship between the items of a programme for a construction project, used in critical path analysis.

Neutral Term sometimes used to describe a **mediator** or other third party who is not directly involved in the dispute at issue and who may therefore be able to help achieve a settlement.

Neutral event An event which can entitle a contractor to an extension of time under a construction contract but not to further payment by way of loss and expense.

New Engineering Contract (NEC) A standard form of contract currently in its third edition. The contract is most well known for its short clauses, lack of legal precision and emphasis on management procedures and early warning of events which may lead to delay or costs increases in the project. The latest (3rd) edition (NEC3) was published in 2005 and an update was published in September 2011 to bring the NEC3 up to date with the changes introduced by the **LDEDCA** to the **Construction Act**. NEC3 comprises a suite of contracts that have nine core clauses. Added to this is one of six main option clauses plus other standard options to suit the procurement requirements of the client. The main option clauses include: (A) Priced contract with activity schedule; (B) Priced contract with bills of quantity; (C) Target contract with activity schedule; (D) Target contract with bill of quantities; (E) Cost reimbursable contract and (F) Management contract.

New York Convention An international treaty relating to the enforcement of arbitration awards.

Newton A unit of force. The amount of force it takes to accelerate one kilogram at one metre per second.

NHBC See **National House Building Council**.

NIA See **Nuclear Industry Association**.

Nickel sulphide An impurity trapped inside glass during its manufacture which can cause it to crack and shatter.

NJCC See **National Joint Consultative Committee for Building**.

No damages for delay clause A contractual term that excludes a contractor's claim for damages for delay. An uncommon provision in the United Kingdom, where it would be subject to challenge under the Unfair Contract Terms Act 1977, but frequently occurring in the United States and sometimes in other Commonwealth jurisdictions.

Node Where lines showing activities on a building programme meet.

No-fines concrete Concrete made from coarse aggregate and cement (ie no sand). The large pores act as a capillary break. Often lightweight, it cannot be nailed, is not usually reinforced (apart from corners) and has good key (roughness) for plaster.

Nogging or **Nog** A short horizontal piece of timber fixed between vertical studs of a timber framed wall or partition. Their purpose is (as with blocking pieces between joists) to stiffen the studs and provide intermediate fixing points for things like switch sockets and data cable points.

Noise Rating (NR) Rating the acceptability of indoor environments for the purposes of hearing preservation, speech communication and annoyance based on curves. Sound pressure levels measured in octave bands are compared with curves from which a noise rating (NR) is obtained. At higher frequencies, heavier noise ratings are given. The NR rating is the highest NR curve touched by the measured octave band spectrum.

Noise reduction coefficient A rating system used to compare the sound-absorbing characteristics of building materials. A measurement of the acoustical absorption performance of a material is calculated by averaging its sound absorption coefficients at 250, 500, 1000 and 2000 Hz.

Nominal damages Damages in a minimal amount which might be awarded for a breach of contract causing no damage.

Nominal dimension Used as a rough guide for the size of something. Its actual size may be larger or smaller by an allowable tolerance. For example, timber when cut.

Nominated subcontractor An employer-specified subcontractor to be appointed by the main contractor, such as a specialist design subcontractor from whom the employer would receive a direct warranty. JCT'98 contained complex provisions for nomination, which were dropped by JCT 2005. Contractors were often opposed to the notion and problems could arise when, using the standard JCT wording, a nominated subcontractor had failed and the employer was required to renominate. Nomination now rarely occurs although there is still provision for this in some other standard conditions (eg ICE 7th edition). ■ **See Named subcontractor**.

Nominated supplier A supplier who is subject to the same process as a nominated subcontractor. The relevant provision has not been included in JCT 2011 though GC/Works/1 still makes provision.

Non-combustibility test A test specified in BS476, Part 4: 1970 which requires the certification of materials that are non-combustible. Materials heated to 75°C which give off a flame for more than 10 seconds or raise the temperature by more than 80°C will not pass. Plasterboard complying with BS1230 Part 1: 1985 or any other material with a non-combustible core at least 8 mm thick having combustible facings (on one or both sides) not more than 0.5 mm thick fully bonded to the non-combustible sub-strata can be regarded as non-combustible, as can materials such as concrete, fired clay, ceramics, metals other than magnesium/aluminium alloys which must be assessed in each individual case, plaster and masonry containing not more than 1 per cent by weight or volume of organic material, and concrete bricks or blocks complying with BS EN 772-2:1998 and BS EN 771-3:2011. A non-combustible double-skinned panel containing thermal insulation other than non-combustible thermal insulation must be edge-sealed so that the thermal insulation material is protected from fire by the non-combustible panel containing it.

Non-completion certificate See **Certificate of non-completion**.

Non-contestable work When installing a new supply of gas, electricity or water, the work can be split into contestable and non-contestable. Non-contestable works include design approval, obtaining statutory consents, inspection of the works that can only be undertaken by the host Distribution Network Operator (DNO). This work can only be carried out by the distributor or transporter. This work comprises the provision of equipment and connection of the new service cable to existing low voltage network, design, project management and future operations and maintenance costs. ■ See **Contestable work**.

Non-disclosure A failure to communicate a matter. Generally, a party entering into a contract is not under a positive obligation to inform the other party of matters about which he has not been asked, but where the contract is one of the utmost good faith (uberrimae fidei), such as an insurance policy, he is obliged to disclose material facts. In the absence of disclosure, the insurer may be entitled to repudiate liability under the policy.

Non-disclosure agreement (NDA) A confidentiality agreement whereby parties who wish to share or make available information which would otherwise be confidential, agree not to disclose that information. It is often used during tender processes.

Non est factum Latin: "the thing has not been done". A defence originally for the enforcement of deeds made by those who were either illiterate or incapable of reading what had been written in Latin. A person who has signed a written instrument is now allowed to say that he did not consent to its terms and it is void. Needless to say, the requirements are strict and the party relying on the doctrine must be under some disability.

Non illegitimi carborundum Latin: "don't let the bastards get you down!"

Non-loadbearing wall A wall that only carries it own weight plus wind, if external.

Non sequitur Latin: "it does not follow".

Non-slip floors Finishes that includes granolithic floor sprinkled with emery or carborundum powder.

Non-trafficable roof Not intended for walking across. Accessible for light maintenance only.

Nosing The rounded edge overhanging stair riser.

Notice Information, particularly in writing as required by the terms of construction contracts, which frequently require a particular form of service such as registered post or recorded delivery (now signed for). Defences based on such provisions can be defeated by a plea of waiver or on their construction, as in *Yates Building Co Ltd v RJ Pulleyn & Sons (York) Ltd* [1975] 237 EG 183 where the Court of Appeal held that a requirement for a notice to be sent by registered or recorded delivery did not apply where the person to be served received the notice in time and the purpose of the requirement being to put the matter beyond doubt.

Notice to admit documents A notice served under a procedure provided for in CPR 32.19 whereby a party may require the authenticity of a particular document to be proved at trial. In the absence of such a notice, the authenticity of disclosed documents is deemed to be admitted.

Notice to admit facts A notice served under CPR 32.18 requiring another party to admit particular facts before trial. The party upon whom the notice is served will be at risk of the costs of proving the facts if they should have been admitted.

Notifiable projects A project is notifiable to the **HSE** if the construction phase will be longer than 30 days, or 500 person days of construction work, except where there is a domestic client. ■ See **Construction (Design and Management) Regulations 2007, SI 2007/320**.

Novation The substitution of one party to a contract by a third party, whereby a third party succeeds to both the rights and liabilities of that party under the contract. The process is achieved by a tripartite agreement between the original contracting parties and the third party whereby the original contract is discharged and a new contract is substituted. It is to be distinguished from **assignment**. The process is usually associated with design and build procurement where, after the preliminary design stage, the employer's design consultants enter into novation agreements and are adopted by the contractor. This is intended to sever the consultants' contractual obligations to the employer although reporting obligations are often expressly retained which may cause a possible conflict of interest. Following the decision in *Blyth & Blyth Ltd v Carillion Construction Ltd* [2001] Scot (CS) 90; 79 ConLR 142, contractors must take care as they could find themselves required to take liability for the design of the works without having recourse to the designers who have prepared the design. In *Blyth*, there was a novation agreement, which purported to place upon the consultant the responsibility for all services performed prior to the novation as services performed for the contractor. The consultant commenced proceedings against the contractor for non-payment of fees.

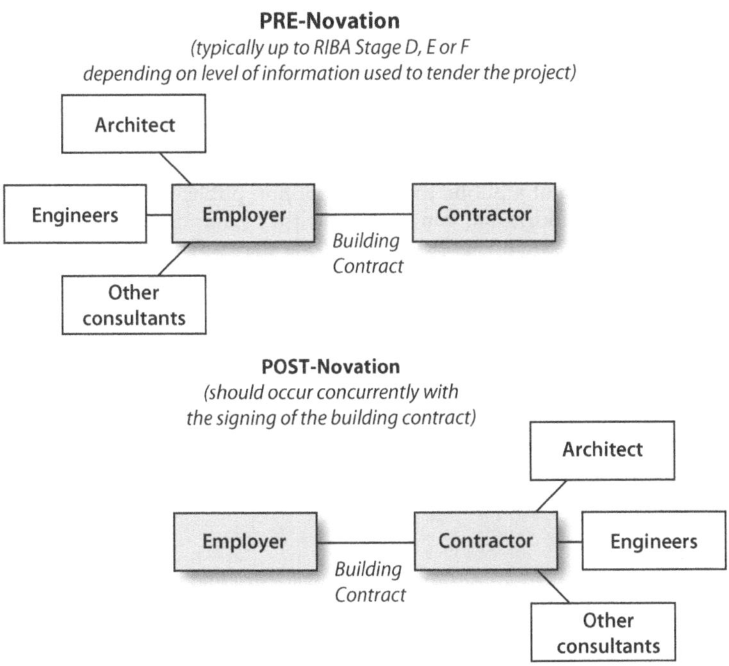

➤ **Figure N1.** Novation

The contractor counterclaimed for breaches of contract that occurred prior to the novation. The court decided that the contractor could not bring proceedings against the consultant, because the contractor had suffered no loss for which the consultant owed a duty to the contractor. ➤ **Figure N1**

Novus actus interveniens Latin: "a new act intervening", which breaks the chain of causation between the breach by the defendant and the damage suffered by the claimant.

NOx Oxides of nitrogen that are a chief component of air pollution that can be produced by the burning of fossil fuels. It is also called nitrogen oxides.

NR Noise-relating

NSC/4 A JCT standard form of nominated sub-contract for use under JCT 98. It can be used as either a lump sum contract or a re-measurement contract. The conditions are contained in NSC/C.

NSCC See **National Specialist Contractor's Council**.

Nuclear Decommissioning Authority (NDA) Set up in 2005 to oversee the decommissioning and clean up of civil nuclear sites across the United Kingdom.

Nuclear energy The energy stored in the nucleus of an atom and released by fusion, fission or radioactive decay.

Nuclear Industry Association (NIA) Trade association of the civil nuclear industry within the United Kingdom.

Nuclear reactor Device for producing a controlled release of nuclear energy.

Nuisance There are three types of nuisance: private, public and statutory. Private nuisance involves unlawful interference with the use or enjoyment of land. This can be in the form of noise, smells or other matters such as overhanging trees or plants. Public nuisance is an act or omission which damages, inconveniences or causes injury to the public such as the obstruction of a public road. An action in public nuisance will only succeed if an individual can show that they have suffered damage or inconvenience which significantly exceeds that suffered by the general public. Statutory nuisance is where an Act expressly prohibits nuisance. Nuisance under the statute usually arises when a certain act required by the statute such as the maintenance of buildings or streets is not adhered to.

O

Oath A formal undertaking invoking the name of God, or in any other lawful manner, to tell the truth when giving evidence. The form is governed by the Oaths Act 1978. Evidence will be admissible if given on oath or by **affirmation**.

Obiter dictum Latin: "something said by the way": a statement in a judgment which is not essential to the court's decision on the question of law under consideration and is not part of the determinative elements of the decision. Case reports may contain helpful discussion of collateral legal issues which are not strictly necessary to the **ratio decidendi**. A statement in a higher court which is obiter may have persuasive effect in later cases in the absence of other authority but is not binding on lower courts. ■ See **Ratio decidendi**.

Objective approach Establishing the mutual intention of the parties to a written contract by the ascertainment of what is to be taken as the intention which reasonable people would have had if placed in the situation of the parties, rather than by direct evidence of what their intention was: *Reardon-Smith Line Ltd v Yngvar Hansen-Tangen and Sanko SS & Co Ltd* [1976] 2 Lloyd's Rep 621; [1976] 1 WLR 989.

Obstruction Improper intervention by an employer in the certification process and a ground for disregarding a certificate or its absence as well as entitling the contractor to terminate under the JCT forms. ■ See **Prevention principle**. ■ See also **Adverse physical conditions**.

Occupancy The physical possession of real property. The legal status of an occupier which will determine his rights in relation to the property may be that of a tenant, licensee or trespasser. Residential occupiers cannot be evicted without a court order. A contractor is usually entitled to possession of the site under a contractual licence for the duration of the works until practical completion.

Occupiers' liability The duty imposed primarily by the Occupiers' Liability Act 1957 on occupiers of premises not to cause injury to visitors caused by dangers due to the state of the premises or to things done or omitted to be done on them. Contractors and subcontractors with a sufficient degree of control over sites to be able to ensure their safety and appreciate that a failure on their part to use care might result in injury to a visitor are likely to be regarded as occupiers, as well as or even in distinction from the owners: *Ferguson v Welsh* [1987] 1 WLR 1553 (HL); [1987] 3 All ER 777.

OCR See **Optical character recognition**.

ODN Ordnance datum Newlyn. ■ See **Above ordnance datum**.

Off site Not on site, in the context of goods and materials intended for use in contract works but stored off site for reasons of space or safety. If properly marked as the property of the employer their cost may be included in interim valuations.

Offer A statement made by a person putting forward terms for a contract. An offer must be certain in its terms and may specify the mode of acceptance, for example that it must be in writing or made within a certain time. It must be made with the intention to create a contract, and not for example as a gratuitous offer of help or to make a gift or as a mere advertisement of products. An offer capable of acceptance can however be made to the public at large, but generally when goods are displayed or advertised the offer is made by the intending purchaser. An offer can be made orally as well as in writing (or both) but a contract must be supported by consideration. ■ See **Consideration, Contract**.

Offer to settle A proposal to compromise a dispute. Offers to settle can be made on the following bases: (1) Open and so capable of being mentioned to the court at any time; (2) Without prejudice and not be referred to in open correspondence or discussions or to the court at any time; (3) Without prejudice save as to costs, to be referred to only when all issues except costs have been disposed of; (4) Sealed, the equivalent of a "without prejudice save as to costs" or **Calderbank** offer in arbitration; and (5) Under CPR Part 36. The usual consequence of a claimant obtaining less by way of judgment or award than the amount of an offer to settle by the defendant which can be referred to, is that of the claimant being directed to pay the claimant's costs from the date of that offer. If a claimant recovers more than the amount of his offer to accept a lesser sum from the defendant, he will usually recover costs on the **indemnity basis from the date of his offer**. ■ See **Open offer, Part 36 offer, Without prejudice, Without prejudice save as to costs**.

Office cost The sum of office and administration overheads and factory cost.

Official receiver A civil servant of the Insolvency Service and an officer of the bankruptcy court whose role is to investigate and manage any bankruptcy or insolvency.

Official referee The title of judges who tried High Court construction cases before the introduction of the TCC: now known as judges of the Technology and Construction Court. ■ See **Technology** and **Construction Court**.

Official referee's schedule A synonym previously used for a **Scott Schedule**.

OHP (OH&P) See **Overheads and profit**.

OJEU The Official Journal of the European Union

OJEU Notice A notice placed in the European Union's Official Journal which indicates that a contracting authority is intending to issue a tender for goods or services

O&M See **Operation and maintenance manual**.

Omissions Work specified in the contract but which the employer no longer requires to be carried out, or which may be superseded by variations to the works. Following an instruction from the architect, the value of the omitted work is calculated and an appropriate adjustment is made to the contract price or valuation of the variation. Provisional sums will also be omitted and the actual cost of work carried out added back in to the final contract sum.

On costs See **Overheads**.

On demand bond A contractual undertaking by a person, usually a bank, to pay a specified amount of money to a third party on the occurrence of a stated event, the wording of which has the result that the liability of the person who has given the bond arises on mere demand by the creditor, notwithstanding that it may be evident that the principal is not in any way in default or even that the creditor himself is in default under his contract with the principal. ■ See **Performance bond**.

One-line programme See **Single-line programme**.

Onerous property Any unprofitable contract and any other property of an insolvent company which is unsaleable or is not readily saleable or is such that it may give rise to a liability to pay money or to perform any other onerous act: Insolvency Act 1986, s178(3). A liquidator has the power to terminate an unprofitable contract unilaterally under the right to disclaim onerous property under s178(5).

Onus Latin: "burden". ■ See **Burden of proof**.

Open book Where the contractor offers full disclosure to the employer of his accounts for a particular project. Often used in partnering contracts where the pricing basis will typically be open book **cost-plus** basis which includes an element of **pain/gain share**.

Open-drained joint A shaped open joint between cladding panels which allows water and in particular wind driven rain to enter the joint and thereby avoid running down the face of the building. The water is prevented from penetrating into the building however by a baffle built into the panel (usually a neoprene or plastic gasket) and an air seal at the rear of the joint. The water follows a path within the joint to a flashing in the horizontal joints which directs it externally to run down to ground level.

Open offer An offer to compromise a dispute which is made on an open basis and can be subsequently referred to in open correspondence or discussions and before the court.

Open plan Layout of premises (in particular offices and schools) without internal partitions to divide floors into rooms, although low demountable partitions to separate work stations may be installed. This permits maximum penetration of natural light and may result in more efficient ventilation and heating and the running of service cables for IT and greater efficiency in conduct of occupier's business.

Open procedure A one-stage tender process where tenders are advertised and any contractor or supplier of services is free to submit a tender for the works without any prequalification. ■ See **Restricted procedure** and **Negotiated procedure**.

Open tendering Where tenders are advertised on behalf of the employer to the public at large, often in trade magazines and other outlets, and any contractor or supplier of services is free to submit a tender for the works without any prequalification. The tendering of public works is subject to the **Public Contracts Regulations 2006, SI 2006/5**.

Opening note and speech In a trial in the Technology and Construction Court, each party's advocate will be expected to provide an opening note, of modest length and proportionate to the size and complexity of the case, outlining that party's case in relation to the issues identified at the pre-trial review. The notes can be exchanged simultaneously or served sequentially and should identify the documents in the trial bundles which the parties consider the judge should read before the hearing.

The claimant's note, which should include a neutral summary of the background facts, a chronology and a "cast list", should usually be served two clear working days before the start of the trial. Other notes, which should be shorter and assume familiarity with the factual background, should normally be served by 1 pm on the last working day before trial. The judge is likely to have had the opportunity to read into the case in some detail before the trial begins, particularly where he is the assigned judge who has dealt with case management. In such circumstances the opening of the case will be comparatively short, with brief statements by each party. Although it is not normally necessary to embark upon legal argument during these speeches, it is helpful to foreshadow legal arguments which explain the relevance of particular parts of the evidence or will assist the court in following a party's case. See para 15.2.5 of the **TCC Guide**. A similar procedure will usually be adopted in an arbitration where there is a full hearing.

Opening up The process of exposing or dismantling part of the works for the purposes of inspection. Construction contracts usually provide that the contractor will bear the cost of doing so if defects are revealed and otherwise the employer will do so.

Operation and maintenance manual (O&M) Operation and maintenance manuals define the requirements and procedures for the effective operation, maintenance, decommissioning and demolition of a building or project. Typically an O&M will provide details of the building's construction, history and/or maintenance as well as instructions for operation and maintenance of any systems within the building as well as guarantees and warranties.

Operational bills Bills of quantities set out by reference to operations rather than trades.

Operative An experienced workman, not possessing a particular trade or skill, but more skilled than a labourer.

Opinion evidence Evidence of a witness's opinion, which is only admissible in the case of expert evidence given with the court's permission: CPR 35.4.

Optical character recognition The process by which images of printed or manuscript text are captured by an optical scanner and converted by software into an encoded format which can then be used to scan, manipulate, store, search and transmit the text by electronic means. A large volume of contract documentation can be stored on disc when scanned: this is also a substantial benefit in the conduct of disclosure for claims. OCR systems have more difficulty in reading handwriting than printed texts.

Optimum moisture content A moisture content which will produce the highest dry density of a soil after compaction.

Oral testimony Evidence provided in person by a witness or expert to a court.

Orange Book FIDIC Conditions of Contract for Design-Build and Turnkey published in 1995. First **FIDIC** contract to introduce a **Dispute Adjudication Board**.

Order A formal direction made by the court.

Order 14 The former Rule of the Supreme Court under which **Summary judgment** could be given on a claim.

Ordinary meaning See **Meaning of words**.

Oriented strand board (OSB) A manufactured board made from strands of wood bonded with resin and wax and compressed. The wood used in manufacture can include material not suitable for timber plank production including undersized trees and is therefore economical to produce. The wood is shredded and then placed in layers in alternating directions. OSB can be sawn and nailed and has good thermal properties. It is often used as a lining material in walls and inside roofs.

O-ring joint A circular ring made of synthetic rubber or thermoplastic material which is seated in a groove in a joint assembly at the end of a pipe and then compressed when a connection is made with another fitting in order to create a watertight seal. Used in tap fittings and drain pipes.

Or other approved An alternative to the product identified which must be approved by the employer or his agent. The expression is often used in specifications and bills of quantities.

Orthographic projection The drawn representation of an object seen from front view, side view and in plan; it may also include a view along each axis of the object (axonometric projection). The purpose is to depict a three dimensional object in two dimensions on the plan. For greater accuracy six sides of the object may be shown as if it were contained in a rectangular box and its appearance in each plane was projected onto one side of the box. Used in engineering design.

OSB See **Oriented Strand Board**.

Outer House The Outer House of the **Court of Session** in Scotland, being the court of first instance in civil matters and the equivalent of the High Court in England and Wales.

Outer string The length of timber which runs diagonally on the open side of a staircase and supports and encases the treads and risers of the stairs. It matches the wall string on the other side of the staircase. ■ See **Wall string**.

Out of ground The stage at which the substructure is complete and construction work reaches above the natural ground level of the site.

Outline planning permission Permission granted in principle for development of a site, enabling an applicant to find out at an early stage whether or not the local planning authority approves a proposed scheme, without having to incur substantial costs for the purchase of the site and the detailed design of the development. Since 2006 the application must deal with key design principles such as the layout of the site, the scale of the development including its height and access points. Where outline permission is granted, a subsequent submission of "reserved matters" (further detailed plans and specifications as requested by the local authority) must be made within three years and approved prior to commencing development. ■ See **Change of use**, **Full planning permission, Planning application, Planning permission**, and **Reserved matters**.

Outrigger Form of scaffolding in which supporting poles or beams are cantilevered out of building windows at right angles to facade and which support plank walkway parallel to wall or other scaffolding. Also an extension to scaffolding at ground level to give greater stability.

Oven-dried timber See **Kiln-dried timber**.

Overcladding The renovation of a façade by the addition of a new skin over the existing fabric: usually carried out on substantial buildings with a repetitive design such as blocks of flats. It may be required to remedy defects in the original construction (spalling and water penetration) but also provides opportunity to improve insulation and waterproofing to modern standard and improves appearance. Materials include panels of aluminium or plastics on a sub-frame or of concrete with a protective render. Water disposal and ventilation between the two skins of the building is essential.

Overflow A pipe or other outlet allowing liquid to escape from a container when it fills to its limit: in particular a pipe which discharges from a water tank or cistern.

Overflow rainwater gutter A hole or scupper to let overflowing rainwater escape from the gutter away from the building.

Overhang Part of a structure which projects beyond the vertical face of its support, such as the eaves which overhang the external walls of a building.

Overheads It is doubtful that a precise definition of overheads is possible. It is a word whose precise meaning varies with the context, but its core element is that it refers to expenses, such as those related to fixed assets which do not vary according to the level of business activity: *British Telecommunications plc v Bell Cable Media (Leeds)* Ltd [2001] BLR 343. It usually refers to the costs of running a contractor's general business as distinct from the site costs of the particular contract. Contractors often claim "loss of overheads" in relation to periods of delay on the basis that they have been prevented from undertaking other work which would have made a contribution to their overheads. ■ See **Head office overheads, Site overheads** and **Preliminaries**.

Overheads and profit A percentage usually applied to the cost of labour and materials to arrive at a price.

Overpanel A timber panel above a door, providing a fixing location for the door opening mechanism: may be glazed as a fanlight.

Overriding objective The underlining principle of civil litigation as stated in Part 1.1 of the CPR when introduced in 1998. The court is required to deal with cases justly, which includes: ensuring that the parties are on an equal footing; saving expense; dealing with the case in ways which are proportionate to the amount of money involved, the importance of the case, the complexity of the issues and to the financial position of each party; ensuring that the case is dealt with expeditiously and fairly; and allotting to it an appropriate share of the court's resources, while taking into account the needs of other cases. The parties are under an obligation to assist the court in achieving the overriding objective. Recognition of the overriding objective may justify the court in departing from traditional case management, for example by limiting the amount of time which each party is permitted to take to present its case.

Oversail To project beyond a vertical wall or boundary: in particular used of a crane whose arc takes its jib beyond the boundary line of adjoining property or the public highway: normally this requires permission from the landowner or the local authority since their rights extend into the airspace above their property.

Oversite concrete A layer of dry-mix concrete spread over the surface of the natural ground in order to seal it prior to construction work: also refers to a foundation slab incorporating a damp proof course laid direct onto natural ground (in contrast to a suspended slab).

Owner A synonym for the employer under a construction contract.

Ownership See **Title**.

Oxidation A corrosion reaction in which the corroded metal forms an oxide; usually applied to a reaction with a gas containing elemental oxygen, such as air.

P

PABX Private automatic branch exchange being a telephone exchange that serves a particular business or office, as opposed to one that a common carrier or telephone company operates for many businesses or for the general public.

Package deal contract A contract, also known as a "design and build contract", under which the contractor undertakes both design and build obligations.

Pad, padstone (1) A block built into a wall or fixed to the top of a pier on which a beam or truss rests; (2) any large block carrying a load.

Pagnan v Feed Products [1987] 2 Lloyd's Rep 601: the parties are to be regarded as masters of their contractual fate in determining what terms are essential. Lloyd LJ said that: "It is for the parties to decide whether they wish to be bound and, if so, by what terms, whether important or unimportant".

Pain/gain share An agreement whereby a contractor has the opportunity to "gain" where the project is delivered below the target cost, but where the contractor will be expected to absorb "pain" where there are overspend costs. ■ See **Contractor's share percentages and share ranges**.

Pali radice An underpinning system consisting of mini piling typically installed in existing basements to strengthen existing foundations which are settling or which can be used to support increased loads.

Pallet (1) A portable platform, usually designed to be easily moved by a forklift, on which goods can be stacked, for transport or storage; (2) a flat base for combining stores or carrying a single item to form a unit load for handling, transportation and storage by materials handling equipment.

PAP See **Pre-action protocol**.

Paralegal A clerical assistant who gives practical backup to members of the legal profession. Many paralegals are in fact legally qualified.

Parametric design Design which links the relationship and function of one object to other objects and specified criteria. Using Building Information Modelling to its full extent employs parametric design rather than basic geometric, computer-aided design whereby the software is simply used as a replacement for the traditional drawing board. For example, when an external wall is drawn, it is given a relationship or "link" to say the windows, eave overhand and doors within that wall. When the wall is moved during the design development process, the windows, eaves and doors change accordingly. ■ See **Building Information Modelling (BIM)**.

Parapet Low wall or barrier at the edge of a balcony, bridge, roof, terrace or where there is a drop. ➤ **Figure P1**

Parent Company Guarantee See **Guarantee**.

Pareto optimality The improvement of an agreement for at least one of the parties while not making the agreement worse for any other party.

Pari passu Latin: "with equal progress", equally. The rule that creditors of an insolvent company must be dealt with on an equal footing.

Sir Lindsay Parkinson (Sir Lindsay) & Co Ltd v Commissioners of Works and Public Buildings [1949] 2 KB 632; [1950] 1 All ER 208:

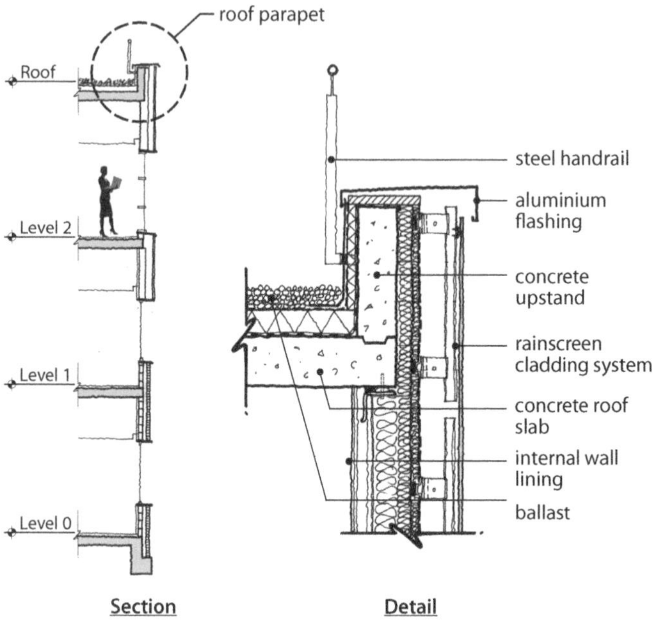

➤ **Figure P1.** Parapet

it was held that an employer is obliged to pay a contractor for any requested work in excess of the contractor's estimate on a **Quantum meruit** basis.

Parole evidence rule The rule that, if a contract has been reduced into writing and is meant in itself to constitute an entire agreement, oral evidence is not allowed to be given of what passed between the parties, either before the written instrument was made or during the time that it was in a state of preparation, so as to add to or subtract from, or in any manner to vary or qualify, the written contract. Thus, evidence of negotiations leading up to the making of a contract cannot be relied on to interpret the contract: such evidence is unhelpful, because where negotiations are difficult, the parties' positions are changing and until the final agreement, though converging, still different, it is only the final document which records a consensus, construction of different expressions in previous documents is a doubtful process and does not help on the construction of the contractual words, and something may be lost by looking back to the use of the same expressions since the relevant surrounding circumstances may be different when there was no consensus of the parties: see *Prenn v Simmonds* [1971] 1 WLR 1381, *per* Lord Wilberforce at 1384H–1385A. The rule only excludes extrinsic evidence for the purpose of drawing inferences about what the written contract means, but not for other purposes, such as resolving an ambiguity or determining the factual matrix or whether or not there has been a mistake or misrepresentation. ■ See **Misrepresentation, Negotiations** and **Rectification**

Parquet floor Polished floor finish of hardwood blocks laid in patterns on a firm base.

Part 7 claim A claim commenced and issued by the court in accordance with CPR Part 7. Part 7 prescribes what is to be filed at court and served on the defendant when such a claim is commenced. This is the general procedure for all claims which are likely to involve a dispute of fact. The Technology and Construction Court has developed a fast-track procedure for the enforcement of an adjudicator's decision which specifies that a Part 7 Claim Form is used. See s9 of the **TCC Guide**.

Part 8 claim A claim commenced and issued by the court in accordance with CPR Part 8. Part 8 prescribes what is to be filed at court and served on the defendant when a claim is commenced. One of the main differences to Part 7 is that the claimant files all evidence upon which it relies when the claim is issued and there are no substantial disputes of fact. As such the Part 8 is only suitable for disputes on law/the construction of a document and is often used during ongoing adjudications to clarify disputes on jurisdiction.

Part 20 Claim A claim other than a claim made by the claimant against the defendant. Formally known as either a counterclaim or third party claim.

Part 36 Offer An offer made by either the defendant or claimant in accordance with the CPR Part 36 which imposes severe costs sanctions in the event that the offeree rejects the offer and at trial fails to recover a higher sum. The offer has to be in writing and open for acceptance for 21 days. If it is accepted within the 21 days, the offeror is to pay the costs of the offeree up until the date of acceptance. In the event that the offer is rejected by the defendant and judgment is granted against him for a higher amount the court can order interest on any sums payable at up to 10 per cent starting from the date the offer was made and for the claimant's costs to be paid on the indemnity basis or with interest not exceeding 10 per cent, or both. If the defendant makes a Part 36 offer and judgment is entered for less than the offer the court will order that the claimant pay the defendant's costs from the last day the offer could have been accepted until the conclusion of the trial.

Partial possession Many JCT standard forms make provide for the employer to take possession of part of the works before completion. Generally, on partial possession: (1) the architect or contract administrator must issue a certificate to that effect; (2) the certificate must state the value of the work taken over; (3) half the retention in respect of the part taken over must be released; (4) the amount of liquidated damages must be reduced in proportion to the value of the work taken over the total contract sum and (5) the contractor's liability, if any, for the insurance of the part is removed. Some JCT forms provide for early use or occupation of part of the site or works with the contractor's consent, which must not be unreasonably delayed or withheld, subject to notification of insurers.

Partiality See **Bias**.

Particle board An engineered wood product manufactured from wood particles, such as wood chips, sawmill shavings or saw dust and a synthetic resin or other suitable binder, which is pressed and extruded.

Particleboard is used as an alternative to conventional wood and plywood in instances where appearance and strength are less important than cost.

Particulars of claim The claimant's statement of case which sets out the legal and factual basis of the claim and the relief sought. The Particulars of Claim are either served and filed along with the Claim Form or filed within 14 days thereafter.

Partition A screen or a non-loadbearing wall dividing a space into parts.

Partner A member of a **Partnership**.

Partnering The forming of a relationship between two or more parties with the intention of improving efficiency and reducing disputes. It was one of the recommendations of the **Latham Report** and several forms of partnering contract have now been published including PPC 2000 and JCT Constructing Excellence. ■ See **Project partnering**.

Partnership An association of persons or organisations joined as partners in business. Subject to the provisions of the Partnership Act 1890 which commences by describing partnership as the relationship which "subsists between persons carrying on a business in common with a view of profit". ■ See **Joint venture**.

Party wall A wall dividing adjoining properties. There are three categories of party wall: (1) where the wall is divided vertically, the whole wall being subject to reciprocal easements; (2) where the wall is divided vertically into strips, one belonging to each adjoining owner; (3) where the wall belongs entirely to one owner, subject to his neighbour's rights to have it maintained as a dividing wall. The basic rights are those of support and user over structure. An owner may demolish his half of the wall so long as he does not disturb his neighbour's right of support. Where one person owns the entire wall, he may do whatever he likes to it, subject to resulting damage in negligence or other statutory liability if he demolishes his building.

Party Wall Act 1996 Strictly the Party Wall etc. Act 1996, this is an Act extending and reforming previous legislation applicable to the Inner London area, which provides a framework for preventing and resolving disputes in relation to party walls, boundary walls and excavations near neighbouring buildings. A person intending to carry out work of the type described in the Act must give adjoining owners notice of his intentions. Where the intended work is to an existing party wall (s2 of the Act) a notice must be given even where the work will not extend beyond the centre line of a party wall. Adjoining owners can agree with that person's proposals or reach agreement with him as to changes as to the manner and timing in which the works are to be carried out. Where there is no written consent or agreement, the Act provides for the resolution of "disputes". The Act covers: (1) work that is going to be carried out directly to an existing party wall or structure; (2) new building at or astride the boundary line between properties and (3) excavation within 3 or 6 m of a neighbouring building(s) or structure(s), depending on the depth of the hole or proposed foundations.

Passing off A common law tort used to enforce unregistered trademark rights. The tort of passing off protects the goodwill of a trader from a misrepresentation that causes damage to goodwill. The law of passing off prevents one person from misrepresenting his goods or services as being the goods and services of the claimant. The tort of passing off also prevents one person from holding out his goods or services as having some association or connection with the claimant when this is false. A successful claim for passing off requires satisfaction of three elements: (1) goodwill owned by a trader; (2) misrepresentation and (3) damage to goodwill.

Passivation A reduction of the anodic reaction rate of an electrode involved in corrosion. The changing of a chemically active surface of a metal to a much less reactive state. ■ See **Activation**.

Passive fire protection A component of structural fire protection and fire safety in a building. Attempts to contain fires or slow the spread, through use of fire resistant walls, floors and doors.

Passive solar heating The reduction of the need for heating through the careful planning and design of buildings to optimise the amount of energy that can be derived directly from the sun. ■ See also **Active solar heating**.

Passivhaus An energy performance standard developed in Germany in the early 1990s by Professors Bo Adamson of Sweden and Wolfgang Feist of Germany. To achieve the standard there must be: (1) a maximum space heating and cooling demand of less than 15 $kWh/m^2/year$ or a maximum heating and cooling load of 10 W/m^2; (2) a maximum total primary energy demand of 120 $kWh/m^2/year$; and (3) an air change rate of no more than 0.6 air changes per hour @ 50 Pa.

Patent ambiguity An ambiguity on the face of a written instrument, as distinguished by Francis Bacon from a latent ambiguity, which arises from extrinsic facts. A number of old authorities suggest that extrinsic evidence was admissible to resolve a latent ambiguity but not a patent one. The distinction has, however, been described as "based on outmoded and highly technical and artificial rules" and "not merely capricious but also … incoherent": see *Schuler (L) A.G. v Wickman Machine Tool Sales Ltd* [1973] 2 Lloyds Rep 53; [1974] AC 235 and *Mannai Investment Co Ltd v Eagle Star Life Assurance Co Ltd* [1997] AC 749; [1997] 2 WLR 945; [1997] 3 All ER 352.

Patent defects A defect that is obvious or easily discovered, as opposed to a latent defect, which is not. Patent defects are also called "detectable defects". It is no defence for a contractor to say that a defect was patent and must or should have been seen by the employer or his construction professional during the course of the works: see *East Ham Corp v Bernard Sunley & Sons Ltd* [1966] AC 406 (HL). ■ See **Defect**.

Patent glazing A proprietary glazing system for opening lights, skylights, etc. Metal glazing bars supporting glass without putty, employed in roofs and walls. Its dry construction enables speed of erection.

Patina The film of oxide which forms on certain metals when exposed to air, such as verdigris on copper.

Pay direct clause See **Direct payment**.

Payless notice Introduced by s144 of the **LDEDCA**, and replacing the **withholding notice**, the pay less notice is a notice given by the payer that the payer will pay less than the sum stated in the payment notice. If the payer fails to give a valid payless notice then the payer must pay the sum stated in the payment notice by the final date for payment without any deduction. If the payer does not, the payee can go to court or first obtain an adjudicator's decision requiring payment. ➤ **Figure P2**

Payment into court Previously, a procedure whereby a defendant could offer to settle a monetary claim by paying a lesser sum into an account held by the court, now superseded by the offer procedure under CPR Part 36. A defendant can still pay money into court if he is relying on a defence of tender, and can also ordered to do so as a condition of being allowed to defend a claim or pursuing an appeal of a judgment against him.

Payment notice A notice from the employer (or any paying party), in accordance with s110A of the **Construction Act** following an application of the contractor which specifies how much they intend to pay. ➤ **Figure P2**

Pay-when-paid clause A clause usually, but not exclusively, found in subcontracts which provides that payment will not be made to the subcontractor until the main contractor has been paid by the employer. Such clauses were ineffective under a construction contract governed by Part II of the **Housing Grants, Construction and Regeneration Act 1996** except where the employer is insolvent and are now outlawed by the **LDEDCA** 2009 which extends prohibition to "pay when certified". Similar statutory provision is made in legislation in other Commonwealth jurisdictions.

PBA See **Project bank account**.

PC item or sum Prime cost sum

PD See **Practice Direction**.

Pea gravel Gravel that consists of small, rounded stones used in concrete surfaces. Also used for walkways or driveways.

Penalty A punishment, the essence of which is a payment of money stipulated as in terrorem of the offending party. The law does not give effect to a contractual provision which amounts to a penalty by obliging a party in breach to pay a sum greater than that which the other party could possibly suffer as a result of the breach. Inaccurately used in the building industry to describe a liquidated damages provision. ■ See **Liquidated damages**.

Pencilling Mortar-joints in brickwork painted to emphasise them.

Pepper v Hart [1992] UKHL 3; [1993] AC 593; [1992] 3 WLR 1032. If primary legislation is ambiguous or obscure, the courts may in certain circumstances take account of statements made in Parliament in construing that legislation. Prior to this decision, making use of Hansard, the record of Parliamentary proceedings, in this way, would have been regarded as a breach of Parliamentary privilege.

Peremptory order An order of the court or arbitral tribunal which applies a sanction for non-compliance. A peremptory order will specify a time limit for compliance which if not adhered to will result in sanctions as to costs or the right to claim or defend the whole or part of the claim. Documents not being admitted in evidence or adverse inferences being drawn from the lack of compliance.

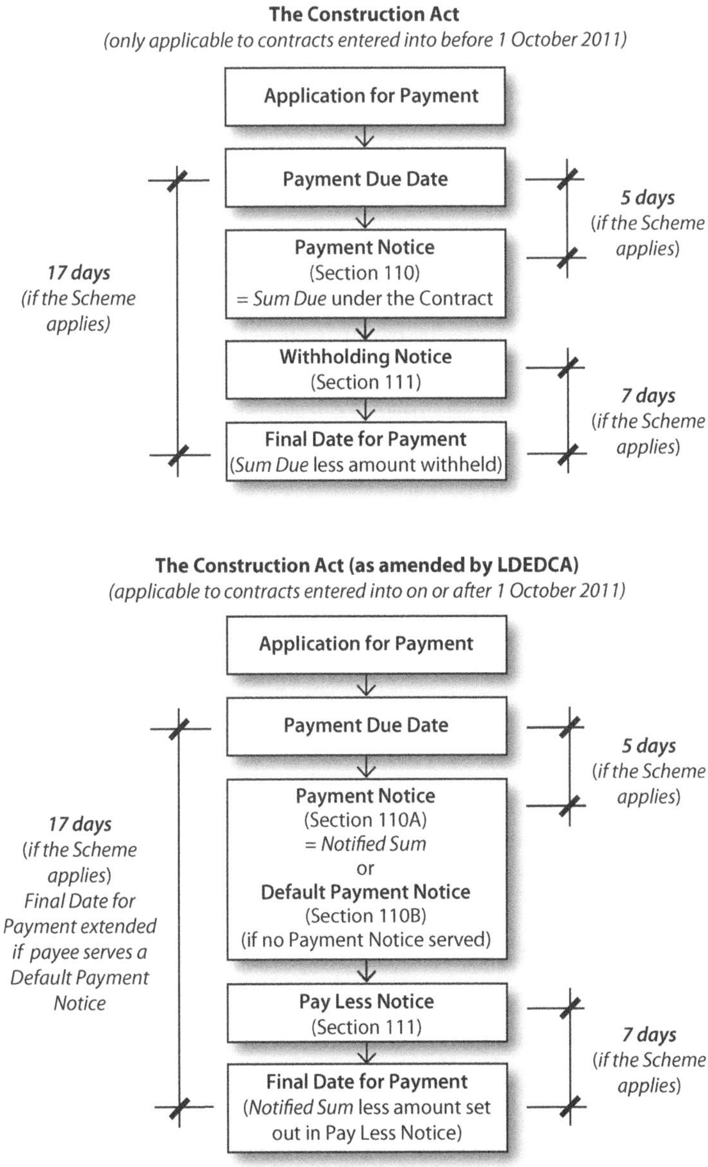

➤ **Figure P2.** Payment under the Construction Act

Perforated brick A brick or block in which holes passing through it exceed 25 per cent of its volume, and in which the holes are not small.

Performance bond or security A contractual undertaking by a person, usually a bank, to pay a specified amount of money to a third party on the occurrence of a stated event, usually the non-fulfilment of a contractual obligation by the principal to that third party. Sometimes the wording of the contract has the result that the liability of the person who has given the bond arises on mere demand by the creditor, notwithstanding that it may be evident that the principal is not in any way in default or even that the creditor himself is in default under his contract with the principal. It all depends on the wording of the instrument. It is often a difficult question to determine whether, on its true construction, a particular contract which provides for payment on demand is a performance or demand bond (where the obligation to pay is triggered by a demand alone or by a demand accompanied by the provision of specified documents) or whether it is a guarantee (strictly so called) where the obligation to pay is of the "see to it" kind, that is, conditional on proof by the creditor of default by the principal: see *VosslohAtkiengesellschaft v Alpha Trains (UK) Ltd* [2010] EWHC 2443 (Ch).

Performance specification A specification directed to a result rather than the standards of workmanship and materials to be used. ■ See also **Prescriptive specification and Specification**.

Performance Specified Work (PSW) A document (first described in JCT 98) which sets out standards to be achieved by a design.

Performance test contract A contract under which the primary design obligation of the contractor is to meet performance requirements.

Peril A fortuitous and unexpected event of the type against the risk of which insurance is usually taken out. In the JCT standard forms of building contract the "specified perils" can also be grounds for an extension of time for completion. ■ See **Specified peril**.

Period of final measurement In former RIBA and JCT standard forms of building contract, a time within which the final measurement and valuation of the works was to be completed before the issue of the final certificate.

Permanent works The works to be constructed under a construction contract and left on site, as opposed to **Temporary works** used as part of the construction process.

Permitted development Development for which planning permission is not required.

Perpend A vertical joint between bricks, stones or blocks in a horizontal course. Perpend also refer to the ends of walls first built-up by bricklayers to provide a level for the courses in between. ➤ **Figure B3**

Person-in-charge A site agent or foreman retained by the contractor to supervise the works.

Perspex, Plexiglas A clear acrylic resin used mainly as a substitute for glass.

PERT See **Program Evaluation and Review Technique**.

PFI See **Private Finance Initiative**.

PFI contract Generally, contract made under the private finance initiative. Specifically, a construction contract are excluded from the operation of Part II of the Housing Grants, Construction and Regeneration Act 1996 by article 4(1) of the Construction Contracts (England and Wales) Exclusion Order 1998, made pursuant to the powers conferred by ss106(1)(b) and 146(1) of the Act.

PFP See **Passive fire protection**.

pH A measure for acidity or alkalinity, meaning "potential Hydrogen".

Phenolic foam A material used to make insulating boards. It is very light and does not burn easily.

Piercing the corporate veil See **Corporate veil**.

Pig A device which travels through a pipeline and which is typically used to either inspect for defects or obstructions or to remove accumulated debris and otherwise clean the pipeline. The name is thought to be an acronym for pipeline intervention gadget or pipeline inspection guage, although some prefer to say that the name is derived from the squealing noise the object makes when going down the pipeline.

Pilaster A slightly-projecting column attached to the face of a wall.

Pile An upright timber post driven into unstable ground to support a superstructure.

Pink Book FIDIC conditions of contract for construction – Multilateral Development Bank (MDB) Harmonised edition.

Pinnel's case The rule in *Pinnel's case* (1602) 5 Co Rep 117 is that a creditor is not bound by a promise to accept part payment in full settlement of a debt.

Pitch Degree of slope given to any part of a roof.

Pitched roof A roof structure where the roof slants to one side of the building.

Plain concrete (1) Concrete without reinforcement or reinforced only for shrinkage or temperature changes; (2) concrete without some other specific admixture or element.

Plaintiff Previously, the claimant in litigation.

Plan A two-dimensional drawing used to demonstrate the horizontal arrangement of a design. More specifically, a horizontal section is taken through the building (or product) and the drawing represents the horizontal view as seen from above. ■ See **Orthographic projection** and **Figure G3**

Planning application A formal application to the local planning authority for permission to carry out development or make a change of use.

Planning conditions Conditions attached to a planning permission which must be fulfilled for the permission to be effective.

Planning permission In accordance with s57 of the Town and Country Planning Act 1990, anyone intending to carry out any development of land must obtain planning permission. Simply put, this is the authorisation from the local council to proceed with the development. Planning permission may be obtained in one of three ways: (1) a development order which negates the need to apply to the local authority for permission; (2) a deemed grant of planning permission; and (3) as a result of an express application made to the local planning authority. In the majority of cases, an express application is required. Those seeking permission may either obtain full planning permission or outline planning permission. ■ See **Full planning permission**, **Outline planning permission**, **Permitted development** and **Planning application**.

Planning supervisor See **CDM Coordinator**.

Plant Equipment used by a contractor, which may include temporary or pre-fabricated buildings, tools, mechanical equipment, goods, scaffolding, dumpers, cranes and materials. The ICE standard forms now refer to "Contractor's Equipment" in place of "Constructional Plant". A construction contract is excluded from the operation of the Construction Act under s105(2) of that Act if the works comprise the assembly, installation or demolition of plant or machinery, or erection or demolition of steelwork for the purposes of supporting or providing access to plant or machinery, on a site where the primary activity is nuclear processing, power generation, or water or effluent treatment, or the production, transmission, processing or bulk storage (other than warehousing) of chemicals, pharmaceuticals, oil, gas, steel or food and drink. There are a number of authorities relating to this exclusion and the meaning of "plant" in this context.

Plant level The level at which the plant for the mechanical and electrical services is located.

Plantroom A room in which the plant for the mechanical and electrical services is located.

Plasterboard A wallboard with a gypsum plaster core bonded to layers of paper or fibreboard; used instead of plaster or wallboard to make interior walls.

Plasterwork Architectural work executed in plaster.

Plasticiser Additives that increase the plasticity or fluidity of the material to which they are added; these include plastics, cement, concrete, wallboard and clay. Plasticisers increase the material's flexibility and allow for a lower use of water.

Plate glass Strong, thick high-quality glass cast in sheets and polished.

Platform floor A raised floor designed to provide access to cables beneath the floor.

Pleading A formal statement of a party's case in litigation and arbitration, now known as a statement of case and the art of preparing such a document.

Plenum A pressurised chamber containing gas or fluid.

Plexiglas A synthetic material used as an alternative to glass.

Plot ratio The ratio of the gross floor area of a building to its site area.

Plumb A line which is exactly vertical or perpendicular to a level horizontal line.

Plumb level A straight bar with a plumb line attached to it.

Plumb line A line from which a weight is suspended to determine verticality or depth.

Plunge column A structural steel (occasionally concrete) section embedded in a freshly poured concrete pile, thus eliminating the need for baseplates.

Plywood A type of manufactured wood made from thin sheets of wood.

Pointing Process of mortar joints in masonry or brickwork.

Point of law An issue of law, particularly one arising from an arbitral award. Under the Arbitration Act 1996, only a question of law may be the subject of an appeal to the High Court from an arbitrator's award, which must be one that substantially affects the rights of the parties.

Points of claim The traditional title of a claimant's statement of case in an arbitration and also in the Commercial Court.

Points of defence The traditional title of a respondent's statement of case in an arbitration.

Poisson distribution A statistical probability distribution which can be applied to the occurrences of events in a fixed time, frequently used by engineering expert witnesses.

Polybutylene A form of plastic resin used extensively in the manufacture of water supply piping from 1978 until 1995.

Polycarbonate sheet (PC) A high-impact strength, light weight and flexible shatter-resistant thermoplastic used as a substitute for glass.

Polyethylene (PE) A type of plastic widely used for packaging.

Polypropylene (PP) A thermostatic material used in a wide variety of applications, including packaging, plastic parts, various types of reusable containers and laboratory equipment.

Polystyrene (PS) One of the most widely used types of plastic. Polystyrene is a thermoplastic substance used extensively in insulation and packaging.

Polytetrafluorethylene (PTFE) A plastic used in plumbing, particularly in the form of tape.

Polyurethane (PU) Polyurethane formulations cover an extremely wide range of stiffness, hardness and densities. Variations of polyurethane include (1) low-density flexible foam, (2) low-density rigid foam (used for thermal insulation), (3) hard solid plastics used as structural parts and (4) flexible plastics used as straps and bands.

Polyvinyl chloride (PVC) A type of thermoplastic widely used in the construction industry. Common applications include (1) insulation on electric wires, (2) piping and (3) ceiling tiles.

Polyvinyl fluoride (PVF) A surfacing material for cladding panels.

Polyvinylidene fluoride (PVF_2) A specialty plastic used primarily in applications requiring high purity, strength, resistance to solvents, acids, bases and heat and low smoke generation during a fire. Commonly used as insulation on electrical wires.

POMI Principles of Measurement International

Ponding The formation of semi-permanent puddles of rainwater, particularly on flat roofs.

Portal frame A method of construction used for design and building of simple structures using primarily steel or steel-reinforced precast concrete. Typically used for construction of warehouses and similar places where large, open spaces are required at low cost and a pitched roof is acceptable.

Porter v Magill [2001] UKHL 67; [2002] 2 AC 357. Lord Hope set out the test for apparent bias as follows: "whether the fair-minded and informed observer, having considered the facts, would conclude that there was a real possibility that the tribunal was biased". ■ See **Bias** and **Natural justice**.

Portland cement The most common type of cement in general use around the world. Typically used in production of concrete.

Portland stone A type of limestone used extensively in the construction of public buildings and memorial in the United Kingdom.

Possession The occupation of land, particularly by a contractor for carrying out works. A construction contract will grant the contractor a contractual licence to occupy the site for the purpose of carrying out the works and the employer will be in breach if he fails to give such possession.

Post and beam construction Timber frame comprising posts supporting horizontal beams.

Postal (or posting) rule A general rule that a postal acceptance of an offer takes effect when it is posted, not when it arrives or is received: *Henthorn v Fraser* [1892] 2 Ch 27.

Powder coating A form of coating applied as a free-flowing, dry powder. Forms of powder coating fall into two categories – thermosets and thermoplastics.

Power float Associated with dense, super smooth concrete floors, common in warehouses and hospitals. A power float is a concrete finishing machine designed to smooth and to some degree level the surface of the concrete to an exceptionally high tolerance.

PPC2000 A Standard Form of Contract for Project Partnering, published by the ACA. ■ See **Association of Consultant Architects** and **Partnering**.

PPP See **Public- Private Partnership**.

PQQ See **Pre-qualification Questionnaire**.

Practical completion A stage of completion of the works under JCT standard forms of contract marked by the issue of a certificate to that effect. The term is not defined by the conditions and can lead to dispute. It has been held to mean: the completion of the works for all practical purposes, allowing the employer to take possession of the works and use them as intended but not down to the last detail, however, trivial and unimportant; the completion of all the construction work that has to be done and there are no patent defects (*Jarvis & Sons Ltd v Westminster Corp* [1970] 1 WLR 637; [1970] 1 All ER 943); and the completion of the works where very minor de minimis work has not been carried out and there are no patent defects (*HW Nevill (Sunblest) Ltd v William Press & Son Ltd* (1981) 20 BLR 78). In the ICE standard forms of civil engineering contract, the expression "substantial completion" is used: see **Substantial completion**.

Practice Direction A direction as to the practice and procedure of any court within the scope of the Civil Procedure Rules (or CPR) issued under s5 of the Civil Procedure Act 1997. Most parts of the CPR are supplemented by practice directions. ■ See **Application and Civil Procedure Rules**.

Pre-action meeting Meeting required under para 5 of the Pre-action Protocol for Construction and Engineering Disputes. The purpose of the meeting is to identify the main issues and the root causes of the disagreements between the parties who are expected to consider whether, and if so how, those issues might be resolved without recourse to litigation or if litigation is unavoidable to considered how best that litigation can be conducted. Whilst the meeting is "without prejudice", the parties can disclose to the court that the meeting took place, who attended and who refused to attend, together with the grounds for their refusal and any agreements concluded between the parties. See s2 of the **TCC Guide**.

Pre-action protocol (PAP) A statement of best practice about pre-action conduct which has been approved by the Head of Civil Justice and listed in the CPR Practice Direction for Pre-Action Conduct. The Pre-action Protocol for Construction and Engineering Disputes is an approved pre-action protocol for construction and engineering disputes which applies to such disputes including professional negligence claims against architects, engineers and quantity surveyors. It requires the service of detailed correspondence between intended parties and a pre-action meeting, non-attendance at which can be disclosed to the court. If, in the opinion of the court, non-compliance has led to the commencement of proceedings, or has led to costs being incurred in the proceedings that might otherwise not have been incurred, the court may make appropriate orders as to costs and the recovery of interest. The court may also stay proceedings where the protocol requirements have not been complied with and there is some prospect that compliance would lead to an early compromise of the action and the saving of costs. The protocol does not apply to certain proceedings, such as those for the enforcement of an adjudication award.

Preambles A series of terms contained in an introductory section to a bill of quantities or specification setting out conditions generally applicable.

Precedent The doctrine that like cases should be decided alike in accordance with previous decisions. Because English law is largely based on case law, a decision will constitute a precedent which must be followed in a subsequent decision on the same point of law, embodied in the Latin phrase stare decisis: "to stand by decisions". Arbitrators and adjudicators are bound by decisions of the High Court, which is bound by those of the Court of Appeal, which is in turn bound by decisions of the Supreme Court (previously the House of Lords). There are exceptions, perhaps the most important of which is the power if the Supreme Court to depart from its (or the House of Lords') previous decisions.

Prefabricated building A type of building which consists of factory-built components which are assembled on site. Typically used on construction sites as temporary office space or accommodation.

Preferential engineering The use of approval procedures to improve the standard of the design or materials and workmanship.

Preliminaries Resources necessary for carrying out a project on site which do not become part of the final works. These may include management of the works, general attendance on subcontractors, temporary site accommodation, plant, and scaffolding, all specifically dedicated to that particular project. Preliminaries are frequently time-related and so where a project is delayed these costs will usually increase and "extended preliminaries" may form part of a claim. It is also known as "**Site overheads**" and "site project overheads".

Preliminary issue An issue, usually one of law, which is to be decided in a separate hearing before the main trial of a claim. Although preliminary issues can be useful, the practice of allowing them to be taken frequently adds to the difficulties of courts of appeal and tends to increase the cost and time of legal proceedings and preliminary points of law are too often treacherous short cuts and their price can be delay, anxiety and expense: see *Tilling v Whiteman* [1980] AC 1.

Pre-patinated Material upon which a patina has already formed or been applied.

Pre-qualification The selection of a shortlist of potential contractors or consultants who will be invited to submit a tender.

Pre-qualification Questionnaire (PQQ) The responses to a PQQ are often used to evaluate potential tenders and so to select those to go forward to the next stage of the procurement process.

Prescriptive specification A specification that provides for a well-defined means and method of construction. It goes further than merely setting out the required performance of the building element. ■ See also **Performance specification and Specification.**

Pressed bricks Bricks moulded under high pressure which have sharp edges and smooth surfaces.

Pressed metal Metal which has been hot-pressed into shape.

Pressetext Nachrichtenagentur v Republik Oesterreich (Bund) (Case C-454/06): the **ECJ** defined what constitutes a **Material change** which would necessitate a new competitive tender process in accordance with EU Procurement Regulations. According to the ECJ, amendments to a contract may be regarded as material where they introduce conditions which, had they been part of the initial award procedure, would (1) have allowed for the admission or acceptance of a tender other than the winning tender; and/or (2) have extended the scope of the contract considerably to encompass services not initially covered and/or (3) have changed the economic balance in favour of the contractor in a manner not provided for in the terms of the original contract.

Prevention principle The principle that a party cannot insist on the performance of a contractual obligation by the other if it is itself cause of the non-performance. Thus the implication of a term into a construction contract that the employer will not do anything to prevent the contractor from performing the contract or to delay him in performing it means that an employer cannot recover liquidated damages where he has ordered extra work or is in breach.

Prima facie Latin: "at first sight".

Primavera Project Planner™ (P3) A project management software package used for scheduling and tracking of projects.

Prime Contracting Where a single company assumes responsibility for the delivery of the entirety of the project.

Prime contractor Main contractor (US).

Prime cost The actual cost of the works to the contractor under a cost contract, which will usually contain a precise definition of what type of cost is recoverable by the contractor directly and what type of cost the contractor is expected to recover within the fee or percentage addition. Typically, definitions of prime cost include all the cost of labour, materials and subcontractors and other costs incurred on the site but exclude head office and administrative costs. Such a definition of prime cost is unnecessary in a lump sum contract, although it can form part of the formula for the valuation of extras.

Prime cost contract A contract where the price is fixed after the work is done by reference to the prime cost of the work done, ie the JCT Prime Cost Contract 2011. ■ See **Cost contract**.

Prime cost (or PC) sum These terms are usually defined in the contract. In the earlier versions of the JCT standard form of building contract, prime cost work or materials could only be carried out or supplied by nominated subcontractors or suppliers, and the cost resulting from the nomination was substituted in the final account for the prime cost sum in the contract. Under the ICE standards forms of civil engineering contract, a PC item is one which contains a sum referred to as Prime Cost which is to be used for the carrying out of work or the supply of goods, materials or services for the works. If there is no contractual definition and where there is no question of nomination, the ordinary meaning of prime cost would appear to be that of an estimate of net cost, with and the intention that the contractor should only charge the employer the actual cost to himself. If this cost is less or more than that stated in the contract the contract sum is adjusted accordingly, subject always to the principles relating to extra work. ■ See **Provisional sum**.

Principal A party for whom an agent acts or a party whose obligations are being guaranteed.

Principal contractor See **Construction (Design and Management) Regulations 2007, SI 2007/320**. The principal contractor's obligations include ensuring site welfare facilities are provided, displaying health and safety information on site and taking reasonable steps to ensure that all site workers are trained and inducted onto the site.

Principal rafter A main rafter in a roof truss, carrying the purlins.

Priority of documents The order of importance accorded to the terms of a contract contained in different documents. In the absence of specific provision (which is no increasingly common) the rules are: that written or typed clauses prevail over printed clause; written words prevail over figures; the terms of a contract incorporating the terms of another document prevail over those terms. A term in the JCT standard forms has for many years given priority to the agreement and conditions over other documents, such as bills of quantities and specifications, to the extent that those other documents do not override or modify the agreement and conditions.

Private automatic branch exchange (PABX) See **PABX**.

Private Finance Initiative (PFI) A method of procurement first developed in Australia and adopted with enthusiasm in the United Kingdom by both Conservative and Labour governments since 1992. Under PFI a public authority can arrange for private sector bodies to provide and own services. Typically, a project company is formed and enters into long term contract (usually 25 years) for the construction of a new asset along with its operation and maintenance. Once the asset has been constructed the government authority pays a specified charge (known as a unitary charge) for the service provided. At the end of the contract ownership of the asset usually reverts to the government authority. See **Appendix 5**.

Privilege A right or duty to withhold evidence in the form of inspection of a document or answering questions on various grounds, the most important of which are likely to be legal professional privilege and the rule against self-incrimination. ■ See ***Three Rivers District Council v Bank of England*** [2004] UKHL 48; [2004] 3 WLR 1274.

Privity of contract A principle of law that dictates that only the parties to a contract or his assignee can enforce it, now subject to the Contracts (Rights of Third Parties) Act 1999. An employer under a construction contract can recover damages for loss suffered by a third party where it is within the contractor's contemplation that such a party would occupy or purchase the works: see *Linden Gardens Trust Ltd v Lenesta Sludge Disposals Ltd* [1994] 1 AC 85; [1993] 3 WLR 408; [1993] 3 All ER 417.

Privy Council The Judicial Committee of the Privy Council, which has jurisdiction to decide certain appeals, particularly from Commonwealth jurisdictions.

Probationary drawing A proposal, sketch or design submitted for approval to the client by a construction professional: see *Moffatt v Laurie* [1855] 15 CB 563.

ProCure 21 An NHS procurement method for publicly funded capital projects, which was replaced by ProCure21+ in October 2010.

Procurement The process of buying goods and services. In the construction industry the term also often refers to the type of contract used to buy those good and services (eg traditional, design and build, construction management, management contracting, etc.). See **Appendices 1–5**.

Procurement Regulations See **Public Contracts Regulations 2006, SI 2006/5**.

Productivity A measure of how quickly a contractor completes the works, expressed as work output divided by resource input. Often an employer will incentivise productivity by offering bonus payments for early completion or completion by the original completion date.

Profiled sheeting Galvanised steel sheeting with a troughed cross-section.

Profit See **Loss of profit** and **Overheads and profit**.

Programme A plan of the works which is supposed to illustrate the timing and sequencing of the various stages of the project.

Program Evaluation and Review Technique A method of analysis used for project planning.

Progress payment An interim payment on account during the course of the works.

Project bank account A bank account with no overdraft facility into which all monies due under a construction contract are paid by the employer and immediately distributed to the main contractor and subcontractors. Such accounts have been used on public sector projects but are comparatively rare in the private sector.

Project manager A party providing management services in relation to a construction project. Variation in the services provided and the qualifications of their providers make it difficult to generalise about the role of a project manager.

Project mediation A process whereby one or more project mediators are appointed at the beginning of a project. The role of the project mediator is to identify and address problems before they turn into disputes.

Project partnering See **Partnering**.

Projecting scaffold A scaffolding platform built out from an upper level.

Prolongation An increase in the time taken to complete the works. The basis for a contractor's claim for loss and expense under express contractual terms or damages for breach where the prolongation is due to some act or omission of the employer, or for an employer's claim for liquidated damages. ■ See **Disruption**.

Proof of debt Document submitted by a creditor to establish a claim in an insolvency.

Property damage insurance Insurance against damage to property, usually covering damage to the works, temporary works, goods and materials and plant and equipment on site.

Proportionality A key concept which influences the manner in which disputes are litigated. The courts are expected to deal with a case in a way that is proportionate to the amount of money involved; the importance of the case; the complexity of the issues and the financial position of each party. ■ See **Overriding Objective**.

Proscenium arch A masonry construction, which is typically curved, for spanning an opening and supporting the weight above it.

Prospective delay analysis An examination of the events during a contract which may cause delay and their likely future impact on the progress of the works by looking back at the delays and their effect at the end of the contract. It may be contrasted with **Retrospective delay analysis** which aims to demonstrate the past impact of delay events on the works.

Protimeter A proprietary trade name which has become synonymous with damp testing meters.

Provisional sum A price for work which may not be carried out or work the content of which is undefined so that the parties decide not to try to price it accurately, and is usually included as a round figure guess. It is included mathematically in the original contract price but the parties do not expect it to be paid without adjustment. Its precise meaning and effect depends on the terms of the individual contract: see *Midland Expressway Ltd v Carillion Contractors Ltd* [2006] 107 ConLR 235 (CA).

Proximity A connection between an injured party and the party causing the injury which will support a duty of care being owed by the latter to the former.

PSW See **Performance specified work**.

PTFE Polytetrafluorethylene

PTR Pre Trial Review. A hearing where the court establishes if and/or the extent to which the parties are (or will be0 ready for trial. See section 14 of the TCC Guide.

Public Contracts Regulations 2006, SI 2006/5 The Public Contracts Regulations introduced in 2006 replaced the Public Services Contracts Regulations 1993, SI 1993/3228, the Public Works Contracts Regulations

1991, SI 1991/2680 and the Public Supply Contracts Regulations 1995, SI 1995/201 and set out revised rules for the procurement of supplies, works and services, above certain thresholds, by public authorities. Often known as the **Procurement Regulations**.

Public–Private Partnership (PPP) A procurement model under which a public agency identifies the need for as well as the scope, timescale, price and services of a project measured against performance indicators and invites the private sector to participate. The participators form a special purpose vehicle which finances, builds, operates and then (after 25 years or so) transfers the project back.

Public procurement Procurement by a public authority (also known as a **Contracting Authority)**, covered by the **Public Contracts Regulations 2006, SI 2006/5**.

Punch list See **Snagging and Snagging list**.

Pure economic loss A category of financial loss and damage suffered by a person such as can be seen only on a balance sheet as opposed to physical injury to the person or damage to property. Not recoverable in the tort for negligence in the absence of a duty to avoid causing such loss. ■ See **Damages**.

Purlin A horizontally oriented beam in a roof supported by the principal rafters.

The Purple Guide See **the Event Safety Guide**.

Purposive construction Originally, the interpretation of a statute by reference to its purpose. The term has subsequently been used to describe an approach to the interpretation of contracts by reference to their intended commercial effect. If a detailed semantic and syntactical analysis of words in a commercial contract is going to lead to a conclusion that flouts business common sense, it must yield to business common sense: see *Antaios Compania Naviera SA v Salen Rederierna A.B.* [1984] 1 3A11 E.R. 229.

Pursuer The Scottish term for a claimant.

Push plate A plate, typically metal, on a door to protect the door finish from dirt or damage when “pushed”.

Putlog scaffold Scaffolding consisting of a single row of standards, parallel to the face of the building and set as far away from it as is necessary to accommodate a platform of four or five boards wide, with the inner edge of the platform as close to the wall as is practicable. The standards are connected by a ledger fixed with right angle couplers and the putlogs are fixed to the ledgers using putlog couplers. The blade end of the putlog tube (or putlog adaptor) is normally placed horizontally on the brickwork being built, taking care to use the maximum bearing area.

PVB Poly Vinyl Butyral. A type of resin used for applications that require strong binding. Most frequently used to produce laminated glass which is effectively a sandwich made of one piece of plastic PVB between two or more sheets of annealed glass.

PVC Polyvinyl chloride

PVCu Unplasticised PVC, formerly known as ‘uPVC’. ■ See **Unplasticised polyvinyl chloride**.

PWR Pressured Water Reactor. A nuclear reactor that uses water as a coolant or moderator.

Q

QA Quality assurance

QC See **Queen's Counsel, Quality control**.

QC clause Common in professional indemnity insurance contracts, under a QC clause, disputes about the conduct of a defence to a claim made against that policy can be referred to an independent **QC**.

QM See **Quality management**.

QS See **Quantity surveyor**.

Quality assurance (QA) Procedure for ensuring that high standards are maintained in a business activity. Based on adopting specified quality requirements and monitoring and recording progress of work at all stages. A QA certificate may enhance the value of the product or service provided in the construction industry. See ISO 9001 and Agrément Certificate.

Quality control Inspection by sampling on a mathematical basis.

Quality management (QM) Process by which the quality of a product or service is emphasised in its design and production by adopting quality controls and QA procedures.

Quality of materials Apart from express contractual provisions, the Supply of Goods and Services Act 1982, s4 implies a condition that the goods supplied under the contract are of satisfactory quality. ■ See **Satisfactory quality**.

Quality of workmanship Subject to express terms, s13 of the **Supply of Goods and Services Act 1982** implies a term that the contractor will carry out the works with reasonable care and skill. A person who takes on work for, or in connection with, the provision of a dwelling owes a statutory duty to ensure that the work is done in a workmanlike or, as the case may be, professional manner, with proper materials and so that, as regards that work, the dwelling, when completed, will be fit for human habitation: Defective Premises Act 1972, s1.

Quantities The amounts of each item in a **Bill of quantities**.

Quantity Surveyor (QS) A person with skills in the specification estimation and measurement of materials required for building work. The designation Chartered QS is confined to members of the RICS. QS services often provided include advice on and drafting contract terms, administration of contracts particularly regarding payments, advising, conducting claims, and resolving disputes.

Quantum (of damages) The amount of any damages, as opposed to the liability of a party to pay them or their measure, which is the basis upon which they are to be assessed. ■ See **Measure of damage**.

Quantum meruit Latin: "as much as he deserved", used in three main senses: (1) The entitlement of a party who has supplied goods or services to another on request, in circumstances, which suggest that the supply was not to be gratuitous, to recover a reasonable price for it. Originally considered to be based upon **Quasi-contract**, this remedy is now regarded as one arising in **Restitution**. (2) A reasonable price recoverable where a contract has been made for the supply of goods or services but the price for them has not been agreed. This result is now reached by application of s15 of the Supply of Goods and Services Act 1982, which provides that where under a contract for the supply of a service, the consideration for the service is not determined by the contract, left to be determined in a manner agreed by the contract or determined by the course of dealing between the parties, there is an implied term that the party contracting with the supplier will pay a reasonable charge. (3) Reasonable remuneration recoverable by a contractor where the contract has been repudiated by the employer, as an alternative to a claim for damages based on the contract price for completed work and loss of profit on the balance: *Lodder v Slowey* AC 442 (PC). This rule has been the subject of academic criticism.

Quantum valebat Latin: "as much as it was worth", bearing a very similar meaning to the first sense of **Quantum meruit** identified above.

Quarry tiles Square burnt clay floor tiles, traditionally red in colour. The name derives from the French for square "carré" and has nothing to do with quarries.

Quarter bend A 90° bend (in pipework).

Quarter-sawn timber Wood cut into planks from timber logs which have been cut into quarters along their length. The resulting timber is less susceptible to shrinkage when drying and has a dense and attractive grain (particularly oak).

Quasi-arbitrator Formerly used to describe the role of a certifier or valuer who must hold the balance between the parties to a contract, but disapproved of by the House of Lords in *Sutcliffe v Thackrah* [1974] AC 727 and *Arenson v Arenson* [1977] AC 405, holding that a certifier or valuer is not an arbitrator enjoying immunity from action.

Quasi-contract Formerly used to describe rights arising out of situations in which a contract was not made but goods or services were provided or payment made. Such rights are now regarded as arising in **Restitution**.

Quatrefoil window A quatrefoil window is a round window that is composed of four equal lobes, like a four-petaled flower. The quatrefoil pattern is most common in Moorish and Gothic architecture.

Queen Anne Architecture Although named after a queen who ruled during the early 1700s, Queen Anne is a Victorian style. It means either the English Baroque architectural style roughly of the reign of Queen Anne (1702–14), or a revived form that was popular in the last quarter of the 19th century and the early decades of the 20th century. The historic reference in the name should not be taken too literally, as buildings in the Queen Anne style can bear as little resemblance to English buildings of the 18th century.

Queen's Counsel (QC) Queen's Counsel are senior lawyers who are recommended by an independent selection panel and appointed by the Crown by letters patent. Appointment is open to solicitor advocates as well as barristers and marks excellence in advocacy in the higher courts: some appointments are made honoris causa. Court dress includes silk gowns, which leads to their colloquial name of "Silks".

Quia timet Latin: "because he apprehends", a type of injunction available where the applicant claims damage will occur to his property unless the defendant is restrained from taking certain action.

Quicklime **Lime** which has not been slaked.

Quicquid plantatur solo, solo cedit Latin: "what is fixed to the soil, passes to the soil", the general principle that any **Personal property**, such as building materials, which is attached to land, or incorporated into works attached to the land, becomes the property of the owner of that land.

Quid pro quo Latin: "what for what", something given for something else, such as the consideration for a promise in return.

Quiet enjoyment Clause found in leases giving the tenant or landowner the right to the undisturbed use and enjoyment of property.

Quiet possession Occupation of the site by the contractor without disturbance or interruption, which, if they occur, may give rise to a claim by the contractor, depending upon the allocation of risk in the construction contract. There is no implied warranty against third parties making unfounded claims challenging the employer's title to land upon which a temporary access road is to be built: *Porter v Tottenham UDC* [1915] KB 776 (CA).

Quoin The external corner of a building: one of the stones used to form that corner. These stones can be both structural and decorative in that they often differ in materials, colour, texture, or size from the masonry or brickwork of the adjoining walls. Usually quoins are toothed, that is set in short courses in a regular pattern of alternating lengths. The term is also applied to a wedge shaped keystone.

Quoin block A distinctive cornerstone made of brickwork, stone or other material, sometimes projecting beyond face of wall.

Quotation, quote An offer to carry out work or supply materials, or both, for a specified sum.

R

Rabbet See **Rebate**.

Radial shrinkage Shrinkage of timber when drying in the direction across the growth rings, from the centre of the tree to the bark.

Radial-sett paving Arrangement of square paving blocks in partly overlapping fan shapes, set out from a centre point.

Radiant heat(ing) Heat directly emitted by electromagnetic radiation by a source such as the sun: usually infrared but may be visible at high temperatures. It heats objects in its path but not the air: heating effect may be measured by black bulb thermometer. Contrast with heating of the surrounding air by convection.

Radiation protection Protection of persons and the environment against harmful effects of particle and electromagnetic radiation: usually involves a shield such as thick concrete or lead to absorb radiation.

Radioactivity The emission of particles by the natural decay of nuclear isotopes: classified into alpha, beta and gamma rays, all of which are harmful to health and protection is required when working with radioactive substances.

Radon A naturally occurring radioactive gas produced by the breakdown of radium, found in the United Kingdom principally in Cornwall. It is harmful to health and as a heavy gas can accumulate in buildings: protection against its effects is provided by depressurisation beneath the floor slab and enhanced ventilation of the building.

Raft foundation A foundation comprising a continuous slab of reinforced concrete over the area of a building, used in poor ground.

Rafter A timber sloping from ridge to eaves of a pitched roof to support the purlins and roof covering. Pre-assembled roof trusses serve the same function. ➤ **Figure T4**.

RAG See **Residential Agency Guidelines**.

Rainscreen or rainscreen cladding An exterior weather facing surface that is attached to, but "stands off" from a building, which is usually ventilated to allow any water penetrating through cladding joints to run out at the base. As its name suggests, it operates as an interruptive barrier between weather and other atmospheric conditions and the structure of a building itself. The rainscreen also has an aesthetic purpose, as well as practical benefits such as reducing thermal bridging, maintaining temperature control, and preventing condensation from forming in, for example, brickwork (which otherwise might occur when warm moist air from inside penetrates the fabric of the building, and condenses, causing damage, when it hits a cold surface such as exposed brickwork). ➤ **Figure P1**

Rainwater outlet A plastic or metal receptacle fixed to flat roof or at end of gutter to provide connection with downpipe: see **Hopper**.

Rainwater pipe A pipe in plastic or metal used to conduct rainwater usually as a downpipe fixed to façade of building.

Raised floor An internal floor finished above the structural level, usually to accommodate services or underfloor heating. The flooring is supported on pedestals and can be removed in sections to give access to services.

Raked-out joint A joint between brickwork and masonry where the mortar is scraped out to a uniform depth. This accentuates the appearance of the joints but increases risk of water penetration.

Ramsar site A wetland site listed under the Ramsar Convention on Wetlands and in United Kingdom enjoys protected status against development as a Site of Special Scientific Interest **(SSSI)** under the Wildlife and Countryside Act 1981, s28 and Schedule 11. The Convention was signed in Ramsar in Iran.

Rapid Chemical Test A test used as an initial indicator to determine if High Alumina Cement (HAC) is likely to be present in a concrete sample: also a test to determine reactivity of concrete aggregates to alkalis or sulphates.

Rapid gravity filter A filter used in water purification where water percolates through coarse sand by gravity or under pressure and flocculent chemicals are added to promote the removal of suspended solids from water. Also known as a rapid sand filter.

Rates The unit prices for items of work or materials in bills of quantities.

Rateable value The official assessment by the Valuation Office of annual value of a business or commercial property used to determine the rate which the occupier pays.

Ratification Confirmation, particularly in the case of a contract made by an agent without the authority of his principal, who may subsequently ratify the contract and be bound by it.

Ratio decidendi Latin: "reason for deciding", the court's conclusions in a judgment or other decision on the essential issues of law raised by a dispute. The ratio of a decision by a higher court may be binding in later cases involving the same or similar issues. Contrast **Obiter dictum**.

RCD See **Residual current device**.

RDSAP See **Reduced Data Standard Assessment Procedure**.

RE See **Resident engineer**.

Ready-mixed concrete A mixture of cement, aggregates and water prepared off-site according to specified strength requirements and delivered by a purpose built vehicle to a worksite: usually has to be placed within a short time after delivery. The use of ready mix has led to much greater efficiency in construction.

Real evidence A physical object produced and verified by a witness or introduced into evidence by agreement between the parties and subsequently referred to by an exhibit number.

Real property Land and the works attached to them, as opposed to personal property such as loose materials which have yet to be incorporated into the works.

Reasonable care and skill The standard of performance to be reached by a party supplying a service under a contract by virtue of a term implied by s13 of the **Supply of Goods and Services Act 1982**.

Reasonable price The price payable under s15 of the **Supply of Goods and Services Act 1982**, which provides that where under a contract for the supply of a service, the consideration for the service is not determined by the contract, left to be determined in a manner agreed by the contract or determined by the course of dealing between the parties, there is an implied term that the party contracting with the supplier will pay a reasonable charge. In addition, a party who has provided services to another may recover a reasonable price in the absence of a contract provided that the circumstances justify the inference that the services were not to be rendered gratuitously, by way of what is now regarded as a form of restitution, formerly known as a **Quantum meruit**. The assessment of a reasonable price is a question of fact.

Reasonable skill and care Shorthand for the standard below which conduct will be negligent. Negligence is the omission to do something which a reasonable man, guided by those considerations which ordinarily regulate the conduct of human affairs would do, or doing something which a prudent and reasonable man would not do: *Blyth v Birmingham Waterworks* [1856] 11 Ex 781.

Reasonable time Where, under a contract for the supply of a service (such as a construction contract) by a supplier (such as a contractor) acting in the course of a business, the time for the service (completion of the works) to be carried out is not fixed by the contract, left to be fixed in a manner agreed by the contract or determined by the course of dealing between the parties, there is an implied term that the supplier will carry out the service within a reasonable time, and what is a reasonable time is a question of fact: **Supply of Goods and Services Act 1982,** s14. In addition, where the employer under a construction contract prevents the contractor from performing the contract or delays him in performing it, any express contractual obligation to complete by a particular time will be replaced by one to complete within a reasonable time in all the circumstances in the absence of a contractual provision entitling the contractor to be granted an extension of time in such circumstances: see **Time at large**.

Reasonableness test See **Test of reasonableness**.

Rebar Reinforcing bar: steel bar used to reinforce concrete structures. ➤ **Figure R1**.

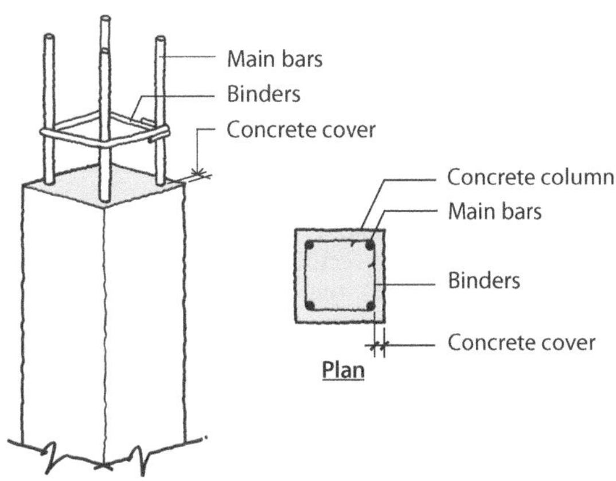

➤ **Figure R1.** Reinforcement Bars (Rebar)

Rebate A step-shaped recess in a piece of timber, usually one used to form a window.

Rebated joint A 90° joint between two pieces of timber where a section is cut out at the end of one piece for half its thickness and equal in size to the cross-section of the joining member: the pieces are then glued and screwed together to form a strong joint.

Rebound hammer test See **Schmidt hammer test**.

Rebuilding The reconstruction of the whole or part of a building substantially in the same form as before. ■ See **Redevelopment** and **Refurbishment**.

Receipts and expenditure method A method of valuation for determining rental or rateable value of a commercial property such as a public house or petrol station by reference to the income and expenditure of the business.

Receptor (1) A shower tray. (2) Anything which is likely to be harmed by a contaminant in soil.

Recessed joint A joint between two sections (such as mortar between brickwork) where the surface of the joint material is finished below the level of the sections joined.

Recharge The run-off of surface water and process by which surface water percolates through the soil to become groundwater.

Re-circulated air Air within a building which has been heated or cooled and is returned to air conditioning plant for cleaning through filters before being returned into the building through ductwork.

Recitals The introductory parts of an Act, Deed, Contract or other legal documents, explaining the background circumstances and the general intentions giving rise to the instrument in question. They may be taken into account as an aid to construction.

Recklessness An alternative to deliberate intent, particularly in relation to fraud. If a party making a false representation does not care whether it is true or false, he/she makes it fraudulently.

Reclaiming The Scottish equivalent of making an appeal to the **Inner House** of the **Court of Session**. Reclaimer is the name given to the appellant.

Reconstituted stone Facing blocks panels and other building components made of precast concrete and surface finished to resemble natural stonework, often incorporating crushed stone dust in surface layer.

Rectification An equitable remedy whereby the court amends a written instrument. A party seeking rectification on the grounds of common mistake must show that: (1) the parties had a common continuing intention, whether or not amounting to an agreement, in respect of a particular matter in the instrument to be rectified; (2) there was an outward expression of accord; (3) the intention continued at the time of the execution of the instrument sought to be rectified; (4) by mistake, the instrument did not reflect that common intention. The requirements for the exercise of the jurisdiction to rectify a contract for unilateral mistake are: (1) One party, A, erroneously believed that the document sought to be rectified contained a particular term or provision, or possibly did not contain a particular term or provision which, mistakenly, it did contain; (2) The other party, B, was aware of the omission or the inclusion and that it was due to a mistake on the part of A; (3) B has omitted to draw the mistake to the notice of A; (4) The mistake is one calculated to benefit B; and (5) It would be inequitable for B to resist rectification into the terms A believed them to be. ■ See ***Chartbrook Ltd v Persimmon Homes Ltd*** [2009] UKHL 38; [2009] AC 1101; [2009] BLR 551; [2009] 3 WLR 267.

Rectification period See **Defects liability period**

Recurring expenditure Expenditure in performing a contract or running a business which is paid on regular basis, for example, head office overheads such as rent insurance and business rates, or wages of employees.

Recycled water Water which has passed through supply system and returned to storage tanks (often for purification) before being recirculated. In ecological systems such water may be reused for less sensitive uses (eg flushing lavatories, irrigation). Also refers to recovery of water after treatment in sewage plants.

Recycling The process of recovering and reusing expended materials, often in a different form: crushed brick and concrete is an important source of aggregate and sub base material for foundations. Statutory regulations control the disposal of waste from building operations such as plastics and plasterboard to encourage recycling of the constituent materials.

Red Book (1)The **FIDIC** conditions of contract for construction where the employer carries out the design; (2) The **IChemE Red Book** for lump sum contracts (3) **RICS** Valuation – Professional Standards, contains mandatory rules and best practice guidance for meeting asset valuations.

Red Judge Term for a High Court Judge. Name derived from the red colour of their traditional robes.

Redevelopment Building on land after the removal of all or most of the existing buildings.

Reduced Data Standard Assessment Procedure A standardised survey procedure for the assessment of energy efficiency of an existing dwelling. The survey is used to produce an Energy Performance Certificate for existing homes.

Reduced groundwater The lowering of the level of water naturally in the ground by dewatering abstraction or percolation.

Reduced level Altitude calculated from an agreed datum, as opposed to sea level.

Reef Rocks, coral, sandbar or other features to be found lying just above or beneath the surface of the sea.

Re-examination Further oral evidence taken from a witness by the party calling him after cross-examination by the opposing party and confined to issues arising out of cross-examination.

Reference A synonym for an **arbitration**.

Reference dose The maximum daily quantity of an ingested chemical such as pesticides to which a human can be exposed for a lifetime without health problems.

Reference specification (1) A standard specification for a product or service provided by the manufacturer or supplier to describe its technical attributes. (2) A document in tender requirements or a project specification to define the characteristics and performance required.

Referral (1) That step in the beginning of an adjudication whereby the dispute comes before the adjudicator after he has been appointed. Referral under s. 108(2)(c) of the **Construction Act** does not mean despatch of the notice of referral. Receipt might occur later. A thing is not referred to another unless that other receives it. It may be sent with the intention of referring it but never received. It has then not been referred. The word is unambiguous. Referral takes place upon receipt of the notice by the adjudicator: *Aveat Heating Ltd v Jerram Falkus Construction Ltd* [2007] EWHC 131 (TCC), [2007] TCLR 3; 113 ConLR 13. (2) A document setting out the referring party's case. (3) The whole process of the adjudication of a dispute, just as the term "reference" is used in relation to arbitration and the word "action" in relation to court proceedings.

Referral notice If the provisions of a construction contract do not comply with the requirements of the **construction Act**, the **Scheme for Construction Contracts** applies, and where an adjudicator has been selected in accordance with that scheme, the referring party must, not later than seven days from the date of the notice of adjudication, refer the dispute in writing (the "referral notice") to the adjudicator. A referral notice must be accompanied by copies of, or relevant extracts from, the construction contract and such other documents as the referring party intends to rely upon. The referring party must, at the same time as sending to the adjudicator the referral notice and accompanying material, send copies of those documents to every other party to the dispute: see Schedule 1, para 7.

Referring party The **claimant** or initiating party in an **adjudication**.

Reflectance The percentage of radiation such as light or electromagnetic waves which are reflected by a surface on which they fall.

Reflective glass Glass sheets manufactured or treated so as to reflect radiation (both light and heat) falling onto its surface: mainly used on external façade of buildings.

Reflective insulation Material (usually aluminium foil on plastic film backing) which reflects heat back into a room and limits its loss: used in lofts to prevent solar heat gain in summer and heat loss from building in winter.

Refractories Heat resistant materials which maintain their strength and shape at very high temperatures and are used as linings for furnaces and kilns: silica, calcium and alumina compounds are used to make bricks and blocks for heat containment vessels.

Refrigerant dehumidifier Plant for removing excess water vapor in air by passing damp air over refrigerated evaporator coils which condense the vapor to water. Often used for drying out after plasterwork and before decoration.

Refuge An area protected by fire-resistant materials within a building which provides a safe waiting area for occupants for a limited duration.

Refurbishment Improvement or modernisation of the whole or part of a building or buildings short of **Rebuilding** or **Redevelopment**.

Regent St disease The name given in London to corrosion of steel-framed buildings built in the first half of the 20th century. It occurs when moisture penetrates a Portland stone façade and corrodes structural steelwork. The steelwork may be treated by cathodic protection reversing the conditions leading to rusting.

Regional Planning Body (RPB) The statutory body responsible for the preparation of the **Regional Spatial Strategy (RSS)**.

Regional Planning Guidance (RPG) Policy guidance issued by the Government to guide development and other uses of land within a region. This was replaced by **Regional Spatial Strategy (RSS)** and now by the **Regional Strategy (RS)**.

Regional Strategy (RS) Policy guidance issued by the Government to guide development and other uses of land within a region. Represents a combination of the **Regional Spatial Strategy**, Regional Economic Strategy and the Regional Housing Strategy.

Regional Spatial Strategy (RSS) A document setting out the Secretary of State's framework for regional level planning in England. It is prepared by regional planning bodies and forms part of the development plan for the purpose of determining planning applications. Now replaced by the **Regional Strategy**.

Register Plate Plates used to seal a stove's fluepipe, or a canopy outlet to a chimney. The register plate prevents loose objects falling from inside the stack into the fireplace and also keeps the flue insulation in place.

Registered land Land (freehold and leasehold) and interests in property whose title has been deduced and registered with the Land Registry. Each registered title is assigned its own unique number.

Registered office The office of a company which is named on the Register at Companies House. It is usually the place to which official correspondence, notices and legal documents are to be sent and is often not the same as the trading address of the company. Part 6 of the CPR states that service of legal proceedings may take place at a company's registered office.

Registers of Scotland Office maintaining the Land Register and other legal documentation relating to property in Scotland including Chancery and Judicial Registers.

Registry of Toxic Effects of Chemical Substances A compilation from published technical literature of the reported effects of chemical substances on humans: formerly produced by the US National Institute for Occupational Safety and Health.

Regolith The layer of loose material (including rock, soil and sediments) on the Earth's surface which lies above the bedrock.

Regularly and diligently A term used to assess whether the contractor is applying sufficient focus and application to a project. To proceed continuously, industriously and efficiently with appropriate physical resources so as to make the work progress steadily towards completion substantially in accordance with the contractual requirements as to time, sequence and quality of work: *West Faulkner v London Borough of Newham* (1994) 71 BLR 1. An obligation to so proceed has been a feature of the JCT standard forms for many years and a ground upon which the

Contractor's employment under such a contract may be determined. ■ See **Hurry-up notice**.

Reinforced concrete Concrete which is strengthened by the incorporation of steel reinforcement around which the wet cement is placed. Concrete used for any structural purpose will be reinforced. The nature and extent of the reinforcement will depend upon the configuration and loads which the completed concrete has to bear.

Reinforced masonry Blockwork, brickwork or stonework strengthened by vertical insertion of steel reinforcement surrounded by concrete through hollow sections or perforations in masonry.

Reinforcement Steel bars, mesh and sheets which are cut, bent, fabricated and placed before being encased by cement poured within shutters to form structural concrete or structural masonry. Reinforcement greatly enhances structural strength and on complex structures will be designed by an engineer. ➤**Figure R1**.

Reinforcement bar See **Rebar**.

Reinforcement schedule List of type and quantities of reinforcement required for the works or a section thereof, usually arranged in accordance with weight, size and length required to assist steel stockholder. ■ See **Bar Schedule**.

Reinforcement spacer Piece of plastic, metal or other material which holds reinforcement in its designed position when structural concrete is poured in order to ensure that sufficient concrete cover is achieved.

Reinstatement The restoration of a building or other structure to its previous condition. The cost of reinstatement is one measure of damage for breaches of contract or tortuous acts causing defective work, the other being any diminution in value. The prima facie rule is that the employer will be entitled to the cost of reinstatement provided that the repair would be a reasonable course to adopt.

Reinstatement basis A basis of insurance upon which the loss is assessed on the cost of repair of the insured property if damaged or rebuilt i or destroyed.

Rejoinder Formerly a **Pleading** in response to the **Reply**. Under the CPR, permission is now required for any statement of case after a **Reply**.

Relationship Used in planning or **Retrospective Delay Analysis** to describe the dependency between activities on site. There are a number of different relationships: (1) finish-to-start relationship where an activity must be completed before another starts; (2) finish-to-finish relationship where the completion of one activity depends on the completion of another; (3) start-to-start relationship where the start of an activity is dependent on the start of another; and (4) start-to-finish relationship where the completion of an activity depends on the start of another.

Relative humidity The amount of water vapour in the air compared with the maximum amount it could hold (fully saturated air) at a given temperature, usually expressed as a percentage.

Relative readings (R/R) Readings of the percentage moisture content of masonry or plaster by a damp meter (see **Protimeter**).

Relevant Events Events identified in the **JCT** standard forms as potential causes of delay to the regular progress of the works which might justify the granting of an extension of time to the Contractor for completion. The events are: **Variations**, **Instructions**, **Deferment of possession**, **Approximate quotation** work, **Suspension by the Contractor**, **Impediment Prevention or default** by the Employer, **Statutory undertaker** work, **Exceptionally adverse weather conditions**, **Specified Perils of** loss or damage, **Civil commotion or terrorism**, **Strike lock-out or local combinations**, exercises of statutory power, and **Force majeure**.

Relevant Matters Matters identified in the **JCT** standard forms as potentially affecting the regular progress of the works materially and causing the Contractor to incur **Direct loss and/or expense**, being: variations, various instructions, suspensions by the Contractor, approximate quantities of work, impediment preventions or defaults by the Employer.

Relief Any remedy sought by a party in an action or arbitration, such as payment under the contract, damages for breach of contract or tortious conduct, a declaration as to rights or an injunction.

Remeasurement The act of measuring the amount of work carried out once it has been completed, particularly where payment depends on the measure of work executed.

Remeasurement contract A contract in which the rates for the work to be carried out are agreed but the amount of work carried out is not finally measured until completion, when the agreed rates are applied to the quantity of work performed. The ICE Measurement Version and JCT 2011 with Approximate Quantities are examples of remeasurement contracts, which are used where the parties cannot be certain how much work will be required to execute the project, particularly in relation to civil engineering works. ■ See **Approximate quantities** and **Lump sum**.

Remedial Treatment Surveys An inspection of property to locate areas where remedial work may be required and to identify the nature of the work required to rectify defects. Often made by building surveyors prior to purchase of property where specific defects such as damp penetration or damage to woodwork have been found.

Remedial work Work to cure **Defects** in design or workmanship. Remedial work may be required by the Architect/CA or Engineer as the works progress and he may also order opening up of completed work to ascertain whether it is defective. The cost of remedial work to reinstate the works is prima facie the measure of damage for breaches of contract or tortious acts or omissions which result in defects. ■ See **Defect, Opening up and Reinstatement**.

Remediation The removal of pollution or contaminants usually from soil or groundwater. Work upon contaminated land to allow it to be used for development under the provisions of the Environment Act 1990.

Remedies Directive Name given to EU Directive 2007/66/EC which introduced a requirement for courts to make a declaration of ineffectiveness where a public sector or utility contract was awarded in breach of certain fundamental EU public procurement rules.

Remedy The basis of any decision to be made by a tribunal in a party's favour. Most construction contract disputes are resolved by a decision either that one party is obliged to pay the other party sums due under the contract or that one party should pay the other damages for breach of contract. Other common remedies include the granting of an **Injunction** or **Rectification** of the contract, as well as **Abatement** or **Set-off**.

Remoteness of damage The principle that some damage and loss may be too far removed in law from the events which give rise to the claim to be recoverable by the claimant, even though they have been caused by those events. In contract following *Hadley v Baxendale* [1854] 9 Ex 341 a defendant is not liable for losses caused by his breach of contract if the damage did not arise naturally or within the contemplation of the parties at the time the contract was made. In tort the defendant will only be liable for damage that was reasonably foreseeable as a result of the wrongful act. Loss and damage which have arisen outside those boundaries are said to be too remote. ■ See **Knowledge**.

Render A thin cementitious layer applied as a wall finish to brickwork or stonework to protect it against the weather and sometimes to improve appearance. Gravel may be added when wet to create a pebbledash finish.

Renomination The nomination of a second subcontractor to carry out work where the first subcontractor nominated has abandoned it, usually because of financial difficulties. In *Bickerton v Northwest Metropolitan Hospital Board* [1970] 1 WLR 607 the House of Lords held that under the then current JCT form the employer was obliged to renominate in such circumstances. The decision is now regarded as largely of historical importance given the decline in nomination of subcontractors.

Renovating plaster Plaster incorporating perlite and cement as well as lime and sand for repair work and to allow passage of damp out of wall: the plaster is therefore said to "breathe".

Rent Payment by tenant for right to possession of business or residential property during a period of tenancy.

Renunciation An **Anticipatory breach** of contract whereby one party informs the other of his intention not to perform the contract or acts in such a way as to render his performance impossible. ■ See **Repudiation**.

Repair Restoration by renewal or replacement of subsidiary parts of a whole: *Lurcott v Wakely* [1911] 1 KB 905. However, the word can have very different meanings particularly in a covenant in a lease when combined with other words such as "amend", "maintain" or "renew" and the circumstances. In the end the question is whether the ordinary speaker of English would consider that the word "repair" as used in the covenant was appropriate to describe the work which has to be done. The cases do no more than illustrate specific contexts in which judges, as ordinary speakers of English, have thought that it was or was not appropriate to do so: *Post Office v Aquarius Properties Ltd* [1987] 1 All ER 1055.

Reply A **Statement of case** served in response to a **Defence**, sometimes combined with a **Defence to counterclaim** where the latter has been served with the defence.

Repointing Renewing the mortar between brickwork stonework and blockwork or the plaster between tiling where the old filling has deteriorated or fallen out. The joint is raked out to a certain depth before the filling is replaced with fresh mortar or plaster.

Representation A statement of fact or law, which, if false, may entitle the party to whom it has been made to relief. ■ See **Misrepresentation**.

Repudiation Circumstances giving rise to an entitlement on the part of one party to regard himself as discharged from further performance and to claim damages from the other, such as: (1) Such a serious breach of a term as would make it unreasonable for the innocent party to continue; (2) Protracted or repeated breach of less serious terms; (3) Express **Renunciation**; (4) Where the contract indicates that breach of a particular term is to have that effect; In conventional terms, the innocent party is said to have a choice of "affirming" the contract or "accepting" the other party's repudiation, thus bringing the parties' primary obligations to an end, and claiming damages for breach.

Request for Further Information A document served by one party to arbitration or litigation on another asking the latter to provide further details of his **Statement of case**.

Request for Information (RFI) A process by which a contractor can seek necessary information from the Architect/CA or Engineer or from the employer regarding the works. Often this involves clarification regarding the drawings or specifications or instructions. Construction contracts often contain express provisions for RFIs. Unscrupulous use of RFIs to justify a claim for an extension of time to mask a contractor-generated delay has been a regrettable feature of some projects in the past.

Rescission (1) A remedy for misrepresentation whereby a contract entered into as a result of the misrepresentation is set aside and the parties are restored to their respective positions before the contract was entered into. The general rule that the representee must communicate his/her intention to rescind to the representor, although this may not be necessary where the representor is deliberately keeping out of the way. Rescission might be regarded as a remedy of "self-help", but the court has a discretion under the Misrepresentation Act 1967 to refuse it, so that it could "annul" a purported rescission by the representee. Other limits on rescission are: (i) The character of any property transferred must remain the same, for example, where mines have been worked out there cannot be substantial restitution. (ii) The representee will be bound by any affirmation of the contract which he has made, for example, an express declaration to continue with it. (iii) Lapse of time may exclude the right to rescind. (iv) A third party's acquisition of rights in the subject-matter of the contract in good faith and for consideration before avoidance of the contract will prevent rescission. (2) The process whereby an innocent party may treat himself as discharged from further performance by reason of the other party's breach of condition (repudiation) and claim damages.

Reserved matters Planning conditions remaining to be decided when a planning authority grants outline permission for a development. Detailed plans drawings and relevant information must be submitted by the applicant for approval in accordance with the list of reserved matters before any site work begins. ■ See **Outline planning permission**.

Reservoirs A location where water or other liquid is collected, in particular water for farming, industrial or residential use. May also refer to an area where water collects undesirably: for example ponding on roofing felt or absorbent insulation material.

Resident engineer (RE) An engineer employed full time on site for a particularly large or complex project.

Residential Agency Guidelines (RGA) RICS guidelines to be followed for marketing, sale or letting of residential property.

Residential occupier A construction contract with a residential occupier is not subject to the provisions of the **Construction Act**: see s106(1)(a). Such a contract is one which principally relates to operations on a dwelling which one of the parties to the contract occupies, or intends to occupy, as his residency: s106(2). "Dwelling" means a dwelling-house or a flat: "dwelling-house" does not include a building containing a flat, and "flat" means separate and self-contained premises constructed or adapted for use for residential purposes and forming part of a building from some other part of which the premises are divided horizontally: 106(2). The authorities on this provision are very few, particularly on the issue as to what may or may not be encompassed by the term "residential occupier": *Shaw & another v Massey Foundation & Pilings Ltd* [2009] EWHC 493 (TCC).

Residual current device Device to detect leakage of electric current and to trip a switch cutting off power to limit harm through electrocution: also known as a residual current circuit breaker.

Residual risk The unquantifiable risk in an activity which remains after a risk assessment and all reasonable steps in mitigation of known risk have been carried out. While works are in progress this risk is likely to fall on the contractor, for example of inclement weather or delays by suppliers.

Resilient flooring Flooring material which possesses a natural spring such as cork, rubber, vinyl flooring, lino and sprung wooden floors. This finish is more comfortable for walking and standing than a rigid floor such as concrete and its surface can usually be treated to make it resistant to stains and damage.

Resin A naturally occurring sticky extrusion from conifers and other plants traditionally used in the production of varnish and adhesives. Also artificial products such as epoxy, polyester and polyurethane resins, used for flooring and many other construction materials.

Res inter alios acta non nocet Latin: "a thing transacted between others does not harm", the principle that an arrangement made between parties cannot work to the disadvantage of another who was not party to it. The shortened version, "res inter alios acta", is sometimes used to denote an agreement made by one of the parties to an action which is irrelevant to the issues of liability or quantum in that action.

Res ipsa locquitur Latin: "the thing speaks for itself", a rule of evidence relied on in claims in tort whereby a state of affairs which prima facie can only be explained in terms of negligence on the part of the defendant shifts the burden of proof to him to show that he was not negligent.

Res judicata Latin: "a thing adjudged", a decision made by a tribunal having jurisdiction over a dispute and the parties which disposes once and for all of the matters decided so that, except in the case of an appeal, the dispute cannot be relitigated between the same parties. The consequences are that the parties cannot dispute the correctness of the decision in later proceedings and the cause of action merges in the decision. A distinction needs to be drawn in the case of adjudication, where a decision cannot be challenged in a further adjudication but can be in subsequent arbitration or litigation. Section 108(3) of the **Construction Act** and para 23 of the **Scheme for Construction Contracts** provide for the temporary binding finality of an adjudicator's decision. More than one adjudication is permissible, provided a second adjudicator is not asked to decide again that which the first adjudicator has already decided. Indeed para 9(2) of **the Scheme** obliges an adjudicator to resign where the dispute is the same or substantially the same as one which has previously been referred to adjudication and a decision has been taken in that adjudication. See HG Construction Ltd v Ashwell Homes *(East Anglia) Ltd* [2007] EWHC 144 (TCC), [2007] BLR 175; 112 ConLR 128.

Resistance The degree of opposition to the passing of an electric current through a conducting medium, usually directly proportional to its length and inversely proportional to its cross-section: copper is normally used for wiring because of its low resistivity.

Resource Any person or thing required for the completion of an activity and any variation which may affect progress.

Resource levelling The reduction in the planning of a project of variation between maximum and minimum resourcing levels by the movement of activities within their required time frame, usually by means of project planning software.

Resourceful losing party Term coined by Mr Justice Coulson in *AC Yule & Son Ltd v Speedwell Roofing & Cladding Ltd* [2007] EWHC 1360 (TCC); [2007] BLR 499 to characterise the approach of parties seeking to resist adjudication enforcement applications who were continually looking for new legal grounds to defend such claims.

Responding party The party against whom the claim is made in an adjudication and who is served with the **referral**.

Response A document setting out the Responding party's case in reply to the **referral** in an adjudication.

Restitutio in integrum Latin: "restitution in whole", the principle that rescission of a contract should place each party in the position in which he was before the contract was made. ■ See **Rescission**.

Restitution A remedy based on the principle by which a person who has received unjust enrichment may be obliged to compensate the claimant even though there is no basis for a claim for damages for breach of contract or tort. Its application in relation to construction disputes is likely to arise where: (1) a benefit has been conferred under a mistake of fact or law; (2) a transaction is too incomplete or uncertain to amount to a contract or otherwise ineffective or failed; and (3) a party has supplied goods and services to another in circumstances which suggest that the supply was not intended to be gratuitous.

Restricted procedure A two-stage procurement process which allows **Contracting Authorities** to draw up a short-list of interested parties by undertaking a pre-qualification stage, prior to the issue of invitation to tender documents. ■ See **Open procedure**.

Restrictive covenant A term in an agreement between parties to limit the development or use of land, including commercial and residential property, which is made for the benefit of other property, such as building on a plot or extending an existing house. The covenant binds subsequent purchasers of the property if it is negative in character. Application may be made to the Upper Tribunal (Lands Chamber) to discharge or modify a restrictive covenant.

Retail Prices Index (RPI) An index of prices of goods and services compiled monthly by the Office of National Statistics and sometimes used in contracts as a basis of adjustment of prices to allow for inflation. The government now prefers the Consumer Price Index.

Retainage Term used in United States for **retention**.

Retaining wall A wall or similar structure built to hold back ground either in its natural state or where exposed vertically as a result of engineering works. Such a wall will be strengthened and may be propped or supported by buttressing. ➤**Figure R2**.

Retention (monies) A percentage of the contract sum (usually 5 per cent) retained by the employer from sums certified for payment to the contractor as a form of security against the cost of remedying defective works. Usually half the retention is released at practical completion and the balance upon the completion of making good defects after the expiry of the rectification or defect liability period. Contracts often provide that the employer holds these monies on a fiduciary basis. ■ See **Fiduciary interest**.

Retention of title The reservation by a supplier of his ownership of goods after they have been delivered and until some event, usually payment in full, has occurred. This result is achieved by the inclusion in the supplier's terms and conditions of sale of a clause (sometimes known as a **ROT** clause) to that effect, known as a Romalpa clause after the first case in which such a device was given effect to, ***Aluminium Industrie Vaassen BV v Romalpa Aluminium Ltd*** [1976] 1 WLR 676 (CA); [1976] 2 All ER 552. The objective of such a provision is to protect the seller in the event of the buyer's insolvency. In the context of construction projects the

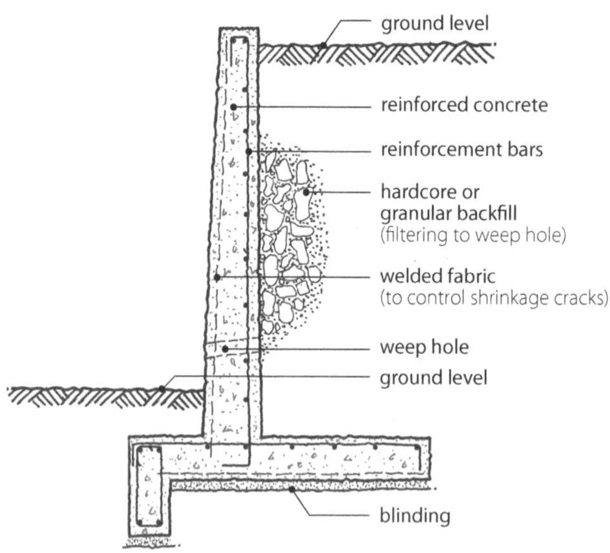

➤ **Figure R2.** Retaining Wall (section)

question of the supplier's rights against the employer or owner to whom the goods have been passed arises and clauses of increasing complexity and scope have been introduced over the years. Two particular difficulties such provisions face are the requirements in the Companies Act 2006, ss860 and 874 for certain types of charges to be registered, and the Sale of Goods Act 1979, s25(2) which allows a main contractor to transfer good title to an employer receiving the goods in good faith and without notice of the provision, although each case will turn on its particular facts.

Retrofit To install a component after the date of the original construction or manufacture in order to upgrade or modernise.

Retrospective delay analysis An examination of the events during a contract which may have caused delay and their actual impact on the progress of the works by looking back at the delays and their effect at the end of the contract, usually by reference to an **As-built programme**. It may be contrasted with **Prospective delay analysis** which aims to demonstrate the likely future impact of delay events on the works. Types of retrospective delay analysis include: **As planned v as built**, **As-planned impacted (baseline adding impacts)**, **Collapsed as built** and **Time impact analysis**.

Return air Air that is returned via vents and ductwork from the space already heated or cooled and ductwork to an air conditioning heating or cooling plant where it is filtered and then recirculated.

Return wall In the United Kingdom, a wall constructed at 90° to the main façade: a side wall. In the United States, an internal wall built to same height as external wall of a building.

Reveal A vertical side of an opening in a wall for a door or window.

Reverberation time The time required in seconds for the sound in a room to become inaudible once a noise source ceases: it will vary according to the characteristics of the room and the extent of sound absorbent materials which cause the reverberant echo of the sound to decay. It may be adjusted by alterations to the room to meet particular requirements such as the playing of music.

Reverse premium A payment or benefit made by one party to induce another to enter into a transaction. For example, a landlord may make a payment to a prospective tenant to induce him to enter into a lease.

Reversible repair or improvement A change to a building which can later be undone to restore the property to its original condition, such as removal of tenant's alterations at end of lease: or where some protection is required but improved restoration techniques in the future are anticipated.

Reversion The legal title of a landlord or other owner to property or goods which are currently in the possession of another person such as a tenant.

Revetment A timber wall or stone construction built along a shoreline or river bank to protect it against erosion by wave action or currents: see **breakwater**. Also a retaining wall to support an embankment or trench and to provide shelter, for example against damage by explosives where stored in magazines.

Revision Amendments to a drawing, specification or other document which may undergo periodic changes during the course of a project and are reissued (usually designated rev A and so on). The revised areas may be highlighted or indicated by a "cloud" shape on the drawing and summarised in a table at the side: the revision date should be stated.

Revocation of offer The withdrawal of an offer to enter into a contract. A revocation takes effect from the time when the offeree becomes aware of it and, unlike an acceptance of an offer, from the date of receipt if sent by post: *Byrne v Van Tienhoven* [1880] 5 CPD 344. ■ See **Postal rule**.

RFI See **Request for Information**.

RH See **Relative humidity**.

RIAS See **Royal Incorporation of Architects in Scotland**.

Rib and block suspended floor Floor constructed of precast shaped concrete beams placed at regular intervals which span from structural walls, with the intervening gaps filled with lightweight concrete blocks. The floor is then covered in a screed with mesh reinforcement. This is a faster method of construction than casting an in situ slab in formwork but may need propping beneath during construction.

RIBA See **Royal Institute of British Architects**.

RIBA Code of Professional Conduct A code setting out the standards of professional conduct which all members of the RIBA must follow. The code defines professional conduct and values with supporting Guidance Notes. Breach of the Code may result in reprimand, suspension or expulsion from the RIBA.

RIBA contract A standard form of building contract originally agreed between the RIBA and the Builders' Society and adopted by the Central Association of master builders of London: see *Clemence v Clarke* (1879) *Hudson's Law of Building, Engineering & Ship Building Contracts* 4th edn, Vol. 2, p 54. The form was subsequently the subject of agreement between the constituent members of the **Joint Contracts Tribunal**. ■ See **JCT**.

RIBA Outline Plan of Work A schedule of work stages prepared by the RIBA which outlines the key stages for procurement design and construction of a project. The alphabetical work stages (A–L) assist in the organisation and management of construction and engineering projects. Consultants often define their services in accordance with these stages, using them as a basis for project management and fee proposal purposes.

RIBA Plan of work 2013 Expected in spring 2013, the first major revision since its inception in 1962, fifty years ago.

RIBA Work Stages The stages in the **RIBA Outline Plan of Work**. Stages A and B are preparation stages: Stages C to E are design: Stages F to H are pre-construction stages: Stages J to K are the construction stages and Stage L is the use stage in the 2007 edition as amended. ➤**Figure R3**.

RICS See **Royal Institution of Chartered Surveyors**.

RICS Code of Measuring Practice Published standards and guidance for measuring land and buildings including standard definitions of terms such as net internal floor area to promote uniformity of practice: ■ see **Standard Method of Measurement (SMM7)**.

Ridge The top line of a sloping roof where the pitched sides meet at the apex: protected by ridge tiles.

Ridge board A wooden board at the top of each slope of a pitched roof to which the upper end of the rafters is fixed. Not required if roof trusses are used to form roof.

Stage	Description
A	Appraisal
B	Design Brief
C	Concept
D	Design Development
E	Technical Design
F	Production Information *F1 - Preparation of information to enable tendering* *F2 - Preparation of further information for construction*
G	Tender Documentation
H	Tender Action
J	Mobilisation
K	Construction to Practical Completion
L	Post Practical Completion

➤ **Figure R3.** RIBA Work Stages

Ridge course A course of slates or tiles next to the ridge on a pitched roof.

Ridge tile A tile which is usually V shaped or half round placed on a bed of cement which covers the **ridge** of a roof to make it weather tight. Ridgeline roof vents may also be used.

Right in gross A legal right belonging to a person that is not attached to specific parcel of land, such as a personal right of access over property or to extract minerals.

Right to light The right of an owner of property to receive an adequate amount of natural light through its windows: this right is normally acquired through prescription (more than 20 years uninterrupted enjoyment) but may be the subject of a grant. It constitutes an easement and an overriding interest. Rights to light ("ancient lights") can sometimes severely restrict the development of adjoining sites.

Right of support (1) A natural right of support for one parcel of land in its natural state from another. Removal of natural support gives rise to a cause of action in **Nuisance**. The adjoining owner owes a duty to prevent damage limited to taking reasonable steps to counter patent risks: *Holbeck Hall Hotel Ltd v Scarborough BC* [2000] BLR 109 (CA); [2000] 2 WLR 1396; [2000] 2All ER 705. (2) An **Easement** often enjoyed by the buildings on an adjoining property and therefore giving rise to a cause of action when disturbed by construction works on a building site. In such a case the employer is liable for the acts of his independent contractor: *Dalton v Angus* [1881] 6 App Cas 740 (HL).

Right of way The right to pass over land owned by another party. This right may be a public right such as a highway or a private right such as a driveway for access to a property: see **easement**. The right may be limited to passing on foot or may include the use of vehicles: it normally does not permit vehicles to be parked or to obstruct the access.

Rights of audience The right of a party or his representative to be heard in court. A litigant in person always has such a right: Solicitors have rights of audience in the magistrates' and county courts, and if qualified as solicitor advocates in the Crown Court, the High Court and the Court of Appeal. Barristers have rights of audience in all courts, including the Supreme Court. The court may permit a lay person (McKenzie friend) to advise a litigant in person in court and a director to represent a limited company.

Ring beam A continuous reinforced concrete beam which supports or strengthens the walls of a building at foundation level, or sometimes at the top of the wall (in timber). Also a circular beam to constrain a dome.

Ring main An electrical wiring circuit which runs in a circular layout around each floor of a building, departing from and returning to the consumer unit and providing the power to individual sockets and appliances. Because it is circular current can pass both ways through the circuit thereby reducing the load.

Riot There are five elements of a riot: (1) number of persons, three at least; (2) common purpose; (3) execution or inception of the common purpose; (4) an intent to help one another by force if necessary against any person who may oppose them in the execution of their common purpose; (5) force or violence not merely used in demolishing, but displayed in such a manner as to alarm at least one person of reasonable firmness and courage: *Field v Metropolitan Police Receiver* [1907] 2 KB 853 (DC). Riot is one of the **Specified Perils** under the JCT standard forms.

Riparian Pertaining to the bank of a river or stream. A riparian owner will usually own the bed of the stream to its mid-point and may have rights over the watercourse including those to abstract water and fishing. The Environment Agency has powers in relation to watercourses which may affect owners.

Rise The height of an individual stair or a complete staircase. ➤**Figure G2**.

Rise and fall clause See **Fluctuations clause**.

Rise over run A mathematical formula for the calculation of slope: used by carpenters for the design of staircases to ensure they occupy available opening with uniform treads and risers and for the pitch of a sloping roof.

Riser (1) The vertical elements between the treads of a stair. (2) A vertical shaft formed from partitions to allow the vertical distribution of services throughout a building. ➤**Figure G2**.

Rising damp Moisture in a brick wall or other permeable material which has been drawn upwards from the ground or other water source by capillary action. It may lead to efflorescence of salts on surfaces as the moisture evaporates and is normally prevented by a **Damp proof course** or other moisture barrier.

Risk allocation The division of potential liabilities between the parties to a contract.

Risk allowance A provision made in pricing a contract or other transaction against the risks which are inherent in the activity but cannot be precisely predicted, such as the impact of bad weather in a building contract. ■ See **Contingency sum**.

Risk assessment The review of a project or activity (1) to ascertain the risks to health and safety which may arise, (2) to categorise those risks according to their likelihood and the severity of their consequences (3) to identify and implement all reasonably necessary measures to avoid such risks from arising. A risk assessment is an important activity on any project: see the Health and Safety at Work etc. Act 1974.

Risk register A formal record of the risks which have been identified in relation to a project or activity and the measures adopted for managing those risks. The register should also identify the time and cost consequences if the risk event occurs. The register must be updated if the project changes or further risks are identified, and a copy must be kept on site.

Risk value The estimated value of a known or identified risk.

Rock A mass of grains held together by a **Matrix**. Civil engineering contracts usually contain express provisions dealing with the methods for the removal of rock as well as the rates to be applied in doing so.

Rock berm A barrier built of stone at the base of an embankment or along a riverbank or shoreline to allow the passage of water but trap sediment.

Rodding Cleaning out a pipe or conduit by passing a drainage rod with attachments along its length.

Rodding eye A removable cover (sometimes at bend in pipe or drain) to allow drainage rod to be inserted along a length of pipework in order to unblock or clean it.

Rolled steel joist (RSJ) A beam with an I-shaped section made by a hot-rolling mill and particularly used to span openings made in existing buildings in the course of refurbishment.

Roller shutter, roller door A shutter for doors, windows and other openings made from thin sections of metal or wood held together with flexible joints which are held on a roller inside the building above the opening when not in use. Heavy shutters may be operated by an electric motor. They provide a higher level of security in warehouse and industrial premises.

Romalpa clause See **Retention of title**.

Ronseal Term used to describe something where the name or description describes exactly what it is. Taken from the advertising slogan: “does exactly what it says on the tin”.

Roof decking Sheets material such as plastic coated profiled metal used as primary roof covering on commercial and industrial buildings: decking may also incorporate the upper waterproof layer. Also slats of wood fibreglass or other materials forming panels or walkways placed on a flat roof to enable it to be accessed and used.

Roof truss An assembly of timber beams in a triangular form to support a sloping roof: usually prefabricated by specialist suppliers according to the requirements of a project.

Roofing felt A bitumen-impregnated flexible waterproof material composed of fibreglass sheet used as top cover for flat and sloping roofs.

Room data sheets A record of the proposed function, finishes, decoration and fittings for each room and other spaces in a building, usually prepared at the design stage.

ROT clause Retention of title

Rough cutting The initial shaping of timber or other materials before they are cut to exact requirements: also cutting to leave a rough rather than a smooth finish.

Rough opening The framed opening within the fabric of a wall to accommodate the fitting of a door or window, made slightly larger than the framing which is to fit into the aperture.

Routledge v Grant [1828] 4 Bing 653: if an offeror promises not to revoke his offer before a specified date such promises are unenforceable unless supported by consideration, that is, something of value in return.

Rowlock course A course of brickwork with the stretcher laid across the width of the wall and the small headers exposed in line: a decorative feature found on the top of walls.

Royal assent The point at which a Parliamentary Bill, having been passed by both Houses, is consented to on behalf of the sovereign and becomes an Act of Parliament. An Act, however, does not necessarily come into force at that point: many statutes provide that they will not be brought into force until the relevant minister has issued subordinate legislation to that effect.

Royal Incorporation of Architects in Scotland (RIAS) The professional body for chartered architects in Scotland.

Royal Institute of British Architects (RIBA) A professional body which was granted its original Royal Charter in 1837. It supports over 40,500 members in the architectural profession and its mission is "*to advance architecture by demonstrating benefit to society and promoting excellence in the profession.*" The RIBA provides its members with training, technical guidance, publications and events. In addition, it sets standards for the training of architects and also works with the government to improve the UK's quality of design. The RIBA also hosts the annual Stirling Prize (in association with the Architects' Journal and Crystal CG) which honours the architects of a building which has most significantly evolved architecture in the course of that year. The RIBA does not regulate the registration of architects. This function is the responsibility of the Architects Registration Board (ARB). Members of the RIBA must comply with its Code of Professional Conduct (2005). ■ See **RIBA Code of Professional Conduct** and **Architect's Registration Board**.

Royal Institution of Chartered Surveyors The professional and regulatory body of Chartered Surveyors in England and Wales, founded in 1868 and granted a Royal charter in 1881. The Charter requires the Institution "to maintain and promote the usefulness of the profession for the public advantage." Qualified RICS members are recognised by designatory letters: (1) FRICS (Fellow); (2) MRICS (Member); (3) AssocRICS (Associate). RICS members are required to keep up to date with current practice through a programme of lifelong learning. Because of the diversity of its membership, the Institution has established various Professional Groups relating to different areas of practice, the most relevant of which for present purposes are: (i) Building control, (ii) Building surveying, (iii) Project management, (iv) Quantity surveying & construction, (v) Dilapidations forum, and (vi) Insurance forum.

RPB See **Regional Planning Body**.

RPG See **Regional Planning Guidance**.

RPI See **Retail Prices Index**.

R/R See **Relative readings**.

RSJ See **Rolled steel joist**.

RS See **Regional Strategy**.

RSS See **Regional Spatial Strategy**.

RTECS See **Registry of Toxic Effects of Chemical Substances**.

Rule of law (1) A rule which operates irrespective of the intention of the parties involved, as opposed to a rule of construction or one of practice. Parties to a contract can modify or exclude a rule of construction, but not one of law. (2) The principle that the executive should only act in accordance with the law.

Rules of construction Established rules which are applied in construing a document to arrive at its legal effect, also known as **Canons of construction**.

Rules of the Supreme Court (RSC) The rules formerly governing procedure in the High Court, now superseded by the **Civil Procedure Rules (CPR)**.

Running bond A bricklaying pattern where each course consists entirely of stretchers, showing the long side of the brick, and the vertical joints are staggered from course to course.

Rustication The use of rough finished blocks of stonework with deep joints on the façade of a building for dramatic effect.

R-value A measure of the thermal resistance of different types of insulation and their efficiency in a building.

RWP See **Rainwater pipe**.

Rylands v Fletcher liability A rule of strict liability first recognised in *Rylands v Fletcher* [1866] LR 1 Ex 265 at 279, affirmed at [1868] LR 3 HL 330, requiring only that a prospective claimant demonstrates an escape from the defendant's land of something which, having been brought there by the defendant, was likely to do mischief if it did escape and which constituted a "non-natural use" of the land. As Lord Moulton put it in *Rickards v Lothian* [1913] AC 263 at 280:

> "It is not every use to which land is put that brings into play that principle [Rylands v Fletcher]. It must be some special use bringing with it increased danger to others and must not merely be the ordinary use of land or such a use as is proper for the general benefit of the community".

In two comparatively recent decisions, the House of Lords declined to abolish the rule and attempted to clarify it. In *Cambridge Water Co Ltd v Eastern Counties Leather plc* [1994] 2 AC 264; [1994] 2 WLR 53, it was held that foreseeability of damage of the relevant type should be regarded as a prerequisite of liability in damages under the rule, so that the courts might feel less pressure to extend the concept of natural use to circumstances such as the storage of chemicals in substantial quantities, and that in due course it might become easier to control that exception, and to ensure that it had a more recognisable basis of principle. In *Transco plc v Stockport Metropolitan Borough Council* [2003] UKHL 61; [2003] 3 WLR 1467; [2004] 1 All ER 589 there was a clear refusal to abolish the rule or to absorb into the law of negligence. The speeches, however, proceeded on the basis of slightly different approaches.

S

Sacrificial coating A method to control corrosion, a surface applied coating, often of zinc, which is applied to steel and iron to give it sacrificial protection. See galvanising.

Sacrificial panel A lightweight panel which can be broken into for access to services or other hidden construction.

Saddle scaffold A scaffold that spans a roof from opposite sides of a building, typically used to provide comprehensive weather protection to facilitate roof and masonry repairs.

Saddle trusses A roofing frame used to provide lateral support for roof trusses where a valley is formed, also known as a valley truss.

Saddle-jib crane A conventional tower crane, whose horizontal (jib) is fixed at one point along its length to a vertical tower: the jib is free to rotate in the horizontal plane. The hoist can traverse the job along a track on the horizontal jib to change different lifting positions. Such cranes are usually electrically powered.

Safe working load (SWL) The total uniformly distributed load that, for example, a **lintel** or lifting beam is designed to support, whilst providing an appropriate factor of safety.

Sale of goods The law relating to the sale of goods, codified in the Sale of Goods Act 1979. The Act does not apply to construction contracts because services are supplied under them as well as goods. The **Supply of Goods and Services Act 1982** governs some aspects of construction contracts.

Same arbitrator provision A contractual provision for related disputes under different contracts to be arbitrated before the same arbitral tribunal, most usually in the case of employer/main contractor/subcontractor disputes.

Sample panel A section of brickwork, tiling or other building material prepared by contractor and submitted to architect to obtain approval for use of material or standard of workmanship and to be used as model for judging quality of work subsequently.

Sanctity of contract The concept that parties are free to contract on whatever terms they choose. A nineteenth century concept that has been considerably eroded by statutory intervention.

Sand bedding A layer of sand spread above sub base as a levelling foundation for paving materials such as slabs or bricks.

Sanderson order A form of costs order first recognised in *Sanderson v Blyth Theatre Co* [1903] 2 KB 533 (CA) whereby a successful defendant's costs are ordered to be paid directly by an unsuccessful defendant, particularly used where there may be doubt as to the claimant's solvency.

Sandwich construction Placement of building material in alternating layers, for example insulation material between internal and external leaves.

SAP rating This is the 'Standard Assessment Procedure' which denotes the overall energy efficiency of a dwelling. It is measured on a scale of 1-100 where the greater the number, the superior the performance.

Sarking felt A waterproof bituminised felt, traditionally with a coarse jute backing, placed beneath roof tile battens to provide a second line of defence against water penetration and wind blown snow.

Sash Window Window(s) which open by dropping vertically and sliding past each other, guided by runners: balanced by weights on each side held by cords within the frame. Compare with **casement window**.

Satisfaction See **Accord and satisfaction**.

Satisfactory quality The standard (previously known as "merchantable quality") to be met under the term implied into a contract for the transfer of the property in goods in the course of a business by s 4 of the **Supply of Goods and Services Act 1982**, as amended by the Sale and Supply of Goods Act 1994. Goods are of satisfactory quality if they meet the standard that a reasonable person would regard as satisfactory, taking account of any description of the goods, the price (if relevant) and all the other relevant circumstances: s4(A).

Save harmless To protect from loss, usually by way of indemnity.

Saving the document A principle of construction by which the court will give effect to a meaning that will validate a written instrument rather than one that will make it void: *WN Hillas & Co Ltd v Arcos Ltd* [1932] 147 LT 503 (HL). The court will also be reluctant to hold a contract void for uncertainty where the parties believe that they have entered into a binding agreement (*Greater London Council v Connolly* [1970] 2 QB 100), particularly where it has been partly performed (*Sudbrook Trading Estate Ltd v Eggleton* [1983] 1 AC 444 (HL)).

Sawn damp course Damp proof course inserted in walls of older building by cutting into horizontal mortar bed in short sections.

SBC See **Standard Building Contract**.

SBEM stands for Standard Building Energy Method and comprises a computer program developed by the BRE for calculating the carbon emissions of buildings other than dwellings. It calculates monthly energy use and carbon dioxide emissions of a building based on inputting a description of the building geometry, construction, use and HVAC and lighting equipment. The user inputs data relating to the building design and the software compares the actual design with a notional building of the same design built to 2002 standards.

SC See **Supreme Court**.

Scabbling The mechanical roughing up of a surface in order to provide a key for a covering layer, for example, of concrete facing to receive a render finish.

SCADA Supervisory Control and Data Acquisition. A software package designed to display information, log data and show alarms, which is used to monitor and control plant or equipment.

Scaffold coupler A metal clamp for joining two sections of scaffold pole where they meet, in a number of configurations, for example, right-angle couplers, swivel, putlog and straight length couplers.

Scaffold, scaffolding A framework of metal or wooden poles erected around construction site to give access to work areas (eg bricklayers) or around existing building to facilitate repair and maintenance. Wooden planks are laid across the scaffolding to provide platforms for working (known as lifts). The erection and maintenance of scaffolding is subject to technical regulations and is normally carried by specialist tradesmen.

Scafftag A proprietary status tagging system for scaffolding and temporary work which by the use of demonstrable 'tags' shows the status of the scaffolding. It provides the user with an audit trail, showing when the scaffold was last inspected and its duty, and contains checklists for harnesses and ladders.

Scale The reduction of a plan, drawing or measurements by a uniform ratio to enable them to be represented on a sheet of paper of convenient size. The scale is stated on the plan. Common drawing scales include: 1:1250, 1:500, 1:200, 1:100 and 1:50. When scaling off a plan, account must be taken of possible distortion resulting from stretching or shrinkage of paper.

Scale fees Fees calculated in accordance with a scale recommended by a professional body, such as the RIBA or ICE. At one time, the members of such bodies were obliged to charge fees but this is no longer the case.

Scaled dimension A measurement which is obtained by scaling off a drawing. Since copying plans may create some distortion, some inaccuracy is possible: see figured dimensions.

Schedule (1) An inventory or list of items. ■ See **Door schedule** or **Schedule of defects**. (2) An American term equivalent to the British word "programme". ■ See **Programme**.

Schedule 2 quotation A quotation to be provided by the contractor pursuant to an Instruction for a Variation under the JCT standard forms. The contractor is not obliged to provide a quotation if he gives notice that he disagrees with the application of the procedure.

Schedule of defects A list of defective and incomplete work prepared by the Architect/CA after his inspection, either to be rectified before practical completion can be certified, or if less significant, as a Schedule of Outstanding Defects or snagging list to be remedied within the rectification period (defects liability period).

Schedule of rates (SOR) A list of rates identified in a tender by a contractor in appropriate units for specified materials or activities, for example, per linear or square metre, which can later be used to value works. SORs contain both composite and elemental descriptions and are now used extensively in the social housing sector as a fully priced composite schedule defining the repair and renewal tasks for day-to-day and void repairs complete for letting a measured term contract.

Scheduled monuments Currently defined by the Ancient Monuments and Archaeological Areas Act 1979, a schedule has been kept by the government since 1882 of monuments and sites considered to be of national importance. It is an offence to damage a scheduled monument or even remove any item which may be of historical interest from the site of a scheduled monument.

Scheme for Construction Contracts (the Scheme) Section 108(5) of the **Construction Act** provides that if a construction contract regulated by Part II of that Act does not comply with the requirements of ss108 (1)–(4), the adjudication provisions of the Scheme for Construction Contracts applies. The scheme is that contained in the Scheme for Construction Contracts (England and Wales) Regulations 1998, SI 1998/64 (as amended). The position on the consequences of non-compliance should now be regarded as settled: if there is any non-compliance with s108 of the Act, the adjudication provisions in Part 1 of the Scheme are brought in – lock, stock and barrel: *Yuanda (UK) Co Ltd v WW Gear Construction Ltd* [2010] EWHC 720 (TCC); [2010] BLR 435; 130 ConLR 133.

Scheme of arrangement See **Corporate Voluntary Arrangement**.

Schmidt hammer test A non-destructive test which tests the surface hardness and penetrative resistance of concrete. It is also known as the **Rebound hammer test**.

Scientific and technical terms The meaning of technical terms in a document may be established by reference to a dictionary but, where it is in dispute, by evidence alone: *Baldwin & Francis Ltd v Patents Appeal Tribunal* [1959] AC 663 (HL); [1959] 2 WLR 826; [1959] 2 All ER 433.

Scissors lift A mechanical or hydraulic lift whose supports beneath are crossed so that its table remains level as it rises.

SCL See **Society of Construction Law**.

SCL Delay Protocol Published in October 2002, the SCL Delay & Disruption Protocol is a proposed agreed procedure regarding the recording and presentation of information concerning delay events and their impact on a contract programme, which considers the most common techniques employed for analysing the effect of delay events and the means to facilitate the resolution of contract disputes concerning time or delay by the adoption of a common approach by the parties. It is of no effect in resolving disputes unless the parties have agreed to be bound by it and is open to the objection that it excuses a contractor from having to prove particular aspects of a claim to the standard applicable in either arbitration or litigation. Although take up of the SCL Delay Protocol has been limited, it remains a valuable statement of many of the principles surrounding delay and disruption.

Scope of works The extent of the permanent works to be carried out under a contract, and a written description of them, often in a summary form at the start of a contract, also known as "workscope". Work instructed outside the scope of works may constitute a variation, depending on the construction of the contract as a whole.

Scott Schedule A schedule which itemises the individual claims a party makes in an action or arbitration, usually a list of defects or items of loss. Column headings set out the defect, its location, the contract term(s) alleged to be breached, the remedial work required or already carried out and the cost of rectification claimed. There is no standard form of Scott Schedule and its format can be flexibly adapted to suit a variety of claims but the version prescribed by TCC Judges is widely adopted. It was first devised by an Official Referee, Mr G.A. Scott QC. ➤**Figure S1**.

Scott v Avery Clause A term in a contract which requires the parties to arbitrate any dispute between them first as a condition precedent to any legal proceedings: in practice this means that any court action is confined to issues concerning the arbitrator's award. Such a clause does not, however, prevent a party to a construction contract making a claim in adjudication. These clauses are now rarely found in contracts: a standard arbitration clause for the resolution of disputes is preferable to avoid arguments over the contractual dispute resolution procedure.

Item No.	Claimant				Defendant	Judge
	Description	Breach	Remedial Work Required	Cost of Remedial Work	Reply/ Comments	
1	Bypass on the third floor heating circuit not installed.	Breach of clause 1.1 and 2.5 of the Contract Conditions. Breach of s4 & s14 of SGSA 1982 (as amended) : failure to use reasonable care and skill.	Install bypass.	£875		
2	Defective compressors (condenser units)	Breach of clause 1.1 and 2.5 of the Contract Conditions. Breach of s4 & s14 of SGSA 1982 (as amended) : failure to use reasonable care and skill.	Replace condenser units.	£4,000		

➤ **Figure S1.** Scott Schedule (defects)

Screed A surface layer of material placed over a floor to achieve a level and smooth surface and to prepare for a final wearing surface, such as tiling, wood block flooring, carpeting or a synthetic finish. Often screed is made of cementatious material but plastic polymer compounds are increasingly used. ➤**Figure E3**

Scrim is a strong, coarse fabric, traditionally hessian but now more commonly synthetic fabric chiefly used in construction of ornate fibrous plasterwork to help inhibit cracking, may also be used to reinforce plaster based mould support cases and also used as a taping and jointing masker, and as a heavy-duty lining or upholstery.

S-curve Portrayal of expected finance for the duration of a project. The shape conforms to an "s" and shows the gradual build up of expenditure and how it is required over the duration of a project. It can also be used to show expected labour man-hours.

Seal An impression made in melted wax or a wafer on a written instrument. The use of a seal was a formality indicating that a document was a **deed** with important consequences, particularly dispensing with the need for consideration for any undertaking made and extending the limitation period for bringing a claim on the instrument to 12 years. The requirement for sealing of deeds was abolished by the Law of Property (Miscellaneous Provisions) Act 1989 and the insertion by the Companies Act 1989 s130(1) of s36A into the Companies Act 1985 (subsequently amended by the Companies Act 2006).

Sealed offer A written offer by a party to settle a dispute proceeding by way of arbitration on compromise terms, the equivalent of an offer made **without prejudice save as to costs**. The time for acceptance may be limited. Traditionally, such offers were placed in a sealed envelope and given to the arbitrator, not to be opened until his award on all matters other than costs was published, but this practice is no longer followed, the arbitrator merely being made aware of the offer and asked to take it into consideration when he comes to deals with costs, usually by way of a separate award. In court proceedings an offer under CPR Part 36 procedure or made **without prejudice save as to costs** would be appropriate. ■ See **Calderbank offer**, **Part 36** offer.

Search order An order, formally known as an **Anton Piller order**, under s7 of the Civil Procedure Act 1997 requiring a party to admit another party to premises for the purpose of preserving evidence. See Part 25.1(h) of the **CPR**.

Seasoning The drying out of timber, which has limited use when first cut (green state) due to its propensity to shrink and warp. The length of time to obtained seasoned timber varies according to the type of wood and the conditions in which it is stored. The maximum permitted moisture content of timber is often specified for particular uses, such as engineered flooring or panelling.

Seat of the arbitration The location where an arbitration is agreed by the parties, or is deemed, to be based. The hearing(s) of evidence and argument will not necessarily take place there, but the procedural and substantive law of the arbitration will be determined by its seat unless the parties expressly or impliedly agree otherwise. The seat of the arbitration may be important in terms of recognition and enforcement of an award.

Second fix or fixing Mechanical electrical and joinery work carried out after the installation of the **First fix** services and plasterwork has been completed. Includes installation of plumbing and electrical appliances, light fittings, hanging doors, grilles and switch plates. ■ See **First fix**.

Secondary fixing The fixing of components or materials to the precise position required once the main framework has been installed, for example, of external cladding panels or other system built products, and the means of making such fixings, such as purpose made clips or channels.

Secondary glazing Glass panels fixed to framework of existing windows to provide better insulation and protection from draughts: now almost always manufactured as integral window units with two or more glass panels held within a single frame and a semi vacuum created between.

Secret fixings Attachment of materials to a framework or backing by means of fixings which are not visible on the completed surface, such as clips mounted on the back or side fixed screws: usually done for aesthetic impact, particularly in shopfitting.

Secret nailing Nailing which is concealed from an external inspection, for example, behind a glued fillet or by the heads of the nails being recessed and covered.

Section A two-dimensional drawing representing the layout through a building or object. ■ See **Orthographic projection** and **Figures G3 & P1**.

Section 106 Agreement S106 of the Town and Country Planning Act 1990. Allows a local planning authority to enter into an agreement with a developer, obliging the developer to carry out certain works which are intended to mitigate the particular impact of the development in question. For example, the developer may be required to provide social or affordable housing and/or recreational facilities.

Section 4 summons An application previously made under the Arbitration Act 1950, s4 to stay a claim issued in court where there was an arbitration clause in the contract, such an application now being made under the Arbitration Act 1996, s9.

Sectional completion The division of a project into sections (usually parts of a building but may be work stages) which each have their own completion date and may be handed over to the employer when completed. Standard form contracts are available containing provisions for sectional completion.

Security A mortgage or other charge taken over assets to secure re-payment of a debt.

Security for Costs A sum of money or other security provided by a claimant to cover the eventuality of an order for costs in a defendant's favour. In litigation, the court may order the stay of proceedings until security is provided on the following grounds under CPR 25.13: (1) the claimant is resident out of the jurisdiction in a state which is not a signatory to certain international conventions concerning the enforcement of judgments; (2) the claimant is a company or other body (incorporated inside or outside GB) and there is reason to believe that it will be unable to pay the defendant's costs if ordered to do so; (3) the claimant has changed his address since the claim was commenced with a view to evading the litigation's consequences; (4) the claimant failed to give his address, or gave an incorrect address, in the claim form; (5) the claimant is acting as a nominal claimant and there is reason to believe that it will be unable to pay the defendant's costs if ordered to do so and (6) the claimant has taken steps in relation to his assets that would make it difficult to enforce an order for costs against him. Security may be paid into court, a separate bank account or held or guaranteed by a third party (such as an on demand bond from bank). It is common for security to be ordered to a certain point in the case (eg completion of disclosure), but permitting the defendant to make further applications. The court will consider the means of the claimant (particularly a limited company) and whether non-payment of the sum claimed has caused the financial difficulty of the claimant. An arbitral tribunal has the power to order a claimant to provide security for the costs of an arbitration under the Arbitration Act 1996, s38(3) but it is not to be exercised on the grounds that the claimant is an individual ordinarily resident outside the UK or a corporation or association incorporated or formed under the law of a country outside the UK or whose central management is exercised outside the UK.

Security of payment The subject matter of legislation which seeks to facilitate cash flow in the construction industry by restricting the payer's right to delay payment or set-off cross-claims against sums otherwise due, at the same time providing for rapid resolution of disputes on an interim basis by **adjudication**. The first statute was the **Housing Grants,**

Construction and Regeneration Act 1996 applicable to the whole of the UK. There is now similar legislation in Australia, New Zealand and Singapore.

Seizure clause A provision in a construction contract entitling the employer to take possession of the contractor's plant and materials and use them to complete the works, or sell them, in the event of some default on the latter's part. The effectiveness of such provisions depends on their precise wording, which, if it creates a floating charge, may be void against the owner for lack of registration: *Re Coslett (Contractors) Ltd* (1998) 85 BLR 1 (CA); [1998] 2 WLR 131; [1997] 4 All ER 115; [2002] BLR 166 (HL).

Selected subcontractor Another term for a **nominated (or named) subcontractor**.

Selective tendering Tender process in which the employer confines the invitation to tender to contractors on an approved list rather than opening the process to public tender. Many public authorities invite tenders on this basis, but will regularly conduct an exercise for those who wish to qualify for the approved list.

Self-climbing tower crane Also known as Self Erecting Tower Cranes (**SETCs**) they are a purpose designed telescoping type of tower crane which use the existing floors of a structure as it rises for support, the boom and mast are raised through floor openings, such as a lift well and secured by wedges and frames. Usually the crane is hydraulically operated with the hydraulic jack at the back of the climbing frame pushing the structure upwards.

Self-curing Concrete or resin products which harden by a chemical reaction (sometimes by use of additives) rather than the external application of heat.

Self-levelling screed Screeding material which is sufficiently liquid to reach a uniform level to the full extent to which it is to be placed.

Semble Latin: "it would seem".

Separable portion A part or stage of a project to which particular contractual terms apply.

Separating floor A floor which separates one dwelling from another in a block of flats. This is required by Part E of the Building Regulations to have a good degree of insulation against the transmission of noise.

Sequence of trades The order in which skilled work is carried out on a project, determined by the character of the development: first fix mechanical and electrical is followed by plastering, then joinery and decoration.

Seriatim Latin: "separately".

Serious irregularity Serious irregularity affecting an arbitral tribunal, proceedings or award and a ground for challenging an award under the Arbitration Act 1996, s68. It means an irregularity of one or more of the following kinds which the court considers has caused or will cause substantial injustice to the applicant party: (1) failure by the tribunal to comply with s33 (general duty of tribunal); (2) the tribunal exceeding its powers (otherwise than by exceeding its substantive jurisdiction: see s67); (3) failure by the tribunal to conduct the proceedings in accordance with the procedure agreed by the parties; (4) failure by the tribunal to deal with all the issues that were put to it; (5) any arbitral or other institution or person vested by the parties with powers in relation to the proceedings or the award exceeding its powers; (6) uncertainty or ambiguity as to the effect of the award; (7) the award being obtained by fraud or the award or the way in which it was procured being contrary to public policy; (8) failure to comply with the requirements as to the form of the award; or (9) any irregularity in the conduct of the proceedings or in the award which is admitted by the tribunal or by any arbitral or other institution or person vested by the parties with powers in relation to the proceedings or the award.

Service The formal communication of a document by delivery to the recipient. The point in time at which service takes place depends on any governing statutory or contractual provisions. The rules governing service of claim forms and other court documents are particularly technical: see Part 6 of **CPR**. Where an Act authorises or requires any document to be served by post (whether the expression "serve" or the expression "give" or "send" or any other expression is used) then, unless the contrary intention appears, the service is deemed to be effected by properly addressing, pre-paying and posting a letter containing the document and, unless the contrary is proved, to have been effected at the time at which the letter would be delivered in the ordinary course of post: Interpretation Act 1978, s7. Construction contracts usually contain detailed provisions relating to the service of documents by each party on the other.

Service lift Lift in completed building designed for movement of goods rather than passengers.

Services Generic term for provision of external supply of water, gas, electricity, telephone and IT.

Services engineer A consultant M & E engineer.

Set aside The cancelling of a judgment or order or a step taken by a party in legal proceedings.

Set off Giving credit for one sum against another. The following rights of set-off are likely to be relevant to construction contracts: (1) **Abatement**, being a common law right to reduce the price payable for goods and services by showing how much less the subject matter of the action is worth by reason of the other party's breach. (2) **Legal set-off**, being a common law right to claim a credit for one liquidated debt or money demand against another, even if unrelated, provided that the amounts can be ascertained readily and without difficulty. (3) **Equitable set-off**, where it would be manifestly unjust for a claim to be enforced without regard to a cross-claim and there is a close relationship between the dealings and transactions which gave rise to the respective claims. (4) Insolvency set-off arising from **mutual dealings** between one party and another which subsequently becomes insolvent, whereby the amount of a debt to the insolvent party can be reduced by the amount of any debt owed by him to the other party under the Insolvency Rules 1986, r4.90. In the case of construction contracts subject to the provisions of the **Construction Act**, a right of set-off can only be exercised after service of a **withholding notice** or **payless Notice**.

Setting aside A remedy made by order of the court for **serious irregularity** in arbitration. The award will be deemed to be of no effect.

Setting out Placing of site markers to show the precise location where wall slabs drains and other components of a building are to be constructed at or below ground level. Usually carried out by building surveyor or experienced site supervisor. Errors can be costly in large developments.

Settlement (1) Movement of ground caused by the application of external loads or changes in the condition or state of stress in the ground for other reasons, such as shrinkage due to tree roots, mining subsidence or adjacent excavation. It has been held that "subsidence" means sinking, downward movement in a vertical direction, whereas "settlement" means movement in a lateral direction, but an insurance policy which identifies the perils insured against as "subsidence and/or collapse" will cover both subsidence and settlement defined in those terms: *David Allen & Sons Billposting Ltd v Drysdale* [1939] 4 All ER 113. (2) A compromise of a dispute. ■ See **Accord and satisfaction**.

Settlement Agreement A document which records the terms of an agreement resolving a dispute. ■ See **Tomlin Order**.

Shared proceeds provision A provision in a sub-contract whereby the parties agree that the proceeds of a claim by the main contractor against the employer are to be shared with the subcontractor: see *Mooney v Henry Boot Construction Ltd* (1996) 80 BLR 66 (CA).

Shear Deformation involving the relative displacement of parallel planes in a parallel direction with adjacent planes sliding over each other. **➤Figure C2**

Shear force A force causing sliding of adjacent layers of a material relative to one another.

Shear plate (1) A round metal plate placed on a timber joist where a metal to wood joint occurs in order to develop shear resistance. (2) A reinforcement plate added to the web of a steel beam to increase its capacity to resist shearing loads.

Shear strain The angular displacement of adjacent parallel planes in a member subject to a shear force, measured in radians.

Shear strength The stress at which a material fails in shear.

Shear stress Shear force divided by the area over which it acts, measured in kN/m^2.

Shear test Any type of test to measure the shear strength of soil. Common types are the box shear test, the triaxial compression test and the vane test.

Shear wall A wall constructed to resist lateral loads, usually by means of bracing by beams and ground fixings and reinforcement in concrete.

Sheathing felt Felt made from fibre impregnated with bitumen used as a separating layer between insulation on roof deck and top layer of asphalt roof sheeting to allow for thermal movement within the roofing system.

Sheet glass Glass drawn from a molten bath into a thin sheet of film, usually by rolling a cylinder of glass, initially produced in plane flat form, exhibiting some imperfections due to ripples, but by using a twin grinding and polishing process before the advent of float glass created **plate glass** used commonly in high-class fenestration.

Sheet metal Thin plates of metal (usually steel supplied in standard sizes) which can be cut on site and used for many purposes (eg formwork for concrete).

Sheet pile A type of pile driven vertically and set closely together with others to keep earth or water out of excavations.

Shell & core The construction of a building (usually commercial) to the stage of completing the main structure and services, but without fitting out the internal space for its intended use. Commonly required by property developer who then sells or leases premises to end user, who employs own contractor for fit-out works. ■ See **Category A fit-out** and **Category B fit-out**.

Shiplap boards Overlapping wooden planks fixed on frame and used for external walls particularly of ancillary buildings, such as garages and stores: sometimes found on dwellings in coastal areas.

Shock absorber clause A clause providing a machinery for the negotiation and resolution of difficulties arising from the occurrence of certain specified events.

Shoe Metal component for holding rails or beams in place, usually bolted to concrete base.

Shop drawing A drawing prepared for the fabrication of components, usually away from site. Such a drawing will often be created by a designer or supplier prior to manufacture to obtain approval from architect to the proposed design, but may also be produced by the architect to give guidance to the contractor on technical details.

Shopping list principle The principle that, in the valuation of a variation of the works under a construction contract, neither party should be allowed to argue that the prices in the contract bill of quantities or schedule of rates were unduly profitable or unprofitable as the case might be: see *Henry Boot (UK) Ltd v Alstom Combined Cycles Ltd* [2005] EWCA Civ 814; [2005] BLR 437 (CA); [2005] 1 WLR 3850.

Shoring Support given to walls or other construction which require propping, either during construction (eg when pouring concrete into high shutters) or as part of permanent works.

Shower tray A receptacle at floor level in vitreous china or plastic to collect waste water from shower, also known as a receptor.

Shutter, shuttering Timber or metal containment to hold wet concrete in place when poured, often known as formwork. When the concrete has set the shuttering is struck and removed and can generally be reused. Special shapes of shuttering may be employed, some of a substantial size and weight which need to be moved by crane. Shuttering needs to be braced to withstand pressure from weight of concrete and wax product or oil applied to face to prevent cement adhering.

SI See **Statutory Instruments**.

Sic Latin: "thus, so", indicating that the original text referred to contains an apparent error.

Sick building A building which suffers from numerous defects in construction or operation which may be costly or practically impossible to remedy, and may be progressive (eg deterioration of structural concrete, inadequate or malfunctioning heating and ventilation).

Signature The mark made by signing a document to authenticate it personally. Signing can be done by affixing, either by writing or with a pen or pencil or by otherwise impressing (such as by using a rubber stamp with a facsimile signature on it) on the document one's name or signature. As a general proposition a person sufficiently signs a document if it is signed in his own name and with his authority by somebody else: *Goodman v J Eban Ltd* [1954] 1 QB 550 (CA); [1954] 1 All ER 763. For an alternative view of the consequences of signing or not signing a document, see *McCutcheon v David MacBrayne Ltd* [1964] 1 WLR 125, 133; [1964] 1 All ER 430 per Lord Devlin:

> "If it were possible for your Lordships to escape from the world of make-believe which the law has created into the real world in which transactions of this sort are actually done, the answer would be short and simple. It should make no difference whatever. This sort of document is not meant to be read, still less to be understood. Its signature is in truth about as significant as a handshake that marks the formal conclusion of a bargain".

Silver Book **FIDIC** conditions of contract for Turnkey Projects.

Simon Carves Ltd v Ensus UK Ltd [2011] EWHC 657 (TCC); [2011] BLR 340; 135 ConLR 96: Mr Justice Akenhead granted an injunction preventing a beneficiary from calling on an **on demand** or **performance bond** in circumstances where the party seeking payment was allegedly in breach of the terms of the underlying contract.

Simple contract Strictly, a contract not made under seal and therefore subject to a limitation period of six years. A simple contract can be written or it may be made orally. Confusingly, the expression has also been used rather imprecisely to mean a contract of which not all of the terms have been the subject of express agreement.

Simpliciter Latin: "simply".

Sine die Latin: "without day", with no fixed date, an expression previously used to indicate that the adjournment of a hearing was likely to be the end of the matter.

Sine qua non Latin: "without which not", a necessary precondition.

Single arbitrator provision See **Same arbitrator provision**.

Single joint expert An expert who has been jointly chosen and appointed by the parties to a dispute to investigate and report on his findings regarding the matters on which he is expert. The court may direct that such an expert is to be appointed where: the cost of adversarial expert evidence may be prohibitive; the technical topic is a separate and self-contained part of the case; there is a subsidiary issue requiring expertise of a relatively uncontroversial nature to be resolved; or testing or analysis is required and can conveniently be done by one laboratory or firm: CPR 35.7, para 13.4.3 of the **TCC Guide**. The expert is required to act impartially and may be asked to answer written questions from the parties and sometimes to attend court to give evidence: his fees will be paid equally by the parties, or as the court directs.

Single-line diagram A diagram of an electrical circuit showing all the components connected by means of a single line. This is a simplified representation of the layout showing only one conductor and does not show other connections. ■ See **Block diagram**.

Single-ply roof Describes a roof system in which the roof is covered by a single layer of membrane, such as the best known proprietary system known as 'Sarnafil', but can be a thermoset (a plastic that stays firm when set, and does not become soft with application of heat) or thermoplastic (a material that becomes pliable over a specific temperature, and reverts to a solid state upon cooling).

Single-stage selective tendering A form of tendering which pre-selects the contractors who will be invited to submit a formal tender. These contractors may be pre-selected on the basis of experience, financial standing, health and safety and current work loads. Once the employer has pre-selected the contractors then price tends to be the sole criteria in awarding the contract.

SIPs are structurally insulated panels of a composite board form consisting of a sandwich of two layers of structural board with an insulating layer of foam set in between. Widely used in the USA and Canada since early 1950's and now prevalent throughout Europe in timber based construction. The board is usually made of oriented strand board (OSB) and the foam either expanded polystyrene foam (EPS), extruded polystyrene foam (XPS) or polyurethane foam. SIPs share the similar structural properties to an I-beam or I-column. The rigid insulation core of the SIP performs as a web, while the OSB sheathing exhibits the same properties as the flanges. SIPs replace several components of conventional building such as studs and joists, insulation, vapour barrier and air barrier. As such they can be used for many different applications such as exterior wall, roof, floor and foundation systems.

Site accommodation Huts transported and erected on site to provide shelter, lavatories and washing facilities and dining area for operatives: also offices for staff. Usually provided by employer for contractor's use. In existing building undergoing alteration site facilities may be provided within part of the building.

Site agent The representative of the employer on site, sometimes engaged where more than one person has an interest in the works, such as a funder or future tenant.

Site boundary The legal or physical extremities of the site. Unless otherwise agreed, the contractor is entitled to possession of the whole site and to use it for the purpose of carrying out the works. Very commonly a site is protected by temporary fencing which may be substantial since the contractor may be liable for losses by theft or personal injury to trespassers.

Site clearance The clearing away and removal from a site of all contractor's equipment, surplus material, rubbish and temporary works leaving the whole of the site and the works clean, as expressly provided for in the ICE conditions, clause 33.

Site clerk Person engaged by employer to keep records on site: see **clerk of works**.

Site diary Written record kept by clerk of works (for employer) or by foreman or site manager (for contractor) recording the work carried out each day, problems encountered and solutions adopted, visitors to site and delays to works and their causes. It may be a valuable factual record in case of subsequent disputes.

Site engineer Engineer retained by employer to complete designs, answer technical queries, carry out inspection of work in progress and sometimes to carry out interim valuations, particularly on large engineering projects.

Site examination An examination of a site to establish the area available for the works and the nature of the subsoil in order to identify the correct foundation design or underground working methods. A construction professional who undertakes a design can work initially on assumptions but has an obligation either to ensure that the necessary additional information is obtained or to give his client an express warning or disclaimer: *Ove Arup & Partners International Ltd (No 2) v Mirant Asis-Pacific Construction (Hong Kong) Ltd* [2006] BLR 187; [2005] EWCA Civ 1585.

Site instructions Directions given on site by the Architect/CA to contractor's foreman, often orally: good practice requires site instructions to be confirmed in writing to contractor's office as soon as practicable.

Site investigations Investigation by engineers with specialist experience of ground conditions including geology and soil mechanics: findings recorded in written report describing ground conditions, any problems they pose (eg contaminated materials) and usually making recommendations as to foundation design. A site investigation is often commissioned by the owner before works are designed and put out to tender and the report often forms part of the tender documents.

Site manager On larger projects, a person employed by the contractor to be present on site and to be responsible for all activities taking place there. The employer may also appoint a (semi) permanent site representative on a large site.

Site overheads See **Preliminaries**.

Site plan A drawing used to locate the site of the project and other site information, such as the location of any buildings, roads, footpaths, boundaries and trees. Site levels are generally shown and dimensions setting out any structures or objects on the site are normally given.

Skeleton argument A written summary of a party's submissions prepared before a hearing which gives notice of the authorities and legal arguments relied on. The skeleton argument is provided to the Judge and other party in advance and is intended to prevent unexpected issues being raised in court, thus making the whole process more open and time efficient. ■ See also **Opening note and speech**.

Skill and care See **Quality of workmanship** and **Reasonable skill and care**.

Skim coat A thin layer of plaster compound applied as a top coat in order to achieve a smooth finish to a plaster wall or ceiling: commonly the first coat is rubbed down and a second coat applied.

Skirt A robust flexible material placed around equipment or machinery to protect operatives: for example, around chute into skip or machine spraying tarmac.

Skirting A board fixed to the bottom of an internal wall to protect the base of the plasterboard from damage. Skirtings are typically 75–100 mm high and can be made of various materials including wood, vinyl and ceramic tiles. A coved skirting is often used with vinyl flooring to minimise water penetration to the flooring substrate: the vinyl flooring is in essence "wrapped" up the wall (to a height of 100-150mm) and supported by a cove former. ➤**Figure A5**

Slab A reinforced concrete base resting on the sub-base to create a foundation or a suspended floor carried by the structural walls of the building, which may be precast or poured in situ into formwork.

Slack See **Total float**.

Slag The waste product from iron and steel production. Sometimes used as a concrete additive or as foundation fill, but if untreated it is liable to expand and should be used with caution.

Sleeper A wooden or concrete beam resting on ground and used as base and support for metal track particularly of railways.

Sleeper wall A low brick wall built off the ground in a sub-floor space in order to support the floor joists.

Slip form A method of construction of large projects in concrete (particularly tower and road construction) where the formwork into which concrete is poured is moved as the previous section hardens, thus saving time which would otherwise be taken in erecting and dismantling formwork.

Slip joint A joint between two building components which allows them to move relative to each other, for example, to allow for thermal expansion. ■ See **Movement joints**.

Slip rule Any provision which allows a tribunal to correct a clerical mistake or error in a direction, order, judgment, award or decision. ■ See ***Bloor Construction (UK) Ltd v Bowmer & Kirkland (London) Ltd*** **[2000] BLR 314** and **Clerical error or mistake**. Section 140 of the LDEDC Act 2009 introduced section 108(3A) of the Construction Act 1996 (as amended). This requires the parties to a construction contract in England, Wales and Scotland to provide in their contract that the adjudicator has the power to correct a clerical or typographical error in his decision arising by accident or omission.

Slump test A site test to establish the workability of concrete by measuring the distance that a standard cone of concrete collapses when the support is removed. It is used for checking the consistency of the mix.

Small and medium sized enterprise (SME) Defined by Recommendation 2003/361/EC as being firms that employ less than 250 people and have a turnover of less than €50m.

Small claims track The CPR track appropriate for claims of small monetary value (generally up to £5,000). There is a fixed limit on the costs which a successful party can recover.

Small works agreement The JCT 2011 Minor Works Building contract.

SME See **Small and medium size enterprise**.

Smith v South Wales Switchgear [1978] 1 All ER 18: a reference in a contractual document to a contract, being subject to conditions "available on request" and brought to the notice of the other party is sufficient to incorporate the current edition of those conditions.

SMM, SMM7 Standard Method of Measurement

Snagging The term snagging has no universally accepted meaning. The process usually describes the process of inspecting construction works to identify any incomplete items or areas or defects in such purportedly complete works. Although snagging is a well-established and recognised procedure in the building industry, it is hardly ever the subject of express contractual provision, leading to confusion during the correction (defects liability/rectification) period.

Snagging list – A snagging list (also known as a **punch list**) is meant to be a schedule of *de minimis* (very minor) items of work (or snags) that are left over at practical completion, although sometimes the length and nature of these lists can vary. The existence of snags is not a bar to the issuing of **practical completion** (see *HW Neville (Sunblest) Ltd v William Press and Son Ltd (1981) 20 BLR 78*). Sub-clause 10.1 of the **FIDIC Red Book** which states that an engineer can issue a taking-over certificate "*stating the date on which the Works or Section were completed in accordance with the Contract, except for any minor outstanding work and defects which will not substantially affect the use of the Works...*" Those outstanding works would be listed on a snagging list.

Soffit The underside of an element of construction, such as a beam or arch: in particular the underside of a floor or ceiling and the horizontal closure of the eaves.

Soft landscaping Planting of trees shrubs and plants in the grounds of a development: compare with **hard landscaping**.

Softwood Wood obtained from pine trees and other conifers. The most common timber used in construction, it is generally easy to work although not necessarily soft: compare with **hardwood**.

Soil pipe A vertical pipe connecting toilets, hand basins, showers, kitchen sinks, washing machines and other appliances producing waste water into the main drain: sometimes known as a soil stack.

Soil stack See **Soil pipe**.

Soil vent The opening at the top of a soil pipe which permits the entry of air into the drainage system and equalises the pressure to prevent siphonage.

Solar-control glazing Glass which is tinted or coated in order to reduce ultra violet light and solar glare in high rise buildings and glass roofs, such as conservatories.

Soldier course Brickwork laid vertically with the short side at the top, often as a feature at the top of a wall, also any pattern of single bricks laid side by side.

Sole plate The beam which forms the bottom of a timber frame, resting on the ground, and which acts as a foundation for the upright timbers resting upon it.

Sole risk clause A contractual clause which expressly places materials or plant at the sole risk of one of the parties. The construction of such clauses where there are stated exceptions can give rise to anomalous results: *Callaghan & Welton v Hewgate Construction Ltd* (1996) 75 BLR 11 (CA).

Solid masonry unit Unit with no unfilled space between the faces of the construction, such as a gate support.

Sound insulation Material incorporated into buildings (often surface mounted on walls) to attenuate or reduce the volume of the noise made by users of the building.

Spacer See **Reinforcement spacer**.

Spalling The flaking of the surface of a building material, such as stonework or brickwork, often caused by damp penetration or a chemical reaction.

Spandrel panel A panel between a window sill and the window head below in a multi-storey building.

Sparks or sparky A slang term for an electrician.

Spars Part of the roof construction used to support a pitched roof covering.

Spearin doctrine A legal principle (propounded in *USA, United States v Spearin*, 248 U.S. 132 (1918)) that holds that when a contractor follows the plans and specifications furnished by the owner, and those plans and specifications turn out to be defective or insufficient, the contractor is not liable to the owner for any loss or damage resulting from the defective plans and specifications.

Special A brick which is not a standard oblong shape: often made for decorative purposes and may be specially made for particular project.

Special case A former procedure, now abolished, whereby an arbitrator made an award on a point of law.

Special condition(s) A term or terms of a contract which have been added to a printed standard form by agreement between the parties. The court will attach greater weight to the special conditions: *Homburg Houtimport BV v Agrosin Private Ltd* [2003] 1 Lloyd's Rep. 571; [2004] 1 AC 715 (HL).

Special damages Damages for losses which must be pleaded and proved in money terms, as opposed to **general damages**, which must also be pleaded or proved but are quantified in money terms by the court. To take a simple example, damages for the loss of a limb are an instance of general damages; damages for the cost of medical treatment are special damages: *Sempra Metals Ltd v IRC* [2007] UKHL 34; [2008] 1 AC 561; [2007] 3 WLR 354; [2007] 4 All ER 657 (HL).

Special Purpose Vehicle (SPV) A limited company, partnership or trust formed in order to carry out a particular development or activity and often dissolved when this has been achieved. SPVs are used where a number of participants are involved in a development and in particular to limit financial risk to the parent companies and to limit tax liability. They are also often used in PPPs and to transfer title to property when a project has been completed.

Specialist contractor A contractor experienced and working in a specific trade: many specialists confine their business to their specialisation and generally work as subcontractors, often using specialist equipment: examples include piling, underpinning, timber treatment, diamond drilling and shopfitting. There is a National Specialist Contractors' Council (**NSCC**).

Specialty A document made under seal.

Specific disclosure An order by a court or arbitrator that a party discloses a particular document or class of documents identified in the order and shown by the applicant to be relevant to an issue in the dispute.

Specific performance An equitable remedy in the form of a court order requiring a defendant to carry out a prescribed action, normally to comply with a contractual obligation, for example, to transfer property. It provides a remedy for breach of contract where damages would not be an adequate remedy, particularly in relation to the sale of land.

Specification A written document which describes the materials to be supplied, the quality of finishes and the standard of workmanship required on a particular project. It provides further information than drawings are able to convey. A specification is typically one of several contract documents and must be read in conjunction with the bills of quantities (if any) and the contract drawings. It is normally written by an architect, engineer or quantity surveyor. Depending on the procurement route and contract choice, specifications may either prescribe the exact work to be carried out, or alternatively describe the performance of the particular building component required to be achieved ■ See also **NBS, Performance specification** and **Prescriptive specification**.

Specified peril Under the JCT standard forms, any event insurance cover for which the employer is obliged to take out in respect of existing structures and contents and loss and damage occasioned by which is a **relevant event** entitling the contractor to an extension of time. The Specified Perils are: fire, lightning, explosion, storm, flood, escape of water from any water tank, apparatus or pipes, earthquake, aircraft and other aerial devices or articles dropped therefrom, riot and civil commotion, but excluding **excepted risks**.

Split brick A brick cut either lengthways or across its width.

Split-face block A concrete block with a decorative surface.

Spon's Price Books A series of commercial guides which provide detailed information on the price of building works broken down into constituent elements, such as the cost of materials and labour. The rates and prices given are derived from recent contracts and suppliers' price lists and are used by quantity surveyors to price tenders or estimates and to value variations. The series includes price books for Architects and Builders, Civil Engineering and Highway Works, External Works and Landscape, and Mechanical and Electrical Services. ■ See also **Laxton's Building Price Book**.

Springer The lowest **voussoir** on each side of an arch, where the vertical support for the arch terminates and the curve of the arch begins.

SPV See **Special Purpose Vehicle**.

SSL See **Structural slab level**.

SSSI Site of Special Scientific Interest under the Wildlife and Countryside Act 1981 as amended by the Countryside and Rights of Way (CROW) Act 2000 and the Natural Environment and RuralCommunities (NERC) Act 2006. The purpose of designating a site to be of special scientific interest is protect that site fromdevelopment, from other damage, and neglect.

Stability Absence of movement: all built structures are required to be stable, though allowance must be made for thermal expansion and contraction and in tall structures for wind pressure. Special precautions are taken in zones susceptible to earthquakes.

Stack bonding A pattern of bricklaying in which all the vertical joints are aligned to give a uniform appearance. Brickwork laid in this way is susceptible to movement and may need to be tied into structure behind.

Stack effect The upward movement of a column of air within a building that results from warm air rising, creating a positive pressure area at the top of a building and a negative pressure area at the bottom of a building and therefore pressure between the inside and outside. The air current is accentuated by vertical elements, such as chimney stacks and staircases.

Stack pipe Vertical pipe usually fixed externally on houses into which waste water pipes connect which drops into sewer below ground level. The pipe rises to eaves height and is open to allow the system to vent.

Stack vent The open end of a stack pipe or other plumbing installation, externally at eaves height. Its main purpose is to maintain equal air pressure through the drainage system to prevent siphonage but it also removes odours.

Staffordshire blue brick/engineering brick A brick made of Etruria Marl clay with a high iron content which gives a blue colour when fired. The engineering bricks are hard and resist frost and water damage: suitable for groundworks, sewer works and retaining walls.

Stage payment A payment made by the employer to the contractor during the course of the works when a specified stage of work has been achieved. ■ See **Interim payment** and **Work stages**.

Stainless steel A steel alloy which does not stain, corrode, or rust as easily as ordinary steel, but it is not stain-proof. Different grades are made to meet the requirements of specific locations, such as swimming pools.

Stakeholder An individual or organisation that has an interest or share in a commercial undertaking or other issue.

Stall riser The fascia at the front of shop premises between the pavement and the windowsill. In the nineteenth century shops sometimes had a hinged stallboard which could be lowered and used for the display of goods.

Stallboard See **Stall riser**.

Stanchion A sturdy upright post usually in metal, used to protect the corner of a building against damage. Also, the main support of an iron street light and other robust columns and pillars.

Standard basis A basis of assessment of legal costs recoverable by a successful party in litigation. The beneficiary of an order for costs to be paid on the standard basis is subject to a requirement of proportionality and it is for him to show that the costs were incurred reasonably. This is to be contracted with the indemnity basis, where there is no requirement of proportionality and in cases of doubt it is for the payer to show that costs were not incurred reasonably: see *Lownds v Home Office* [2002] EWCA Civ 365; [2002] CP Rep 43; [2002] 1 WLR 2450; [2002] 4 All ER 775; *Sinclair Roche and Temperley v Somatra* [2003] EWCA Civ 1474; [2003] 2 Lloyd's Rep 855. ■ See **Indemnity basis**.

Standard Building Contract (SBC) The suite of contracts first published by the JCT in 2005 (now superceded by the 2011 editions) comprising SBC with quantities, with approximate quantities and without quantities. These are intended to supersede the former Standard Forms of Building Contract published in 1998 (and earlier). There is also a Standard Building Sub-contract Agreement.

Standard Commercial Property Conditions of Sale (2nd edn) Terms providing standard clauses for transactions in respect of commercial property: adapted from the Standard Conditions of Sale (4th edn) which is used for residential properties. Conveyancers usually incorporate the appropriate Standard Conditions in their contract with any necessary amendments.

Standard form A printed form of contract in common use, such as the JCT Standard Forms of Building Contract, the ICE Conditions, the FIDIC Form and the New Engineering Contract. Increasingly the publishers produce versions adapted for specific uses and often amend and revise the text, though the changes are not usually substantial. Contracting parties are free to amend and supplement the terms of a standard contract to meet their particular requirements but this exercise must be done with care to avoid inconsistencies, as the standard terms are detailed and interdependent in their clauses. Their clauses have often been the subject of judicial consideration and are largely certain in their legal effect. The court will be very reluctant to disturb an established construction of such forms: *Federal Commerce & Navigation Co Ltd v Tradax Export SA* [1978] AC 1 (HL). ■ See **FIDIC, ICE Conditions, JCT Standard Forms and New Engineering Contract**.

Standard method claim A claim arising from contractual provisions, such as those contained in the JCT and ICE standard forms, stating that bills of quantities have been prepared on the basis of the **Standard Method of Measurement**. Unstated departures from the Standard Method may be the subject of correction, alteration or modification by instruction and treated as variations. There is a long history of ingenious claims by contractors on the basis that a particular item has been omitted from the description in the bills, thus entitling the contractor to further payment.

Standard method of measurement (SMM, SMM7) A publication by the RICS providing standard rules for the measuring of buildings, building works and the preparation of bills of quantities. It embodies good practice and provides standardisation when bills are prepared in accordance with its provisions. If an item of work has not been measured in accordance with the rules of SMM7, this must be expressly stated in the bills. The last edition is SMM7. ■ See **Bill of quantities**. In April 2012, the RICS introduced the *New Rules of Measurement (NRM): Order of cost estimating and elemental cost planning*. The NRM suite is said to provide a common measurement standard for cost comparison through the life cycle of cost management. The suite has been developed as a result of industry collaboration to ensure that at any point in a buildings life there will be a set of consistent rules for measuring and capturing cost data, thereby completing the cost management life cycle and supporting the procurement of construction projects from cradle to grave. At the time of press, the 2011 editions of the JCT Standard Building Contract (all three versions) and the JCT Intermediate Building Contract (with and without design) refer to SMM7 in their definitions of "Standard Method of Measurement". Depending on advice from the project quantity surveyor (PQS), the parties may now elect to update this.

Standard of care The standard against which an allegation of negligence is to be measured. ■ See **Reasonable skill and care**.

Standard of proof The level of proof which must be achieved in order to make good a claim. In civil disputes, the standard is that of establishing the fact or facts in question on a balance of probabilities, so that the tribunal concludes that facts in question are more likely to have happened than not. Not to be confused with the criminal standard (traditionally "beyond reasonable doubt") or the **burden of proof**, which is the obligation on a party to prove his claim.

Standard special Any brick that is not a rectangle. As if to confuse non-bricklayers, there are "standard specials", such as bullnoses, cants and radials, and "special specials" such as cills and quoins. Otherwise a piece ordered to standard dimensions but not supplied unless specifically ordered, used for decoration and finishes.

Standby letter of credit A guarantee issued by a bank that their customer will perform his obligations under a contract (often for purchase of goods overseas) with the beneficiary. In the event that the customer fails to comply the bank will pay the beneficiary, provided the conditions of the guarantee are fulfilled, within a limited time. Synonym used in some Commonwealth jurisdictions to describe an "on demand" performance bond.

Standing offer An offer to supply goods and services as and when called for. The nature of the relationship arising from such an arrangement depends on the wording used, but it usually does not oblige the other party to order any particular quantity. ■ See **Term contract**.

Standing seam Metal profile sheets (steel, aluminium, copper, zinc) for roofs and wall cladding where sheets interlock and seal along their length at the edge to create a waterproof joint.

Standpipe A detachable vertical pipe connected to a street hydrant to provide water when the domestic supply is cut: also a pipe used for dewatering ground: a vertical water pipe in a building for occasional use, for example, as a connection for fire hoses.

Standstill agreement An agreement between parties to a dispute whereby the limitation period is not to run during a specified period, usually to allow the parties to negotiate. Also known as a **tolling agreement**.

Standstill period Also known as the **Alcatel** period. The period proscribed by the **Procurement Regulations** (of at least 10 days) between the notification of a contract award and the conclusion of that agreement.

Star rate A rate (a sum of money per measurement unit) inserted against a new item in a valuation or final account because that item was not included in the priced bill of quantities or schedule of rates. The rate is traditionally identified by applying an asterisk so that the other party's QS can easily identify the rate and agree it, or negotiate an acceptable rate.

Stare decisis Latin: "to stand by decisions", the principle of judicial precedent by which inferior and equal courts are bound to follow earlier court decisions on issues of law. ■ See **Precedent**.

Start-to-finish relationship See **Relationship**.

Start-to-start relationship See **Relationship**.

Starter bar Lengths of metal reinforcement partly embedded in foundation concrete at the base of a wall or other structure: higher reinforcement is fixed to the top part of the starter bar before further concrete is poured to form the wall or vertical section.

State of the art Is taken to mean the normative or usual professional practice on a particular point and a set point in time against which an allegation of negligence is based. The 'State of the Art' defence can form a limitation on a designer's liability. This means that a designer is only expected to design in conformity with the accepted standards of the time. These standards will generally consist of Codes of Practice, National Standards and any authoritative published information.

It is now well established that the designer has a duty to amend his design if it appears to be defective during construction: ***London Borough of Merton v Lowe* (1981)**, but, following the Abbeystead case (***Eckersley & Others v Binnie & Partners, Edmund Nuttall Ltd. & North West Water Authority*** [1990] 18 ConLR 1, it seems that the designer has no duty of care to continue to warn of potential dangers once his initial involvement has ended except in carefully defined life and limb cases. If a designer uses untried materials or methods of construction, he will be just as liable for design failure as if he makes a mistake in using traditional techniques. In ***Victoria University of Manchester -v- Hugh Wilson & Lewis Womersley and Pochin (Contractors) Ltd* (1984),** the late Judge John Newey QC held that it is not itself wrong for designers to use untried or relatively untried materials or techniques, but that it would be wise to warn their clients specifically and get their express approval.

Statement of affairs A statement containing a summary of assets and liabilities, which shows the estimated financial position of a debtor or a company that may be unable to meet its debts.

Statement of case The term adopted in the CPR to replace the term *pleadings* and to describe the following documents: Particulars of claim, defence and counterclaim, reply, Part 20 claim (request for) further information. It is also used in arbitration and adjudication to describe similar documents presenting each party's claim.

Statement of claim The previous name for **Particulars of Claim**.

Status quo Latin: "the state at which", the existing situation.

Statute See **Act of Parliament**.

Statute barred The prevention of the pursuit of claims by operation of the Limitation Act 1980, which specifies the time limits within which actions must be brought. The court will not raise the statute of its own motion: limitation is a defence which should be raised by the defendant at the earliest point of pleading. If the time limit has expired the claim (although not the underlying cause of action) is statute barred and cannot succeed. However, there may be circumstances (such as concealment of the cause of action or where the claimant is under a disability) in which the time period may be extended by the court. ■ See **Limitation Act**.

Statute of Frauds 1677 Long-standing legislation, s4 of which, requires that an agreement for a guarantee is in writing and signed by the guarantor. Notwithstanding the date of the statute, a valid guarantee can be created by a chain of emails (*Mehta v J Pereira Fernandes SA* [2006]

EWHC 813 (Ch); [2006] 1 WLR 1543) and an electronic signature is a valid signature (*Golden Ocean Group Ltd v Salgaocar Mining Industries PVT Ltd* [2011] EWHC 56 (Comm); [2011] 2 All ER (Comm) 95).

Statutory demand A written demand for payment made by a creditor to a debtor company or individual in accordance with the Insolvency Act and the Insolvency Rules 1986. If the debt exceeds £750.00 and is not paid or disputed within 21 days the creditor can use that as proof of the debtor's insolvency. If liability is disputed the court will have to consider whether the sum demanded is due. Although sometimes used as a form of debt collection it can lead to costly satellite litigation. ■ See **Bankruptcy** and **Insolvency**

Statutory duty A duty imposed by an Act of Parliament which if breached may give rise to an action in tort for damages or to criminal liability. Examples include the duties under the Defective Premises Act 1972 and the Health and Safety at Work Act 1976.

Statutory instruments Delegated legislation often in the form of regulations which supplement statutes.

Statutory scheme See **Scheme for Construction Contracts**.

Statutory undertaker A local authority or other body invested with powers by legislation to carry out works, particularly those that might affect construction works. Most construction contracts provide for the granting of an extension of time for completion where the progress of the works is affected by statutory undertakers' work. There have been a number of statutory definitions of statutory undertakers, such as that in the Housing Act 1985, s611(6)(a). The 2011 JCT form's definition is that of "any local authority or statutory undertaker where executing work solely in pursuance of its statutory obligations, including any persons employed, engaged or authorised by it upon or in connection with that work". However, see also the suggestion by Mr Justice Coulson in *Fenice Investments Inc v Jerram Falkus Construction Ltd* [2011] EWHC 1935 (TCC) that the traiditonal test may need to be revisited following the extensive privatisation of the utility industries which has occurred since 1980.

Stay of execution Where a judgment is given or an order made for the payment by any person of money and the court is satisfied on an application made at the time of the judgment, or order, or at any time thereafter by the judgment debtor or other party liable to execution that there are special circumstances which render it inexpedient to enforce the judgment or order, the court may by order stay the execution of the judgment or order either absolutely or for such period and subject to such conditions as the court thinks fit: RSC Order 47, which remains part of the CPR by operation of Part 50. The probable inability of the claimant to repay the judgment sum (awarded by the adjudicator and enforced by way of summary judgment) at the end of the substantive trial, or arbitration hearing, may constitute special circumstances within the meaning of Order 47 r1(1)(a) rendering it appropriate to grant a stay in enforcement proceedings. If the evidence of the claimant's present financial position suggested that it is probable that it would be unable to repay the judgment sum when it fell due, that would not usually justify the grant of a stay if: (1) the claimant's financial position is the same or similar to its financial position at the time that the relevant contract was made; or (2) The claimant's financial position is due, either wholly, or in significant part, to the defendant's failure to pay those sums which were awarded by the adjudicator. See *Wimbledon Construction Co 2000 Ltd v Vago* [2005] EWHC 1086 (TCC); [2005] BLR 374; 101 ConLR 99 as qualified in *Mead General Building Ltd v Dartmoor Properties Ltd* [2009] EWHC 200 (TCC); [2009] BLR 225; [2009] BPIR 516. ■ See **Adjudicator**, **Enforcement** and **Referring Party**.

Stay of proceedings The suspension of the litigation process or timetable for directions. This may be requested by the parties or ordered by the court to provide an opportunity for settlement discussions, or because some other case which may set a precedent or resolve relevant issues needs to be decided first. The court may also stay proceedings until security for costs has been given if ordered or if there has been some default by the claimant which requires correction such as failure to disclose documents. A defendant will be entitled under the Arbitration Act 1996, s9 to a stay of court proceedings brought in breach of an agreement to arbitrate disputes.

Steel Metal formed from refining of iron with additives dependent on character of product required.

Steel-fibre-reinforced concrete Concrete reinforced with fibres of steel rather than traditional steel bars.

Steel sections A term used in **CAD** to describe the set of commonly used steel sections including angles, channels and box sections.

Step-in rights An entitlement conferred on the funder in a funding agreement allowing him to complete the development in the event of default by the developer.

Stepped footing A brick foundation where the width of the base increases with depth below the ground to give greater stability.

Stick system A form of external cladding in which the pre-engineered projecting framework is visible and the panels are fixed within it.

Sto render A proprietary name. ■ See **Render**.

Stock brick A standard clay brick: in London they were yellow in colour from the clay in Kent from which they were made.

Stockpile A collection on site of building materials such as bricks which may be purchased in bulk and then used as required.

Stop bead Plastic or metal strip fixed as edging piece for plaster or render to protect edge and give clean line, or to divide area to be plastered or rendered into sections.

Stop notice Issued to prevent the carrying out of an activity on land to which an **enforcement notice** relates, when a council considers that an activity should cease before the expiry of the period for compliance with that enforcement notice.

Stopcock Valve or tap on pipe carrying liquid which when turned blocks flow: in particular on rising water main serving property, cutting off water when leaking occurs or repairs are carried out.

Strain The distortion, usually an increase in length, of a material by a force acting on it, expressed as a percentage.

S-trap Section of waste water pipework curved in an S shape on outflow of toilets or washbasins. The depth of the curve retains water and avoids sewer smells rising up the pipe. Now generally replaced by U or P bend.

Stress The force per unit area acting on a material, usually expressed in Newton's per square millimetre, N/mm^2. ➤**Figure C2**.

Stretcher course or bond Brickwork laid horizontally with long side of brick (stretcher) exposed and joined end to end: in the course below and above the vertical joints are staggered. This is a conventional but not especially attractive pattern of brickwork. ➤**Figures B3 & H1**.

Strict construction A more intense interpretation of a written instrument whereby the court must be satisfied that the intention of the author(s) is clear, unambiguous and incapable of misleading: *Mannai Investment Co Ltd v Eagle Star Life Assurance Co Ltd* [1997] AC 749; [1997] 2 WLR 945; [1997] 3 All ER 352. The technique is used where the court is unwilling to construe a document to mean something that would have an unfair effect, as in the case of an exclusion clause.

Strict liability Liability in civil or criminal law for a wrongful act or breach of duty which is imposed without having to prove that the defendant was at fault. It is no defence to a strict liability offence that the defendant took all reasonable care or was acting on the advice of others. Many offences under the Health and Safety Act 1976 and other regulatory codes are matters of strict liability. In civil law torts such as trespass causing damage do not require a clamant to prove that the defendant was aware that his action was unlawful, and damage arising from the defendant keeping dangerous substances on his land (Rylands v Fletcher cases) is a matter of strict liability.

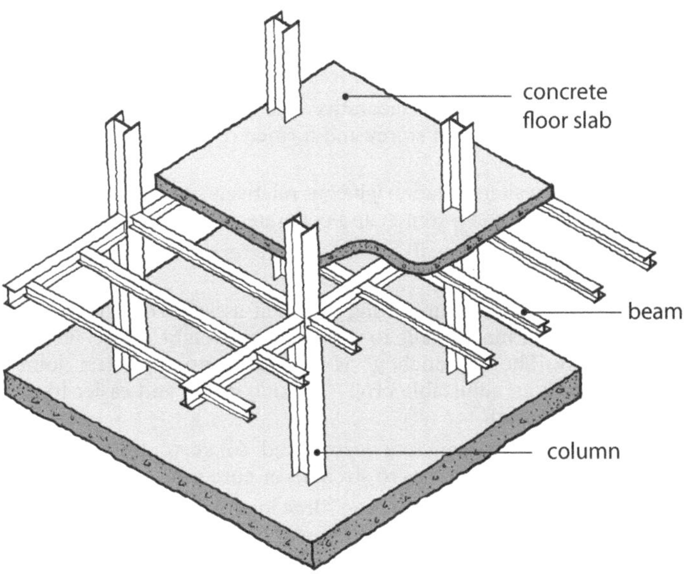

➤ **Figure S2.** Structure

Strike A concerted stoppage of work by men done with a view to improving their wages or conditions, or giving vent to a grievance, or making a protest about something or other, or supporting or sympathising with other workmen in such endeavour: *Tramp Shipping Corp v Greenwich Marine Inc* [1975] 2 All ER 988. Most construction contracts provide for the granting of an extension of time for completion in the event of a strike. Under the 2011 JCT forms the Relevant Event is: "strike, lock-out or local combination of workmen affecting any of the trades employed upon the Works or any of the trades engaged in the preparation, manufacture or transportation of any of the goods or materials required for the Works or any persons engaged in the preparation of the design for the contractor's Designed Portion".

Striking The removal of scaffolding. Also, the act of removing formwork from a concrete construction when it has cured. It may be necessary to strike the formwork sharply to secure its release.

Striking off The removal of a solicitor's name from the roll of solicitors of the Supreme Court, usually due to a serious level of professional misconduct. Other professional regulatory bodies can exercise a similar sanction in respect of their members.

Striking out The deletion by court order of part or all of a statement of case pursuant to CPR Part 3. This is done most commonly where there has been repeated failure by a party to comply with court orders: so a claim or defence may be struck out and thereby determine the case. Claims may be struck out where they disclose no cause of action or defence, or where some material is scurrilous or prolix. In cases where the striking out relates to substantive issues the court will normally give a party an opportunity to amend. ■ See **Application** and **Statement of case**.

Striking time The length of time required for concrete to cure before the formwork can be safely struck.

String A board at either side of the treads and risers of a stair.

String, stringer course A decorative line on the façade of a building usually at the level of each storey and formed of projecting brick or stone work.

Strip footing A wall foundation which is relatively narrow and constructed by placing hardcore in a trench and concrete over it. ➤**Figure E3**.

Stripping out The removal of internal fixtures and fittings prior to redevelopment.

Strongboy A structural supporting tool that assists when fitting a lintel, RSJ or beam within a wall, to support the weight above while work is performed. The "Strongboy" is knocked into a mortar joint and supported with an adjustable prop – making it safe and easier to remove the masonry beneath.

Structural concrete Concrete formulated so as to be suitable for a specific structural purpose as to strength or cure time.

Structural drawings Construction drawings (sometimes prepared by the Engineer) which provide the design and information for building the main structure of a building.

Structural engineer A person who is qualified in structural engineering. The UK's professional body is the Institution of Structural Engineers which has a world-wide membership. Fellows and members are entitled to the designation *chartered engineer.* ■ See **Institution of Structural Engineers**.

Structural glazing Glazing with glass, composite or metal sheets bonded to supporting metal framework to create a smooth façade without visible frames: the glazing and framing carries only its own weight. Produces contemporary look, easier to clean and reduces thermal bridging and air and water penetration.

Structural polychromic Colour coming from the structural component.

Structural slab level (SSL) The top level of the concrete slab from which the vertical levels of the building are typically dimensioned and set out. Any screed, raised floor or floor finishes are above this level. ■ See also **Finished floor level** and **Figure E3**.

Structural steelwork Steel beams which form the load bearing structure of a building: this may comprise a complete framework (as in many industrial buildings) or beams and other steel components which carry a load such as lintels over openings in walls.

Structure The load-bearing part of a building or engineering construction, made from materials such as reinforced concrete, steelwork, timber and blockwork. Internal or finishing elements which are not load bearing such as cladding, decorative finishes and joinery are usually not considered to be a part of the structure. ■ See **Substructure** and **Superstructure**. ➤**Figure S2**.

Strut A length of timber or metal usually fixed diagonally to a framework or adjacent members in order to brace and strengthen them and prevent movement. ➤**Figure T4**.

Stud A vertical length of timber used as a post or in series for wall construction.

Stud partition Describes a partition or non load-bearing wall dividing a space using timber or steel framing. It is used in residential applications, both in new housing and refurbishment, and in commercial and off-site applications. These are also called stud walls. Timber framing is fixed to the perimeter, abutments, and to frame any openings, using suitable fixings. Timber studs are fixed at specified centres. Services are normally installed after one side is boarded. Timber noggings (timber blocking pieces) are fixed horizontally to support recessed switch boxes/socket outlets.

Sub-base The lowest level of construction material on site, usually hardcore, crushed concrete or aggregate such as crusher run. It may also include lean mix concrete or bitumen in order to bind the material. It rests on the sub-grade and is consolidated by being rammed or rolled. Its purpose is to support and spread the load of the construction above. The Department of Transport Type 1 granular sub-base is often specified.

Subbie A colloquial name for a subcontractor.

Subcontract A contract between the main contractor and another contractor to carry out all or more commonly part of the works which the main contractor is obliged to complete under its contract with the employer. The main contractor generally remains liable to the employer for the quality of the work carried out and there is no contractual relationship between the employer and the subcontractor. ■ See, however, **Nomination** and **Named contractors**.

Subcontractor A contractor employed by the main contractor to carry out part of the contract work on behalf of the main contractor. Many subcontractors perform specialist trades and are employed for this reason and it is increasingly common for them to undertake some element of design responsibility. Many contracts require prior written consent from the employer before work can be subcontracted. Subcontractors may be domestic (chosen by the contractor) or named (formerly nominated) by the employer.

Sub-floor The void space beneath a suspended floor which may be used to run services if accessible through access points: needs to be ventilated to avoid dampness.

Sub-frame A frame to carry cladding or a door or window, attached to the main building frame.

Sub-grade The natural underlying ground material at a construction site once the topsoil has been stripped. The sub-grade may be excavated to construct basements or foundations or slabs and stabilised or consolidated if necessary by a capping layer. Its capacity to bear weight is determined according to its CBR. The excavated depth is the formation level, onto which sub-base material such as hardcore will be placed. The excavated sub-grade material may also be used for site infill or the construction of embankments. ■ See **California bearing ratio**.

Subjective intentions See **Parole evidence rule**.

Subject to contract Neither party will be bound unless the terms of a formal contract are agreed and executed. In contracts for the sale of land a formal written agreement is almost invariably made but in construction the execution of a standard form contract is by no means necessary to constitute an enforceable agreement. Standard forms, however, do frequently make such provision in the designated form of tender to be submitted, such as in the ICE Conditions. Even where such a term has been used, the parties can agree to be bound by agreed terms without the necessity of a formal written contract or, put another way, agree to waive that requirement: *RTS Flexible Systems Ltd v Molkerei Alois Muller Gmbh* [2010] UKSC 14; [2010] BLR 337 (SC); [2010] 1 WLR 753; [2010] 3 All ER 1.

Sub judice Latin: "under the judge", and therefore under trial or before the court.

Sublet The further letting of works by a main contractor to another contractor to carry out (part of) the work for which the main contractor is responsible. Many contracts contain restrictions on the subletting of work without prior written approval from the employer or his agent. ■ See **Subcontract**.

Sub-level The area beneath an identified level, often as stated on a drawing.

Sub-network A group of activities or durations in a contract programme which are linked.

Subpoena An abbreviation of subpoena ad testificandum or subpoena duces tecum, Latin for "to testify under penalty" and "bring with you under penalty" respectively, the writs whereby formerly a person could be summoned to give evidence in or bring documents to court, now replaced by a **Witness summons** and the revised rules for **Disclosure**.

Subrogation A transfer of rights from one person to another, without **Assignment** or assent of the person from whom the rights are transferred and which takes place by operation of law in a whole variety of widely different circumstances: *Orakpo v Manson Investments Ltd* [1978] AC 95; [1977] 3 WLR 229; [1977] 3 All ER 1 (HL). The most common examples are those of an insurer or a surety who has made payment for the benefit of their insured or principal and will be entitled to exercise a right of subrogation and bring a claim against a third party in the name of their insured in order to recover their payment.

Subsidence Sinking, downward movement in a vertical direction. Strictly speaking, "settlement" means movement in a lateral direction, but an insurance policy which identifies the perils insured against as "subsidence and/or collapse" will cover both subsidence and settlement defined in those terms: *David Allen & Sons Billposting Ltd v Drysdale* [1939] 4 All ER 113.

Subsidised housing scheme works contracts Contracts for subsidised housing schemes which are subject to the Public Contract Regulations 2006, SI 2006/5. There is no statutory definition, but the term must refer to public sector or social housing.

Substantial completion The stage where contract work has been completed in all significant respects so that the development is ready for use. This term is commonly used in engineering contracts: compare with **Practical Completion** under standard building contracts.

Substantial performance A doctrine developed by the courts to mitigate the rule that a party was not entitled to recover payment under an **Entire contract** until the completion of his performance. Under the doctrine, a contractor is entitled to recover the price if he has supplied all that he agreed to supply but what he supplies is subject to defects of so minor a character that he can be said to have substantially performed his promise: *Hoenig v Isaacs* [1952] 2 All ER 176.

Substantial remedy If a contract does not include a "substantial remedy" for late payment of money that may be due under that contract then the statutory rate of interest, currently set at eight per cent above base rate, will be substituted into the contract by virtue of the Late Payment of Commercial Debts (Interest) Act 1998. ■ See ***Yuanda v WW Gear Construction Ltd***.

Substation Electrical power unit to reduce (or occasionally increase) the voltage of the supply of mains electricity by means of transformers before it is connected to consumers. A large development may require its own substation to be installed by the electricity supplier. A substation may contain other equipment such as switchgear and circuit breakers.

Substituted contractor A new contractor who takes the place of the original contractor after a termination or repudiation. The liability of the new contractor will obviously depend on the terms upon which he agrees to complete the works, but it is possible for him to be liable for delay by the original contractor: *Re Yeadon Waterworks Co v Wright* [1895] 72 LT 832 (CA).

Substructure That part of the structure of a building which is located below ground (ie foundations) and supports the superstructure. ■ See **Superstructure**.

SUDS Sustainable Urban Drainage Systems made up of one or more structures built to manage surface water runoff, used in conjunction with good management of the site to prevent overwhelming of public sewage and storm water systems. The increase in pavement/hard standings in towns and cities has resulted in conventional drainage being overburdened in heavy rainfall. SUDS commonly comprise attenuation cells, (also known as Storm Cells, Soakaway Modules, and Storm Crates). They are the modern equivalent of a soakaway. They allow surface water to be contained in one location and gradually released back to the ground, over time, at a pace the ground can accommodate, rather than in one abrupt deluge, as occurs during a storm. In effect, the transfer of water from the surface to the ground is attenuated, i.e. slowed down and stretched out over a longer period.

Sui generis Latin: "of its own kind", peculiar to itself.

Suitability See **Fitness for purpose**.

Sulphate attack It is responsible for the deterioration of concrete, for example, heave and cracking, in a wide variety of structures. Occurs when sulphate solutions (which can be internal, i.e. derived from a constituent in the concrete such as **aggregate** or external, i.e. water) penetrate and react with the calcium aluminate hydrates present in the hardened cement.

Summary assessment The **Assessment of costs** on a summary basis by the court, usually after the hearing of a short matter, such as a procedural application.

Summary judgment A court procedure under CPR 24 to decide a case without a full hearing where it appears that there is no real prospect of a successful defence (or conversely no real prospect that the claim will succeed). Normally decided on witness statements and documents only without oral evidence: the court can give judgment for the claimant (or for the defendant on his defence or counterclaim) without the need for a full trial. The court may give the defendant permission to defend on stated conditions, such as paying (part of) the disputed sum into court if there is a limited prospect of success. Where the application is made by the claimant, the judge must carry out the necessary exercise of assessing the prospects of success of the defendant. If he concludes that there is "no real prospect", he may decide the case accordingly. The judge is making an assessment, not conducting a trial or fact-finding exercise. Whilst it must be remembered that the wood is composed of trees some of which may need to be looked at individually, it is the assessment of the whole thing that is called for. The criterion which the judge has to apply is not one of probability: it is absence of reality (*Three Rivers D.C. v Bank of England (no. 3)* [2003] 2 AC 1, 282, (HL)).

Summons A document issued by the court requiring a person to attend court to give evidence or to produce documents. A summons may also be obtained from the court to require a witness to attend an arbitration hearing. The former writ of summons beginning a High Court action has now been replaced by the claim form.

Sunday and night working Working at such times which, under the ICE conditions of contract, requires the Engineer to give permission for the contractor to do so.

Sun pipe/sun tube These are reflective tubes designed to bring natural light into deep plan spaces with no access to natural light where this might not otherwise be possible. These tubes extend through adjustable bends with an internal mirror finish that reflects natural daylight, delivering free outdoor light to a room or area below.

Sunset date A date identified in a contract at which the employer will be entitled to terminate in the event of non-completion.

Superplasticiser A concrete chemical admixture which increases its workability while the water content is reduced and enables early strength in the concrete to be achieved. Often used on heavily reinforced structures where adequate vibration is not easily achievable due to the spacing of the reinforcement. ■ See **Admixture**.

Superstructure The main framework of a building above ground, such as the external walls floors and roof or the steel frame of a building: it is supported by the foundations or substructure. ■ See **Substructure**.

Supervising officer A contract administrator. Now infrequently used, the term used to appear in JCT Local Authority standard forms where the Contract Administrator was not a qualified architect.

Supervision The service to be provided by a construction professional charged with administering a construction contract. The three relevant areas relate to: the prevention, detection and correction of defects; intervention concerning the contractor's working methods; and correction of design. ■ See **Design, Inspection** and **Working methods**.

Supervisor Appointment made under the **NEC** form by an employer. The supervisor's role, is to check that the works are carried out in accordance with the contract. ■ See also **Clerk of works** and **Resident engineer**.

Supplier A party who enters into a contract to supply goods and materials to the main contractor under a construction contract, to be distinguished from a **subcontractor**, who will also carry out work.

Supply and fix A contract or item within a contract bill or specification requiring the contractor to obtain, deliver and install goods and materials, often of a specialist nature. Title to the goods will pass to the employer on payment for the goods or their fixing to the works, whichever is the earlier, subject to the express terms of the contract.

Supply chain The activities and/or organisations involved in transforming goods from the raw-materials stage to the final product. The chain itself can consist of many separate stages including sourcing and procurement, production and production scheduling, storage and ultimately transportation to its final destination.

Supply of documents Construction contracts usually make express provision for the supply of various documents by each party, beginning with the contract documents themselves. Under a conventional contract, a construction professional retained by the employer will usually provide documents such as drawings containing information about the works or variations. The JCT forms now contain express provision for an information release schedule and require further drawings, details and instruction to be provided or given at the time it is reasonably necessary for the contractor to receive them, having regard to the progress of the Works. In the absence of express provision, there is an implied term that necessary information will be supplied at a reasonable time: *Neodox v Swinton and Pendlebury BC* (1958) 5 BLR 38.

Supply of Goods & Services Act 1982 An Act codifying the law concerning the terms to be implied into certain contracts for the hire or supply of goods and the supply of a service, subsequently amended by the Sale and Supply of Goods Act 1994. The terms covered relate to title, description, quality and fitness for purpose and on those who carry out services to do so exercising reasonable care and skill, within a reasonable time (where not agreed) and at a reasonable cost (where not agreed). Such terms were previously implied into supply and construction contracts at common law, but the Act prohibits the implication of terms other than those identified in its provisions in relation to quality or fitness: s4(1).

Supply only A contract for goods or materials to be supplied, but not to be installed on site. Such contracts are subject to the implied terms of the Supply of Goods and Services Act 1982.

Supra Latin: "above".

Supreme Court (1) The highest court of appeal in the United Kingdom. The 12 Supreme Court Justices hear final appeals in civil and criminal cases for the whole of the United Kingdom (except for criminal cases from Scotland). The Supreme Court replaced the Judicial Committee of the House of Lords on 1 October 2009. It is located in the former Middlesex Guildhall, on the west side of Parliament Square. (2) The title formerly given to the Court of Appeal and the High Court of Justice: the Supreme Court Acts have now been renamed The Senior Courts Acts.

Surety A person who contracts with an actual or possible creditor of another to be responsible to him by way of security, additional to that other, for the whole or part of the debt: *Rowlatt on Principal and Surety*, 4th edn, p. 1. ■ See **Bond, Guarantee** and **Subrogation**.

Surface coefficient A measurement of friction of a material at its surface: also of heat transfer from the surface of a material.

Surface retarder A chemical compound painted or sprayed onto surface of concrete in order to delay the setting of the mortar and to achieve an exposed aggregate finish when retarder is washed or brushed off.

Surface water attenuation Attenuation consists of the temporary storage of surface water in a suitable chamber (now often proprietary systems) below ground level. This chamber needs to be of sufficient size to capture the run-off during peak periods of rainfall. The stored water is then gradually released in a controlled manner via a hydro brake into a surface water or combined drainage system etc, effectively reducing the risk of flooding.

Surveyor See **Building Surveyor, Chartered Surveyor** and **Quantity Surveyor**.

Suspended ceiling A ceiling usually comprising a metal lattice suspended by wires or straps from soffit of floor above. The framework is filled with light weight ceiling tiles but also diffusers and spot lights and air conditioning outlets, which have their own suspension systems. A suspended ceiling is often required to accommodate air conditioning ductwork and other services, but may also be built to achieve a balanced appearance to room. Common in office buildings but not in houses.

Suspended floor Floor carried by joists bearing on the flank walls of a room, leaving a void beneath for ventilation: otherwise resting on supports such as brick piers or sleeper walls built off the sub floor (at ground floor level). May be constructed of joists and floorboards in timber, or concrete beam and block flooring. Upper floors of a building are of necessity suspended.

Suspension The temporary cessation of work on a contract before it is completed. This may be done by agreement: some standard forms permit the employer to suspend work for a limited period of time, but this will incur additional costs. The contractor has no right to suspend performance on the grounds of non-payment at common law, but is entitled to do so under s 112 of the Housing Grants, Construction and Regeneration Act 1996 after having given at least 7 days' notice of intention to do so.

Suspension bridge In their simplest form made from rope and wood, the deck of the bridge is supported at intervals by cables, which extend from one end of the bridge to the other.

Sustainability Sustainability rests on three pillars, economic, environmental and social, albeit that it is the second of these which tends to take prominence. Whilst the attempt to define sustainability has memorably been described as an "exploration into a tangled conceptual jungle where watchful eyes lurk at every bend" (by Timothy O'Riordan in 1985), sustainability refers to the use, development and protection of resources in such a manner that enables both current and future needs to be met.

Sustainable development In 1987 the Bruntland Commission defined Sustainable Development as "development that meets the needs of the present without compromising the needs of future generations to meet their own needs". Sustainable development typically refers to the environmental and social impact of actions taken in the present on future generations.

Sutcliff v Thackrah [1974] 1 All ER 859: an architect or professional consultant has a duty to act impartially when deciding questions between the client and the building contractor. Lord Reid said: "The building owner and the contractor make their contract on the understanding that in all such matters the architect will act in a fair and unbiased manner and it must therefore be implicit in the owner's contract with the architect that he shall not only exercise due care and skill but also reach such decisions fairly, holding the balance between his client and the contractor".

Swan neck The double curved section of a drainage pipe: also applied to a curved decorative feature in metalwork or in joinery at the end of a staircase handrail.

Sweating The appearance of condensation on cold surface inside a building, generally on hard surfaces such as metal pipes or ducts and stonework, but also possible on walls and ceilings: caused by excessive humidity and cured by improved ventilation. The term is also used for soldering of pipework.

SWIFT Structured what-if checklist technique. A method of identifying potential hazards through structured brainstorming by a team looking for potential risks. See **HAZID** and **HAZOP**.

Switchroom A room containing electrical switchgear and transformers to reduce voltage of incoming electricity supply for distribution through building: it also often contains electrical control equipment for systems such as power and lighting, telephones and IT.

SWL See **safe working load**.

10% Syndrome The problem that the last 10% (or maybe 1%) of anything takes longer than the rest. Phrase sometimes used by disgruntled employers who feel that once contractors have been paid the vast bulk of their fee, they take forever to finish off the works.

T

T&Cs Terms and conditions of a contract.

Take-off or Taking off The estimation of quantities for a contract from plans and drawings which are then recorded in the bill of quantities.

Take or pay agreement A contractual arrangement whereby one party must either take delivery of goods in question and pay for them or, if it does not take delivery of the goods, pay a specified sum.

Take over or Taking over The passing of possession of works or a section from the contractor to the employer. This is not a formal term used in contractual documents, which tend to refer to the employer "taking possession" of the works after **practical completion** or **partial possession** before that date. Also known as **handover** or **handing over**.

Taking Over Certificate (TOC) Certificate issued following **take over**.

Tanking The waterproofing of a structure below ground level such as a basement, achieved by the application of bituminous or other impermeable coatings to the inside or outside of vertical walls and waterproofing the slab by means of damp proof course, alternatively with a cavity wall construction and an impermeable membrane within the cavity.

Tap-off unit Electrical equipment for connecting secondary power cabling for appliances to mains power circuit.

Target contract A contract with a price agreed as a target figure. The employer and contractor share the benefit of any savings and the additional cost of any expenditure above target in proportions agreed when the contract is made. Variations to the works remain at the employer's expense, so the project needs to be well defined to benefit from this collaborative form of working. NEC Options C & D provide a target price contract. The target may include the period for completion of the works, providing an incentive to complete early.

Target cost contract See **Target contract**.

Target price contract See **Target contract**. ■ See **Burgundy Book** and **New Engineering Contract**.

Taxation See **Assessment of costs**.

TBM See **Temporary benchmark**.

TECBAR See **Technology and Construction Bar Association**.

TeCSA See **Technology and Construction Solicitors' Association**.

TCC See **Technology and Construction Court**.

TCC Guide The Technology and Construction Court Guide, the 2nd edn, 2nd rev, of which was published in October 2010. An invaluable guide to practice in the TCC.

Technical query (TQ) A written question raised by a contractor concerning technical issues relating to a project, such as a design query affecting construction or mechanical and electrical services. Usually directed to the architect, engineer, M & E consultant or other technical expert advising the employer, both the query and the response are usually recorded in writing. They may be raised at tender stage or during construction.

Technical terms See **Scientific and technical terms**.

Technology and Construction Bar Association (TECBAR) Professional association of barristers practising in the Technology and Construction Courts and in arbitration, adjudication, mediation and other dispute resolution procedures and providing advice and drafting contract documentation relating to building, engineering and technology projects.

Technology and Construction Court (TCC) A specialist list under Part 2 of the **CPR** designated as such by Part 60 and managed by the judge in charge of the Technology and Construction Court in conjunction with the court manager. In the High Court, the list forms part of the Queen's Bench Division, but there are also TCC lists in the County Courts for Birmingham, Bristol, Cardiff, Central London, Exeter, Leeds, Liverpool, Manchester, Newcastle and Nottingham. Claims which can be brought as Technology and Construction Court claims are: (1) building or other construction disputes, including claims for the enforcement of the decisions of adjudicators under the **Construction Act**; (2) engineering disputes; (3) claims by and against engineers, architects, surveyors, accountants and other specialised advisers; (4) claims by and against local authorities relating to their statutory duties concerning the development of land or the construction of buildings; (5) claims relating to the design, supply and installation of computers, computer software and related network systems; (6) claims relating to the quality of goods sold or hired, and work done, materials supplied or services rendered; (7) claims between landlord and tenant for breach of a repairing covenant; (8) claims between neighbours, owners and occupiers of land in trespass, nuisance, etc; (9) claims relating to the environment (eg pollution cases); (10) claims arising out of fires; (11) claims involving taking of accounts where these are complicated; and (12) claims relating to decisions of arbitrators in construction and engineering disputes including applications for permission to appeal and appeals. Claims for personal injuries and public nuisance which are factually or technically complex, as well as procurement disputes relating to the Public Contracts Regulations 2006, SI 2006/5, are also dealt with, as well as claims for legal professional negligence concerning planning, property, construction and other technical disputes. The TCC has produced an invaluable guide to dealings with the court: the **TCC Guide** or Technology and Construction Court Guide, the 2nd edn, 2nd rev (October 2010). ➤ **Figure T1**

Technology and Construction Solicitors' Association (TeCSA) The professional association of solicitors practising in the areas with which the TCC is concerned. Established in 1991 to promote the interests of solicitors and their clients involved in litigation in the TCC, TeCSA produces its own protocols in relation to adjudication, ADR and IT disputes.

Tell-tale A device attached over the path of a crack as a crack monitoring device. Usually made of sliding perspex tell-tales to monitor both horizontal and vertical movement are either screwed or fixed with epoxy resin. The interpretation of such gauges should be assessed by a chartered structural engineer or chartered building surveyor. Sliding perspex tell-tales are either screwed or fixed with epoxy resin to each side of the crack. The calibrated

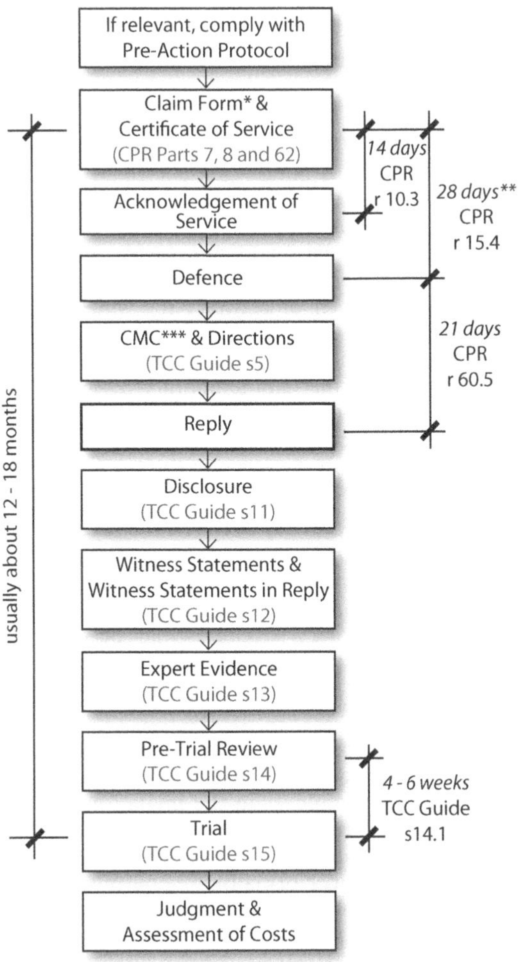

* If Particulars of Claim (PoC) are not served with the Claim Form, must be served within 14 days.

** From service of the PoC & only if the Defendant files Acknowledgment of Service.

*** On occasion, the Case Management Conference (CMC) may be held before service of the Defence.

➤ **Figure T1.** Litigation in the Technology and Construction Court (TCC)

scale on the face of the tell-tale is then monitored to establish extent and direction of movement. (See 'Differential settlement crack').

Tempered glass Heat-treated glass subjected to high temperature and then rapidly cooled in 1991 to harden and strengthen it. If damaged it breaks into small pieces rather than jagged shards: it is widely used in buildings for doors, windows and glass features such as atria and glass walling where strength and safety are required.

Temporary benchmark (TBM) A secondary level used in surveying once the primary benchmark has been established from OS marker or plan. A TBM is often marked by a steel pin driven into a solid surface and is used to set out levels on a building site.

Temporary disconformity A phrase first coined by Lord Diplock in his dissenting speech in *P & M Kaye Ltd v Hosier & Dickinson Ltd* [1972] 1 WLR 146, 165; [1972] 1 All ER 121, suggesting that the argument that such discomformity of any part of the works with the requirements of the contract even though remedied before the end of the agreed construction period constituted a breach of contract for which nominal damages would be recoverable did not make business sense. He went on to say that, provided that the contractor put it right timeously, he did not think that the parties intended that any temporary discomformity should of itself amount to a breach of contract by the contractor. The theory has not found favour and was criticised in *Lintest Builders Ltd v Roberts* (1978) 10 BLR 120 (CA), although there is some overseas authority approving it: *Adkin v Brown* [2002] NZCA 59.

Temporary works Works necessary to enable the permanent construction to be built such as scaffolding and formwork and temporary foundations, but which are removed prior to completion: generally the contractor is responsible for their design installation and operation. In engineering projects substantial temporary structures may be built and these may be designed by the engineer. The definition in the ICE conditions of contract is: "all temporary works of every kind required in and about the construction and completion of the Works".

Tender An offer by a contractor to carry out work, specifying the price and usually the time required. The form which the tender takes is often laid down by the employer in the invitation and may include a breakdown of the rates and prices and a programme showing planned progress and technical details if some responsibility for design is imposed on the contractor. Normally the contractor bears the cost of preparing the tender as part of his overhead costs. A competitive tender process is intended to enable the employer to select a contractor best suited for the project by reference to price and other criteria such as commercial record. The description of a price as an "estimate" does not prevent it from amounting to a tender, which can give rise to a binding contract if accepted by the employer: *Crowshaw v Pritchard* (1899) *Hudson's Law of Building, Engineering and Ship Building Contracts* 4th edn, Vol. 2, 274. ■ See **Award of Tender, Invitation to Tender** and **Tendering**.

Tender deposit A sum of money placed with the employer as a condition of being entitled to submit a tender, which may be forfeited in the event of withdrawal of the tender.

Tendering The competitive procedure by which an employer chooses a suitable contractor for his project. The employer (with the support of his design team) defines the scope of the works to be carried out, usually in the form of drawings, specifications and/or bills of quantities. This package is issued to selected contractors who price the works and return their Tender (or offer) by a specified date. The Tenders are opened simultaneously and assessed: usually but not always the contract is awarded to the contractor putting forward the lowest Tender. Procurement by a public authority is covered by the Public Contracts Regulations 2006, SI 2006/5, which impose strict procedural requirements. There are a variety of tendering procedures in the construction industry: see **Award of Tender**, **Open Tendering**, **Single-stage selective tendering**, **Tender** and **Two-stage selective tendering**.

Tenon The projecting part at the end of a length of timber which fits into the mortise (chiselled out to the same size) in the wood to which it is to be joined in a mortise and tenon joint.

Tensile Of or pertaining to a pulling force.

Tension A force that tends to pull a body apart. A beam in tension is the act or process of stretching it, e.g., the cables in a suspension bridge. It describes the condition of so being stretched, the tautness. ➤ **Figure C2**

Term contract A contract (usually for services) to be carried out over a fixed period, particularly one which continues for a specified number of years, for example between a public authority and a contractor to carry out maintenance work as required at agreed rates over a fixed period of time.

Terminal float The period of time between planned completion and the contractual completion date.

Termination See **Determination**.

Terms of art Some expressions in common use in documents dealing with legal rights or obligations which have acquired in a legal context a special meaning different from, or more precise than, their meaning in common speech: *Prestcold (Central) Ltd v Minister of Labour* [1969] 1 WLR 89.

Terms of reference An initial document prepared by an arbitral tribunal with the cooperation of the parties setting out the issues to be decided. This procedure, which can be time-consuming, is hardly ever adopted in domestic arbitrations but is not uncommon in international disputes.

Terrazzo Terrazzo is a floor or wall covering consisting of chips of marble, granite or glass set in concrete as a binder that is cementitious and polished to give a smooth surface. 'Modern' terrazzo was invented by Venetian contractors as a low cost flooring in the fifteenth century using marble cast offs remaining from the custom made marble slabs, to surface the terraces around their living quarters. The workers would usually set them in clay. Production of terrazzo became much easier after the 1920s and the introduction of electric industrial grinders and polishing equipment. The word comes from the Italian for terraces and has been used since Roman antiquity as a flooring medium.

Terrorism A **relevant event** under the JCT standard forms which may entitle the contractor to the grant of an extension of time. The full phrase used is "civil commotion or the use or threat of terrorism and/or the activities of the relevant authorities in dealing with such event or threat". Under s1(1) of the Terrorism Act 2000 terrorism means 'the use or threat of action where the use or threat is designed to influence the government [or an international governmental organisation] or to intimidate the public or a section of the public, and the use or threat is made for the purpose of advancing a political, religious [racial] or ideological cause.'

Terrorism cover Insurance under the JCT 2011 standard forms for physical loss or damage to work executed and site materials or to an existing structure and/or its contents caused by terrorism.

Tessellated pavement A mosaic consisting of tesserae, pieces of marble about half-inch square, in mortar.

Test piles Piles installed at specific locations and subjected to loading tests to establish their viability for proposed works.

Test pit See **Trial pit**.

Testimony Evidence given by a witness, particularly oral evidence given on oath or affirmation as oath of court proceedings.

Test of reasonableness The test to be satisfied under the Misrepresentation Act 1967, the Unfair Contract Terms Act 1977, by a contract term which excludes or restricts liability in order to have effect where one of the parties deals as consumer or on the other's written standard terms of business. The matters to which regard is to be had in particular are any of the following which appear to be relevant: (1) the strength of the bargaining positions of the parties relative to each other, taking into account (among other things) alternative means by which the customer's requirements could have been met; (2) whether the customer received an inducement to agree to the term, or in accepting it had an opportunity of entering into a similar contract with other persons, but without having a similar term; (3) whether the customer knew or ought reasonably to have known of the existence and the extent of the term (having regard, among other things, to any custom of the trade and any previous course of dealing between the parties); (4) where the term excludes or restricts any relevant liability if some condition was not complied with, whether it was reasonable at the time of the contract to expect that compliance with that condition would be practicable; (5) whether the goods were manufactured, processed or adapted to the special order of the customer.

Thaumasite Is a sulphate attack of concrete, of which many cases were reported between 1995 - 2002 concerned with cracking of bridge and pier structures of motorways. It occurs where water containing dissolved sulphate penetrates the concrete. The reaction only occurs where there is a combination of very wet, cold conditions; a source of sulphates, for example clay soils react with the calcium carbonate in the concrete. This produces a soft, crumbly mineral known as thaumasite. Existing sulphate-resistant Portland cement appears to provide no answer to the problem.

Theft The dishonest appropriation of property belonging to another with the intention of permanently depriving the other of it: Theft Act 1968. There is an implied term of a construction contract that the contractor will take reasonable care with regard to the state of the premises where he is working if he leaves them during the performance of his work and if he fails to do so and a theft occurs, he will be liable for the loss: *Stansbie v Troman* [1948] 2 KB 48 (CA).

Thermal break A thermal break describes the use of an element of low thermal conductivity placed in a construction detail, such as a window, door, wall or framing system to reduce or prevent the course of thermal energy between conductive materials thereby minimising cold spots and interstitial condensation. For example, early aluminium and steel Crittall window systems suffered through the lack of use of thermal breaks.

Thermal bridge See **Cold bridging** and **Linear thermal bridge**.

Thermal movement The expansion and contraction of building materials with temperature: materials like stone have low thermal movement, most metals and plastics have a higher coefficient of expansion.

Thermal resistance The ability of a construction material or an entire building to resist the transfer of heat through the material: the opposite to thermal conductivity. Its measurement is known as the R-value of the material.

Thermal stress breakage Damage caused to building materials by expansion through heat, in particular damage to glazing caused by differences in temperature between the exposed centre and shaded edges of tempered glass panels.

Thermal transmittance The transfer of heat through a construction material: its measurement is known as the **U-value**.

Thermoset A polymer product which is applied in a plastic form but which sets hard either when heat is applied or as a result of a chemical process.

Third fixing The final fixing of joinery items such as doors.

Third party A party who is not participating directly in a transaction between two other parties, such as a contract or a claim. A third party can only acquire rights under a contract between others by agreement of those others, assignment of rights by one of those parties, or under the **Contracts (Rights of Third Parties) Act 1999**. In litigation, if a defendant makes an additional claim against an additional party or a counterclaim against the claimant and an additional party, the additional party is referred to in the title of the proceedings as a third party: CPR Practice Direction 20 para 7.4.

Third party debt orders A court order under CPR Part 72 directing a third party owing money to a defendant (such as a bank or an employer) to pay money to a claimant in satisfaction of his judgement against the defendant. For example, a subcontractor (following a successful claim against the main contractor) could serve a third party debt order on the employer so that all sums owed to the contractor would be paid to subcontractor until its judgment was satisfied.

Third party proceedings The former (and now informal) name for an additional claim by a defendant against an additional party.

Third surveyor A surveyor appointed to resolve differences between surveyors acting for the building owner and adjoining owner respectively under the **Party Wall etc. Act 1996**.

Thixotropic The property of a liquid that can alter its viscosity, such as paint that thickens in its can but thins after stirring. This property is used in grouts. Cohesive thixotropic masonry repair grout for bonding, crack stitching reinforcement bars into brickwork and masonry walls.

Three Rivers District Council v Bank of England [2004] 3 WLR 1274: The House of Lords reversed the decision of the Court of Appeal and held that the documents containing legal advice were privileged. For reasons of public policy they considered it to be essential for a client to be able to seek legal advice freely and to be frank with its solicitor without fear that these matters would later be disclosed. Without this approach the solicitor cannot give sound advice to the client. Unless clients are able to obtain sound legal advice they cannot go about their affairs in an orderly way. Legal advice privilege protects clients' rights in this regard. ■ See **privilege**.

Three rules of mitigation There are three rules of mitigation following a breach of contract: (1) You cannot recover damages for a loss which could have been avoided by taking reasonable steps, for example as you would in the ordinary course of business; (2) However, if you do take steps which you could not reasonably have been required to do, and thereby avoid the potential loss, you cannot recover the potential loss as damages; but (3) You can recover any losses or expenses incurred in taking reasonable steps to mitigate the loss due to breach of contract, whether they are successful or not. ■ See **Mitigation**.

Threshold (1) A length of timber or other material which forms the floor of a doorway and over which a person passes to enter the building; (2) the point which triggers an entitlement to an (increased) payment or other contractual benefit or penalty.

Threshold jurisdictional error A fundamental error as to jurisdiction, particularly in the case of adjudication, which might invalidate the entire proceedings and can occur when an adjudicator embarks on a reference where: (1) there was no relevant construction contract or construction operation; (2) there was no construction contract in writing; or (3) The claiming party has purported to refer a dispute when the subject matter of that purported dispute has yet to crystallise into a dispute between the parties. See *Joinery Plus Ltd v Laing Ltd* [2003] EWHC 3513 (TCC); [2003] BLR 184; 87 ConLR 87.

Tie beam The lowest horizontal timber of a roof truss, tying the feet of the rafters.

Tier-1 supplier Term used in procurement to represent a supplier of goods and services at the top end of the supply chain. Term sometimes used to mean **main contractor**.

TILOS Planning software for managing linear construction projects, such as roads and railways. ➤ **Figure T2**

Tilt-and-turn window A window (usually metal framed) which has hinges on two sides of the frame which are engaged in turn by operating a handle. This enables the window to be opened either by tilting on its lower edge or central pivot or by opening as a casement on the hinges at the side.

Timber Any wood used for building, but usually in large cross-section. "Wood" is not a word generally used in the construction industry.

Timber Research and Development Association (TRADA) An association of companies and professionals engaged in the timber industry, supplying manufacturing or working with wood products including contractors and designers. It provides technical information and carries out research into the use of timber and its development as a building material, for example in the use of engineered floors.

Time-at-large A consequence of the application of the **prevention principle**, whereby a contractor who has been prevented from completing the works by the contractual completion date, for which delay he is not

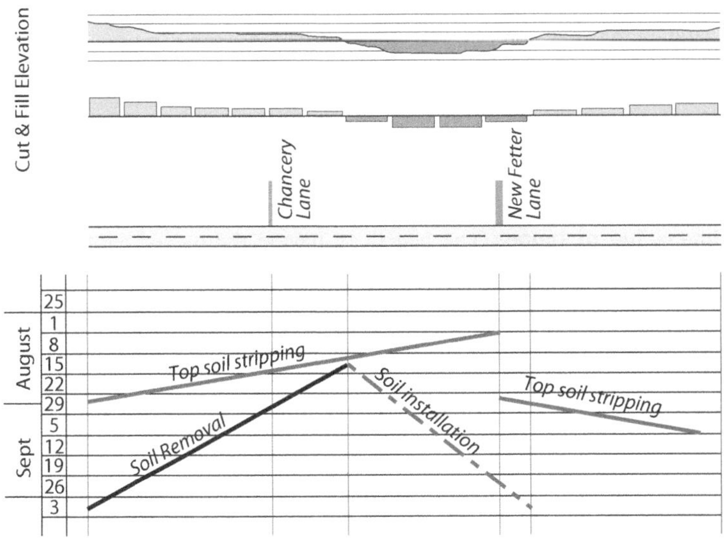

➤ **Figure T2.** TILOS (simplified extract of linear programme for road construction.)

entitled to an extension of time, is only obliged to complete within a reasonable time and the employer cannot enforce the liquidated damages provision. See *Multiplex Constructions (UK) Ltd v Honeywell Control Systems Ltd* [2007] EWHC 447 (TCC); [2007] BLR 195; 111 ConLR 78. ■ See **Extension of time**.

Time bar A clause in a contract, for example subclause 20.1 of the **Red Book**, which (1) gives a party a set number of days or deadline to submit a notice of claim for additional cost or an extension of time and (2) seeks to prevent a party from making such a claim unless it complies with the deadline. ■ See **Condition precedent**.

Time immemorial The time of legal memory, which is fixed as 1189 the beginning of the reign of Richard I. Also known as legal time.

Time of the essence The effect of a contractual term or subsequent notice making performance by a stated date an essential requirement, failing which the contract may be terminated. Such a term would hardly ever be found in a construction contract, which will usually contain provision for extensions of time and liquidated damages for delay. Theoretically, an employer could serve a notice making time of the essence on the basis that a failure to complete for so long would evince an intention no longer to be bound by the terms of the contract, but there is normally express provision for termination on the grounds of poor progress.

Time-impact analysis A method of analysing the effect of a delay event on the progress of the works by examining the actual progress achieved to date and programming the project from the date of the delay to assess the additional time required to complete the project and thus the delay caused. This is a prospective analysis and depends upon the availability of detailed information regarding progress.

Times Law Reports A series of law reports published between 1884 and 1952, not to be confused with the case summaries which appear in *The Times* newspaper.

Time-related costs Heads of claim by a contractor, such as extended preliminaries or loss of overheads, the amount of which depends in part on the length of time for which there was disruption or delay.

Time value of money The benefit of having the use of money over a period of time, for the loss of which a claimant may be compensated by an award of damages or interest. ■ See **Interest**.

Title The legal right to ownership of property.

Title block The blocked corner of a drawing (usually bottom right) which identifies it, describing the location of the project and contents of the drawing, the maker (including the name of the professional practice), the date of creation, approval and revision and the drawing number (and revision). ➤ **Figure T3**

TLC Through life cost, i.e. the cost not just of construction but of running and maintaining the completed building.

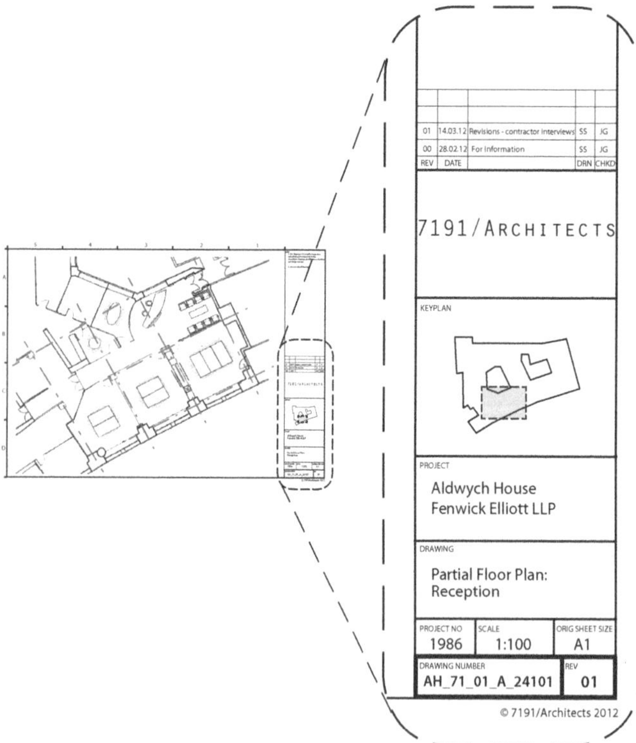

➤ **Figure T3.** Title Block

TLR See **Times Law Reports**.

TOC See **Taking Over Certificate**.

Tolent clause Named after the case of *Bridgeway Construction Ltd v Tolent Construction Ltd* [2000] CILL 1662, a Tolent clause in a contract requiring the referring party in an adjudication to pay all the legal and expert costs of both parties. Following the case of ***Yuanda (UK) Co Ltd v WW Gear Construction Ltd*** [2010] EWHC 720 (TCC); [2010] BLR 435; 130 ConLR 133, it was thought that such clauses would be considered contrary to the **Construction Act** and s141 of the **LDEDC** was certainly intended to outlaw such clauses. However, the true meaning of that section has attracted some controversy, particularly following the case of Profile *Projects Ltd v Elmwood (Glasgow) Ltd* [2011] CSOH 64 and it is possible, that the new legislation has not achieved its desired outcome.

Tolerance A stated allowance for deviation from the precise requirements of a specification in respect of goods and materials: for example standard bricks are manufactured to a tolerance stated by the manufacturers and steel is cut to a stated tolerance.

Tolling agreement See **Standstill agreement**.

Tomlin order Form of settlement order, named after Mr Justice Tomlin who made the first order in the case of *Dashwood v Dashwood* [1927] WN 276. A Tomlin Order stays an action on terms agreed by the parties which are set out on an attached schedule.

Tongue and groove joint Technique for joining two sections of wood edge to edge in a flat joint, for example with floorboards. One edge is machined to leave a protruding central part (tongue) and a slot is cut along the length of the adjoining timber in the centre (groove) so that they fit together without the use of adhesive.

Tooling Fabricating components or equipment for a project, often for a specific use: also equipping workmen with tools. Some tradesmen still provide their own tools.

Toothing out The act of leaving stretchers left protruding at the end of a wall or a wall opening, like teeth in alternate courses, as a bond for future work.

Top chord See **Chord**. ➤ **Figure T4**

Top-down construction (1) Sequence of construction for deep underground works in which retaining diaphragm walls are piled into ground, which are then excavated to form upper slab at ground level, with access sections through: these then enable excavation and construction to continue downwards with less disruption and also for building to continue upwards. (2) Once the main framework of a development has been built, the installation of internal fittings and decoration is started on the top floor and tradesmen work down the building towards the ground floor. There is this benefit of avoiding unnecessary movement across completed floors.

Top-hung window A window hinged along its top edge so that it opens outwards at the bottom.

Topping-out Traditional ceremony by the workforce and invited guests at completion of main structure of building usually involving drinking a toast.

Torpedo A claim made before a tribunal expected to accept jurisdiction in order to prevent the dispute from being pursued elsewhere.

Tort A wrongful act or omission constituting a breach of a duty primarily fixed by law towards people generally, as opposed to a contractual duty arising from the consent of the parties and owed to a specific party.

Tortfeasor A person committing a tort.

Total float The total allowance made by the contractor for unforeseen contingencies, giving the contractor a degree of flexibility in the organisation and timetabling of the contract works. Also, the amount of time an activity can be delayed without affecting the planned completion and reducing the **terminal float**.

Total loss claim See **Global claim**.

Total rise The overall height of a staircase, from the floor where the staircase begins to its top tread.

Toughened glass Float glass which has been heat treated or annealed in order to give it greater resistance to damage by impact. All modern glass is toughened to some extent. Widely used in buildings where there is a risk that occupiers or visitors will come into contact with it or will be injured if the glass breaks.

Tower crane The classic crane arrangement with a tall mast supporting a counterbalanced **jib**, which is able to swing through 360° and with a hoist able to travel the length of the **jib**.

Tower scaffold Prefabricated scaffold sections forming a square or rectangular tower often used independently to gain access to roof or gutter level for maintenance.

Town planning System for controlling development including construction operations and change of use. The current legislation is contained in the Town and Country Planning Act 1990 and numerous statutory orders. Responsibility for granting planning permission is normally held by District Councils but larger projects may be called in by Secretary of State. Appeals against refusal of permission or unreasonable conditions are made to the Secretary of State and are generally heard by a planning inspector. There is an increasing emphasis on strategic planning at a regional level, and on developers providing funds for projects to benefit local communities when development takes place under a **s106 agreement**.

TPO See **Tree preservation order**.

TQ See **Technical query**.

Trabeation The use in a building construction of beams rather than arches or vaulting.

Trace heating A method of heating pipework against the risk of freezing or to maintain a required temperature by attaching an electric cable along its length beneath insulation and passing a low current along it.

Tracery The decorative stonework framing windows in medieval and later buildings.

Track allocation The decision by the County Court (normally by a District Judge) as to whether a case is to be tried as a small claim (claim less than £5,000), on the fast track (claim up to £25,000 able to be tried in one day) or the multi-track. The decision is taken after the parties have completed an allocation questionnaire and depends upon the amount claimed or counterclaimed and complexity of issues. The track allocation will determine the number of preliminary steps leading to trial, the timetable for preparation, the length of trial and recoverable costs. Track allocation does not apply in the High Court.

TRADA See **Timber Research and Development Association**.

Trade contractor See **Works Contractor**.

Trade usage See **Custom and usage**.

Traditional contract Traditionally a building contract requires the employer to provide the contractor with the specification, drawings and all the design information which the architect engaged by the employer produces and the contractor is responsible for building the project. If problems arise, this can sometimes result in a confrontational rather than a co-operative approach to the works, since responsibility for finding solutions for design problems rests solely with the employer and his architect, and the contractor can be entitled to make significant financial claims. The expertise in building techniques which many contractors possess may not be fully utilised. Some traditional contacts may require the contractor to carry out some of the design, which is termed a Contractor-Designed Portion. ■ See **Contractor-Designed Portion**.

Traditional procurement route Usually the employer engaged and relied upon his architect, engineer, quantity surveyor and other construction professionals to specify and design the works and prepare documents for tender, ignoring the possible design and cost advantages of earlier contractor involvement. Modern procurement practice generally involves the contractor at an earlier stage (eg by two stage or negotiated tendering) and imposes design obligations upon the contractor (often through novation of the professional team or by the employment of specialist sub-contractors) and greater involvement in the preparation of sub-contract packages. See **Appendix 1**.

Trafficable roof A roof whose construction allows the passage of workmen and others, often on purpose made walkways or decking. Flat roofs are often designed to maximise use for example as recreational areas or for the installation of plant.

Transcript A typed record of a hearing, usually prepared on the basis of stenographers' work. Transcripts are usually provided on a daily basis at the expense of the parties where the hearing lasts several weeks.

Transfer of proceedings Proceedings may be transferred between courts under CPR Part 35. An application for the transfer of proceedings to the Technology and Construction Court list must be made to a TCC judge under CPR 30.5(3) (see para 3.6.1 of the **TCC Guide**). A Technology and Construction Court judge has jurisdiction to order proceedings to be transferred to or from the TCC list whether from or to the Chancery, Queen's Bench or even Family Divisions (*NATL Amusements (UK) Ltd & others v White City (Shepherd's Bush) Ltd Partnership & others* [2009] EWHC 2524 (TCC) paras 25–28; [2010] BLR 24; [2010] 1 WLR 1181). A party applying to a Technology and

Construction Court judge to transfer a claim to the TCC specialist list must give notice of the application to the court in which the claim is proceeding, and a TCC judge will not make an order for transfer until he is satisfied that such notice has been given (CPR Practice Direction 60 para 5.3).

Transmission The passing on of information, for example by the architect to the employer and the contractor. Where documents are intended to circulate to a number of people it is common to add a circulation list to be ticked when read and passed on.

Transom A horizontal beam separating the lights of a window or a door from the fanlight over it.

Transparency An obligation imposed by the **Public Procurement Regulations** to ensure that **contracting authorities** do ensure equal and fair treatment of all tenderers during the procurement process.

Transparency International Founded in 1993, Transparency International is a global civil society organisation whose mission is to create change towards a world free of corruption. Publishes an annual index ranking countries and territories according to their perceived levels of public sector corruption.

Trap A chamber in a waste pipe designed to intercept and retain waste which should not be discharged into the public sewer, such as fat from a kitchen or petrol from a forecourt.

Tread The horizontal part of a step. ➤ **Figure G2**

Tree preservation order (TPO) An order made by a local planning authority under statutory powers forbidding the felling or lopping of identified tree(s) or woodland without permission, usually because of their size, age and contribution to the landscape. It is a criminal offence to breach a TPO and substantial fines may be imposed. The offence is one of strict liability. In general, the law in relation to TPOs can be found in Part VIII of the Town and Country Planning Act 1990 and in the Town and Country Planning (Trees) Regulations 1999, SI 1999/1892. ■ See **Strict liability** and **Tree Preservation Orders: A Guide to the Law and Good Practice (2000)**.

Tree Preservation Orders: A guide to the Law and Good Practice (2000) with amendments (2009) A guide which sets out the government's guidance and policy advice on the system of tree preservation orders (TPOs) taking into account the Town and Country Planning (Trees) Regulations 1999, SI 1999/1892. The guide is also commonly known as "The Blue Book". ■ See **Tree Preservation Orders**.

Trench-fill foundation Building foundation formed by excavating a trench in the ground along the line of load bearing walls and filling it with hardcore and concrete to within 150 mm of ground level. The width and depth of the trench will depend upon the load to be applied and the nature of the ground. Trench fill foundations are generally deeper and narrower than strip footings.

Trespass Unlawful interference with the possessory rights of an owner of land by direct physical entry. A trespass will occur if any part of a new building is constructed beyond the boundary of the employer's land. An injunction may be granted to restrain acts of trespass but if an owner delays, his remedy may be limited to damages under the equitable doctrine of **laches**.

Trial pit A small pit excavated to establish ground conditions, also known as a **test pit**.

Triaxial compression test A procedure in which a load is applied by a piston to a sample of soil in a rubber bag surrounded by liquid under pressure.

Tribology The science and technology of interacting surfaces in relative motion. It includes the study and application of the principles of friction, lubrication and wear. The word "tribology" derives from the Greek ("tribo") meaning "rub" and ("logos") meaning 'principle or logic'. In construction and engineering disputes, experts in tribology are often called where reciprocating machinery like motors, generator sets or HVAC equipment is concerned.

Trimmer beam Where ceiling or floor joists are cut short in order to create an opening, for example to accommodate a staircase, the trimmer beam is a wood or metal beam installed at right angles to the shortened floor or ceiling joists. The ends of the shortened joists are attached to the trimmer by joist hangers or fitted into and carried by the trimmer beam, which is supported at each end by a load bearing part of the building such as the walls.

Trunking Ducting used to carry and conceal wires and pipework around a building on walls, along skirting boards and in floors and voids. Often made from PVC because of its flexibility, but also galvanised steel where a more robust finish is required. Trunking may be rounded or rectangular in section or divided into compartments to separate a number of cables.

Truss A building component made from timber or steel which is triangular in shape with straight sides and therefore possesses structural stability. ➤ **Figure T4**

Trussed rafter A rafter assembly triangular in form with two sides forming rafter on either side of sloping roof and fixed bottom chord maintaining stability. The points where the sides meet are held together by connector plates. ➤ **Figure T4**

Trust An obligation to hold property or exercise rights on behalf of others or for the achievement of an object. Trusts take many forms, many of which are not directly relevant to construction contracts. The most important of these for practical purposes is an employer's fiduciary interest in retention monies. ■ See **Fiduciary interest**.

TRV Thermostatic radiator valve.

Tubular scaffolding Scaffold poles of 5 cm external diameter made of steel or light alloy.

Tunnel boring machine A machine with a circular rotary cutting plate with teeth attached capable of cutting through rock. May be lowered into a shaft or assembled on site. Able to excavate through the ground in a continuous operation and direct excavated spoil to surface by conveyor belt. Substantial savings can be made on major tunnelling projects: the diameter of such machines is often substantial and they enable the excavation and subsequent support of the tunnel to be fully mechanised.

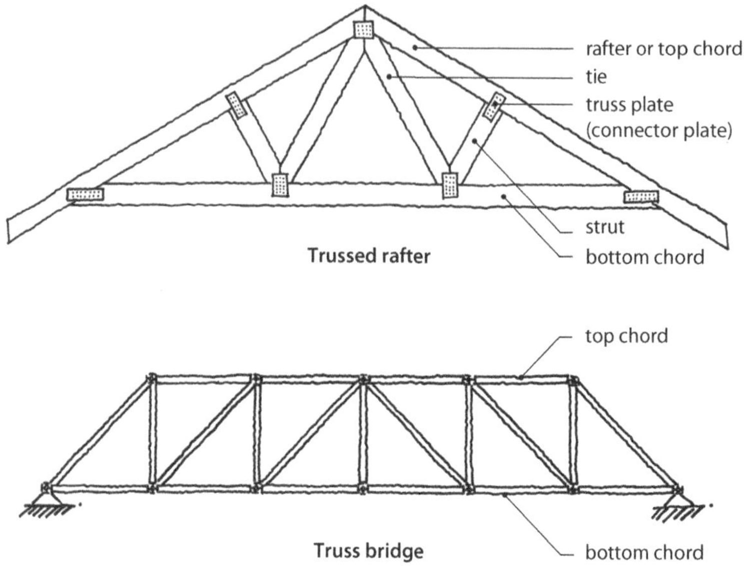

➤ **Figure T4.** Truss

Turriff Construction Ltd v Regalia Knitting Mills Ltd (1971) 9 BLR 20: In **obiter** comment, Judge Fay QC provided guidance on what a **letter of intent** is, stating that it is "no more than an expression in writing of a party's present intention to enter into a contract at a future date. Save in exceptional circumstances it can have no binding effect … . A letter of intent would ordinarily have two characteristics, one, that it will express an intention to enter into a contract in future and two, it will itself create no liability in regard to that future contract".

Turnkey contract A project in which the developer is responsible for carrying out not only the construction of the building but also its fitting out and decoration so that it is handed over in a completed state to the employer ready for use, so that he has only to "turn the key". This method of procurement has the advantage that the contractor takes full responsibility for the operation of the building but may mean that the employer has less control over detailed decisions. The term is now synonymous with **design and build**.

Turnover discount A percentage reduction in the prices charged (eg by a supplier to a contractor) which varies according to the volume of business done by the contractor with the supplier.

Tuck pointing Tuck pointing is a very precise brick pointing method producing the appearance of fine tight bed joints. It is employed now days in the conservation and restoration of existing brickwork.

Two-stage selective tendering A tender process suitable for large or complex projects which involves the contractor at an early stage. The first stage is the selection of a contractor on the basis of limited information about the project: the contractors invited to tender may be asked to price their required overhead and profit and preliminaries and to provide schedules of rates. In the second stage the chosen contractor helps to develop the design and to prepare and obtain tenders for the main subcontract packages. The contractor may be paid a fee for his services during the second stage and required to enter into pre-construction services agreement. Once approximately 70–80 per cent of the works by value have been tendered by subcontractors the contractor enters into a lump-sum sum contract for the whole of the works. The **NJCC** published a Code of Procedure for two stage selective tendering.

Typical detail A drawing or other description of an area of work, which is repeated at many locations in the project. Such details may be produced during RIBA Outline Plan of Work Stages D or E in order to inform the project Cost Plan. This detail may be repeated without change, or may be modified in some respect for a specific location: this would generally be covered by a note on the typical detail or alternatively a new specific detail would be created. A typical detail may be a standard detail regularly used in a particular design practice: manufacturers of engineering or building products also often supply typical details of their product. ■ See **Detail drawings** and **RIBA Outline Plan of Work**.

Typical floor A floor whose design is repeated on other floors throughout the building: the architect and/or engineer need only to draw and detail the plans for a typical floor: this may be supplemented by further plans where other floors in the building differ in detail. ■ See **Floor plan** and **Typical detail**.

Tyrolean finish or render An external render with a rough textured finish supposedly inspired by the chalets of the Tyrol.

U

Uberrima fides Latin: "the utmost good faith", a characteristic of certain contracts whereby one party who has knowledge of material facts is required to disclose them. The most common example of a contract uberrimae fidei (of the utmost good faith) is that of an insurance policy. Construction contracts are not contracts uberrimae fidei.

Ultra Latin: "above" or "beyond".

Ultra vires Latin: "beyond the powers", used to describe a decision or action which lies beyond the powers of the body which took it. Government departments, local councils, statutory bodies, limited companies and many other legal persons whose powers and functions are prescribed by statute or written articles may be limited as to the actions they are authorised to take. Decisions made in breach of any procedural or regulatory requirements may also be invalid.

Ultraviolet radiation Part of the sun's radiation which breaks down plastics under prolonged exposure. It is also known (inaccurately) as ultraviolet light.

Umbrella deed A master agreement between the parties involved in a large project, setting out their rights, duties and relationships.

Umpire A third arbitrator appointed by two arbitrators who cannot agree on a matter relating to an arbitration as envisaged by the Arbitration Act 1996, s16.

Unbonded screed A concrete screed which does not adhere to the underlying surface. This may be a matter of design, for example, where the screed is laid on a damp proof membrane or other non-adhesive surface or may result from failure to adhere to the underlying surface through loss of key, becoming detached: sounds hollow when tapped. The cause may be an incorrect mix or conditions when laid or a failure to prepare surface.

Uncertainty A lack of clarity in a contract or one of its terms which may prevent a contract from being made or the term being of any effect. The contract or term may make no sense, or one of several meanings cannot be preferred, or further agreement is required. A contract or a term within it may be held to be void for uncertainty, although the court will normally try to find its intended meaning. ■ See **Void**.

UNCITRAL The United Nations Commission on International Trade Law, which has produced a Model Law on International Commercial Arbitration and Rules of Arbitration. The Model Law influenced the drafting of the Arbitration Act 1996.

Unconditional bond See **On-demand bond**.

Unconscionable bargain A transaction which is substantially unfair to one party parting with property for much less than its true value or getting nothing out of it and where the other party has behaved in a morally reprehensible manner. The authorities usually involve young, inexperienced or ignorant individuals and not commercial parties. There is no general principle that relief will be granted in the case of a harsh and unconscionable bargain. ■ See also **Duress**.

Undercertification The issue of a certificate under a construction contract on the basis of a valuation of the works which is below the value in accordance with the terms of the contract.

Undercroft A cellar or storage room which is often brick-lined and vaulted.

Underfloor space The area beneath a suspended floor. In traditional building where there is no foundation slab, the floor joists are carried on load-bearing walls and a space remains above natural ground level. This is ventilated by air bricks in the walls.

Underground services Services provided through pipework ducts or cables running beneath ground level, such as water, electricity, gas and telecommunications. Precautions are necessary when carrying out groundworks in their vicinity.

Underlay A padded layer of material placed under carpeting or other flooring in order to protect it against excessive wear, to make it more resilient and to provide thermal insulation. Underlays were formerly made of felt, but are now usually rubber or plastic compounds. Underlay may also be placed beneath wood flooring and vinyl tiles.

Underpinning Remedial work below ground level to an existing load-bearing wall or other foundation. Various techniques may be employed: short alternating sections of the foundation are exposed and supported by additional brickwork/reinforced concrete to a greater depth. In other methods, liquid cement (grout) is pumped into the cavity below the foundation, or an independent foundation is constructed parallel to the existing wall and the load transferred by pins. Work of any complexity is carried out by specialist subcontractors. The need for underpinning may arise because uneven settlement has occurred, or loading of the existing structure has been increased or the adjacent ground levels have been lowered (eg by construction of a basement next to an existing structure).

Undertaking A formal promise made by a party to the court to carry out or refrain from a specified action: for example, not to enter upon neighbouring land until a boundary dispute has been resolved. Court undertakings are usually negative in substance but a positive obligation may be undertaken, for example, to pay a sum of money. Undertakings are generally made in the course of litigation prior to the determination of the substantive rights of the parties. Breach of an undertaking may constitute a contempt of court. Undertakings are not given in arbitrations because an arbitrator lacks the coercive powers of a court. Also a professional agreement by a solicitor to carry out a specified action in a transaction, for example, to pay money to a named recipient out of the proceeds of sale of a property. A failure to perform such an undertaking is a breach of the Solicitor's Code of Conduct.

Undisclosed principal A principal neither the existence or indentity of whom is disclosed by his agent. Any contract with a third party is made with the agent, but the principal can bring a claim on it, subject to the third party's right to claim against the agent.

Undue influence The courts will set aside transactions obtained by undue influence but have refused to define either undue influence or the relationships of trust and confidence from which the presumption that there has been such influence might arise. It is highly unlikely that such a presumption could arise in relation to a construction contract. ■ See also **Duress**.

Uneconomic working Work carried out more expensively in changed circumstances from those anticipated when the contract was made, for example, when work has to be performed out of planned sequence leading to less efficient production. This may result in a claim by the contractor for loss and expense due to delay and disruption caused by the employer, either under an express contract term permitting such claims or as a claim for breach of contract.

Unenforceable contract A contract on the basis of which neither party can bring a claim because its terms do not comply with statute, such as the Statute of Frauds 1677, s4, which requires an agreement for a guarantee or some memorandum or note of it to be in writing and signed by the guarantor.

Unfair Contract Terms Act 1977 A statute imposing restrictions on contract terms which limit liability in contract and in negligence or are otherwise unreasonable. Liability for causing death or personal injury by negligence cannot be excluded by a contract term, and any other loss caused by a negligent act can only be excluded if a notice or term satisfies a reasonableness test. The Act has a greater impact on businesses dealing with a consumer. A party dealing on its standard terms of business cannot restrict liability in respect of a breach or be entitled to render a contractual performance substantially different from that which was reasonably expected, or to render no performance at all, except insofar as the contract term satisfies a reasonableness test. No clause can exclude the effect of the seller's implied undertakings as to title under s12 of the Sale of Goods Act 1979. Reasonableness test guidelines are set out in Schedule 2 of the Act which takes into account the bargaining position of the parties, whether there was an inducement to agree an exemption clause and whether the customer ought reasonably to have known of the term. ■ See **Test of reasonableness**.

Unfixed materials It includes goods, materials and equipment which have not yet been incorporated into the works. Many contracts provide that the cost of such materials when brought to site or specifically identified may be included in an interim valuation. Property in such materials passes to the employer where it can be demonstrated that the price of the materials has been included in the valuation for a particular payment.

Unforeseen ground conditions See **Adverse physical conditions**.

Ungley order Named after Master Ungley who devised them in clinical negligence cases. An Ungley Order requires that parties to a dispute consider whether the dispute is suitable for mediation. ■ See **The Halsey Guidelines.**

UNIDROIT See **International Institute for the Unification of Private Law**.

Uniformity The rule of construction that a legal draftsman aims at uniformity in the structure of his draft and uses the same words throughout a document to express the same thing or concept, and consequently if he uses different words, the presumption is that he means a different thing or concept. Thus, where the draftsman has made express reference to subcontractors, their servants and agents both in the clause under consideration and elsewhere in the contract, "the contractor" is not to be understood as including subcontractors and their servants and agents: *John Jarvis Ltd v Rockdale Housing Association Ltd* (1986) 36 BLR 48 (CA).

Unilateral contract See **If contract**.

Unincorporated association A body such as a member club or trade association formed by agreement between individuals and sometimes defined by a constitution and rules. It has no separate legal identity from that of its members and is not incorporated as a limited company. ■ See **Partnership**.

Uniplex (UK) Ltd v NHS Business Services Authority (Case C-406/08, 28 January 2010): the **ECJ** clarified the position on limitation period relating to actions for breaches of public procurement regulations: the period for bringing proceedings should start to run from the date on which the claimant knew, or ought to have known, of the alleged breach. A provision of national law that allows a national court to dismiss proceedings as being out of time on the basis that they were not brought "promptly" (even though within the three-month time limit) breaches the principles of certainty and effectiveness and is therefore not compatible with the **Remedies Directive**.

Unit price, unit rate The price of material goods or services given in a measurement appropriate to the product, such as linear, square or cubic metres, or an hourly or daily rate, from which the cost of any measured item can be calculated: commonly used in bills of quantities.

Universal beam (UB) section A standard steel beam which has an I shape in cross section with wide flanges at top and bottom and is able to resist both bending and shear loads. ➤ **Figure U1**

Universal column (UC) section A standard steel column which is H shaped in cross section: the flanges are generally thicker than the UB.

Unjust enrichment The mischief for which the law of restitution provides a remedy, namely the obtaining of a benefit by one person at the expense of another in circumstances where it is unjust that he should retain it. This benefit might arise through the beneficiary's own wrongful conduct or through the acts of the other person or a third party. ■ See **Restitution**.

Unless order See **Peremptory order**.

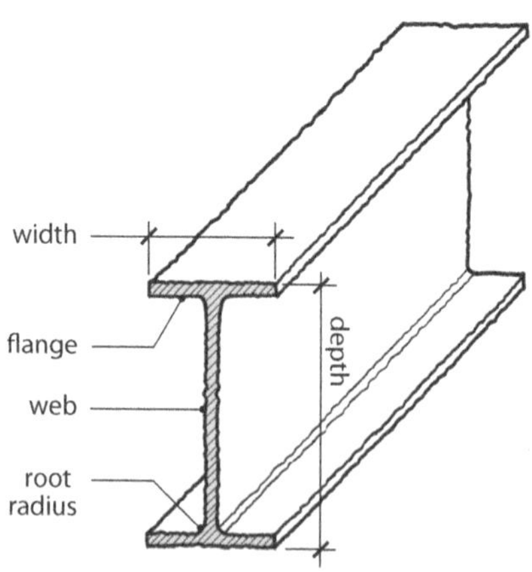

➤ **Figure U1.** Universal Beam

Unliquidated damages Damages for loss which are not quantified in the contract which has been broken but remain to be decided by the court or arbitrator according to the evidence of loss, including **general damages**. ■ See **Damages** and **Liquidated Damages**.

Unplasticised polyvinyl chloride (uPVC) A material used for window frames and piping which does not deteriorate on exposure to **ultraviolet radiation**. Now more commonly known as PVCu in accordance with Continental usage.

Unreasonably Notice of termination by a contractor is given unreasonably unless a reasonable contractor, circumstanced in all respects as was the particular contractor at the time when he gave notice to terminate, would have thought that it was unreasonable to give such notice: *John Jarvis Ltd v Rockdale Housing Association Ltd* (1986) 36 BLR 48 (CA).

Untrimmed floor A floor which is supported by common joists alone.

Uplift An increase in a rate or price for work to compensate for changed conditions in which it is carried out or additional obligations which have arisen, often expressed as a percentage increase.

Uplighter A source of illumination either above head height or from a concealed location which throws light upwards onto the walls and ceilings, a form of indirect lighting which avoids glare.

Upon notice Having previously informed the other party or parties to a dispute of an intended course of action, usually an application to the tribunal for a particular order or direction.

Upside-down roof A form of roof construction in which the waterproof membrane is placed directly on top of the roof deck and the insulation is placed above the membrane topped with gravel or paving. Locating the insulation externally has the advantage of avoiding extremes of temperature within the roof construction.

Upstand A vertical component in construction, often describing the backing to a horizontal surface or where material is turned up against a vertical face. ➤ **Figure P1**

Upstand beam A beam with a pronounced vertical element, for example, at the edge of a building frame to contain the floor construction: also the vertical side of a beam cast in an L shape thereby ensuring structural strength. Often used in foundation design when upstand supports walls built above.

uPVC See **Unplasticised polyvinyl chloride**.

Usage See **Custom and usage**.

Utilities Contracts Regulations The Utilities Contract Regulations 2006, SI 2006/6, which govern procedure where a utility seeks offers for proposed works. The utilities in question are those relating to gas, electricity, water, transport, post and fuel extraction. The regulations do not apply where the activity is subject to competition in unrestricted markets (reg 9).

U-value A measure of heat transfer through a building and the efficiency of insulation. A calculation is made of the transfer of heat (thermal energy) measured in watts through one square metre of a building component resulting in a temperature difference of 1°C. A low U-value means that the component is an efficient insulator of heat.

V

Vacate (a date) To cancel the date for a hearing.

Valley The junction of two slopes on a roof where water is directed and collects and runs off to the gutter. Traditionally lined with lead, now rubberised and fibreglass composites, valley troughs are now often made with aluminium, copper, zinc or glass-reinforced polyester.

Valuation The ascertainment of the monetary worth of work in accordance with the rates and prices in the contract or with reasonable rates. Valuations may be either interim or final. Interim valuations are carried out at intervals prescribed in contract (usually monthly) and will be superseded each month. An initial valuation will be made by the contractor applying for a payment, usually followed by a valuation on behalf of the employer, generally by a quantity surveyor or, on smaller projects, the certifier. Where a certificate is to be issued before payment, this will reflect the employer's valuation. In other cases, the contract may provide that payment is to be made on the contractor's valuation and application, although in such a case the employer would still be able to dispute the amount subject to the notice provisions of the **Construction Act**, see ss110 and 111. ■ See also **Variations**.

Value Added Tax (VAT) A statutory tax charged by a registered seller on the supply of goods and services. In most cases, the seller will have to account to Her Majesty's Revenue and Customs (HMRC) for the VAT on a quarterly basis whether the payment has been collected or not. The seller is entitled to set-off the VAT payments he has made to others against his liability to pay the VAT he has received. It is customary within the building industry to quote net figures of VAT. The problems relating to VAT which can arise in the construction industry include the following: (1) Whether a contractor's quoted price includes VAT: it has been held that it does where the quotation is to a private individual: *Franks & Collingwood v Gates* [1983] 1 ConLR 21. (2) Whether the works are subject to VAT. (3) Whether any sum included in a judgment, award or decision is sum due under the construction contract (which would attract VAT) or for damages for breach of contract (which are not subject to VAT). (4) Whether any sum agreed by way of compromise of a claim is inclusive or exclusive of VAT. (5) Whether any sum agreed by way of compromise of a claim is subject to VAT.

Value engineering (VE) The process of examining the function of an intended project and choosing the most cost-effective means of delivering the desired result, usually at the design stage of a project.

Vane testing Vane shear testing is one of the most common *in situ* methods for the estimation of the undrained shear strength of the soil as a pre-development activity.

Vapour barrier A material which prevents or limits the movement of water vapour through its thickness; usually made of polyethylene or similar plastics or metal foil. There may be a greater degree of permeability than with a damp proof membrane, which is normally a heavier material.

Vapour control layer A material to limit the movement of air into a warm roof system and to reduce condensation, for example, within the roof space caused by the meeting of cold and warm air.

Variable air volume systems (VAV) Feature of air conditioning or heating and cooling systems in which the volume of air supplied through ducts is varied to meet the current requirements of the building. These are determined by sensors which change the speed of the fans and operate a damper which restricts the flow of air to each area. This system reduces the cost of operation.

Variant bid A bid that differs from the specific requirements set out by the **contracting authority** in the tender documents.

Variation An alteration in the previously described work to be provided by a contractor by addition, omission or substitution of different work; also known as a "change". Virtually all construction contracts will expressly authorise variations to be instructed. The contractor is not entitled to vary the works to suit his own convenience unless he obtains the employer's agreement. The grounds entitling the contractor to payment for a variation or change have been summarised as follows: (1) The work is outside the agreed scope of the contract; (2) The work has been ordered by or on behalf of the employer; (3) The employer has agreed to pay for the work by words or conduct; (4) The work has not been voluntarily provided by the contractor; and (5) The work was not necessary through the contractor's fault. See *Watson Lumber v Guennwig*, 79 Ill. App. 2d 377; 226 N.E.2d 270 (1967) before the Appellate Court of Illinois, cited in *Hudson's Building & Engineering Contracts* 12th edn, at 5-024. The valuation of variations is a source of considerable dispute, but general principles are difficult to extract from the authorities because they turn on the effect of express provisions. Most clauses concerning such matters proceed from the basis that the contract prices are applicable, subject to alteration to reflect changed circumstances to the rather unsatisfactory concept of a "fair valuation".

Variation in cost clause See **Fluctuations clause**.

Variation of price clause See **Fluctuations clause**.

Variation order An instruction issued under the contract for a variation to the works. Such orders may be given in writing, or if given orally on site, be confirmed in writing by the architect, engineer or contract administrator as soon as possible. There may be limits on the extent to which the works can be varied if they significantly change the character of the project, but in practice this problem is rarely encountered. ■ See **Variation**.

VAT See **Value added tax**.

VAV Variable Air Volume. See **Variable air volume systems**.

VE See **Value engineering**.

Veneer Thin slices of hardwood applied to timber backing for decorative effect, particularly on furniture and domestic and office fittings and panels. Also, thin stone and brick cladding to walls and concrete structures.

Veneered wall A wall faced with thin layer of brick, stone, tile or other decorative finish, attached to brick concrete or masonry wall behind by wall ties or other non-corroding metal fixings.

Ventilating brick A clay or terracotta brick perforated across its face and for full depth to allow the passage of air. Such a brick is usually of standard size to permit it to be incorporated in a brickwork wall, often to ventilate sub-floor space or kitchens and bathrooms.

Ventilation The movement of air in a building, particularly the admission of fresh air from outside. This may be achieved by natural air circulation caused by differences in temperature and draughts or enhanced by an air conditioning system or other mechanical means such as ceiling fans.

Ventilation pipe, vent pipe An open top vertical pipe which allows the escape of gas and smells from an otherwise sealed system such as a public sewer or household drain and the venting of any pressure within it. It normally terminates at a height at or above the top of the building and is protected by a cowl.

Venting The process of a party to a dispute expressing anger or other emotions, usually at the beginning of a mediation.

Verba chartarum fortius accipiuntur contra proferentem Latin: "the words of an instrument shall be taken most strongly against the party employing them". ■ See **Contra proferentem**.

Verbatim Latin: "word for word".

Verdigris The green **patina** which forms on copper when exposed to air.

Verge The edge of a roof that projects over a roof **gable**.

Vermiculite A lightweight insulating aggregate used in screeds and plaster.

Vesting The passing of ownership of property from one party to another, particularly that of goods and materials used in construction projects.

Vesting clause A contractual term in a construction contract dealing expressly with the passing of ownership of goods and materials between the parties.

Vertical production method See **Line of balance**.

Vexatiously With an ulterior motive to oppress, harass or annoy: *John Jarvis Ltd v Rockdale Housing Association* (1986) 36 BLR 48.

Vicarious liability The liability of a party for the tortious acts and omissions of another, arising from the relationship between them. Thus, a company will be liable for the negligence of its employees in the course of their employment.

Videlicet Latin: "Please see", meaning namely, often abbreviated to viz.

View An inspection of real or personal property by a tribunal. On a view in a case in the Technology and Construction Court, the judge is usually accompanied by an expert instructed by each party or a representative of each party. The matters viewed will form part of the evidence, but anything said to the judge will not be taken into account in reaching his judgment, unless there has been an agreement or order to that effect: *Technology and Construction Court Guide*, 2nd edn, 2nd Rev. (October 2010), para 15.8.2.

Vis major Latin: "a greater force" or irresistible violence, which may be a defence to a claim in tort. It is not interchangeable with **force majeure**: *Lebeaupin v Crispin* [1920] 2 KB 714. An act of God has been said to be an instance of vis major: *Nugent v Smith* (1876) 1 CPD 423. Its use is now extremely rare.

Vitiate To make ineffective or invalid date: for example, fraud will vitiate an agreement.

Viz See **Videlicet**.

Void (1) (noun) an empty space, for example, within roof space or under the floor; (2) (adjective) of no legal effect, sometimes found in the expression "void ab initio", meaning invalid from the start.

Voidable An agreement which is capable of being set aside (avoided) as legally invalid by a party to it, for example, because of misrepresentation or mistake. Unlike an agreement which is void from the outset, voidable agreement remains valid until expressly set aside. In some instances it may be necessary to apply to the court to set the agreement aside or declare it invalid. ■ See **Misrepresentation** and **Mistake**.

Volenti non fit injuria Latin: "no injury is done to a willing person", the principle that someone who voluntarily assumes a risk cannot then make a claim for any damage suffered as a result, a defence to claims in tort. There are significant qualifications to this general rule.

Volume control damper A damper used to fine tune the volume of air in a mechanical system during the commissioning process.

Voluntary arrangement See **Company Voluntary Arrangement**.

Volute A curled decoration (in stone or wood) at the top of a column in classical design.

Vomitory/vomitorium A passage situated below or behind a tier of seating in an amphitheatre or stadia through which crowds can exit at the end of a performance.

Voussoir Wedge-shaped piece, usually made of stone, that makes up part of a vault or arch. See **Keystone** and **Springer**.

W

Wainscot Panelling lining the lower half of an interior wall from the skirting board to the dado or chair rail for decorative effect, nearly always made of wood but other linings such as stone panels are occasionally found.

Waist The middle section of a building structure where it narrows, for example, the narrowest part of a chimney flue or flight of stairs.

Waiver The giving up of a legal or procedural right, either by choosing between two inconsistent alternatives (waiver by election) or by conduct (waiver by estoppel) showing that a particular entitlement will not be pursued. Waiver may be express or inferred from conduct. For example, a contractor who is entitled to suspend work because he has not been paid certified sums but chooses to continue working may have waived his right on this occasion to stop work, although he will still be entitled to rely upon later breaches by the employer. If the waiver is supported by contractual consideration moving from the defaulting party to the party that has waived its right, this will irrevocably alter the initial legal right. If not, the waiver may be withdrawn on reasonable notice. ■ See **Estoppel**.

Wall anchor A heavy duty fixing into a wall enabling weight to be attached or loads applied; for example, the attachment of a harness for building inspection or a fire escape. Expanding bolts are often used to secure the anchor.

Wall plate (1) A wooden beam fixed and/or strapped horizontally along the top of an internal or external wall of a building on which the ends of joists and rafters rest. It may also connect to posts and studs below to complete the upper section of timber frame. (2) A shaped piece of wood fixed to the vertical surface of a wall as a base for a light fitting or bracket.

Wall string A length of timber set against the wall (or closed) side of a staircase. ■ See **Outer string**.

Wall tie A short usually galvanised metal connector between two leaves of a cavity wall, ordinarily secured in mortar in the horizontal joints as the wall is constructed, but may be drilled and fixed after construction. Also employed to hold facings and cladding to backing structures to provide stability and restraint and Is usually made of stainless steel.

Wallboard Also known as drywall, wallboard is sheets of plasterboard made of gypsum plaster lined **with heavy** paper and used to construct internal walls and ceilings when fixed to wooden studs or joists. Magnesium oxide and fibreglass may also be used to make wallboard.

War Although at common law a state of war between the United Kingdom and a foreign state does not exist until a formal declaration of war has been made by the Crown or hostilities have been begun by the Crown, in the particular context in which the word "war" is found in a contract, it must be construed, having regard to the general tenor and purpose of the document, in what may be called a commonsense way: *Kawasaki Kisen Kobushiki Kiasha of Kobe v Bantham Steamship Co Ltd (No 2)* [1939] 2 KB 544 (CA). A declaration of war does not prevent the performance of a contract, but acts done in furtherance of the war may prevent performance, such as the illegality of trading with the enemy: *Finelvet AG v Vinava Shipping Co Ltd* [1983] 1 Lloyd's Rep 503; [1983] 1 WLR 1469. In accordance with this approach, construction contracts usually concentrate on the potential effects of government intervention rather than the fact of war itself, although insurance cover is normally required for resulting loss and damage. "War" is part of the definition of All Risks Insurance against the Specified Perils under the JCT standard forms of contract. The full phrase is: "any consequence of war, invasion, act of foreign enemy, hostilities (whether war be declared or not) civil war, rebellion, revolution, insurrection, military or usurped power, confiscation, commandeering, nationalisation or requisition or loss and destruction of or damage to any property by or under the order of any government *de juris* or *de facto* or public, municipal or local authority". Loss or damage occasioned by any of the Specified Perils is a **relevant event**, which can entitle the contractor to an extension of time.

Warm roof A roof construction whereby the waterproof membrane is installed beneath the insulation. The advantages include greater heat retention, less condensation, as the roof construction is warm, and no need to lag pipes and tanks.

Warning A method of construing a potential exclusion clause by giving effect to it as a warning rather than an effective exclusion of liability.

Warranty (1) A term of a contract breach of which by one party would merely give the other party a right to damages, as opposed to an entitlement to regard himself as excused from further performance (breach of condition). (2) A separate contract between the parties to another contract or between one of the parties to that contract and a third party. ■ See **Collateral warranty**. (3) An undertaking, sometimes described as a "guarantee", by a manufacturer or installer of goods to the end user, which may be enforceable if there is consideration.

Wasted cost order A court order for costs made under the Senior Courts Act 1981 s51(6) and CPR 48.7 against a party's legal representative personally because his conduct has been improper, unreasonable or negligent. The order may either disallow the legal representative's costs or order him to meet wasted costs. Such orders should, if possible, be considered by the judge who hears the proceedings and only be made in a clear case.

Wasted expenditure A head of consequential loss recoverable for an anticipatory repudiatory breach of contract: *Anglia Television Ltd v Reed* [1972] 1 QB 60 (CA); [1971] 3 All ER 690. This may extend to payments made under the contract in a case of part performance. Where a contractor has accepted a repudiatory breach by the employer, he may be entitled to the value of the works assessed on a quantum meruit: *Lodder v Slowey* [1904] AC 442 (PC), a decision which has been the subject of criticism.

Water bar A metal bar installed in a threshold to prevent the ingress of water.

Water content The percentage of water by weight or volume within a building material. This must be ascertained to ensure that timber is sufficiently seasoned before use and the performance of other materials, such as cement and plaster, may depend on their water content. The water content of the ground in which construction takes place will also be significant.

Waterproofing The treatment of parts of a building to prevent the ingress of water. Techniques include tanking basements, damp proof membranes in ground bearing slabs and in walls, sealing of openings and waterproof membranes in roof construction. Moisture within building fabric can cause extensive damage, such as rot in timber, breakdown of plaster and efflorescence. ■ See **Tanking**.

WBP (Weather and Boil Proof) timber There are different types of plywood available, including standard, plastic-faced and wood-faced. If the wood is for external use, a more expensive ply laminate that is waterproof – known as exterior WBP (Weather and Boil Proof)-graded – is available. This means that the adhesives used in its construction are waterproof. There is another waterproof type on the market known as marine plywood that is also suitable for exterior use. Plywood can be used for many jobs in the same way as solid wood. It is stronger but more expensive than chipboard, and often has a more attractive surface, which can be either varnished or painted.

Weather See **Exceptionally adverse weather conditions**.

Weatherstripping or Weather-stripping The sealing of doors, windows and the perimeter of other external openings of a building against the ingress of wind and rain by fixing a draught-excluding strip. This may be an adhesive-backed rubber or plastic strip, or a more complex gasket or spring metal strip. The metal bar in a threshold also serves the same purpose.

Wednesbury grounds A decision being so perverse that no reasonable tribunal, properly directing itself as to the law to be applied, could have reached such a decision, traditionally justifying interference by the courts: *Associated Provincial Picture House Ltd v Wednesbury Corporation* [1948] 1 KB 223 (CA); [1947] 2 All ER 680. This test has been modified to one of proportionality where the Human Rights Act 1998 applies.

Weekly Law Reports (WLR) A series of law reports published in weekly parts by the Incorporate Council of Law Reporting for England and Wales.

Weephole A small drain hole for water or moisture/interstitial condensation commonly found in retaining structures, like concrete and masonry walls or glazing structures to channel ground water built up behind the structure.

Wet rot Timber decay as a result of alternating wet and dry conditions, caused by various fungi. It is preventable by preservative treatment.

Wet trades Building activities using products containing water, particularly concreting, screeding, bricklaying and plastering. A suitable interval is required to allow a building to dry out before trades susceptible to damp such as joinery and decoration are begun.

Whereas clause See **Recitals**.

White Book (1) FIDIC Model Services Agreement; (2) Civil Procedure Rules and Forms published for High Court use.

WHRB Waste heat recovery boiler

Whole life costs The total relevant costs and revenues associated with the acquisition and ownership of an asset.

Wickham test A test for a contractor's right to head office overheads and profit proposed in the US case *Wickham Contracting Co v Fischer* (1994) 12 F.3d 1574 (Fed. Cir. 1994), which is that the contractor could not have practically reduced his overhead costs or acquire replacement work to absorb the overhead.

Wild cat arbitration See **Copy-cat arbitration**.

Wilful misconduct Either an intention by someone to do something which that person knows is wrong or a reckless act in the sense that the wrongdoer is aware that loss may result from his or her act and yet does not care whether loss will result or not. ■ See Longmore J in *National Semiconductors (UK) Ltd v UPS Ltd* [1996] 2 Lloyd's Rep 212.

Williams v Fitzmaurice [1858] 157 ER 709: it was held that under a **lump-sum** contract, if it is discovered that "indispensably necessary" additional work is required to complete the whole work, the courts will infer that this work is included in the contract price and thus cannot be regarded as a variation.

Wind load The force exerted on a structure by the pressure of the wind.

Winding up The statutory procedure by which a limited company is put into liquidation. It begins by a petition to the Companies Court, either by the company (voluntary) or by a creditor (compulsory) including HM Revenue and Customs. The court order winding the company up may also appoint a liquidator, who takes over the affairs of the company in place of the directors. The liquidator collects the assets of the company, pays the creditors and distributes any balance according to the Insolvency Rules. Finally, the company will be dissolved and its legal existence ceases. ■ See **Liquidation** and **Liquidator**.

Window board A board fitted horizontally from the interior at the sill level of a window.

Windows analysis A form of delay analysis which provides a snapshot at the point at which the analysis takes place. It is a method of discovering the effect between a particular event and series of events within the time frame and the effect of one or more events on the total contract period. HHJ Toulmin CMG QC noted that: "Windows analysis, reviewing the course of a Project month by month, provides an excellent form of analysis to inform those controlling the Project what action they need to take to prevent delay to the Project. Without such analysis those controlling the Project may think they know what activities are on the critical path but it may well appear after a critical path analysis that they were mistaken." *Mirant Asia-Pacific Construction (Hong Kong) Ltd v Ove Arup and Partners International Ltd* [2007] EWHC 918 (TCC); [2008] BLR D1.

Winter working (External) work carried out during the months of winter when low temperatures and adverse conditions such as ice and snow may limit productive work, particularly ground excavation and the setting of concrete. Work may be condemned by the architect if damaged by frost. Contractors' claims often arise when work planned to be carried out in summer or autumn is delayed by events beyond the contractor's control into the winter months.

Win-win situation The resolution of an issue to the advantage of both parties.

Wingman A co-arbitrator.

Wireframe A wire frame is a visual presentation of a three-dimensional or physical object. Today it is typically used to describe a visual illustration of the content and links that need to appear on an individual web page.

Wire gauge A device for measuring the diameter of a length of wire to establish its tensile strength or the electrical current it can carry.

Wire-cut bricks Bricks formed by the extrusion of clay in a shaped length that is then cut by wires into individual bricks of equal length before being fired. The cutting may create a pattern on the end of the brick. ■ See also **Pressed bricks**.

Wired glass Sheet glass incorporating a wire mesh within its thickness: if the glass is broken, the mesh should hold the glass in place. Wired glass is sometimes used in glazed doors and windows where risk of breakage is high, but is considered reliable for fire-resistant purposes.

With costs The successful party's costs to be paid by the unsuccessful party, as in "application dismissed with costs" or "appeal allowed with costs".

Withholding notice A notice in writing given by an employer to a main contractor (or by a main contractor to a subcontractor) stating the sum(s) which the payer intends to deduct from the sums certified for payment or otherwise due, giving the calculation of the proposed deduction and the reasons why it is said to be justified, including the contractual or other basis. The provisions of s111 of the **Construction Act** require the notice to be given not later than the prescribed period (usually seven days) before the final date for payment: important amendments were made by ss143 and 144 of the **LDEDCA** regarding payment of the notified sum. Failure to serve a withholding notice on time (or at all) precludes the payer from making the deduction, though it may be deducted against future payments before they fall due. Often adjudication claims involve consideration of whether a withholding notice has been correctly issued. ■ See **Pay Less Notice** and **Figure P2**.

Without prejudice Confidential to the parties and not to be referred to in court or in documents disclosed to the court. This convention can only arise when a dispute has arisen and the exchanges are without prejudice to the formal position as to facts and law, which each party adopts in the dispute.

Without prejudice save as to costs Confidential to the parties and not to be referred to in court or in documents disclosed to the court, except in relation to costs when all other issues have been decided. ■ See **Calderbank offer**.

Witness A person who gives evidence in court proceedings or an arbitration or other dispute resolution procedure. Traditionally, a witness attends a hearing in person in order to give **oral testimony**: the almost invariable practice today is for his evidence to be written down in advance in a witness statement. The witness may only be required to attend for the purpose of **cross-examination** if his evidence is contentious. A witness who knowingly gives factual evidence which is untrue may be guilty of perjury.

Witness conferencing See **Hot tubbing**.

Witness purdah The rule that a witness should not discuss his evidence or the dispute with another person during any adjournment of his oral testimony.

Witness statement A written statement of the evidence, which a witness is able to give. The judges of the Technology and Construction Court have emphasised that witness statements must: (1) as far as practicable, be in the witness's own words; (2) indicate which of the statements are from the witness' own knowledge and which are matters of information and belief; (3) include a statement by the witness that he or she believes the matters to be true; and (4) should be no longer than necessary and not argumentative. See para 12.1.3 of the **TCC Guide**. The Court normally directs that a witness' statement should stand as his evidence-in-chief.

Witness summary A resumé of the evidence, which a party anticipates that a witness will be able to give which may be produced to the court under CPR 32.9 in circumstances where it is not possible to obtain a signed witness statement. The witness may still have to be called to give oral evidence in order for the matters stated in the summary to be accepted. In practice, this procedure is rarely used.

Witness summons A document issued by the court under CPR 34.3 requiring the person named in it to attend court on a specified date for producing documents in his care or control or to give oral evidence (or both). Deliberate failure to attend is a contempt of court. Some potential witnesses employed by third parties (such as central or local government employees) may request that a witness summons be issued so as to avoid any impression that they favour the party calling them. The court may fix a date for the witness to attend prior to the main trial hearing so that the parties are aware of the evidence the witness can give or the documents he holds. A witness who is summoned is entitled to be paid his travelling costs (conduct money) and some payment for his time. On the application of the parties or the arbitrator, the court may issue a summons requiring a witness to give evidence in an arbitration under the Arbitration Act 1996, s43.

Witney Town Council v Beam Construction (Cheltenham) Ltd [2011] EWHC 2332 (TCC); [2011] BLR 707; [2011] TCLR 8: Akenhead J defined the nature of a dispute for the purposes of adjudication in particular reference to a party seeking to avoid enforcement of an adjudicator's decision on the basis of a multiple dispute argument.

WLR See **Weekly Law Reports**.

Woolf Report The report entitled "Access to Justice" produced by Lord Woolf in 1996 whose recommendations led to the CPR. It introduced the concept of the **overriding objective** and encouraged cost- and time-effective case management by track allocation and for parties' representatives to adopt a less adversarial and more collaborative approach.

Work person A generic term covering anyone working on site, for example, in the context of health and safety: more particularly, the contractor's employees engaged in working on site.

Workability The level of ease or difficulty in mixing or applying a building material, such as a concrete mix or plaster.

Working drawings Drawings showing sufficient detail to allow manufacture or installation to take place.

Workmanship The execution of works, as opposed to their design. Both form part of the spectrum of the process of construction and absolute distinctions cannot be made, for example, where the contractor selects materials. ■ See **Quality of workmanship**.

Works The permanent construction to be carried out on site. ■ See **Temporary works**.

Works contractor Name given to a **trade contractor** who enters into a contract with a management contractor. ■ See **Management contract**.

Works information Under the **NEC** form of contract, the works information determines the extent of the contractor's obligations by defining what is required from the contractor in order to complete the works.

Writ The formal document by which a claim was initiated in High Court before the introduction of the CPR: now replaced by **Claim Form**.

Writ of execution See **Fieri facias**.

Writing Typing, printing, lithography, photography and other modes of representing or reproducing words in a visible form, and expressions referring to writing are to be construed accordingly: Interpretation Act 1978, s5, Schedule 1.

Written clauses Clauses which form part of a contract negotiated between the parties and which have been written (or typed), as opposed to printed clauses forming part of a standard form which has also been incorporated into the contract. As a general rule, the written clauses will take precedence over the printed clauses in a case of inconsistency between them.

Written submissions Documents containing a party's submissions reduced to writing, most often used where the issue is limited or for closing submissions after the end of a hearing.

X

Xeriscapeâ Xeriscaping is derived from the Greek word "xeros", meaning "dry" and combined with "landscape"; xeriscape means gardening with less than average water. A trademarked term referring to water-efficient choices in planting and irrigation design. It refers to seven basic principles for conserving water and protecting the environment. These include: (1) planning and design; (2) use of well-adapted plants; (3) soil analysis; (4) practical turf areas; (5) use of mulches; (6) appropriate maintenance and (7) efficient irrigation.

Xestobium rufovillosum See **Death-watch beetle**.

XPS Extruded Polystyrene A closed-cell, thermal plastic material used in building insulation and construction.

Xylonite Fibrous vegetable matter (eg cotton and flax waste and old rags), which formed a substance called *Parkesine*, named after its inventor, Edmund Alexander Parkes (1813–1890), of Birmingham. In its liquid state, it was applied as a waterproofing agent, in its plastic form for insulation, and, with the addition of oils, glues, and colour, for making objects, for example, tubes and architectural enrichment.

Xylotechnigraphy An architectural term for a decorative treatment to wood. By staining, finishing and graining, the wood appears more expensive or of finer type. In 1871, the process was patented in England.

Y

Y-value A measure of the total heat loss expected from **thermal bridge** losses in new homes.

Yard Yard of concrete – Imperial measure used for volume as in one cubic yard of concrete is 3" × 3" × 3" in volume, or 27 cubic feet; broadly one cubic yard of concrete will pour 80 square feet of basement/garage floor.

y2k Term referring to computing and/or control apparatus prepared to accurately process date and time data between and into the twentieth and twenty-first centuries. No longer an issue and a greatly exaggerated problem, an industry was grown from it to avoid a largely illusory issue.

YCMS Ltd v Grabiner [2009] EWHC 127 (TCC); [2009] BLR 211; 123 ConLR 202: it was held that a correction to an adjudicator's decision must be made within a few days of the decision. The correction, which can only be of a clerical mistake or error, can arise either on the adjudicator's initiative or on application by one of the parties. However an adjudicator cannot use this rule to correct his award because he has had second thoughts about his decision. ■ See **Slip rule**.

Year Either a calendar year or a period of 12 months reckoned from another date, depending on the context. It has been held that each meaning applied in the same contract in different places: *IRC v Hobhouse* [1956] 1 WLR 1393.

Yellow Book See **FIDIC Yellow Book**.

Yett An open metal wrought iron grid, hinged to form protection for a doorway, a sort of portcullis.

Young's modulus See **Modulus of elasticity**.

Youngman's board Term used to describe a working platform board commonly timber, but now often aluminium, circa 450mm wide with origins in a proprietary staging and platform company of that name.

Yuanda (UK) Co Ltd v WW Gear Construction Ltd [2010] EWHC 720 (TCC); [2010] BLR 435; 130 ConLR 133: the **TCC** held that (1) a ***Tolent*** clause in the parties' contract conflicted with s108 of the **Construction Act** because it fettered the referring party's right to refer a dispute to adjudication "at any time"; and (2) a contractual rate of interest for late payment did not necessarily fail to meet the "**substantial remedy**" test set out in the Late Payment of Commercial Debts (Interest) Act 1998 merely because it was lower than the statutory rate. The Construction Act 2009 has subsequently attempted to outlaw the provision of Tolent clauses at s108A.

Yurt A yurt or ger is a portable, felt-covered, wood lattice-framed circular in plan dwelling structure traditionally used by Turkic and Mongolic nomads in the steppes of Central Asia like Kazakhstan. It provides a good level of insulation and strength.

Z

Z-bar Z-bar flashing is a bent, galvanised metal flashing that is installed above a horizontal trim board of an exterior window, door or brick course. It prevents water from getting behind the trim/brick and into the property.

Z clause Found in the **NEC** form of contract, Z clauses are used to insert terms and conditions which are not dealt with by the existing standard contract form wording.

Zealous witness A witness demonstrating partiality towards one party.

Zero-sum game A situation in which any advantage gained by one party must of necessity be lost by the other party: the opposite of a **win-win situation**.

Z-form See **Z-section**.

Zinc roofing A metal roof covering: zinc (usually alloyed with lead) has the advantage of being malleable and resistant to corrosion but may become rather dull in appearance and without insulation will lead to heat loss. It is generally used for roofing of smaller buildings and flat roofs.

Zipper clause See **Entire Agreement clause**.

Zone of influence The area surrounding a pipe where pressure can bear.

Zoning The division of a locality into distinct areas with specific characteristics, particularly in planning where areas may be designated as industrial, commercial or residential zones. In building a large development, the property may be divided into zones where different activities are carried out or standards apply: for example, private and social housing.

Z-purlin A horizontal or inclined tertiary roof member supported by the rafters, which in turn supports the roof sheeting and finishes. Made of galvanised steel, Z-shaped in cross section to enable fixings for cladding.

Z-section Sometimes referred to as Z-form. Name given to Z-shaped sheet piles and to a type of horizontal beam or trim made of wood, metal or reinforced concrete. ■ See **Figure A4**.

APPENDICES: PROCUREMENT DIAGRAMS

1. Traditional Procurement Route 318
2a. Design & Build Procurement Route (Pre-Novation) 319
2b. Design & Build Procurement Route (Post-Novation) 320
3. Construction Management 321
4. Management Contracting 322
5. Private Finance Initiative (PFI) Procurement 323

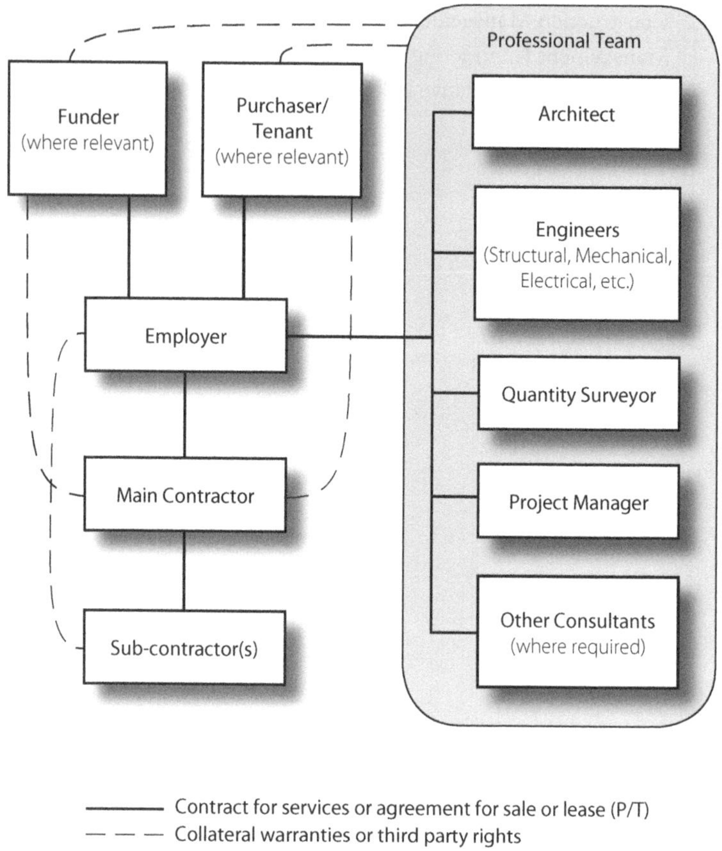

➤ **Appendix 1.** Traditional Procurement Route

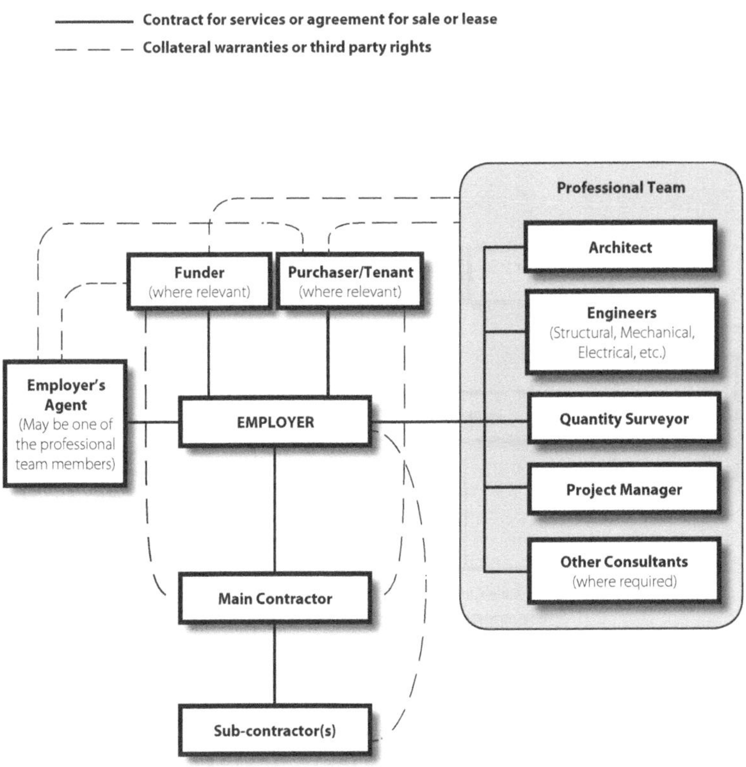

➤ **Appendix 2a.** Design & Build Procurement Route (Pre-Novation)

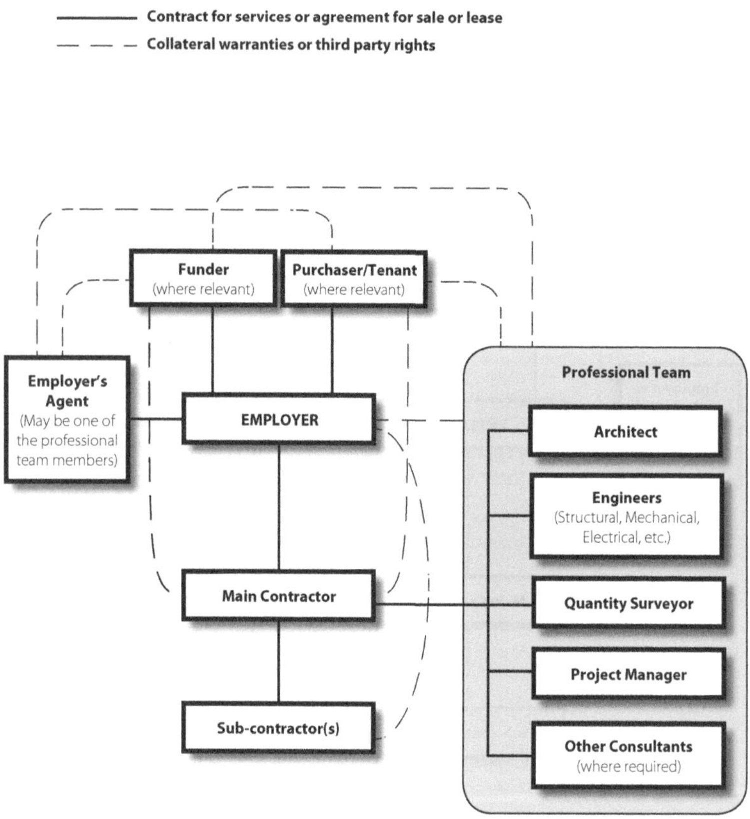

➤ **Appendix 2b.** Design & Build Procurement Route (Post-Novation)

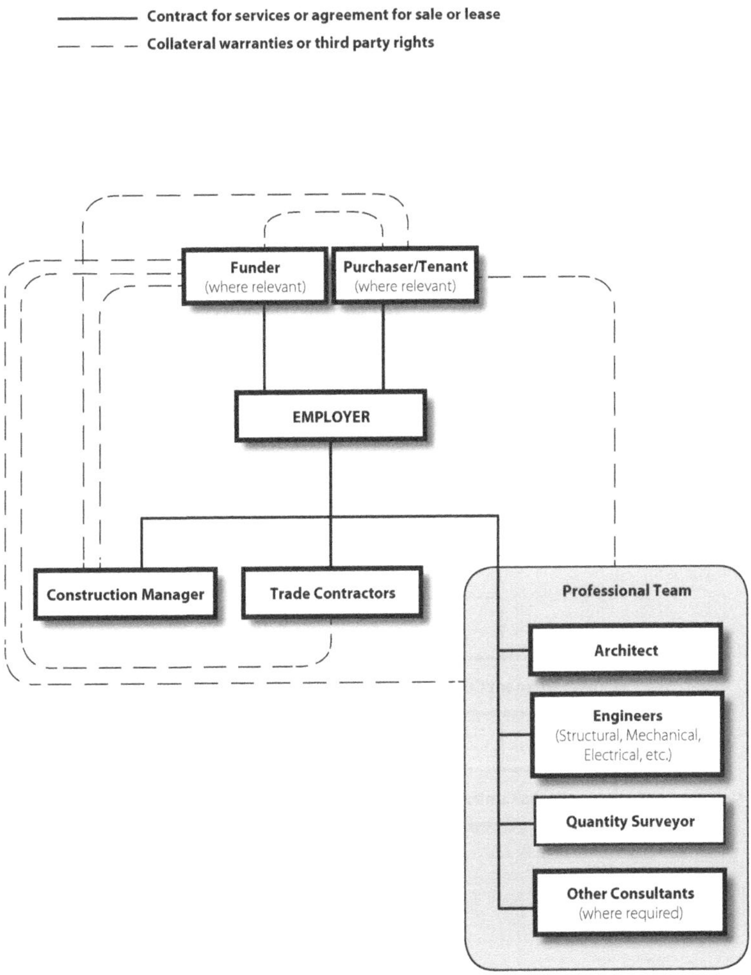

➤ **Appendix 3.** Construction Management

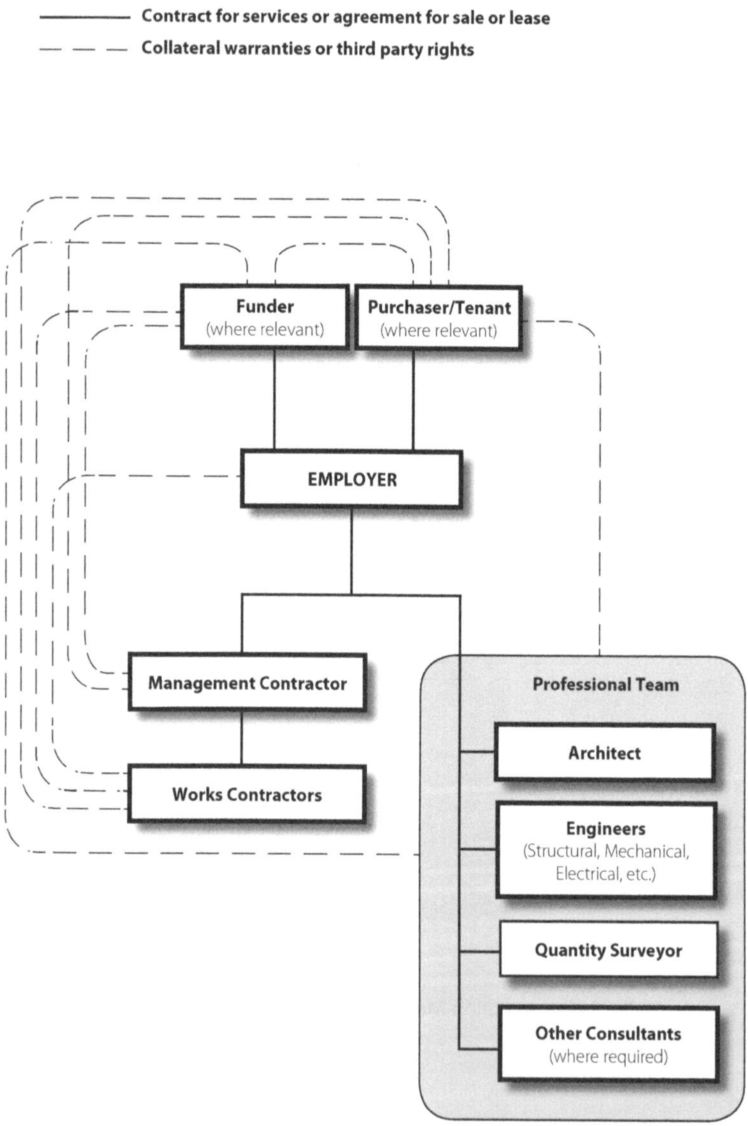

➤ **Appendix 4.** Management Contracting

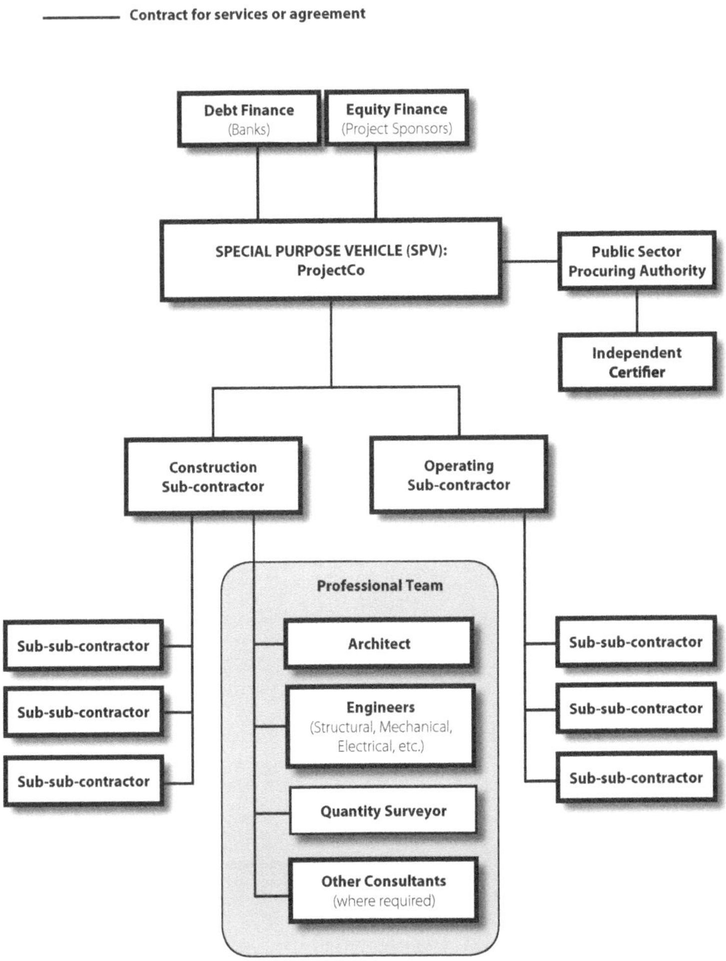

➤ **Appendix 5.** Private Finance Initiative (PFI) Procurement

For Product Safety Concerns and Information please contact our EU representative GPSR@taylorandfrancis.com Taylor & Francis Verlag GmbH, Kaufingerstraße 24, 80331 München, Germany